Abiding by

Sri Lanka

PUBLIC WORLDS

Series Editors: Dilip Gaonkar and Benjamin Lee

QADRI ISMAIL

Abiding by

Sri Lanka

On Peace, Place, and Postcoloniality

PUBLIC WORLDS, VOLUME 16
UNIVERSITY OF MINNESOTA PRESS
MINNEAPOLIS LONDON

Published by the University of Minnesota Press
111 Third Avenue South, Suite 290
Minneapolis, MN 55401-2520
http://www.upress.umn.edu

Library of Congress Cataloging-in-Publication Data

Ismail, Qadri.
    Abiding by Sri Lanka : on peace, place, and postcoloniality / Qadri Ismail.
        p.   cm. — (Public worlds ; v. 16)
    Includes bibliographical references and index.
    ISBN 0-8166-4254-0 (hc : alk. paper) — ISBN 0-8166-4255-9 (pb : alk. paper)
        1. Sri Lanka—Ethnic relations.   2. Ethnology—Sri Lanka—Philosophy.
    3. Political violence—Sri Lanka.   4. Sri Lanka—Social conditions.   5. Sri
    Lanka—Politics and government—1978–   . I. Title. II. Series.
        DS489.2.I84 2005
        954.9303'2—dc22

                                                                    2005017713

Printed in the United States of America on acid-free paper

The University of Minnesota is an equal-opportunity educator and employer.

12 11 10 09 08 07 06 05   10 9 8 7 6 5 4 3 2 1

≈

For Appa

Contents

Acknowledgments

If a project like this has a beginning, then it began with my grandfather. Every Saturday morning he would take me to Cargill's. We would buy two books, three if I was lucky, to be followed by steak and kidney pie at Pagoda. Eventually, Appa introduced me to the canon.

Many years later, Ian Goonetileke made me aware that there were other books. At the University of Peradeniya, Thiru Kandiah showed me how one could love the canon and learn from it without succumbing to it. Kumari Jayawardena—her middle name is generous—always encouraged me intellectually but insisted at the same time that there were things to be done. If I know anything about politics, it is because of her. Edward Said, at Columbia University, powerfully reinforced that message about doing while warning me never to lose sight of the canon. He will always be an inspiration and I am grateful he gave me some of his time. Gayatri Spivak, quite simply, taught me how to read—or tried. It's a lesson I'm still learning.

Just about every statement here, though they may not recognize it, bears the trace of exchanges, meals, and maybe a drink or four with Sanjay Krishnan, Milind Wakankar, Ajay Skaria, and Pradeep Jeganathan. I also owe immeasurably Newton Gunasinghe, Aamir Mufti, John Archer, David Scott, Ram Manikkalingam, Tony Anghie, Anne McClintock, Joe Cleary, Rob Nixon, Zaineb Istrabadi, Mala de Alwis, Vasuki Nesiah, Tim Watson, Fenella MacFarlane, Mazen Arafat, Neville Hoad, Arjuna Parakrama, Ramani Muttetuwegama, Mangalika de Silva, Dayan Jayatileke, Chandan Reddy, Colleen Lye, Sonali Perera, Bruce Robbins, Sumi Kailasapathy,

Ananda Abeysekera, Ruvani Ranasinha, Joseph Massad, Jean Howard, Joy Hayton, and Gayatri Gopinath. Ranajit Guha, Shahid Amin, Partha Chatterjee, Arjun Appadurai, Gyan Prakash, and Gyan Pandey took the time to encourage a graduate student, and it was a privilege to have been able to learn from them. The conversations with all of these friends are ongoing. Alas, they are not with Chanaka Amaratunga, Ravi John, Rajani Thiranagama, and Richard de Zoysa, who taught me, in different ways, how to abide by Sri Lanka.

The arguments that began in Colombo and continued at Columbia flourished in Minneapolis. Without the patient mentoring of John Mowitt, this would have been a very different book; every new professor should have a friend like him. Adam Sitze and Premesh Lalu were in the first graduate seminar I taught at the University of Minnesota and are now among my most cherished interlocutors. Jani Scandura, Vinay Gidwani, Lisa Disch, Charlie Sugnet, Bruce Braun, and Tom Wolfe read and made valuable suggestions on various chapters. They almost made me forget the cold, as did Gloria Raheja, Maria Damon, Paula Rabinowitz, Rod Ferguson, David Bernstein, Jigna Desai, Ananya Chatterjee, Shiney Varghese, Divya Karan, Rose Hendrickson, and Keya Ganguly. I also owe special thanks to everyone at the SSA, Colombo, and to Allen Isaacman, Bud Duvall, and the MacArthur Program. Carrie Mullen and the rest of the staff of the University of Minnesota Press were a real pleasure and unbelievably easy to work with.

My parents, Shakir and Fazeera Ismail, were very supportive during these years, as was my family generally: my sister Luthfiya, Fahardeen, and the kids, Seyyid and Saabira, my brother Eithquan, my uncle Fahmi Markar, Hamim and Fathuma Magdon-Ismail, Fiaza and Riza Haniffa, Hanan and Wimala Ismail, and Alavi and Sithy Ismail. Salma and Zamil Zarook and the boys (Sadir, Shezan, and my man Qadir) made me want to keep returning to Colombo after we sold our own house. Nizam Cader deserves special mention for asking, after years of frustration: why are you taking so long to finish your book? Are you writing only one sentence a day?

Shreen quit her job in Sri Lanka, which she loved, and came to the freezing cold of Minneapolis to help me finish this book. No system of justice exists that can compute my debt to her.

Introduction

Abiding by Sri Lanka

I would rather think of the text as my accomplice, than my patient or my analysand.

> —Gayatri Spivak, "The New Historicism"

Acknowledging Inheritances

Newton Gunasinghe, in his 1984 essay "May Day after the July Holocaust," made a cortical, if now almost forgotten, intervention into the Sri Lankan debate on peace. He contended, about what was beginning to be called the "ethnic conflict":

> It is now clear that the anti-Tamil riots of July '83 constitute one of the most important turning points in the recent history of Sri Lanka. A particular equilibrium within the Sri Lankan social formation has been irrevocably lost and a new equilibrium is yet to be achieved. Within the context of a heightened ethnic consciousness among the masses, the left and the democratic forces are in *a situation of theoretical disarray*. One symptom of the disarray is the dominant tendency in the old left to sweep the ethnic issue under the carpet, and to raise "safe" economic and class slogans.[1]

Elements of this formulation could be quibbled with. It does not, for instance, quite escape the grasp of empiricism. Surely, to an Althusserian like Gunasinghe, any determination of a conjuncture cannot be a matter of self-evident clarity. To read him thus might appear, at least to some, as a not particularly comradely thing to do. Why, somebody might ask, criticize a friend, and in public at that? Why begin a book by so doing? But it is a part of the argument here that comrades can and must disagree, openly if necessary. Otherwise, one subscribes to a notion, always dangerous, of leftist infallibility; one risks being dogmatic; one refuses to work with difference (or, more precisely, singularity). That said, let me acknowledge here Gunasinghe's commitment to Sri Lanka and the left, a lifetime's struggle trying to make the country more egalitarian, not just from within the academy but also from within trade unions and other allied organizations. And I also acknowledge that these pages owe to Newton's intellect, commitment, courage, guidance, generosity, humor, and—most of all—example, much more than they might reveal, as they do to the same in his if anything even more generous colleague at the Social Scientists' Association, Kumari Jayawardena. Recognizing that, the first point to be taken from his essay is that Gunasinghe made the case there for understanding what one might term the post–July 1983 conjuncture, understood not as a historical but an epistemological moment, as "overdetermined." Class contradictions were no longer the primary questions the Sri Lankan left had to address in this changed conjuncture, this new state of disequilibrium; ethnic ones had assumed greater urgency. The task, therefore, was not to represent "the current view most popular amongst the masses," or "tailism," but to produce "a far-sighted strategic line, together with the tactical steps necessary to pursue it."[2] The most important element of this "line," its goal, would be an "optimum political solution to the ethnic problem."

Gunasinghe is not cited at the very beginning of this study because we have both been inspired by Marxism, although not of the orthodox or dogmatic kind but rather that of Louis Althusser. Neither is it sought here, by invoking the name of a leftist academic and activist, to imply that what follows, while academic, is also activist (despite my employment in the Western academy). Unlike Gunasinghe, the concern here is not to produce a strategic line, or even a tactical one. This study sees itself as interventionist, but it seeks self-consciously to intervene in an academic debate, even while it is informed and influenced by others, and seeks to influence them, too.[3] Besides, it does not hold the position, somewhat fashionable within cultural studies, that academic work is also activist; it has a much more modest conception of such practice. Indeed, it holds rather strongly that one completely misrepresents academic knowledge production if one finds it synonymous with the work of those who actually take risks. Rather, I begin this study by invoking Gunasinghe's name to acknowledge an inheritance (which is also, and there really is no paradox here, a debt I can never repay). This study would quite simply not be possible without his example, without his work, and that of many others.[4] But, then, the question arises, why this particular essay of Gunasinghe's? Why not another better known or more substantial one? "May Day after the July Holocaust" is the most apposite text, or accomplice, with which to begin advancing my own position, making my own intervention because, for a start, it too is interventionist and situates itself explicitly on the left. Second, and more important from the perspective of what is to come, Gunasinghe's response to what he understood as a changed *political* situation, one that has apparently confused the left he is a part of, or abides by, is to call for *theoretical* reflection.[5] Such theory must lead to changed practice, of course; the ultimate goal is a far-sighted strategic line, a solution to the ethnic problem. But the cardinal need of the moment as he identifies it is not what might be called knee-jerk activism but theory. To paraphrase John Mowitt's reading of Marx's second thesis on Feuerbach here, the strength of Gunasinghe's formulation is that he refuses to separate politics from theory, without conflating the two.[6] What he considers the old political realities can no longer be taken for granted. New concepts are called for as a response.[7]

That precisely is the claim being advanced here, too. Or, to use a different vocabulary, that not just the current political moment confronting Sri Lanka, in the form of the question of peace, but the current epistemological or *disciplinary* moment—which I prefer to characterize as postcolonial and postempiricist rather than poststructuralist but, it must be stressed, without any prejudice or hostility to the latter term—requires that these theoretical advances be considered and, more importantly, *consolidated*, affirmed, abided by, not taken for granted or abused by casual reading and lazy citation, as all too commonly happens in social science and literary criticism inspired by it.[8] For such consolidation to occur in an abiding fashion, the postcolonial/postempiricist *reader*—and all three terms in this position are of equal importance—must make the social sciences in general, and anthropology and history most particularly in the Sri Lankan instance, account for their complicity in naturalizing a certain, ultimately empiricist and even colonialist, understanding of the social and this moment and account for their complicity in naturalizing the apparent fixity of the present. But it cannot stop there. It must also put "into question the system" or the episteme that enables such understanding.[9] Sri Lanka, in other words, is not simply a political problem, one to be addressed by the

discipline of conflict management. The question of peace, in my understanding, is a politico-epistemological problem. As will be argued in the
Conclusion of this study, after a reading of both Sinhalese and Tamil
nationalist texts, and leftist or "oppositional" interventions on peace, Sri
Lanka demands, perhaps even desperately, the formulation and deployment of "new" concepts. The current, rather narrow debate needs to be
broadened. That is the inescapable burden facing both the leftist and the
postcolonial/postempiricist thinker of peace.

What, though, is meant by postempiricism? It is an inelegant term,
yes, but more exact than "postmodern" (and resonates, serendipitously,
with "postempire"). By deploying it instead, I want to signal that the
break to be made—which cannot be a complete or clean one, since the
"post" signifies that one is still quarreling with, trying to displace, and
therefore complicit with, empiricism—is not so much with the concept
of structure but empiricism, and its postulate, the empirical. As Jacques
Derrida reminds us, in his critique of Lévi-Strauss, structuralism promised such a break but did not deliver. Empiricism, as he puts it there, is
the "matrix of all faults" infecting the social sciences.[10] So postempiricism
refers, very broadly, to those literary critical persuasions that begin from
this position, to those that take reading and/or textuality and/or semiotics as their point of departure. Empiricist understandings of language, of
course, hold that language can, without too much difficulty or any kind
of mediation, capture or represent the real, the event, the social. They
operate within what Barthes called the "referential illusion." Language, in
that understanding, has no significatory function. Even if self-consciously
influenced by "postmodernism," as in much contemporary social science,
including the "interpretive" tendency, the object, to empiricism, is conceived as transparent, outside language and the process or play of signification, whereas the postempiricist reader does not conceive of herself as
an autonomous or agential subject, conceives of her object as also subject,
as simultaneously subject and object. Most important, she works toward
the demise of this opposition.

But what connection does postempiricism have, you may wonder, with
Gunasinghe's argument or my object of study, the question of peace in Sri
Lanka? What do the social sciences (especially anthropology and history)
and empiricism have to do with Sri Lanka? To these questions, this reader
would respond with other questions that would get to the heart of what is
at stake in insisting on consolidating the gains of postempiricism: what is
this object, Sri Lanka, in the first place? What kind of a place is it? Do
you know it? Really? How do you know it? Did you hear or see or read

about it? Why are you convinced that what you heard or read or saw was persuasive? Did it occur to you, to anticipate my argument somewhat, that Sri Lankans and Westerners, for instance, might comprehend it differently? Did you pause, consider, however briefly, that *different disciplines might produce it differently?* That anthropology might see one thing, produce a certain object when it apprehended Sri Lanka, history another, and literature yet another? Is Sri Lanka a country in which people are domiciled, as the social sciences—geography, anthropology, area studies—and their applied allies—the census, encyclopedia, journalism—by and large claim? Is it a state that issues passports—and kills its citizens, routinely and randomly? Or, as the postempiricist might want you to consider, might it be comprehended differently, textually? Is its "conflict" best understood as about "ethnic" or nationalist violence, things that separate us (the "nonviolent" West) from them, or about peace and democracy, concerns we all share (or are at least supposed to)? By what criteria does one decide? What is at stake in the difference? And to pose a more provocative question: might those disciplines that are still empiricist actually be an obstacle to peace—*not to be understood as homonymous with the absence of war*—in Sri Lanka? Can reading textually, patiently, make a difference? Can it not just complicate, or supplement social science understandings of, but actually enable a reconceptualization of the question of peace?

These are not, of course, quite the same questions as those posed by Gunasinghe. But, in one crucial sense, they are not very different. Our concerns, one might say, rhyme (*rhyme* in the *OED*: "Agreement in the terminal sounds of two or more words or metrical lines, such that . . . the last stressed vowel and any sounds following it are the same, while the sound or sounds preceding are different").[11] He, too, asked the "old left," as he put it, How do you understand Sri Lanka? You say that, to the left, it is about class conflict. I beg to differ; to me it should be comprehended today as about ethnic conflict. The reader will notice that, in so saying, the grain of the text emerges as postempiricist. That is, Newton Gunasinghe—and this is where our projects rhyme intellectually—wasn't so much making a different interpretation of the country but an intervention within it; his text wants to produce a different *object* when the leftist thought "Sri Lanka," an object he also conceives of as subject because he grants it, rather than his own thoughts/subjectivity/agency, or career for that matter, primacy, an object he wants to *intervene* within and so change. As does this study, and in so doing, it wants to produce a different object not only for the leftist and the Sri Lankan but for the postempiricist and the postcolonial. For whoever reads this book, I seek to produce Sri

Lanka as an object that cannot be grasped empirically, one that, when grasped textually, will not be conceptualized as merely object and existing outside the investigating subject but as also subject and existing in language. This may sound like the repetition of old-fashioned terminology that we have left behind. After all, such a conception of the object is now, to those who think time through the calendar, many decades old. But the stakes in so doing are actually huge—especially at this epistemological moment when a Terry Eagleton can declare that theory is over. In bringing the gains of the critique of empiricism, and of colonialism understood as a politico-intellectual project, to the study of not just Sri Lanka but of non-Western "place," which is another way of saying the critique of anthropology, it is sought here to "finish" the critique of Eurocentrism inaugurated by postcoloniality.[12] In our current disciplinary moment we seem to take for granted that certain intellectual victories have been won permanently—against the West (or Eurocentrism). I am not so certain. *This book proceeds from the conviction that postcoloniality—and postempiricism—still has a lot of work left to do,* despite the arguments of those who hold that the project of postcoloniality has been superseded, whether by globalization theory or our historical moment. They forget, of course, that the object of the latter is very different. Globalization theory's emergence and current trendiness are to be actually welcomed by those with a serious commitment to the study of colonialism and its effects. For if it is no longer quite fashionable, as globalization studies clearly is, one can happily let those runway-driven academics who so desire strut to the beat of a different designer; the rest of us can, undisturbed, continue with the work that lies ahead, for postcoloniality still has many questions to conceive, let alone address or answer; many positions to disappear; many others to make axiomatic. Thus it must be (de)fended: fostered, nurtured, protected; its gains consolidated; its indispensability for the current disciplinary moment (re)articulated and, if necessary, reconceptualized.

Included here is the indispensable enterprise of rethinking, from a minority perspective and from that of the critique of social science and of representation, the problem of democracy; of considering whether representative democracy, understood not as an egalitarian mode of government or as the best possible system one can conceive but as a structure of dominance (not hegemony), enables the minoritization, the making insignificant and of no count, of minorities. Reading the Sri Lankan debate leads, almost inevitably, to asking a question about not just the necessity or practicality but the very ethicality of what is arguably the founding structural principle of representative democracy: majority rule. My argument then is that displacing Sri Lanka, producing a different object when it is thought, an object that is also conceived as subject, leads not only to reconceptualizing peace in this particular place but to addressing a much larger problem, one that must concern leftists everywhere, perhaps even as a matter of some urgency; one that anthropology, given its constitutive inability to see politics but only culture (gone crazy and violent) in postcolonial places, cannot notice. This question is visited somewhat in chapter 2, and at slightly greater length in the Conclusion of this study. But, ultimately, I can only gesture toward the directions that my argument compels me, for taking on the question of representative democracy, of majority rule, seriously, adequately, and responsibly would require a book of its own. However, since the problem does emerge when thinking peace in Sri Lanka, it must at least be raised, placed on the table, and the questions that occur at least asked.

In the rest of this Introduction, the task of "displacing" Sri Lanka is begun, a task continued in the next chapter. *Displacing* is used here in two senses. On the one hand, I attempt to push aside, to replace, if not to delegitimize, the dominant account of the country produced by the Western academy that sees it, as Pradeep Jeganathan has argued, as a place of violence caused by culture and not politics.[13] In this disciplinary moment that account is authorized by anthropology, the discipline that has dominated recent intellectual production on Sri Lanka in the conjuncture Gunasinghe would call post–July 1983. Thus, both the anthropological story of Sri Lanka and anthropology more generally *must* be scrutinized, critiqued, displaced before another object, also called Sri Lanka, could be produced. Or, rather, the displacement of the one would be the emergence of the other. In its second sense, the place—and place as a concept—is understood not geographically, or through its ally, area studies, but as a debate; not as an object that exists empirically but as a text, or a group of texts, that is/are read. These texts constitute the object, Sri Lanka. Some of these texts are anthropological. Others, as explained later, abide by the country, see it as subject (and also object), and are opposed to the anthropological, which only informs the West about the place, continues its objectification, and cannot conceive of it in any way as subject. Understanding place thus brings into play the question of reading textually, postempirically. In chapter 1, what is at stake in making that move, for the possibility of reconceptualizing the question of peace in Sri Lanka, is discussed, and it is concluded by (re)conceptualizing postcoloniality. The concept of postcoloniality has been accused by many critics of lacking substance, real content, even of having outlived its usefulness in this moment of globalization. Such a conclusion is much too hasty; indeed, it constitutes a surrender to Eurocentrism. From the perspective of this study, postcoloniality, or the critique of Eurocentrism, has been most effectively articulated in the work of Frantz Fanon and *Subaltern Studies* book series—most powerfully by Gayatri Spivak and Partha Chatterjee. (Re)reading their efforts offers a way of reinfusing the term with a new energy. Consolidating the gains of *Subaltern Studies*—rather than treating it as a once-fashionable enterprise whose time has passed—involves the challenge of reading it creatively, putting it to work, articulating what really is at stake in that project, which is by no means limited to the critique of imperialism or of colonial and nationalist history, or of giving voice to subaltern consciousness. In short, my contention is that the concept, postcoloniality, must be retheorized from the perspective of our current disciplinary moment. By so doing, I seek to make its emergence worthwhile, and thus the projects of postempiricism and postcoloniality come together, become accomplices, comrades.

My most abiding disciplinary concern in this study, however, is with history, not anthropology; with how and why the postempiricist/postcolonial reader must necessarily work against history's authority, which enables, in the Sri Lankan instance, both Sinhalese and Tamil nationalisms to claim that not only is the "ethnic conflict" shaped by the objective working out of the historical process but that this working out also suggests incontrovertible methods of resolving it. Opposed to this, it will be asked whether reading textually, privileging not the empiricist but the literary, whether learning from the singular and the unverifiable, from what could be termed the minority perspective, might allow us to reconceptualize the very question of peace. But the first task, given the commitment to postcoloniality and finishing the critique of Eurocentrism, is to distinguish this project from the discipline that most enables and underwrites the epistemological dominance of the West: anthropology, which is still very influential, and not just within the discipline, in this moment that otherwise appears to be postcolonial. It functions, structurally, to represent or speak for the other, to inform the West about the non-West; it sees its object as only object and works to maintain this relation of dominance. It is an epistemological enterprise that emerged within colonialism and continues to this day to reproduce those relations of knowledge production—if only, as Fanon might say, in new forms. Opposed to anthropology, committed to reading after the critique of empiricism, I would rather conceive of my object—the question of peace in Sri Lanka—as also subject (and also object, simultaneously; to just seek to make an object subject is to merely make a gesture of inversion, to work within the logic of nationalism, or identity politics). This is a theoretical position that I both begin from and arrive at after reading the texts of Ernest Macintyre, Kingsley de Silva, Kumari Jayawardena, Ambalavaner Sivanandan, and Jeyaratnam Wilson. To put this differently, a distinction is made between texts that anthropologize Sri Lanka and those that abide by it. The latter kind of text—Gunasinghe's being an exemplary instance, despite his being an anthropologist by training—intervenes in the Sri Lankan debate, the debate or text that is Sri Lanka, addresses its concerns, takes sides in its quarrels, refuses to stand above and sound objectivist. That kind of text doesn't want to wash its hands of the place, write about it one moment, forget about it the next. To say this is not to imply that Jayawardena, Macintyre, Sivanandan, Wilson, and de Silva share a politics. They do not. What they do have in common is a desire to get involved with the present, to try to shape thinking about the future of the country. In very different ways, they want to intervene on the question of peace. In so doing, they abide by Sri Lanka.

One final word is necessary here. Much of what follows is written in a polemical spirit. To Michel Foucault,

> The polemicist . . . proceeds encased in privileges that he possesses in advance and will never agree to question. On principle, he possesses rights authorizing him to wage war and making that struggle a just undertaking; the person he confronts is not a partner in the search for truth, but an adversary, an enemy who is wrong, who is harmful and whose very existence constitutes a threat. For him, then, the game does not consist of recognizing this person as a subject having the right to speak, but of abolishing him, as interlocutor, from any possible dialogue; and his final objective will be, not to come as close as possible to a difficult truth, but to bring about the triumph of the just cause he has been manifestly upholding from the beginning.[14]

This may sound like a description of a jihadist, but, as often in Foucault, the immediate adversary here, unnamed, is Marxism. Of course, it also constitutes a more general argument against polemics as such. Should it give me pause? Are all polemics bad, if not dangerous and anti-intellectual by definition? Do they prevent, if not prohibit, "dialogue"? Perhaps. However, the trouble with this position, at least to the postcolonialist perspective I seek to advance here, is that postcoloniality proceeds from the conviction—not from a truth, but a conviction—to put it crudely, that colonialism was a bad thing. What constitutes colonialism, how it should be conceptualized, is open to question, to debate. That its lingering effects, if not its strong aftermath, must be opposed is not. This is not a "privilege" it possesses in advance. Rather, it is something postcoloniality must both take as axiomatic and argue for. From such a conviction certain things follow. I am, as I hope the next chapters will demonstrate, always prepared to grant Sinhalese and Tamil nationalisms, however opposed the Sri Lankan leftist might and must be to them, however much leftists may wish their abolition, a hearing, and I would ask they grant my position a hearing, too. Peace would not be possible without such a conviction. But it is impossible, just impossible, to grant the same privilege to colonialism and its intellectual heirs, especially anthropology.

Insider, Outsider, Abiding

This book, then, responds to a compulsion: to address the question of peace in Sri Lanka, to intervene in that debate, from an explicitly leftist, postcolonial, and postempiricist perspective. Coded as such, or as the ethnic conflict, as the problem of war, terrorism, or genocide, this question—or something like it—is discussed every day in what geography, abetted by anthropology, area studies, and political science, not to mention Sinhalese nationalism, identifies and authorizes as a place called Sri Lanka and is discussed less frequently in places geography would identify as outside it.[15] *Abiding by Sri Lanka*, while it doesn't see itself as unrelated to these conversations, while it is certainly informed by and hopes in turn to inform them, while it would be impossible without them, and is thus also a part of them, is not directed at them. At least, not directly. Relevance is not the driving impetus behind this study, although it doesn't seek to be irrelevant, either. Rather, it endeavors to intervene in a more academic, conceptual argument. Not by asserting the ontological privilege of the citizen or "insider"; the nativist, in any shape or form, is not the ground from which I wish to, or can, speak. And not either from the Archimedean, implicitly objective, perhaps even imperial distance asserted by the "outsider." To the postempiricist reader these are untenable distinctions. I want to address Sri Lanka by taking into account both my insiderness or citizenship (inadequate terms that will be replaced soon) and outsiderness or what for lack of a better term could be called my employment (something not, in my understanding, synonymous with location) in the Western academy. Given the latter, given the commitment to contesting Eurocentrism, to opposing anthropology, I must confront (at least) the following questions: What might it mean to read Sri Lanka, and write it, from the Western academy?[16] What might be the implications,

the consequences, of so doing? How could making just another contribution to Western or anthropological, in the structural sense, discourse
on Sri Lanka be avoided? What needs to be taken into account by a self-
proclaimed postempiricist/postcolonial leftist Sri Lankan reader who
wants to avoid doing so? Can it be avoided, in good faith, by someone
employed in the Western academy? Does such employment inevitably,
inescapably, make me an effective outsider to Sri Lanka, imply or impose
upon me a politico-intellectual position complicit with the West or, worse,
with bourgeois capitalism, as some critics of postcolonial studies like Arif
Dirlik have charged? Is my claim to be on the Sri Lankan left, an academic
in the footsteps of Jayawardena and Gunasinghe, self-serving and unpersuasive? Could someone employed in the Western academy also be on
the Sri Lankan left?

But the first question to be asked, before any of the above, must concern the production of Sri Lanka by this enterprise from which I seek
to distinguish my project: Western/anthropological discourse. Shouldn't
its contours be demarcated, its concerns specified, its categories identified, its inadequacies cataloged? Its dominant strain addresses what it calls
the ethnic conflict—and what this study prefers to term the question of
peace, so as to produce a different object—from the outside, through the
mechanical, routinized protocols of conflict management. It proceeds by a
very predictable move, from diagnosis (identifying the causes of conflict,
the antagonists, and their mutually exclusive demands) to prescription,
a way of making these antagonists compromise upon these demands so
that they become mutually inclusive. Peace, to this perspective, is the
absence of war. This can be seen, to cite a convenient instance, in I. B.
Watson's preface to a recent collection of essays on Sri Lanka (convenient because it was selected randomly from my bookshelf).[17] Watson's is
the type of generic text that produces and reproduces Western discourse
on Sri Lanka, that makes *authoritative* statements, the type that therefore
must be taken into account, displaced, pushed aside, and deauthorized
in order to articulate my own position. The significance of this argument
for the study cannot be stressed too much: *the anthropological account of Sri
Lanka must be displaced, deauthorized, so that the postempiricist/postcolonial reader can
write.* For anthropology (and area studies), in my understanding, is the *différance* of abiding: it is what defers, delays, and of course the opposite of,
what differs most radically from, abiding. Watson's text is an exemplary
instance of such anthropology; it announces the questions that invariably
occur from the discursive/disciplinary location of the "outsider":

The conflict, often so incomprehensible to an outsider . . . has been a profound shock. No less of a shock has been the awareness that Sri Lankans
I know, while quiet, quick and gentle in themselves and with their immediate circles, are strongly partisan, vigorously intractable in their attitudes towards their opponents. Why has this situation arisen? What are
its characteristics? Who are the leaders and what are their motivations?
What are the consequences, both immediately and into the future? What
can be done to ameliorate these consequences, to establish different para-
digms under which to resolve at least the major conflicts?[18]

It is important to stress here that, to Gunasinghe, the conflict was not
in the least incomprehensible. In fact, what was going on, the changed
reality, was very clear. But that might be the result of the special insight
available to the insider, which Watson proclaims he is not. If his questions are those of conventional political science, one can also see the impress of geography and anthropology in the description of his object. For
one thing, he understands Sri Lanka empirically, as a place on the map of
the world where people (unlike him) reside, a place that he is—by definition to the empiricist—outside. For another, he understands it through
the protocols authorized by anthropology: he will make generalizations
about *all* of the natives, about their personality and character, based on
some of them, based, indeed, on his "experience" (does this count as "par-
ticipant observation"?) of some of them.[19] The logic here is metonymic;
the part can represent the whole; his experience of a few natives enables
him to make proclamations, without blush, about the native character or
condition as such.

This is the kind of knowing, of course, one expects to find in living
rooms, not common rooms. Dismissive, or just plain ignorant, of the critique of essentialism, this perspective does not subscribe to the slightest
doubt that the individual could be unrepresentative of the species or that
the part may not describe the whole. It cannot consider the possibility
that there might be other ways of reading the social, other ways of understanding or coding difference, those that emphasize the singular, ways
of reading that could be deemed characteristic of a minority perspective. And beneath its ostensible concern for the natives can be noticed
one of liberalism's most disturbing structural features: it must other, in an
anthropological spirit, those toward whom it would be benevolent. Sri
Lankans, to Watson, are both "gentle in themselves and with their immediate circles" and the opposite, "*strongly* partisan, *vigorously* intractable
in their attitudes towards their opponents." If uttered by a journalist, this

could serve as a summary description of most fans, otherwise known as fanatical supporters, of sports teams, whether in Brisbane, Baltimore, or Bogambara. But Watson produces such behavior as, amazingly enough, unfamiliar, downright incomprehensible, indeed shocking. He sees Sri Lankans as culturally different, as having a split personality; they are—and there's really no other way of reading that unit—schizoid, sick, suffering. A conservative Westerner might conclude from this that Sri Lankans languish from an incurable condition, that there's something in the culture, if not the water—the country is an island, no?—that makes them thus. But Watson, clearly a good and concerned liberal, is not such a pessimist; he wonders how this affliction could be ended or at least ameliorated, which signifies that he doesn't see it as a permanent condition or the natives as suffering from an incurable disease. Thus he insists that someone find out what kind of medicine can terminate it. For, while the conflict may be incomprehensible, it is only so to an "outsider" like himself; the contributors to the volume he prefaces—"insiders," presumably, or at the very least experts—can be trusted to fill the prescription.

But what, then, makes this an instance of Western discourse on Sri Lanka? Watson does not identify his writing or location as such, so is it a fair or proper characterization? By what criteria is it made? Would his employment in the Australian academy make it Western? Would the publication of the article down under make it Western? Geography would respond to such assertions with predictable laughter. Australia is not a Western country, at least not in a geographical sense. But, of course, this is not a question to be settled by turning to the map. From my perspective, the Westernness of Watson must be identifiable through a reading of the text. It turns out to have two related strands, one more important than the other. First, Watson presents himself as "outside" Sri Lanka. This alone does not necessarily make his text Western. It could, after all, be Indian.[20] But it is a significant element of anthropology, the discipline that produces authoritative knowledge of Sri Lanka in this epistemological moment, the discipline that, more than political science, makes Watson's text possible. Even in its most "sophisticated" variant, the so-called interpretive turn, anthropology cannot proceed without producing itself as outside its object of study and speaking for or objectifying it. (Indeed, as will be seen soon, the insider-outsider distinction is crucial to the very possibility of anthropology.) Is it, then, an irredeemably Western way of knowing? Yes, but only provided one comprehends "West" not in geographic, sociological, or essentialist terms but sees it, rather, as the *producer and authorizer of disciplinary knowledge, an "epistemological space."*[21] The second element of

Watson's text's Westernness, following from the above, is its disciplinary allegiance: it approaches Sri Lanka anthropologically. It may desire a solution to the ethnic conflict but leaves that work to others; it will make no demand on or, in Spivak's phrase, "speak to" Sri Lanka.[22] All it will do is make disciplinary statements, inform the West about the non-West, maintain its object as only object.

If Watson's is an instance of the troubleshooting strand in Western discourse, what of the others? Are there others? Like Watson, the anthropologist Jonathan Spencer also produces himself as writing from "outside Sri Lanka"; his subject-position is well within his discipline, which he does not seek to exceed. However, he has actually performed "fieldwork" in the country and so makes a good example of the foreign expert. Then, and most significantly, despite his allegiance to a discipline with a long racist career, Spencer calls himself a postorientalist. This suggests, at the very least, an awareness of the bind between knowledge and power. That, after all, is one of the most important arguments made by Edward Said in *Orientalism.* So Spencer produces himself as politically correct. Additionally, the essays in his collection, *Sri Lanka: History and the Roots of Conflict*—also selected from my bookshelf, but not randomly[23]—are said to be different from "that kind of political history which is based almost entirely on English-language sources and seeks its explanations only within the actions of the English-speaking elite." Unlike those histories, the essays here "employ local sources and attend to the voices of people many miles from the capital."[24] This, of course, is a self-authenticating move: my book is true because its authors have taken the trouble to converse with real people, not the elite. It should be pointed out, however, that more than half the essays in the volume do not actually "attend" to village voices—or any voices at all, in the sense Spencer uses the term; they analyze documents, are archive derived. Still, there is no great necessity to pause too long over this; after all, it is always possible that Spencer may not have actually read the essays in his collection. The question to ask is whether Spencer comprehends the conflict differently from Watson, or do both outsiders see it similarly? To Watson, the parties to the Sri Lankan conflict are "obvious": "the supporters of Tamil Eelam and the equally intransigent Sinhala nationalists."[25] Spencer finds the "conflict [to be] between the majority Sinhala population and the minority Tamil population . . . often presented, not least by the antagonists themselves, as the inevitable outcome of centuries of hostility."[26] Unlike the antagonists, the contributors to his volume do not share such a "primordialist" perspective of the conflict, but, partly because these antagonists themselves emphasize the significance of history, they feel a necessity to address this question. Thus the subtitle of the book: *History and the Roots of Conflict*. Leaving for later consideration the question of history and its significance, the point to take from his statement is that, at least when it comes to identifying the parties to the Sri Lankan conflict, Spencer is not very different from Watson. Both outsiders, expert and nonexpert, see the conflict in binary terms, as between two entities: the Sinhalese and the Tamils, the difference being that Spencer calls one a majority and the other a minority.

I could, at this stage, keep reaching for my bookshelf—with a view perhaps to exhausting it—after which I could surf the World Wide Web, looking for Western writing on Sri Lanka, from newspapers to Web pages. Indeed—if I felt sufficiently energetic—I could follow that with an excursion to the archives or, if I was fortunate enough to receive a grant, the British Museum, throw the dust off old files, solicit books not checked out in a century, and investigate the colonial roots of this discourse. And then, to bring the argument up to date, I might realize a lifelong dream and do some fieldwork—among faculty and graduate students in selected villages—oops I meant to say anthropology departments—and ask them how they think about Sri Lanka, how the country was produced for them in their classes, courses, and reading lists.[27] But Watson and Spencer are read here as symptomatic texts. So the reader should be prepared to concede, without further citation, that the elements of a discourse on the Sri Lankan "conflict" can be identified, at least provisionally, within Western academic production, which produces itself as situated outside the conflict and sees it as composed of two "antagonists," the Sinhalese and the Tamils. That much, at least, appears to be common to the empiricist/outsider perspective shared by Watson and Spencer. Even if the Sinhalese are identified, alternatively, as nationalists or as the majority, and the Tamils as separatist or as the minority, the conflict, evidently, is between two and only two parties.

Now to the "insiders." How do they comprehend the "conflict"? Do they see it in binary terms? Are nationalism and history important in their understanding? Rather than return to Gunasinghe—who did not identify himself as an insider, to whom the question would not have arisen—Valentine Daniel's *Charred Lullabies: Chapters in an Anthropography of Violence* seemed an appropriate place to address these questions. Daniel calls his book an "anthropo*graphy*." That is to say, he is concerned with graphing, the problem of writing, with writing as a problem; he situates himself within the "interpretive turn" in the discipline. His work, unlike that of

Watson and Spencer, to whom words are things and to whom signification is not an issue, appears to be somewhat postempiricist. His is an important book, for ethico-political reasons; he does not want to do business as usual, to simply represent. Situating himself explicitly as an insider, he says *Charred Lullabies* is about "the violence between Sri Lanka's two major ethnic groups, the Sinhalas and the Tamils."[28] Here, a difference of crucial importance to this study can and must be noticed from Spencer: even though Daniel, like the foreign anthropologist, sees the conflict—a violent one—as between only two groups, he does not characterize one as a majority and the other a minority but both as "major groups." This is a cardinally significant difference. To the empiricist, "majority" and "minority" are straightforward terms, simple facts of number or arithmetic, a matter of things that are self-evidently different, that can be and are grouped together, counted. To the postempiricist, in contrast, language matters: Spencer's terminology places the Tamils at the bottom of a binary in relation to the Sinhalese; it displays a partiality, however subtle, toward the Sinhalese or, more correctly, sees Sri Lanka in Sinhalese (nationalist) terms (perhaps a consequence of uncritically attending to only some of those voices outside the capital). In contrast, Daniel's usage asserts equality between the two groups; he refuses, one might say, to minoritize the Tamils. ("Minority," as I argue later, is not a descriptive term simply reflective of number, but an indice in Barthes's sense, a metaphor loaded with meaning, demanding interpretation.)[29] Daniel, that is, revises or rewrites Spencer, or the Sinhalese nationalist perspective on Sri Lanka. Can it be concluded, then, from this single instance, that the writing of outsiders and insiders, that Western or "outside" intellectual production on Sri Lanka differs significantly from that of the "inside"?

Actually, what the above discussion suggests is something the postempiricist reader knew to begin with: that easy, line-in-the-sand-style distinctions between insider and outsider, inside and outside, cannot be drawn; that the border that separates Western from Sri Lankan intellectual production is not hermetic. Spencer may produce himself as writing from the outside, but he sees the Sri Lankan conflict, at least in one important respect, through the terms of Sinhalese nationalism. This coincidence of perspective signifies, of course, that Spencer is not really "outside" Sri Lanka, or, rather, that to make the claim one must have a naive, empiricist, objectivist, and antidiscursive understanding of place, authorized by geography and area studies. Whereas, if Sri Lanka in particular, and "place" more generally, is understood textually, as it is by this study, then no "person" who produces knowledge of it, including Watson, can be considered "outside" it.[30] Indeed, the Watsons and Spencers of this world, despite being employed as they are by the Western academy, are very much "inside" Sri Lanka, for they are the experts who produce authoritative, disciplinary knowledge of the place—which also makes their texts Western (something with which, given my employment and disciplinary allegiance, I am also unavoidably complicit, even as I seek to contest this in my own work). But Spencer, although he claims to have read *Orientalism*, has an objectivist understanding of the production of knowledge:

> This book, most definitely, is not an attempt to rewrite Sri Lanka's national past. The aim is not to disprove or discredit any particular view of the national past . . . Instead the book seeks to analyze the appeal and effect in the present of certain dominant interpretations of Sri Lankan history . . . The broad orientation of this volume is toward the asking of new and unfamiliar questions . . . not the provision of fixed and definite answers.[31]

To this perspective, knowledge is objective; one can "analyze" without "rewriting"; ask questions without answering them, even implicitly; produce knowledge that is outside power, that will have no impact on its object. Indeed, it works hard to keep its object at a sanitized distance. Epistemologically speaking, this is consistent with his empiricism; he works to maintain his object as only object.

Is Daniel's text any different? It certainly wants to be—which is why it is given the extended attention it deserves here. It is a serious and thoughtful attempt at being different. But is it? Does it escape the trap of the anthropological, of speaking for? Though a "naturalized American," he was "born to Sri Lankan parents," and he says he writes with "a gentle prejudicial tilt, self-confessedly willed, in favor of the point of view of Sri Lanka's Estate Tamils."[32] This admission of "bias" or nonobjectivity, so rare in social science, so rare and thus refreshing, certainly produces the writer as an insider.[33] Indeed, Daniel takes great pains to let the reader know how much inside Sri Lanka he really is, despite having "lived more than half my life in the West": he speaks, for instance, not one but two dialects of Tamil; Sinhalese, too (and of course English, the language of the elite). Thus, when doing his fieldwork, he was "taken into the prejudices of all three ethnic (sub)groups," who told him their experiences freely.[34] In other words, Daniel had access, through a few informants, to the *entire*, representative Sri Lankan story. (This, of course, presupposes essentialism, that his informants were representative of their groups.) He may be an insider, he may even be partial to one point of view, but that is a justifiable bias based on a knowledge of the whole story. His ethnicity, his subjectivity, was an aid to interpretation, not a hindrance. Still, the reader must ask, are Daniel's proclamations about being an insider enough to make him one? Does the text move in a direction consistent with the claims of its putative author? For a start, the reader would have noticed that Daniel understands place empirically, not discursively; he lived more than half his life in that geographic entity called the West. Then, in a crucial passage early in his narrative, explaining why he decided to publish the stories of his informants, mostly UpCountry Tamil victims of "collective violence," Daniel tells his reader,

> I took upon myself the responsibility of telling a wider world stories that they told me, some at grave risks to their lives, only because they believed there was a wider world that cared about the difference between good and evil. The charge to tell a wider world also betrays these victims' despair over their own narrow world that has lost the capacity to tell the difference.[35]

This is the voice of orthodox anthropology to which, at least since Franz Boas, the insider-outsider distinction is indispensable: the scholar travels from the West ("wider world") to nativeland ("narrow world") and returns to inform the West about the natives. The scholar in question might be "native" himself, but that is not a significant difference, because native informants don't reside only in the "field." The most basic, foundational *structural* elements of (colonialist) anthropology identified above are reproduced here without the slightest self-consciousness or irony: distinguishing empirically between inside (non-West) and outside (West), informing this West about the non-West, informing an authoritative or powerful place about the powerless, and, perhaps most damningly, reinforcing the epistemological powerlessness of the powerless or relations of knowledge production that emerged during colonialism.

It was Daniel, after all, who took upon himself the "responsibility of telling a wider world" the stories his informants told him; they themselves did not demand it (even if they believed the wider world cared about them). Daniel, in this regard, does not sound very different from Spencer and Watson. Indeed, by reproducing the claim that Sri Lankans have lost the capacity to tell the "difference between good and evil," he makes his natives sound sick and rhymes with Watson. Daniel, that is, might be an insider on one register, but his work produces him as an outsider. Or, rather, since these terms aren't very useful, this could be phrased differently: the most significant element in Daniel's intellectual production, that which enables it to be characterized as belonging in the same category as the intellectual production of Watson and Spencer and not of the scholars, dramatists, and novelists discussed later, is not that, like the avowed outsiders, he lives and/or is employed outside Sri Lanka, or even that he shares their foreign citizenship. What is at stake here is that *his text does not intervene in a Sri Lankan conversation,* or argument, or brawl perhaps; rather it seeks to *interpret* the country to a "wider world," presumably the West. This debate in the wider world is certainly *about* Sri Lanka but, in a very strict sense, it is not *of* it. Daniel might be an insider, he might interview other insiders and collect their stories, but it is outsiders to whom he explicitly wishes to relate and interpret them; it is outsiders whom he feels can recognize their value, only outsiders—and I will stop using these terms momentarily—that he, like Spencer and Watson, finds intellectual-political community with. They may "attend" or "listen" to Sri Lankan voices, travel miles from the capital, no doubt at great inconvenience and without running water, in order to do so, but it is to the epistemic space of the West, and only that space, that their work is addressed. Spencer, after all, is not interested in "rewriting" Sri Lanka's past; that would be an interventionary act. All he wants is to comprehend, to "analyze" without getting involved. This produces intellectual activity as a sanitized exercise. Whereas, to a Gunasinghe, as already noted, the very purpose of intellectual, or theoretical, production is not comprehension or interpretation but involvement, getting one's hands dirty, taking the risk of being interventionary. To be entirely fair by Daniel, he does seek the same, at least in one sense: unlike Spencer, he wants his work to have an explicitly ethical level. He is not concerned with being considered objective. He wants to be on the side of the good. But, alas, he locates that good outside Sri Lanka. In so doing, he "incarcerates" Sri Lanka, in Arjun Appadurai's term, keeps it in its place, imprisons it as a place of difference.[36]

If, then, the terms themselves, insider and outsider, do not turn out to be very productive in helping understand questions such as these; if they are not even a convenient shorthand; if they cause more problems than they solve, another is needed—to capture the difference signified by Watson and Spencer; the difference that emerges from reading Daniel; the difference between the kind of intellectual production that produces itself empirically and objectively, as about mere understanding, or empirically and subjectively, as about biased understanding, both of which seek to comprehend, master the object, and then inform the West about Sri Lanka, or the non-West; and the kind, like Gunasinghe's, that seeks to intervene in Sri Lanka. Between the kind of intellectual production that proclaims itself to have no great stake in its object but only in its discipline and that to which the stakes—*understood as ethical and political as much as epistemological*—are huge. Between, in short, the colonial and the postcolonial. Even if the former inevitably informs the non-West's perceptions of itself; even if the latter, that is, is inevitably shaped by the powerful, authoritative, Western discourse. Put differently, Gunasinghe cannot be considered outside the West; no one who cites Althusser can. His work must be understood as speaking to both Sri Lanka and the West, though not equally. A Daniel would not be compelled to cite Gunasinghe's work—and doesn't; even though he must cite that of the anthropologists like Spencer who objectify Sri Lanka. So, then, if insider and outsider are not useful, a more supple term, I suggest, is abiding. It does much work for this study. And, quite serendipitously, finds its way into the title.

To the *OED*, to "abide" is to "wait, stay"; "pause, delay"; "tarry over"; "remain (after others have gone)"; "continue"; "sojourn . . . dwell"; "to stand firm by . . . hold to . . . remain true to"; to "endure . . . encounter, withstand, or sustain"; and, finally, to "suffer," even. To abide by a place, then, cannot be to physically reside in it. One cannot, after all, physically relate to a text. Rather, it means to display a commitment to attending to its concerns, to intervening within its debates, to taking a stand—to sticking one's neck out if necessary, even at the risk of what might seem like permanent frustration (thus making it an accomplice of Spivak's calls for "transnational literacy" and responsibility).[37] It means to display patience, to stay with it, endure it, work with it, even if it appears—and I speak, of course, of the question of peace in a textual object called Sri Lanka—unbearable, unending, unendurable. For, as anybody who has endured Sri Lanka over the past few decades could attest, it has been a tremendously frustrating affair. So, abiding by Sri Lanka also means suffering it, whatever the consequences. Daniel's informants, the attentive reader would have noticed, apparently did so, apparently spoke to him "at grave risks to their lives." His position, of course, is quite different. His text does not seek to stand by Sri Lanka (perhaps with good reason; he has nothing to say to a place that cannot tell the difference between good and evil). Neither does Spencer: the writers in his collection, apparently, are objectivist; they do not, as noticed earlier, intend "to disprove or discredit any particular view of the national past."[38] Abiding by Sri Lanka would require this, would require a stand. Unlike those of outsiders, to whom a relationship to place is temporary or unabiding, nonbinding, who, to be exact, comprehend place empirically, as an object (of study), texts that abide conceive of place as subject. Or, to be precise, texts that abide see Sri Lanka as simultaneously object (of knowledge) and subject (of intervention). These texts not only abide by Sri Lanka, they are also, in a certain sense, abided by it.

It also follows from all this, if you insist on asking the question, which really doesn't make much sense to a postempiricist, that a "person" can be physically "domiciled" in a place, to use a term favored by Walter Perera, without abiding by it and abide by a place without being domiciled in it. (The question does not make sense because what concerns this study is scholarship not scholars, texts not authors. This paragraph is included, at some risk, in the interest of clarity.) Fieldwork, however long in duration, attending to native voices, however far they may be from the capital or dangerous the enterprise, is not central to the question of abiding by. Neither is subjectivity. The pivotal factor, quite simply, is whether the *text* addresses, feels itself accountable and responsible to, the questions and concerns *only* of the powerful epistemological space of the West or to those of Sri Lanka as well. That is to say, my concern in this study is not with the subjects who produce arguments but with the arguments alone, not with the author but the text. How exactly these questions and concerns matter will be made evident in the pages that follow. I will conclude this opening salvo with a few examples of other intellectuals and their relationship to Sri Lanka; it will help, again at some risk, establish my claim. The science fiction writer Arthur C. Clarke would be someone who, according to geography, has been domiciled many decades in Sri Lanka, has indeed taken citizenship, without abiding by it; he is not in the habit of speaking out on the question of peace. He has published copiously in these decades but avoided what goes by the name of the ethnic conflict. In this same sense, Gananath Obeyesekere has all his adult and professional life abided by Sri Lanka. Even though he has resided and been employed primarily in the United States, he has consistently—and courageously—intervened within its debates, spoken to its concerns, refused to simply represent the country to the West and to address merely Western questions.[39] This is to be seen not only in his critiques, over the decades, of Sinhalese nationalism but also, for instance, when deploying psychoanalysis to explain the "work of culture" in Sri Lanka; he doesn't simply apply it to the country but recasts Freud creatively. Other names to be mentioned here include David Scott, Michael Roberts, and, to cite a perhaps perverse one, Adele Balasingham.[40] To move away from Sri Lankan examples, Fanon comes immediately to mind. Though born in Martinique, he abided by Algeria, if not Africa. And, to cite one of the most inspiring intellectuals of our moment—Edward Said, in relation to Palestine—even though exiled from the place, even though enjoying the privileges of U.S. citizenship, Said spoke to Palestine consistently, often at great personal and professional risk, producing work that challenges not only Zionism and its (imperialist) allies *and* elements of the Palestinian resistance simultaneously but also challenges our conceptions of community, of the necessary conditions for peace, of what we may need to forget or forgo, to forget *and* forgo, in order to achieve it. His intellectual production and interventions, over a long and consistent career, serve as an exemplary instance of what it means to abide by a place.

But, now, this argument should perhaps be rephrased somewhat more precisely, since it is cortical to the entire study. Abiding is a *concept* that allows a distinction between *texts*. The distinction is one the texts themselves call for, thus making abiding a "level" of the text. The term is needed because, having read texts that proffer Sri Lanka as their object of study, a difference emerges between them. That is to say, I noticed the difference only after reading the texts themselves, after, as it were, reading Watson after reading Gunasinghe. Some see the country empirically, objectively, antidiscursively, as existing outside the text, and work to maintain this distinction, thus contributing to the further objectification of the country, to its production as only object, to its incarceration. They have a stake in, or abide by, only the West; these texts, regardless of their particular disciplinary allegiance, are anthropological in the structural sense: they distinguish between (intellectual) subject and native (informant), then *speak for* the native, take her place, rather than address her concerns; the debates they wish to address are Eurocentric. Thus they reproduce relations of knowledge production that emerged with colonialism and cannot be considered postcolonial in the strict sense—regardless of their publication date. Others intervene within Sri Lanka, have a stake in the country, produce it as both object of study and as the subject of intervention. They *speak to* the problem of Sri Lanka. Explicitly or otherwise, these texts make the emergence of postcoloniality worthwhile. To capture this difference, which emerges from my reading and the texts themselves call for, I deploy the term "abiding," understood as an epistemological relation to, or intervention within, a place that foregrounds, explicitly or otherwise, the ethical and political interests at stake in such a relation/intervention,[41] as opposed to those that foreground the merely disciplinary, which present themselves either as objectivist and noninterventionary (Spencer) or as subjectivist and noninterventionary (Daniel). It should be stressed here, to repeat a point previously made, that place is understood by this study in textual, not cartographic, terms. That is to say, Sri Lanka is not just a place on a map, a self-contained, discrete entity in which events (by and large) do not exceed its borders. Sri Lanka is a problem, an intellectual and political problem—ultimately for the theory of democracy, not of violence, and not, either, for a theory of difference and one of the disciplines that authorizes it, area studies.

That said, it cannot surprise the reader that texts that abide by the country are the ones that really concern this study. It is in these texts—which constitute the country as a specific place—that the question of peace emerges as a problem in a manner that I want to address. But the one kind of text cannot be read without also reading the other, the Western/anthropological, those that objectify Sri Lanka, produce it as a place of violence. Given their authority, they inevitably shape the questions and contours of texts that speak to the country; indeed, they even help shape the contours of what is understood by peace. These other texts, of course, must be considered a part of the discourse of Eurocentrism—however much their "authors" might protest such categorization. Their texts represent Sri Lanka in the sense of being a proxy, put themselves in its place, make themselves a substitute for the country, rather than speak to it; indeed, they actually ignore the Sri Lankan debate, even erase it. In so doing, they reproduce a structure of knowledge production that emerged with colonialism, most exemplarily in the discipline of anthropology. They are, therefore, to be exposed, they must be opposed, by the postempiricist/postcolonial Sri Lankan leftist reader, as a matter of necessity, not of choice. For one thing, as said before, anthropology is the discipline that has dominated academic knowledge production on Sri Lanka in this epistemological moment. For another, casting one's lot with postcoloniality does not leave an alternative. Therefore, in the next chapter, Daniel's *Charred Lullabies* is more closely scrutinized and situated wherein the text places itself, the so-called interpretive turn in anthropology. So doing enables further clarification of what is at stake to this study in the distinction between that kind of text, which produces itself as the work of a concerned native but turns out to be that of a native informant, and the kind produced by a Gunasinghe, which abides by the country. Between those texts that, when they see Sri Lanka see violence as the problem to be explained, produce Sri Lanka as a problem for a theory of difference and those that find the problem to be about politics, something that should concern us all. It also enables closing, if only provisionally, the critique of anthropology, without which this study cannot proceed. For what unites Watson, Daniel, and Spencer is an essentially anthropological understanding of their object, of place and intellectual production. Without displacing such a conception of Sri Lanka, I cannot advance my own. To displace such a conception is to advance my own. In the next chapter, I also seek to (re)theorize postcoloniality. Strangely enough, the concept has not been adequately theorized by its advocates. Indeed, one might say it has not been theorized at all—except by its opponents. Arif Dirlik and his fellow travelers, of course, find it complicit with capitalism. This kind of thought, if it really can be called so, criticizes an idea not on its own terms but by talking of economics, of class. It is categorically confused. A far more intellectually honest critique of postcoloniality is offered, from roughly the same position, by Neil Lazarus, and I discuss his work at some length in the next chapter. After which, finding inspiration in Fanon, Spivak, and Chatterjee, I offer my own understanding, a (re)theorizing of the concept and the work it has still left to do.

Reading Abiding

But how, you may wonder, were the texts that abide by Sri Lanka chosen in the first place? By what criteria was it decided that a certain text does so and another does not? Do some texts come stamped "abiding by"? Or do I, despite my disclaimer, actually work within a notion of an insider? Even worse, am I performing some kind of police function? My only honest answer is that I did not choose the texts, they chose me. They insisted that they be read. For reading—conceived in opposition to interpretation—is not an agential activity. A discourse already exists on Sri Lanka. If one wants to intervene within it from a leftist perspective, or make an interventionary reading such as this—and want, again, is not to be understood as an agential term, since I am the product of my inheritances—the texts more or less select themselves, distinguish themselves from the Eurocentric, thrust themselves upon the reader, demand her attention. The nationalist histories, for instance, impose themselves because they constitute themselves as the true account of what really happened in the country. They dominate the discourse and so simply cannot be ignored. Just as much as one had to displace the anthropological account to properly situate these texts, one has to read the nationalist histories, come to terms with how they produce their arguments, then critique them if one wants to make a case—always in relation to these texts, not from a position outside them—about a different, a leftist, a more enabling notion of peace. And it is here that literature becomes indispensable, not just to the leftist reader but also to the postempiricist seeking to learn from the unverifiable, as opposed to the empiricist/verifiable and, to that way of knowing, social science, which finds significance in number instead of the singular. For, as will be seen, the literary texts do not exist as original works, hermetically sealed, outside of a relation to the social sciences; they are entangled with them, argue with them, support them sometimes, contest them at others. Taken together, all these texts constitute an object that, in a sense, I have assembled, as a postcolonial/postempiricist leftist reader seeking to intervene in Sri Lanka, just as much as they constitute me, the would-be abider, as their own object (of interpellation).

Kingsley de Silva's thesis about the question of peace in Sri Lanka, what he calls the ethnic conflict in *Reaping the Whirlwind* (and which the present text will read in chapter 2) is straightforward: the Sinhalese, the Sri Lankan majority, are the victims of centuries-long historical injury at the hands not only of colonialism, as one might expect, but of the Tamils before that.[42] Finally, with decolonization, they were able to begin healing these wounds—by exercising the democratic right of any majority to rule and to set the rules by which its country should function. The Tamils, a minority that was hugely privileged, economically and otherwise, during colonialism, did not accept their place after the British left, did not concede to the will of the majority as they should have, as any minority should in any democracy; instead, they made extravagant demands unwarranted by a minority. The most important of these have been conceded by the Sinhalese, who are not and have never been a tyrannical majority. For instance, the Sri Lankan government made both Sinhalese, the language of the majority, and Tamil, that of the minority, equal official languages of the country in the 1980s. Yes, this took place only after the Tamils protested that making only Sinhalese the official language, which is what originally happened in 1956, was unfair. That is to say, the Sinhalese may be insensitive, sometimes, to the concerns of the minority; they may act, sometimes, without consulting it; they have certainly made mistakes, but they are also always prepared to listen, to make fair concessions, to make amends for their mistakes. Nevertheless the Tamils continue to insist upon a separate state for themselves, on breaking up Sri Lanka, using bogus historical claims about the northeastern part of the country being their "traditional homeland" and equally bogus political claims about discrimination and military oppression to advance their case. It is a case supported by the West, which, incredibly enough, refuses to see that the Sinhalese have been behaving democratically, just like any majority anywhere. However, if you place the Sri Lankan situation in a long historical frame—which the West is reluctant to do, since that would bring the question of colonialism back into play—then it becomes quite clear that the Sinhalese, the majority, are the actual victims of the story. That is why, without history, without taking colonialism into account, a proper understanding of the conflict is impossible. Peace in Sri Lanka can only come about when the Tamils get this, realize what their place is, what the place is of any minority in any democracy—and accept it.

Jeyaratnam Wilson's thesis, made in *The Break-Up of Sri Lanka* (read in chapter 3), is as straightforward as de Silva's: the Tamils are not a minority but a nation; indeed, they are an oppressed one reluctantly exercising the internationally recognized right of every sovereign nation to self-determination.[43] The nationness of the Tamils is to be seen not only in their discrete language and culture but also in their history: they had an independent kingdom in northeastern Sri Lanka, the part of the country they dominate numerically to the present day and consider their traditional homeland, for centuries. This kingdom was never overthrown or conquered by a Sinhalese ruler but only by the Portuguese. Even then, that part of Sri Lanka was administered separately, by the Portuguese and then the Dutch, until the British eventually unified the government of the island. That is to say, the Tamils had no history of living together with the Sinhalese until colonialism forced such an eventuality. Despite this, and also despite severe suspicions of the Sinhalese elite at the moment of decolonization, who were giving clear signals that they intended to dominate the country, the Tamils were prepared to live together with the Sinhalese, as the British insisted they should. Only, though, if the majority recognized them as equals. The Sinhalese, however, consistently let them down; they made many promises to flatten the Sri Lankan playing field, grant them equal rights, respect their interests and desires, but broke every single one. Sinhalese leaders signed many pacts—but didn't implement even one. For instance, they promised to grant the Tamil language equal status to the Sinhalese in 1956 but didn't do so till the 1980s, by which time Tamil political demands had escalated and the Tamils were also being militarily oppressed. So the Tamils eventually resorted to separatism, to desiring a state of their own called Eelam, slowly and reluctantly, as the only means of saving their nation from political insignificance, perhaps even physical elimination. They did not want to do this. They had to. The Sinhalese gave them no alternative—as all Western human-rights groups and governments recognize and have been trying to make the Sinhalese recognize, too. Peace in Sri Lanka, therefore, can only occur when the Tamil right to self-determination is granted.

When read against the anthropological account, three things stand out about Wilson's and de Silva's texts, which are read as symptomatic chapters in the autobiography of Tamil and Sinhalese nationalisms, respectively. For a start, neither finds Sri Lankan events incomprehensible; in fact, to both, emplotting the Sri Lankan story is a matter of no difficulty—what the facts reveal is self-evidently, indeed superabundantly, clear. Second, culture and/or the trope of violence does not inform in any significant way, let alone dominate, their narratives; there is what the empiricist would call "violence" in these accounts, but what's at stake in them, the object to be described and interpreted, intervened within, abided by, is understood to be—and this is the third difference—political. The conflict is understood by both as being about the rights, privileges, and obligations of the majority and minority in a democracy. Thus both texts make claims, if implicitly at times, about how the conflict is to be resolved; in so doing, they intervene within the debate called Sri Lanka, take sides, abide by the place—if from very different, though sometimes also quite similar, positions. Western and Sri Lankan texts, then, clearly see the place very differently. But, you may ask, is the comparison fair? Won't two nationalists, committed as they are to certain political projects, inevitably see politics when they see Sri Lanka, whereas anthropology, being about the production of disciplinary knowledge, must necessarily differ? Not necessarily, for neither de Silva nor Wilson—academics both—produce their texts as making political arguments. Indeed it is crucial for de Silva, a trained historian, to insist that his text is pure disciplinary history, untainted by other concerns. The history he writes may have political implications or consequences. It certainly suggests that the Sinhalese claim to hegemony in postcolonial Sri Lanka is justified. But those things happen despite him. All he does in his work is provide an objective account of the record. Wilson, in contrast, admits an ethical—as opposed to a political—level to his text, to its being the product of a member of an oppressed group unable, in the later 1980s, to countenance Sinhalese atrocities any more. Nevertheless, he too insists that his arguments are historical and a disciplinary refutation of the Sinhalese nationalist account of Sri Lanka, a correct account of the facts, rather than determined by the ethical level. If the story of Sri Lanka implies that the Sinhalese and Tamils will inevitably separate, that is because history itself suggests this.

Several questions arise as a consequence of this difference. Most important, how does the reader evaluate the rival and quite incompatible claims advanced by both histories? Is there a neutral, Archimedean ground from which to do so? To the postempiricist, leftist or otherwise, calling for an alternative account, a better reading of the record, is not an option. That would be to work within empiricism. So Wilson and de Silva are read closely, to see how their texts work within the limits of the narrative form, to scrutinize whether they are in fact pure disciplinary history or—as the theory of the text suggests—informed by other levels. But what is meant by a "level"? The term itself, used for want of a better, is borrowed from Althusser and deployed catachrestically: in his usage, "level" characterizes the articulated *heterogeneous* elements of the "social totality."[44] The term is useful precisely because it enables the text to be understood as heterogeneous, as shaped by many disciplinary and other knowledges, perspectives, politics—elements of the text that, unlike for instance its actants or events, are not a manifest component of the written but emerge as a consequence of reading. To say this is only to acknowledge an axiom of textuality. A level, then, to paraphrase Mowitt, may be understood as brought to the text by its reader from elsewhere but also, equally and crucially, solicited by the text of its reader from this elsewhere.[45] Consequently, its levels are not to be understood as inherent to the text; noticing their presence is not the result of discovery, of making the latent manifest, but of the meeting between reader and written, of a symptomatic reading of the texts. Of, in the final analysis, a reading that might be understood as interventionary—as opposed to academic work that only seeks to "understand" (Spencer) or "interpret" (Daniel).

To interpret, of course, is to accept the existence of the object, and consequently of the subject, and to make a statement about the object from a subject-position (usually self-consciously) outside it. It is, therefore, to maintain, reinforce, the subject-object distinction. Interpretation cannot proceed without so doing. To intervene, at least in the sense being advanced here, is to put this distinction into question; indeed, it is to question, also, implicitly or otherwise, the notions of both subject/ivity and object/ivity. To interpret is to explain the object without wanting to transform it; it is to hold that the object somehow is, in its integrity, and cannot be transformed (since it would cease to be that same object if it were). Interpretation, then, does not ultimately break with empiricism, despite being opposed to objectivism. To intervene, in contrast, is to be postempiricist and most determinedly seeks to change the object. This commitment is its imperative, its driving force, its source of energy, that which compels it forward and, sometimes, holds it back. To interpret, however, despite its commitment to the integrity of the object, or perhaps because of it, is to find that object unclear and to seek to render it clearer (making the interpreter's chief tool, effectively, something like a dust cloth or, perhaps in this day and age, a vacuum cleaner). Thus there is something arrogant about interpretation, which presents itself as somehow better, if not more perfect, than its object, or at least necessary to perfect its object. To intervene is not to be faced with the problem of comprehensibility and certainly not to seek perfection. To interpret, in a sense, is to mediate between the object and its understanding. To intervene is to participate in the object, not mediate from outside it. To interpret is to understand the object as different, as other—and as eventually knowable, masterable, however difficult the task. To intervene is not to seek mastery, or understanding, and most definitely not to other. To interpret, ultimately, and paradoxically enough, is to be disinterested, to seek to make a truth claim of some sort about the object. To intervene is to be very interested and, obviously, not to make truth claims but statements that, eventually, take sides, statements that can and must be evaluated—on ethical and political grounds, not on those of accuracy or fidelity to the object.

The question is also raised, toward the end of chapter 3 and after reading de Silva and Wilson, of deauthorizing history. The question arises because, to the postempiricist, neither de Silva nor Wilson could be said to have written "bad" history. For that would also suggest, in contrast, a category "good" history, imply that an accurate account of what really happened in Sri Lanka, one faithful to the record and not to any politics, is possible. Whereas the concern exists and must be faced: how could two different academics, both trained professional historians, visit the "same" events and produce radically differing accounts of them? If history is the real narrating itself, how could this be possible? Does it tell the reader—especially if she is familiar with what, for want of a better term, might be called the French critique of history—something about the discipline itself?[46] What would be the consequences of such a realization—both for the understanding of Sri Lanka and of history itself? Michel Foucault has argued, quite powerfully, that we inhabit the age of history, that, within the Western episteme, thinking historically is actually a very new habit, that historicism became naturalized, but only since modernity, as the way to think, even in the discipline of biology.[47] Postempiricism, of course, must call historicism into question, for it implies a refusal of the very authority history—as the real narrating itself, what Barthes calls the "referential illusion"—has managed to assert over the present, over the apparent fixity of the present. For, if history is understood, in contrast, as narrative, as writing, as text, and not as the real telling itself, then the past can have no determining claim upon the present.[48] And the leftist desiring peace in Sri Lanka need not look to history, to Wilson or de Silva or even a leftist historian, and be frustrated because history cannot determine politics, but to ethics and politics and perhaps even literature, in order to address this question.

The reader might also have noticed, in the summaries above, an important similarity emerges between Wilson and de Silva and the anthropological texts they have been opposed to. While the first two certainly abide by Sri Lanka, intervene within its debates, all of them see the conflict in binary terms, as between just two parties, the Sinhalese and Tamils. What might be termed the dominant depiction of the Sri Lankan "problem," then, is shared by Western and Sri Lankan texts (which shows again the defectiveness of the insider/outsider distinction). To the leftist, however, this is an inadequate characterization of the conflict, which must be seen as also involving Muslims and UpCountry Tamils. On what basis, though, is this claim made? Not, of course, by insisting that such is empirically the case. Rather, it becomes necessary upon reading the narratives of Wilson and de Silva. De Silva produces the conflict as "complex," explicitly identifies four parties to it, including Muslims and UpCountry Tamils; put differently, there are four cardinal actants in his story. He then proceeds to narrativize it, despite his own claim to the contrary, as a conflict between just two "principals," the Sinhalese and Tamils. Wilson's text works similarly: Muslims and UpCountry Tamils also emerge there as having substantial stakes in the conflict, but he, too, while admitting this, cannot narrativize their perspectives. Nevertheless, they come into view through the fissures of the texts and make their demands upon a reader with a perspective such as mine. For the postempiricist critical of social science cannot place significance in number, cannot be concerned only with "principals" or major groups—just because they appear on the top columns of the census—and the leftist, working from egalitarian ground, arguing for equality and against domination, cannot see one group as more important than the other. The former, in a sense, is also the claim advanced, if suggestively, in Sivanandan's novel *When Memory Dies,* that the question of peace in Sri Lanka must be conceived as concerning all Sri Lankans, not just those numerically greater or dominant. And the latter is most definitely the claim advanced by Macintyre's *Rasanayagam's Last Riot,* that the question of peace concerns both men and women, but differently.

But why, after holding that an alternative history to those produced by Wilson and de Silva is impossible to the postempiricist, does this study turn to fiction? Am I simply boosting my own discipline? What can literature do that social science cannot? Literature, understood, if you will allow me the conceit, not as a noun but a verb, not as a material object but as a method, as synonymous with reading and the text, allows one to learn from the problems it stages: at its strongest, most articulate, most imaginative, it presents problems, not answers.[49] Such problems become the task of the patient reader, who has taken the trouble to become familiar with the Sri Lankan debate, to spell out. Spivak has argued that "training in literary reading is a training to learn from the singular and unverifiable" and that such training is a "species of patient reading."[50] The crucial terms in that formulation are "singular" and "unverifiable"; they are discussed in chapters 2 and 3. Here, a word or two about "patience." In my understanding, it rhymes with abiding by and, therefore, is the antonym of speaking to and with only the West, of ways of knowing structured and authorized (in that famous last instance?) by anthropology. For, in a very precise sense, patience is exactly what anthropology lacks, indeed, what it must constitutively lack in order to go about its business. Colonialist anthropology, or the enterprise of representing the Third World to the West, cannot have patience, cannot stay in a place, cannot pause, delay, tarry over, and get to know it, become familiar if not intimate with its questions and concerns, learn how to speak to it. It cannot endure. Rather, it is always impatient, always in a hurry, perennially in a rush—to craft some swift, sexy sound bite about the native condition (like Daniel's clash between the ontic and mythic) before the next conference or publishing deadline. Patience, on the other hand, takes time, and not just in the chronological sense. It can't happen with the guarantee of a return ticket, as opposed to the text that seeks as its purpose, its project, responsible engagement. It takes effort, not the kind involved in traveling miles out of the capital looking for authentic natives but the kind involved in abiding by.

Sivanandan's novel, discussed in chapter 4, does exactly this, intervening in the brawl between Wilson and de Silva. Patiently. It could, of course, be seen as just a story of Sri Lanka in the twentieth century, enjoyed or not accordingly, and then placed back on the shelf. (I must admit, in all honesty, that after its first hundred or so pages the novel does require a lot of patience to be read through.) Or it could be read, in the context of de Silva and Wilson, Gunasinghe and Jayawardena, as doing things they cannot do, for where the Westerner sees the country as constituted by culture gone to violence, Sivanandan sees politics. Where, to the nationalist, history can settle the debate, the postcolonialist insists that, after the epistemic violence of colonialism, history is impossible—except as fiction. Where, to the historian, significance can be located only in the empirical/verifiable and in quantity/number, or the logic of arithmetic, the novelist asks the leftist to learn from the singular and the unverifiable, from the minor, from the product of the imagination, that which never happened, and from quality, if you like, or the logic, to take a set of terms from Aristotle, of geometry.[51] Where social science leads the leftist to an impasse—since there is no ground to settle the rival historical arguments—literature offers an alternative to frustration. It cannot end war, of course. It has no blue-helmets on its side. (Just a sign or two!) However, it might help, just help, might be an accomplice, in the sense of a partner in breaking the law or rules, of doing something not quite sanctioned, in the reconceptualization of peace. But how does this study understand peace? Following Theodor Adorno somewhat catachrestically, it is understood as the "state of distinctness without domination with the distinct participating in each other"[52] (a formulation that will eventually be supplemented by Emmanuel Levinas). The texts of both de Silva and Wilson do not allow for such a possibility. Their conceptualization of a peaceful Sri Lanka, or Sri Lanka/Eelam in Wilson's case, does not anticipate, or desire, an end to domination or call for mutual participation. De Silva wants the Tamils to accept the Sinhalese (majority's) right to hegemony, hegemony being, as Ranajit Guha might remind us, a relation, ultimately, of dominance.[53] Wilson does seek an end to domination but only of the Tamils by the Sinhalese; if the Tamils were to find themselves in a position of dominance, say over the Muslims, in Eelam, he has no ethical quarrel with that happening. Majorities will dominate. That is a fact of life. Wilson—and this is one of the most crucial similarities in their two positions—does not disagree with de Silva over this general fact or structuring principle of representative democracy. His problem is that de Silva does not recognize a particular fact: the Tamils are a nation. *When Memory Dies*, in contrast, works within the logic of geometry, or the incommensurable, not that of arithmetic, the easily compared. Where social science can find significance only in "principals," this novel has actants from four ethnic groups. They are not all cardinal. In fact, the UpCountry Tamil is not given a speaking part and the Muslim barely speaks. But they matter to the text, or, more precisely, their figures can be put to work by the reader, whereas these groups don't really count to Wilson and de Silva. Sivanandan's plot, or emplotment, in contrast, is staged around the fates of all these actants—who participate in each other. In so doing, he asks that the novel be read, in the robust sense of the word deployed here, which needs now to be explained at somewhat greater length.

Reading, as said before, citing Barthes, is to be understood as a "productivity," as a meeting between the reader and the written.[54] It is also, importantly, not the consequence of the work of an agential subject. Yes, any reader inevitably brings her own inheritances—what is colloquially called baggage—to any particular reading, but such reading is also determined by what she reads, or the written. Thus comes the contention that reading is not an autonomous or agential practice; it is always a relational one, which (like peace negotiations?) produces something new, unanticipated—or, at least, should aim to do so. But what is at stake in insisting upon this, upon reading Sri Lanka? How might reading help reconceptualize the question of peace? Two further arguments of theorists of textuality will help here. To Barthes the text is always already interdisciplinary; it is shaped by many knowledges (or levels). Mowitt, in his reading of Barthes, deems the text to be an *anti*disciplinary object, emerging to work against the very notion of disciplinary knowledge.[55] If one is persuaded by these two positions, then part of the task involved in reading textually is to expose the work of the disciplines. Thus the importance of demonstrating that de Silva, for instance, doesn't produce pure, untainted disciplinary history but that his text is shaped by many levels. So doing, of course, is to make primarily an academic argument, or intervention in an academic debate. But my doing so is also motivated by a politics. It is my conviction that reading thus, reading texts that shape the contours and (re)produce the categories of our politics by paying close attention, apart from their "content," to how their rhetoric, structure, and movement shapes and sometimes deconstitutes this content, could significantly nuance, if not substantially guide, how we, leftist academics (re)thinking the questions of history, theory, and politics in this postempiricist disciplinary moment, especially those of us who characterize our work as postcolonial, rethink the question of representative democracy, and how, more particularly, those of us invested in Sri Lanka, who seek to abide by it, might conceptualize the contours and categories of a new leftist intervention into its longstanding and demanding debate on peace, on how we might shift the terrain of this debate and thus more effectively come to terms with the intellectual-political projects of Sinhalese and Tamil nationalisms. That is to say, I do not subscribe to the notion that right-wing intellectual production must simply be opposed (which in effect is to ignore its intellectual content). It is critical to the task of the left to come to terms with such work, not just with its positions and demands but the ground upon which it rests, its categories of analysis, its emplotment and narrative strategies. Otherwise, the left risks mirroring the right—operating, as it were, in enemy terrain. Whereas the task might be to shift the very terms and terrain of debate.

This study proceeds, then, against the argument, made in the context of the Sri Lankan debate and of postcoloniality, by Scott, that we inhabit a conjuncture in which the old divisions between left and right have lost their efficacy. But what exactly might it mean to be left in Sri Lanka at this politico-epistemological moment? I do not wish to answer this question dogmatically, by drawing clear lines that separate friend from foe, ally from enemy and accomplice. My understanding of being left isn't an exclusive one. (Besides, anthropology is the only politico-epistemological object I have a dogmatic position on!) So, given the commitment to abiding by Sri Lanka, and given even more the distinguished career of the left in the country, let me turn to a Sri Lankan for an answer, though not to one of its better-known names. Reflecting on the career of the Tamil or northern left, Santasilan Kadirgamar recently argued:

> A "left-wing" position in modern politics would involve leaning towards such positions as the following in some mix or other. These would include nationalization or control of industry, land reform, state control of the economy, and tax policies that favor the low- and middle-income groups. Also included would be pacifism or arms reduction, egalitarian policies in education, universal health care, a preference for ecological rather than industrial expansionist policies, and positive discrimination in favor of women and minority groups. In the Third World one would add a strong commitment to the rights of peasants and workers, human rights, civil and political rights, and especially social, economic, and cultural rights. It would also include the struggle against imperialism and neo-colonialism and in the contemporary context exposing and resisting First World domination in its political, economic, social, and cultural dimensions . . .
>
> Every left movement would have to be defined in the specific situation both in time and place where it emerges and functions. In the Lankan context one defining factor is whether the movement has taken a stand against national, especially majority, chauvinism and a political program that favors justice to the minorities.[56]

This, of course, is a historicist and empiricist, not a theoretical, articulation of being left. And, as in the case of Gunasinghe, elements of it could and should be quibbled with. Human rights, for instance, isn't a problem only for the Third World. The strength of Kadirgamar's argument, however, lies in its lack of dogmatism. To be left, here, is to have certain convictions and commitments, but not to be inflexibly devoted to them. Rather, it is to "lean toward" them, and not necessarily all of them, either, just in "some mix or other." Nevertheless, one commitment is required in Sri Lanka in the contemporary conjuncture: what Kadirgamar calls "justice to the minorities." Where one stands on the question of peace, then, would distinguish right from left. This would be, as they say somewhere, a necessary though not a sufficient condition. To put it differently, Kadirgamar could be read as having a theorizable position, not just an empiricist one. Being left, to him, is not simply a matter of a checklist. He holds that to be left is to read the world as structured hierarchically and to confront, contest, and combat hierarchization, oppression, and exploitation, a contestation that might very well entail a calling into question, when and where necessary, of the very understanding of hierarchization and exploitation. It is not to have a guarantee about the outcome of such contestation, but it certainly means to know in advance its general contours—or where, what kind of a position, one intervenes from (otherwise, one could not have an ethics). It might also, in this seemingly most pessimistic of moments, in this conjuncture marked by political and epistemological uncertainty, entail faith, an optimism of the will, a belief that things can be different, that "something that has never yet existed," in Marx's felicitous phrase, can be brought about.[57] In other words the stakes, for those of us who would insist on maintaining the distinction between left and right, are immense. Surely, it is unnecessary to point out that a possible future we anticipate or desire, if sought to be "refashioned" in the belief that oppression and exploitation must be opposed, would be a very different one from a future sought to be refashioned in the belief that these things are inevitable, a fact of life (as a de Silva might insist) and therefore to be accepted as inescapable.

It is in this task of "refashioning," or reimagining, that literature, understood as a verb, offers an opening that social science does not, for it is only after reading them, closely, patiently, that the arguments of Wilson and de Silva, Sinhalese and Tamil nationalism, appear incompatible with peace. A more mainstream or dogmatic leftist would find just political difficulties with them; a Neil Lazarus, for instance, would probably call them conservative or bourgeois nationalisms, would insist, perhaps, that an alternative radical nationalist history of Sri Lanka was possible, on the basis of which a different form of community could be conceived.[58] But the postempiricist reader would argue, in contrast, that nationalism itself is the thing to be contested, as such. For, as *Subaltern Studies* reminds one, nationalism always produces exclusivist notions of community and might be understood as a structure in dominance—things, surely, unacceptable to the leftist.[59] Thus the turn to the singular and the unverifiable, to the minority perspective, for alternative reconceptualizations of the question of peace. Of course, without a theory of reading, understood now as an interventionary practice, not an interpretive one, so doing would not be possible, for that, essentially, is what I have been doing here and seek to do in the rest of this study: intervene in a set of debates. The first is an anthropological debate, which has to be displaced, its Eurocentrism revealed for another way of coming to terms with Sri Lanka to be produced.

The second is a historical debate, in which works of (Tamil and Sinhalese nationalist) history that abide by Sri Lanka are read and after which the question is raised of deauthorizing history. The third is a literary debate, in chapter 4, where, following from the argument that history cannot determine (leftist) politics, the question is posed whether literature, reading with an emphasis on the singular and unverifiable, offers an alternative way of conceiving of the kinds of community, and of the relations between communities, that might constitute a more productive understanding of peace.

1

Better Things to Do:

(Dis)Placing Sri Lanka,

(Re)Conceptualizing Postcoloniality

We have better things to do than . . . imitate Europe.
                    —Frantz Fanon, *The Wretched of the Earth*

The "Interpretive Turn" in Anthropology

At the beginning of his narrative, Valentine Daniel lets the reader
know how he stumbled upon Sri Lankan violence as an object of study.
When he thought up his project in 1982, he had planned to write about
UpCountry Tamil workers and to produce an alternative account of
their history. He wanted to listen to their songs and use the lyrics to
challenge the official, and quite abject, version of their story. He arrived in Sri Lanka a year later, in 1983, "on the heels of the worst anti-
Tamil riots known to that island paradise to find that none of my singers
were in a mood to sing."[1] Although his singers may not have wanted to
sing, his informants told him their stories of being victims of the riots.
Consequently, his project changed: he felt he had to address the question of violence even if he didn't understand it, at least initially. It was not
easy to do so from a distance, from the United States. Indeed, he often
thought of doing nothing, but his conscience compelled him. He wanted,

perhaps, to abide by Sri Lanka, stand by it, support it. He certainly seems to have suffered it. So far, so good. Inspired, therefore, he returned repeatedly to the country, hunting and gathering more stories of violence. By 1989 things had gotten worse, far worse: "Kelani Ganga and Kalu Ganga, Sri Lankan rivers of exquisite beauty . . . were clogged with bodies and foamed with blood." Given this and other analogous happenings, Daniel found it difficult to write. "The [general] flow of events in Sri Lanka," he sighed, sounding like an astrologer, was "unpredictable." He bemoaned, with almost Conradian fervor, "the magnitude of its meaninglessness."[2] The country was not just incomprehensible but incredibly so, not just impenetrable but extraordinarily so. How, he wondered, could he produce meaning out of all this; how "does an anthropologist write . . . an anthropography of violence without its becoming a pornography of violence?"[3]

The difference between Gunasinghe and Daniel couldn't now be any clearer, even to the most determinedly Eurocentric reader. Both understand the 1983 "riots" as of pivotal significance to postcolonial Sri Lankan history. To that extent, their positions coincide. But, it is important to stress, they do not rhyme. Gunasinghe's response to the riots, which he did not find in the least incomprehensible, was not to call for comprehension as an end in itself but for theoretical reflection that would lead to new practice, to intervention that would produce social change (in Sri Lanka). His essay concludes with an insistence that the need of the moment is thinking of a solution to the ethnic problem. Daniel, in contrast, is not interested in politics in Sri Lanka; he simply wants to figure out a nonpornographic way to tell some stories, to interpret, to write (for the West). But, you may wonder at this point, don't I too? This study has been presented as an academic endeavor, not an activist one. Indeed, unlike Gunasinghe and like Daniel I am employed by the Western academy. So, surely, my own efforts must be identified as belonging to the same category as Daniel's, not Gunasinghe's? Such indeed would be the case if it were not sought here to speak to Sri Lanka, to intervene within its debates, to ponder its quandaries, to address its texts and concerns, rather than just Western ones. Daniel—and this is the first significant difference between us—merely seeks to inform the West about a place so amoral that it is unable to discern between right and wrong; he no doubt cares about the future of Sri Lanka, but that does not find a place in his text, which does not address the question of peace or Sri Lankan debates. He gathers his stories and leaves, intellectually and politically. His object emerges from his resultant text as only object. And the second difference: this study, while certainly directed at "Sri Lankans," understood as those who abide by the country, also addresses disciplinary practitioners, Westerners in the strict sense. *It wants to change the way they conceive of Sri Lanka and their relation to it.* It invites, indeed it urges those with an investment in Sri Lanka—and, by extension, any other Third World place—not to continue to objectify it but to take on the difficult and challenging task of speaking to it, abiding by it. Daniel, however, does not enunciate a project of this kind, having no quarrel with his discipline, indeed producing work that reinforces the disciplinary objectification of Sri Lanka. That is why this study must expose the bad faith, not of Daniel the author, but of the subfield of anthropology that he inhabits, its so-called interpretive turn, which represents itself as postorientalist, as having thought and worked through the critique of its career, its intimate association with colonialism, which produces its new practice as no longer objectivist, objectifying, or speaking for the native but as speaking *with* her and therefore being politically correct, as being no longer paternalistic but democratic and—finally—on the side of the good guys, as being, in short, no longer colonialist but postcolonial. Once that is done, one can return to *Charred Lullabies.*

If the best-known figure of this movement is James Clifford, the interpretive turn begins, of course, with the work of Clifford Geertz. His most important essay in this regard, where he explains what is at stake in his move, is "Thick Description," the introduction to his collection, *The Interpretation of Cultures.*[4] What initially appears different—and appealing—about Geertz's argument, at least to a reader like me, is his insistence on understanding culture semiotically, not empirically, and in antiessentialist terms. He presents his conception as opposed to the one dominant within anthropology to that date, the nineteenth-century definition of E. B. Tylor: "Culture or Civilization, taken in its wide ethnographic sense, is that *complex whole* which includes knowledge, belief, art, morals, law, custom, and any other capabilities and habits acquired by man as a member of society."[5] This thoroughly empiricist and essentialist conception has exhausted its usefulness, and a new, "theoretically more powerful" one is necessary, which must take into account recent intellectual developments like semiotics. It must recognize that what anthropologists "actually do" is *write,* or "inscribe" accounts of culture, not reproduce or represent another culture or "complex whole" in their texts by studying just a part of it—an essentialist enterprise. Thus interpretive accounts are to be understood as incomplete, contestable, and at a remove from their object: "culture exists in the trading post, the hill fort, the sheep run, anthropology exists in the *book*."[6] The book, or anthropology, is writing, or more correctly, interpretation, or even more precisely, "our constructions of other people's constructions of what they and their compatriots are up to."[7] This makes anthropology not representations of culture—which is what the discipline thought it was doing, from Tylor to the present—but "second and third order interpretations" of it.

At a first glance, this might appear attractive to the postempiricist. Anthropology is a semiotic practice; it is against a notion of totality and essence; it does not seek to capture a whole or produce the last word about a culture, only an interpretation. It is not a reproduction of the real but, one might say, something that exists in an analogous relation to it. It is antirelativist and accepts that—against Boas—one cannot interpret another culture on "its own" terms. Nevertheless, the reader would have already noticed a problem with Geertz's formulation: culture actually exists, empirically—in the trading post and so on. It is anthropology, writing about culture, that is called interpretive. Geertz's conception of his object—culture, that is—in one of its cardinal elements is not very different from Tylor's, even if his understanding of anthropology is. Which raises the question: how does he conceptualize anthropology—as writing or interpretation? If not representative of the real, what relation does it bear to it? "Doing ethnography is like trying to read (in the sense of 'construct a reading of') a manuscript—*foreign*, faded, full of ellipses, incoherencies, suspicious emendations, and tendentious commentaries, but written not in conventional graphs of sound but in transient examples of shaped behavior."[8] This, quite simply, is a very bad analogy (though there maybe no such thing as a good one, either). The cardinal difference between reading, at least in the textual sense, and Geertzian interpretation is that, as Barthes would remind one, the former is conceived as a productivity, a "meeting" between the reader and the "written." This meeting exists in language, the "writing" of which is not understood as a physical activity and is not therefore synonymous with "inscription." It does not seek to produce an object. Equally important, another reader, if unpersuaded—or even if intrigued—by a particular reading of a text can always refer to the written in order to be persuaded or, if not, to produce a different reading of the text. Such an object, of course, is not available to anthropology, which in this understanding has to deal with "transient" things. But, in the last analysis, it still deals with things, objects. For an interpretation is always an interpretation of some*thing*, an object. As the *OED* might remind one here, to interpret is "to expound the meaning of something abstruse . . . to render clear or explicit," even "to translate."

The very notion of interpretation, or hermeneutics, presumes an object.[9] Geertzian ethnography, then, is a very different enterprise from reading textually or postempirically. The two are simply not comparable.

Geertz is also stumped by the question of verification. Writing, to him, produces interpretations, constructs, "culturescapes," fictions—but fiction in the sense of something "fashioned," made up, not something false. If the "content" of a novel must be understood as unverifiable, because none of the "events" depicted in it actually happened, because its characters never existed, and so on, ethnography is not conceived in this fashion. And this is where Geertz's argument, like hermeneutics more generally, begins to deconstitute itself. For it is crucial to this disciplinary project that its product be conceived as verifiable. It cannot allow or sanction what it considers "chaos" or anarchy, something that might sound like relativism, accounts of culture that are all possibly "true" because all are by definition ultimately unverifiable. Some interpretations must be better than others:

> If anthropological interpretation is constructing a reading of what happens, then to divorce it from what happens—from what, in this time or that place, specific people say, what they do, what is done to them, from the whole vast business of the world—is to divorce it from its applications and render it vacant. A good interpretation of anything . . . takes us *into the heart* of what it *is* the interpretation.[10]

Geertz's argument, here, is not uncontaminated by a notion of essence or, of course, by empiricism, for the difference between a good interpretation and a bad one is that the former will take the reader "into the heart"—what could this be, if not the essence?—of some*thing*, or an object, that *is*, that exists, empirically. But how would a reader of an ethnography know that the account it contains is good? By what criteria does one evaluate ethnography? To an empiricist, to a Tylor or Boas, or Spencer for that matter, the answer would be straightforward: if the reader visits the culture under study, she would—or must—see the exact same thing the anthropologist saw; until the reader can make that journey for herself, she must trust the anthropologist. The interpretive anthropologist, however, cannot take this route, because, of course, two people could very well interpret the "same" thing differently. Does this inevitably imply relativism, all interpretations being equal? To some it might. In Geertz's case, coherence and consistency demand that it cannot. By, first, defining the very object of study as existing empirically and, second, defining the task of the study as the interpretation of that object, he implies that some interpretations *must* be better than others. If his theory of interpretation were not bound to the authority of the real, this problem would not arise. All interpretations would be equal, in the epistemological sense, and unverifiable; this would be, intellectually, a most radical move. However, Geertz does not take that step; once an interpretation is understood, as it is by Geertz, as an interpretation of an objectively existing entity, it follows that the two can be compared with each other, and with other interpretations—and some found to be better analogies, or interpretations, or interpretations of interpretations. This, of course, makes the claim that ethnographies are, by Geertz's criteria, incomplete and contestable, impossible to sustain. Those that take us to the "heart" of the culture being studied must surely be considered, by this logic, if not less incomplete, certainly less contestable. To further compound the confusion, Geertz elsewhere defines a "good account" as drawing upon "the power of the scientific imagination to bring us into touch with the lives of strangers."[11] The resort to the imagination would have been, again, a radical move if Geertz grounded his argument upon it—and worked, consequently, outside the logic of the verifiable. In not doing so, he only contradicts himself. For, a good interpretation, in one formulation, will take the reader to the heart of the culture or object; in another, it will be determined not by reference to the culture, or object, but to a vague and untheorized "imagination" outside it.

The reader would also have noticed in that statement Geertz's understanding of the purpose of anthropology: "to bring *us* into touch with the lives of *strangers*." Such statements are iterated by the text, culture once being termed "*our* formulations of *other* peoples' symbol systems."[12] This could be considered refreshingly honest and is indeed one of the things that is initially appealing about the interpretive turn. At least in this incarnation it does not pretend to be transparent, to be letting the native speak unmediatedly (although, in the famous essay on the Balinese cockfight, he does say that the Balinese think of themselves as animals). On the other hand, of course, Geertz ends up ventriloquizing, or speaking for, the native. He finds the purpose of anthropology to be "the enlargement of the universe of human discourse." But such enlargement will always happen as a consequence of *us* studying *them*. To Geertz the converse is inconceivable, as is the possibility that "they" might not want to be studied or that they might want to speak for themselves, without mediation if possible, or, for that matter, that they might not want to speak (to the West) at all. Thus my contention that the project of such anthropology is to reproduce the logic of colonial knowledge production, to "render *them* accessible." Geertz, that is, only speaks to, and from, the West. This position is strongly reinforced in the essay's concluding statement: "The essential vocation of interpretive anthropology is not to answer our deepest questions, but to make available to us answers that others . . . have given and thus to include them in the consultable record of what man has said."[13] Like Watson, this is Western liberalism at its benevolent best: we know they say interesting things; we know they do intriguing things, so we will include them in our records—after having interpreted them. For not only can we understand them on our terms, but they can't really understand themselves. From this follows, of course, that there can only be one agent at work in this project: the "we" who keep the records. "Their" fate is to be forever recorded. The force of Chatterjee's argument that anthropology is irredeemably, unrecoverably, structurally Eurocentric—he doesn't say so, but the implication is clear—because it can never allow, as he puts it, a "Kalabari ethnography of the white man," because it will always be about (powerful) us writing of (powerless) them, should now be evident. It is a largely unremarked-upon passage in a deservedly influential book and must be quoted at some length, both because of its own importance and its significance for this study:

> The scientist is always one of "us": he is a Western anthropologist, modern, enlightened and self-conscious (and it does not matter what his nationality or the color of his skin happens to be). The objects of study are "other" cultures—always non-Western . . . It could be argued, of course, that when we consider the problem of relativism, we consider the relations between cultures in the abstract and it does not matter if the subject-object relation between Western and non-Western cultures is reversed: the relations would be isomorphic.
>
> But it would not: that is precisely why we do not, and probably never will, have a Kalabari anthropology of the white man. And that is why even a Kalabari anthropology of the Kalabari will adopt the same representational form . . . as the white man's anthropology of the Kalabari.[14]

Chatterjee's argument is clear enough not to need too much of a gloss. Anthropology cannot escape its career: structurally, it will *always* reinforce relations of knowledge production that emerged with colonialism; it will always be us writing of, speaking for, them. Indeed, the discipline could be conceptualized as impossible without the inside/outside distinction, as always representing or speaking for an other, whether understood as located in the geographic West or outside it. This makes all anthropology, in a structural sense, colonialist. To put that differently: structurally, anthropology has been unable to displace its emergence within, its intimate implication with, a colonialist mode of knowing. It always represents, speaks for; it cannot abide by.

My conclusion, then, is that the interpretive turn's claim, at least in Geertz, to be radically different from that to which it is opposed, empiricist anthropology, is unpersuasive. It may stress the interpretive (and ultimately uncertain nature) of its descriptions, but it cannot do without an intimate dependence on empiricism, on the existence of the object. It may produce itself as a practice inspired by semiotics, but this turns out to be a novel semiotics—unlike that to be found in linguistics after Saussure—that works within a notion of human agency. ("Man is an animal suspended in webs of significance *he has spun*.")[15] As such, this is opposed to, not just different from, the understanding of signification in the postempiricist perspective. And it continues, like all anthropology, to operate within the inside/outside distinction, to objectify its object, to represent or speak for the native, to work within an epistemological matrix that emerged with colonialism. Inasmuch as the task of postcoloniality is to finish the critique of Eurocentrism, as will be argued later, it has an obligation, a duty, a responsibility not to compromise with the West, understood as an epistemic space, but to work, however frustrating the exercise, to make these things impossible. Working with/in postcoloniality leaves such as myself no other choice.

The charge of elitism, of speaking for, of taking the place of the other, was laid against anthropology most powerfully in the work of Edward Said and Johannes Fabian.[16] Since James Clifford produces himself as an anthropologist who has accounted for this charge, producing work that is no longer colonialist, it is to him, and the Introduction to the book where the new and improved interpretive turn apparently began, *Writing Culture*, that I now go (but not before noting that, throughout its career, from its early beginnings in Tylor and Boas to the present, anthropology has always depicted itself as antiracist!). Here's Clifford:

> No longer a marginalized or occulted dimension, writing has emerged as central to *what anthropologists do* both in the field and thereafter. The fact that it has not until recently been portrayed or seriously discussed reflects the persistence of an ideology claiming transparency of representation and immediacy of experience.
>
> The essays collected here assert that this ideology has crumbled. They see culture as seriously *contested* codes and representations; they assume that the poetical and the political are inseparable, that science is in not above historical and linguistic processes . . . Their focus on text making

and rhetoric serves to highlight the *constructed*, artificial nature of cultural accounts.[17]

Clifford, here, clearly seeks to distance himself from Geertz. The question of writing, he says, has not been discussed in anthropology until "recently." Geertz, of course, did so more than a decade before. Nevertheless, the citation of Geertz in Clifford's argument is evident, even if not made explicit: no longer taking experience as transparent, or culture as an empirically existing object, anthropologists now understand what they *do* as writing, or constructing, accounts that are, by definition, contested and, no doubt, contestable. This much, then, can be taken for granted after postcoloniality: business as usual is over; indeed, it has crumbled. Anthropology has come to terms with the challenges posed by (post-colonial) literary theory—and history. However, two significant differences between Geertz and Clifford must be identified. First, Clifford does not understand culture semiotically; he has no theory of the sign or of signification. Second, and perhaps more important from my perspective, is the political, and indeed ethical, claim made by this allegedly new turn in anthropology, that it does not seek to objectify the native and that it is sensitive to the relation between power and knowledge. Geertz did not even address the question of power; it did not occur to him. Or, rather, it was not raised as a problem; postcoloniality was barely emergent in his disciplinary moment. Thus he could continue to blithely objectify the native. The new anthropology, in contrast, defines itself as after postcoloniality. It must therefore account for the critique of colonialism and anthropology's profound implication with it; it must take the discipline away from its history; indeed, it must historicize the discipline. So—and this is perhaps the most significant difference between Clifford's position and Geertz's—it will no longer see the native as object but as subject. Where Geertz would speak *for* the native, Clifford would work *with* her. Consequently, the new and improved anthropology becomes not just politically correct but, in Clifford's phrase, "potentially counter-hegemonic." Given the career of the discipline, that is a tremendously audacious claim, one that must be scrutinized carefully.

The objectifying exercise of speaking for, then, was characteristic of the old, bad anthropology: "the predominant metaphors in anthropological research have been participant-observation, data collection, and cultural description, all of which presuppose a standpoint outside—looking at, objectifying . . ."[18] In contrast, the new, good anthropology sees those the discipline once considered "informants" as "coauthors." A decentering is promised here of the authority of the West, as is a critique of the inside/ outside distinction. Consequently, culture, the object of study, is "not [seen as] an object to be described . . . [or] a unified corpus of symbols and meanings that can be definitively interpreted. Culture is contested, temporal, and emergent. Representation and explanation—both by insiders and outsiders—is implicated in this emergence."[19] This sounds extremely promising. The postcolonial reader notes with satisfaction that the critique of objectification has been grasped by anthropology. It knows what it is accused of. That is most certainly an advance. It promises that it will work with those once seen as informants, relating to them now as coauthors, equals, subjects, not as inert, unthinking resources. But the postempiricist reader will also notice that Clifford cannot actually do without the inside/outside distinction. The anthropologist may no longer see himself as standing outside and representing, might produce himself as working with insiders/coauthors. Nevertheless, he is still an outsider, even if one who, paradoxically enough, does not stand completely outside since he writes with, rather than about, those "coauthors" on the inside. The inside/outside distinction clearly cannot be moved away from.[20] Place continues to be understood empirically. As in Geertz, Clifford, too, presumes an object that is interpreted by a subject. As stated before, that is inherent in the concept of interpretation, which cannot call the subject/ object distinction into question. What does this reveal about the interpretive turn?

That, of course, Clifford hasn't really broken with empiricism either. (Hermeneutics cannot.) That, more importantly, Chatterjee is right, not empirically but structurally: anthropology is about us producing knowledge of them.[21] This makes Clifford's position, the "interpretive turn," an act of utter bad faith. Geertz at least did not pretend not to be anthropologizing the native. But Clifford would have it otherwise, that he is really different. Why am I not persuaded that he sees the native differently? For one thing, if informants are actually coauthors, instead of simply being proclaimed to be such, then their names should be on book covers, copyright and royalty agreements, and the like; they should be allowed to teach classes, be considered for, if not granted, tenure, invited to conferences, entitled to frequent-flier miles, and so on. Anthropology, that is, is not simply about writing. To hold so is to have the most naive understanding of a discipline. But the more important question to ask of Clifford is the one posed to Daniel: does the anthropologist's assertion that the informant is now an author, or coauthor, automatically effect such a transformation? How is this to be determined? One does not actually have to go in search of copyright agreements or lists of conference participants to do this. The careful reader will notice that Clifford is betrayed by his own rhetoric. This is how the Introduction to *Writing Culture* opens, with the description of a photograph:

> Our frontispiece shows Stephen Tyler, one of this volume's contributors, at work in India in 1963. The ethnographer is absorbed in writing—taking dictation? fleshing out an interpretation? recording an important observation? . . . An interlocutor looks over his shoulder—with boredom? patience? amusement? In this image the ethnographer hovers at the edge of the frame—faceless, almost extraterrestrial, a hand that writes. It is not the usual portrait of anthropological fieldwork. We are more accustomed to pictures of Margaret Mead exuberantly playing with children in Manus.[22]

The reader does not need access to this photograph to get the point to be made here, though it would help because, among other things, it will show that the ethnographer dominates the image, even if he is at the "edge" of the frame. Tyler is in the light; the informant, in shadow, almost blending into his hut, into the natural. But we could let that pass. To Clifford, both Tyler and the unnamed Indian in the photograph are "interlocutors" ("One who takes part in a dialogue, conversation, or discussion"[OED]). Implicit in the term, as in its accomplice "coauthors," is the suggestion that both participants in this dialogue or discussion are equal. But, of course, only one of them—the "white" guy—is granted the courtesy, or perhaps the privilege, of a name in Clifford's text. More significantly, they are not depicted interlocuting or in dialogue, and, indeed, *only one of them—again the same "white" anthropologist—is said to write.* Clifford may proclaim that the new anthropology is a collaborative exercise; his own text, though, suggests otherwise: it is a partnership—if one at all—between unequals. One, the subject, writes, the other, the object, just informs; one is active, the other passive. For the picture to actually mean what Clifford says it does, surely it should show both "interlocutors" writing? For the interpretive turn to be a truly collaborative exercise, should there not be a relationship of equality between the partners, a disturbance, at the very least, of the subject/object distinction? But, quite apart from the photograph, Clifford's own narration signifies that there isn't one. On the other hand, reading somewhat against the grain, he could be seen as correct. The photograph can be read as exemplary of the interpretive turn in anthropology. It shows the object of the discipline—after the dialogue, perhaps—squatting, doing not very much more than "looking," and its

subject writing, producing meaning, interpretation, perhaps even ethnography. To the postcolonial reader, nothing significant has changed.
A decentering is promised, but it cannot, quite literally, be seen in the
photograph. "Representation" (speaking for), as Spivak put it in that famous essay, "has not withered away."[23] My point is quite simple: there
is no *structural* difference between the interpretive turn and ethnography
in its colonial incarnation. Both speak to the West. The difference with
the interpretive turn is that it *works by passing: passing a metaphor or relation
of substitution, speaking for or taking the place of the native, as a metonym or relation
of continuity, and speaking with the native.* The bad faith of this allegedly good
new anthropology lies here, in this passing, in this narratological trick, in
presenting an enterprise profoundly complicit with Western hegemony
as counterhegemonic.

A few further points need to be made, in conclusion, about Clifford.
First, what my study is calling for, in inviting anthropology to "speak to"
place, is *not* for a more genuinely collaborative ethnography, not for the
questions and concerns exclusively of the West to be brought to another
place, but for this West to respond to the questions of the other place,
to speak to it, to lose control—and, in so doing, to begin what might be
called the process of deauthorizing itself, of completing its autocritique
(after which, quite frankly, the only honorable thing left for anthropology
to do is to retire—preferably to the museum.)[24] For one of the most difficult things about abiding by Sri Lanka, in this disciplinary moment, has
been resisting the temptation—and I say this as a lover of food—to fast
unto death as a gesture of protest against the publication of one after
another after another after another, much in the manner of Tennyson's
brook, anthropological article on the country. "Will this ever end?" I have
often thought. Should one dare hope? Could something that has never
yet existed come to be? Disciplines, of course, don't just give up and roll
over at the first sign of trouble. Still, one hopes. Second, it must be noticed that, while this turn may consider anthropology writing, it doesn't
raise the same possibility about history. Ethnography, to Clifford, "is in
not above historical and linguistic processes." In this formulation, history
is understood empirically, as outside "linguistic processes," whereas it is
essential to postempiricism to see history as also writing. Third, writing
emerges here as a physical activity, as inscription, as opposed to a semiotic one. That is what the photograph signifies to its postempiricist reader.
Clifford may quote Barthes, but the resort to the self-evident "message" of
the photograph—denotation without connotation—to establish his point
suggests that writing and writer are distinguished by the interpretive turn,

a position, of course, consistent with its commitment to the inside/outside distinction. But it is not one that would be held by Barthes, to whom, quite simply, writing cannot be captured by an image. That is the quite obvious implication of the position that the text exists in language. Indeed, it doesn't seem to occur to Clifford that, by turning to a photograph—as he sees it, a self-evident, uninterpretable representation of the real—to rest his case, he contradicts his claim to be indulging in an interpretive act. For writing, here, emerges as a physical act, not very different from Geertz's "inscribing." And the postempiricist might insist, again, that in her understanding "to write" is an intransitive verb; *it does not produce an object*. Finally, and to point out another inconsistency, the very notion of a "coauthor" is allowed to coexist here with a theory of culture as writing/textual, whereas it is an axiom of the theory of textuality that the author is, as the famous formulation has it, "dead," that texts have scriptors or narrators—"a mere grammatical pronoun," Paul de Man might remind one—not authors. Like the inside/outside distinction, anthropology cannot let go of the notion of author or subject, because, and it doesn't take much to figure this out, with the author lies authority. Disappear it and with it would disappear the authority of the discipline itself, the hegemony it enjoys over the production of knowledge of postcolonial places.

Derrida, of course, made a similar argument about the discipline a long time ago. That "ethnology . . . is primarily a European science employing traditional concepts, however much it may struggle against them. Consequently, whether he wants to or not . . . the ethnologist accepts into his discourse the premises of ethnocentrism at the very moment that he denounces them. This necessity is irreducible; it is not a historical contingency."[25] In other words, even the interpretive turn cannot avoid being complicit with the structural Eurocentrism of a discipline that emerged to enable speaking for the other and continues to operate so as to continue to enable it. Derrida is cited here to remind us that this argument has been made, even if a while ago—and has not been superseded. We cannot, and should not, forget it and proceed with business as usual—and ignore, with a shrug, the pretenses of the so-called interpretive turn. It must do so, yes. But the postcolonial/postempiricist cannot. Consolidating the gains of the critique of empiricism means, among other things, exposing the discipline's profound and continuing complicity with a colonial way of knowing. This complicity can be seen in its "father," Edward Burnett Tylor, who explicitly evaluated the savage (native) from the perspective of the civilized (Westerner). It can be seen in Franz Boas, who refused to be absolutist, who substituted the less severe term "primitive" for "savage," who wanted to study the native on his own terms and insisted that the discipline should do so, too.[26] But then, how many primitives ever called themselves such? This can be seen in Malinowski, Lévi-Strauss, Geertz—throughout, that is, the career of the discipline, including, as argued above, the allegedly politically correct good new interpreters. This is why, of course, the stakes to the postcolonial in the critique of anthropology, in working to make it impossible, are very high.[27] But to say this is not to hold that I write from a pure space, a position outside anthropology. To work with it, even if only to critique it, is to be inevitably complicit. To speak of Sri Lanka to the West, even while critiquing such speaking of and about, even while seeking to abide by, is to inevitably play the part of the native informant, to some extent. Such complicity, if agonizing, bitter even to admit—and, believe me, it took me a long time to make this statement—is inescapable. The least one can do is be aware of it.

On Violence

Daniel's contention is that "one of the structural conditions for collective violence [in Sri Lanka] is to be found in the discordance that obtains between . . . epistemic and ontic discursive practices."[28] Daniel's substantive argument cannot be given much attention here for two reasons. As said before, it doesn't abide by Sri Lanka or address the question of peace. Like Spencer, and Steven Kemper, whose work is glanced at in the next chapter, the work Daniel does for this study is to enable a distinction between kinds of texts. Furthermore, and amazingly enough in this disciplinary moment, his argument is premised upon metonymy, or essentialism, and culturalism. Sinhalese and Tamils have two very different "dispositions" toward the past: the Sinhalese is "epistemic," a way of seeing that privileges history; the Tamil is "ontic," a way of being that privileges what he calls heritage. Now an argument critical to this entire study is that one of the most significant things *both* Sinhalese and Tamil nationalisms share is that they *produce themselves*, in the literally hundreds of texts available for reading by those who seek to abide by Sri Lanka, as battling not just over claims to the present, or politics, but over the past, or history. Both nationalisms insist that what must determine Sri Lankan politics today is the correct understanding of history.[29] But Daniel blithely ignores such Tamil texts, and, indeed, his ignorance of Tamil nationalism is staggering. The Tiger symbol, for instance, from which the Liberation Tigers of Tamil Eelam take their name, was that of the powerful (southern Indian) Chola Dynasty. Daniel produces his claim about the dispositions as an "informed hypothesis," informed, that is, by "random" interviews with students, one hundred Tamils, twenty Sinhalese—plus one Sinhalese tour guide. I point this out not in order to say that Daniel should have interviewed more informants, or done it with the help of a statistician as opposed to doing so randomly; rather, this mode of knowing has no ground from which to rebut me if I claimed to have interviewed the same number of Sinhalese and Tamil students, or hundreds more for that matter, and reached the exact opposite conclusion. Unlike Geertz, what is epistemologically radical about the new interpretive turn is that it doesn't address the question of verification. It is mortally susceptible, at least in this instance, to the claim that it produced nothing but fiction because it does not provide the criteria by which its contentions and positions can be evaluated, criteria that can, ultimately, only be ethical and political.

The other element of Daniel's argument that demands comment is his commitment to essentialism. All Sinhalese and Tamils, he implies, share these "dispositions." If this is unexpected from an avowedly interpretive anthropologist, given that the interpretive turn, from Geertz on, is explicitly premised on its opposition to essentialism, even more unexpected is Daniel's defense of it:

> Essentialism has come to be the bad word of late modernity. The human sciences have rushed to embrace and expound upon the constructedness of practically everything . . . Much good has come out of these constructivist exercises, some so brilliant so as to deserve the adulation of generations to come. The scholarship that most obviously merits such adulation is of course that of Michel Foucault . . . But there is to be found in some constructivist scholarship at least two unintended, not so very salubrious, effects. Both concern the uncanny resemblance that certain schools of constructivism bear to [essentialism].[30]

Foucault would have been surprised to see himself characterized as a constructivist. Discourse, after all, is not conceptualized as a construct, but that is somewhat beside the point. To Daniel, since just *some* constructivist scholarship is essentialist—and his claim would be easier to take if he told the reader exactly which body of texts he had in mind—the *entire* critique of essentialism becomes mala fide and he can continue being an essentialist in good conscience. This proceeds on the assumption that the critique of essentialism is homonymous with constructivism. Such a position, to say the least, is unpersuasive, especially since it doesn't cite even one instance of constructivist essentialism.

Besides, given the terms important to this study, his text doesn't seek to intervene in Sri Lanka but to interpret it. Such a claim is also the basis of Pradeep Jeganathan's critique of Daniel, even if he doesn't phrase it in exactly these terms. Jeganathan situates Daniel within the anthropology of Sri Lanka, "which is now dominated by the category of violence."[31] Jeganathan specifies "now," as opposed to before the "riots" of July 1983 that Gunasinghe found pivotal. Or, to phrase it differently, the study of Sri Lanka in this epistemological moment is dominated by the discipline of anthropology. Sri Lankanist anthropology, continues Jeganathan, stayed in the village until 1983 and concentrated "on categories such as caste, kinship, and marriage." The discipline that treated the state, indeed dominated intellectual production on Sri Lanka after independence, was political science. According to its narrative, which will be encountered in the following chapters, too, in de Silva and Wilson, Sri Lanka was an exemplary instance of the transformation of a "model colony" into an equally modular modern Third World democracy. Then came what Jeganathan calls that "massive event," the riots: "July 1983 . . . positioned in a narrative of Lanka's possible modernity, is distinguished by its incomprehensibility to political and administrative discourse."[32] Given the narrative it had already produced, of a country steadily progressing toward modernity, political science could not explain what it saw as the horrors of the riots, the total disintegration of the Sri Lankan state in and after 1983, and the consequent demise of modernity. The country's story could no longer be emplotted in exemplary terms.[33] The discipline found the phenomenon, in a word, incomprehensible. How, it asked itself, could a model democracy produce such horror? And it had no answer; its categories were unequal to the task: modernity, after all, presumes the rational exercise of politics (not "irrational" violence). Anthropology, argues Jeganathan persuasively, was also initially at a loss for an explanation; it, too, responded with incomprehension to the riots (as was seen with Daniel). Then it moved, as it were, from the village to the city, gave this phenomenon a name—"violence"—and produced culturalist explanations for it. S. J. Tambiah, for instance, saw the "riots" as the consequence of Sinhalese Buddhism, a nonviolent religion, "betraying" itself. To Daniel, it had to do with the clash of ontic and mythic dispositions toward the past. In other words, when anthropology saw Sri Lanka, it found culture at work, culture turned violent—and not politics.

So, what exactly is at stake here, you wonder? Violence took place and then it was written about. This is a self-evident happening. Disciplines respond to events; that is what they are supposed to do. Why political science failed to address violence is a banal question because it is well known that poli sci has trouble explaining culture, whereas culture is what anthropology is all about. However, as Jeganathan points out, postcolonial Sri Lanka featured at least two other "massive events" that could be considered violence within the logic of empiricism: the 1958 "riots" against the Tamils and the 1971 insurrection against the state. Political science explained both quite easily: as a crisis for the state and as a leftist insurgency, respectively. In other words, and this is the crux of Jeganathan's argument, all mass killings in Sri Lanka were not seen as violence; they were made sense of differently. But 1983 was different; political science found it incomprehensible, leaving a disciplinary vacuum to be filled by anthropology. How was it able to do so—and without much effort? Because, argues Jeganathan, the *study* of 1983 coincided with the emergence of "violence" as a global phenomenon—Rwanda and Bosnia were also being studied as places of violence—which anthropology as a discipline had to explain because it happened in strange non-Western places. Again it is crucial to Jeganathan's argument to notice that, from an empiricist perspective, violence could be considered to have been happening globally for a long time. He cites the war in Indochina "that extinguished more than two million lives." That, of course, was not called violence but politics: U.S. imperialism, communist adventurism, national liberation, Marxist revolution, depending on one's perspective. (One might make a similar point about Bush's adventure in Iraq.) Violence, concludes Jeganathan, is not something that names itself as such but a name given to some "events" and not others. It is not self-evident that events in Sri Lanka are "violence"; they could always be considered politics. What, then, made Sri Lanka, Rwanda, and Bosnia violent, different from Vietnam—and, indeed, comparable to each other in the first place?

> "Violence" in this [anthropological] view is an analytical name for events of political incomprehensibility, events of horror, events that challenge ideas of humanness and humanity, without a countervailing and intelligible political meaningfulness . . . Is there "more" "violence" now in Rwanda, Bosnia, and Sri Lanka than there was in Indo-China? My answer is categorical, not empirical: the war in Indo-China had a political name . . . What is called "violence" today is different, for it cannot be easily placed under a political sign.[34]

Cannot, I would add here, by anthropology. Therein lies the difference— surprise, surprise—between Daniel and, on the other hand, Gunasinghe, de Silva, and Wilson. When Daniel sees Sri Lanka, he sees the object produced for him by his discipline. It is violent, horrible, and, at least initially, impenetrable. But then he managed to make sense of it, partly by comparing it to other violent, horrible, and incomprehensible places, like Bosnia and Rwanda. He made sense of Sri Lanka not by attending to its concerns, its debates, its singularity, but through analogy (which can only work by a certain confusion of arithmetic and geometry); he found significance in number.

De Silva's and Wilson's texts, as will be seen, cannot do without analogy, either. But the place to which de Silva's text most significantly compares Sri Lanka is Malaysia—which does not have exemplary status, as Jeganathan might remind one, in the emergent anthropological canon on violence. To de Silva, a Sinhalese hegemonist, Malaysia is an instance of a multiethnic country at peace because, he is convinced, its principal minority accepted, consented to, the hegemony of the majority. (Other accounts of Malaysia are, of course, available; what de Silva's position shows, really, is the inadequacy of understanding peace as the absence of war.) Wilson, a Tamil separatist, compares the Sri Lankan Tamil case to— again unsurprisingly—Bangladesh, within his terms a successful instance of separation. Both comparisons are examined in the next chapters. The point to be made here is quite straightforward: like Gunasinghe, when de Silva and Wilson see the country, they see their object, that which is to be understood, grappled with, and explained, the problem or conflict in Sri Lanka, to be about *politics* and as pivoting around the question of the rights and privileges of the majority and minority in a representative democracy. Anthropology—Daniel, Tambiah, Spencer, Watson—sees incomprehensibility, then violence and horror, things caused by *culture*. (And I hope I don't have to remind the reader of this, but it won't hurt: it doesn't matter what the place of birth, or employment, or "skin color," of the particular anthropologist might be. Scott, an anthropologist by training but in fundamental conflict with his discipline, sees politics in Sri Lanka.) Therein lies the most significant distinction between the production of Sri Lanka by those texts that abide by the country and those that speak to the West. Anthropology sees Sri Lanka as non-Western, as outside it in more than one sense; what happens there—in a word, carnage—is not to be found in the contemporary West. It is, in other words, a problem to be explained by a theory of difference. To the abider, as it were, Sri Lanka poses an intellectual and political problem—and a serious one, at that—for the theory of (representative) democracy, for its justification of majority rule as ethical. This, of course, is not something that makes the place radically different from the West. Making this case, that the "problem" of Sri Lanka is not a problem for a theory of difference, makes the place therefore of interest not just to the Sri Lankanist but to the postcolonialist more generally.

Reconceptualizing Postcoloniality

Throughout its brief career, and despite its impressive intellectual successes, or perhaps because of them, postcolonial studies has also been the object not just of critique but of attack, often of the vitriolic variety. Its profound epistemological challenge to more established—modern, empiricist, historicist—ways of understanding the social, the literary, and the cultural, it would appear, is threatening in some fundamental way. If the attacks from the conservative right—whose sentiment could be summed up in the position implicit in the statement usually attributed to Saul Bellow that, if there were a Zulu Tolstoy, he would read him—were only to be expected, because the canon itself is at stake in that debate, those from the conservative left were not (yes, these two positions share something deeply conservative: they are both committed to continued epistemological dominance by the West). But dogmatic Marxism and its historicist allies clearly have declared what amounts to war on postcolonial studies; thus one imperative to defend it. In pathetic parodies of a Leninist polemic, Aijaz Ahmad, Arif Dirlik, and Terry Eagleton, unwilling or perhaps just unable to take on the substantial arguments made by this field of study, resorted to mud slinging as a response. Their approach is based on the belief that if you throw enough muck at those making the arguments, the arguments themselves might disappear. The vacuousness of such a strategy has, of course, been thoroughly exposed. Indeed, one of the best responses to Ahmad's venomous attack on Said has come from within dogmatic Marxism itself. In a most careful reading, Lazarus argued that Ahmad's animus against Said had to be personal, not intellectual or political.[35] Similar critiques have been made of Dirlik[36] and could be made of Eagleton, but his rant is best ignored. Dirlik's position, in sum, is this: "the popularity that the term 'postcolonial' has achieved in the last few years has less to do with its rigorousness as a concept, or the new vistas it has opened up for critical inquiry, than it does with the increased visibility of academic intellectuals of Third World origin within the area of cultural criticism."[37] This, of course, is not an intellectual response to postcoloniality; such a response would take on the actual arguments, not those involved in making them. And it, too, is a racist statement, for in holding that postcolonial studies in general has not "opened up" any "new vistas" at all, Dirlik implies, as does his fellow traveler Bellow in relation to postcolonial literature, that this by-now most impressive body of scholarship is of no value at all. This slander could be responded to at length, but others have done so more than adequately, so I will restrain myself to just two words: *Subaltern Studies.*[38] Indeed, taking inspiration from a certain tendency within that collective's truly door-opening body of writing, and from Fanon's *The Wretched of the Earth*, I'll articulate my own take on post-coloniality, one that seeks to (re)theorize the concept, for Dirlik is right in one respect: the concept has not been adequately theorized. Taking both the "post" and the "colonial" in "postcolonial" seriously means arguing that the concept still has a lot of hard labor left on its plate, that it hasn't been superseded by globalization theory. Why does this study find inspiration here and not in the output, more fashionable in postcolonial studies, of metropolitan scholarship? Because the latter, in structural complicity with anthropology, only addresses the West. Because the former, and this is the critical difference, abides by the places it works from and speaks to: India in the first case, Algeria/Africa in the second.[39] Fanon, to state the obvious, was never about addressing the West (except incidentally, if not unavoidably), though he was able to think Africa and the West simultaneously and, in so doing, provide a model for such scholarship. Likewise with *Subaltern Studies*: it emerged as a critique of both colonialist and Indian nationalist historiography; it demonstrated that one cannot think the latter without reference to the former. Both took very seriously the debates, the specific questions, of the places in which they found themselves and in which they intervened. Both may not have and indeed did not think their projects through the rubric of postcoloniality, but such a possibility lies implicit in the work—and it is the task of the (symptomatic) reader to make it explicit.

But, before getting there, one should ask if dogmatic Marxism does in fact have a case. To do so, I will turn to the (alas) only properly intellectual argument made against postcolonial studies from within such Marxism, that of Lazarus.[40] Properly intellectual because, unlike Dirlik and company, Lazarus actually examines the texts he seeks to engage, critiques those he disagrees with, but also finds allies in unexpected places—some of Guha's work, for instance—and acknowledges this, instead of making blanket condemnations of the entire field.[41] Unlike his comrades, Lazarus takes his protagonist seriously, respects it enough to discuss it, which is why, unlike his comrades, Lazarus must be engaged. But why do I call this Marxist position "dogmatic" instead of the more common "orthodox"? Because, like his comrades, Lazarus, who often sounds like a moralist, is inflexible. He believes, without being open to the possibility of disagreement, in "right" and "wrong" readings. His chapter on postcolonial studies is riddled with formulations like the following: "Fanon is simply incorrect"; "Fanon's error"; "Clegg's analysis rings true"; "Taylor quite correctly"; and so on.[42] The move, here, is to distinguish between true and false. Reading becomes not very much more than the issuance of decrees. What should be understood as a matter of agreement and disagreement becomes a matter, quite simply, of true and false. As such, then, his method is opposed to reading in the sense deployed in this study.

Lazarus's argument could be reduced to two points. One, inspired by Lenin, is that there are good (anticolonial) and bad (Western/imperialist) nationalisms. Postcolonial criticism does not recognize this, does not differentiate between nationalisms but seeks, ahistorically, to condemn them all, even the good: "In much of the work currently issuing from this field, the massive nationalist mobilizations of the decolonizing years are thoroughly disavowed."[43] To Lazarus, following from this, the task of postcoloniality is synonymous with that of anticolonial nationalisms; it must continue to seek inspiration from those movements, rather than "disavow" them. This position, of course, is political rather than intellectual; it implies that the task of the academic is to be an activist, something I find both irresponsible and, actually, quite immodest, making the academic into something more eminent than she should or could be. In taking such a position, Lazarus also assumes that the history of anticolonial movements is known, recognized as heroic, and cannot be revisited, revised, or rethought—as *Subaltern Studies*, which most decidedly did not disavow those movements, has done. And, most unacceptably, it collapses the postcolonial into the anticolonial, giving the first term no substance, or a signified. For, the question arises: if "postcolonial" is homonymous with "anticolonial," why have the term "postcolonial" at all? If Lazarus's argument is persuasive, the term itself should be retired, its emergence deemed worthless or at best the self-serving demand, à la Dirlik, of migrants in the metropolis. Additionally, it is critical to notice here, his position is grounded on the empirical and prevents theorizing—in this instance of nationalism. To him, there are "pertinent distinctions to be drawn between different nationalist projects—whether [they are] conservative or revolutionary, bourgeois or socialist."[44] Perhaps, but to hold so is to remain within empiricism. Theory would insist, however, that nationalism itself, as such, could—and should—be conceptualized.

An argument about the nature of theory could be made at some length here but, in the interest of economy, let me fall back on Spinoza's famous statement, cited by Althusser: "the concept dog cannot bark."[45] For, if one wanted to understand "dog"—or any other object, for that matter—there are two ways of so doing. The strict empiricist would observe dogs in the street, or the field perhaps, or even the laboratory for all I know, take a random sampling of many of the animals and conclude, predictably, that all dogs are different: dachshunds are cute, dalmatians spotted, Doberman pinschers scary, and so on. The postempiricist, in contrast, would not have to observe. She would conceptualize, would perhaps hold, with Spinoza, that dog is a concept, understood as an animal that barks (something that happens in language). Or, to make the more general argument, with Althusser: "theoretical practice is indeed its own criterion, and contains in itself definite protocols with which to validate the quality of its product."[46] Theory is the production of concepts that are either useful or useless—to think with. Concepts, in turn, have no referents. ("World peace" is an excellent example here: it is certainly a concept, and nobody, I think, will argue that it exists. A leftist, a liberal, an Islamist, and a conservative would, however, disagree on what exactly it signifies.) In the strictest sense, the concept is outside politics. To confuse the two, as Lazarus does, is to misunderstand its work. Theory maybe useful for politics. Politics maybe impossible without it. And theory may even complicate politics—as I argue in the Conclusion—just as much as politics may complicate theory. But, to recall Gunasinghe's argument from the beginning of this chapter—or was it Mowitt on Marx?—the two are not the same.

Nationalism, then, could be theorized as such. It is a trivial position to hold that all nationalisms are different; one learns very little, *intellectually*, about one's object from doing so, for if one could distinguish, following Lazarus, between conservative and revolutionary nationalisms, then it should also follow that every instance of "conservative" nationalism would be different from every other instance. This would make the category itself unstable, for the only ground upon which conservative nationalism could be categorized would be a political, not an intellectual, one. Whereas, if one concedes the category "conservative nationalism," then, at the risk of stating the obvious, methodological rigor demands that the possibility of the category "nationalism," too, could be conceptualized. Thus the postempiricist would take the risk of conceptualizing nationalism as such; for instance, it could be conceptualized as a structure in dominance that hegemonizes women, minorities, and the subaltern classes, and excludes queers, tribals, and so on.[47] Indeed, it is precisely here, in the task of conceptualizing nationalism, that the work of *Subaltern Studies* becomes vital, because it revisits the question of history and asks,

Is the nationalist account of the anticolonial movement persuasive? Did it have a seamless, metonymic relationship, as asserted, with the masses? Did nationalism actually produce one united nation as it claims? Did those masses mobilize in the name of the nation? Or is it better understood as a structure in dominance? Through meticulously detailed histories, which I cannot summarize here, *Subaltern Studies* has demonstrated that those "massive mobilizations" of Lazarus, while appearing nationalist and anticolonial from an elite perspective, may have had an entirely different logic when seen from that of the subaltern. After all, the project of the collective, as Guha put it in the first volume, was the "study of . . . [the] *failure* of the nation to come into its own."[48] An argument he developed in a later text, which Lazarus ignores, has it that nationalism, like colonialism, is to be *theorized* as a relation of dominance without hegemony and that the subaltern classes were not seen as equals by the nationalist elite but as groups to be disciplined under the control of the elites.[49] The inescapable implication of the work of the collective as a whole, then, is that the nation as such is a dominating, not egalitarian, and so a disabling form of community. But Lazarus cannot admit this, and in so doing, not just the Eurocentrism but the conservativeness of his position becomes clear. Lenin had the last word on nationalism, in Europe, in the early twentieth century. The work of no group of Indians can alter that. One can only learn particulars from Indians, and that, too, only if they work within the categories of Lenin and the Enlightenment.

Strangely enough, though, given his commitment to context, to history, to particularity, Lazarus writes from nowhere. He has no commitment to a particular place, even one understood empirically. He may assert that "no abstract or a priori assessment of nationalist politics is credible," but that is precisely his own position:[50] that anticolonial nationalism, as such, must continue to be supported. Anywhere and everywhere. If this is not an abstract or theoreticist position, I wouldn't know what is, even though, paradoxically enough, it comes from a position that is effectively anti-theoreticist. (But then, this is the structural weakness of much of Lenin, is it not: his work draws intimately upon theory in order to make purely strategic, and therefore antitheoretical, arguments.)[51] This is where the difference between this kind of attitudinizing toward the Third World reveals its starkest difference from *Subaltern Studies*. The work of Amin, Chatterjee, Guha, Pandey, and Prakash attend to place in a meticulously detailed way. Their texts abide by India. Lazarus's abides by no place. Again, a strange position for a historicist to occupy, but not, of course, strange at all from someone writing from the center. Lazarus's argument, then, is a classic instance not just of speaking for but what would be called, in another debate this study does not really have a stake in, rootless cosmopolitanism. His commitment is not to anything resembling a historical moment in the present but to an abstract entity called anticolonialism—that, surely, nobody can claim is an ongoing historical project. (Once more, a strange position for a historicist.) Structurally, his work resonates more with that of the metropolitan critics he condemns than with the postcolonials with whom he desires to ally.

Lazarus's second move, predictably enough from a Leninist-vanguardist, is to defend representation: (Western) intellectuals must speak for the subaltern, the other, the non-West. That is the "burden" of the intellectual (or just the white man, perhaps?), a responsibility that cannot be avoided. Being consistent, he also defends representation in conventional anthropology—he positively cites an ethnography of an African tribe that straightforwardly speaks for the natives—and yet presents himself as anti-Eurocentric![52] Having already taken on this position in relation to anthropology, there is no need to rehearse that argument. But one element of Lazarus's critique of Spivak's critique of representation needs mention. To him, Spivak, who refuses to advocate representation or intellectual leadership, "claims too little for intellectual practice."[53] That, of course, is precisely the point. Academic activity, as Spivak has insisted all along, cannot and should not be confused with activism. Indeed, to repeat myself, I would hold very strongly that one does a tremendous disservice to those whose efforts might be characterized as struggle to misrepresent academic knowledge production, especially when it comes with the security of tenure in the Western academy, as synonymous—or even comparable, for that matter—with the efforts of those who often put their lives on the line. On the other hand, if Lazarus, Benita Parry, or anybody else who holds this position actually wants to hear the voice of the subaltern, or make her speak, then what he should do is get her a computer and a publishing contract and ask her to write (not send Western anthropologists or literary critics out there to speak for her—even if they get consecrated as insiders). If she is illiterate, they should begin, patiently, by establishing schools, but they should never, ever, seek to take her place. By not so arguing, Lazarus reveals what is really at stake in this battle: the elitist desire of the Western intellectual to continue to represent, to speak for, to take the place of, to lead the Third World. (Indeed, with touching humility, Lazarus actually wants to "assume the burden of speaking for all humanity."[54] Difference, clearly, is not a category in this episteme.)

But then Derrida has taught us what is actually at stake in representation. In his reading of the Declaration of Independence, he points out that, "In signing, the people say—and do what they say they do, but in differing or deferring themselves through the intervention of their representatives."[55] To Lazarus, there is a seamless, metonymic relation between representer and represented. Indeed, he speaks of himself as a "converted" intellectual, presumably to the cause of the Third World, which implies that he is not of it, even if for it. But for it how, exactly? How do we understand representation after Derrida? One: as a relationship of difference, not continuity. As, like in anthropology, a metaphor passing or representing itself as a metonym. Structurally, then, the representer is to be understood as different, not the same, as the represented, as someone who takes her place, a substitute. Two: as a relationship of deference in both its senses. To defer, states the *OED*, is to "set aside . . . delay . . . postpone . . . withdraw." Structurally, again, to represent is to delay, hold up, slow down the possibility of the represented ever speaking for themselves (if such a thing is possible) or representing themselves or perhaps even to withdraw, withhold, such a possibility, make it impossible. And, the *OED* continues, to defer, at least in English, if not the French, is to "submit." Inscribed, absolutely, in the structure of this relationship, then, is the notion that the represented must submit, surrender if you like, to the authority of the representer, thus making the relation an elitist one.[56] How on earth, I ask wringing my hands, can anyone committed to postcoloniality, or to egalitarianism, or anybody who sees herself as ethical for that matter, accept such a relationship, want others, if not the other, to yield, even surrender? Representation is not a burden, as Lazarus holds; it is better understood as an act of substitution, of exclusion, and most disturbingly, an assertion of authority. It is not just an elitist but an authoritarian act that forces the represented to submit.

Spivak, of course, implies the same in that notoriously misunderstood essay, that representation even in its most "innocent" incarnation, as description or portrait, is inevitably, inescapably, bound to, or complicit with, representation as substitution or proxy. Her advice to a Lazarus, no doubt, would be "to learn to *speak to* (rather than listen to or speak for) the historically muted subject."[57] But this would involve, she continues, the metropolitan intellectual systematically unlearning privilege. However, as I have been arguing all along, privilege—which he codes as a burden— is something Lazarus cannot let go, for more than one reason. It appears to me that there is something more fundamental going on than the desire to represent, to control, to substitute, to mute, that fuels dogmatic Marxism's attacks on postcolonial studies: the threat of the very loss of its object. For, in this politico-epistemological moment after feminism, after critical race theory, after queer theory, Marxism has lost its patent, as it were, on representing the oppressed. Some Marxism has come to terms with this, acknowledging that a single way of knowing, a simpleminded understanding of forms of domination, is no longer adequate to the task of capturing the complexity of the social. Digging its heels in, however, dogmatic Marxism has refused to do so, has refused to even recognize some forms of oppression as political, dismissing them instead as cultural.[58] But it also came to realize that all it had left to represent, after what is sometimes called the new social movements, was the Third World; all it could still seek to speak for was the wretched of the earth. Then came postcolonial studies. For one thing, it challenged the epistemological ground of Eurocentrism, the Enlightenment, and Eurocentric Marxism. For another, it threatened—*threatens!*—to permanently take away (as it should) the very possibility of the West speaking for the non-West. For, if it does not seek to give some content to the "post" in "postcolonial," if all it desires is to continue to be anticolonial, or anti-imperialist, the concept itself would have very little work to do. And even if postcoloniality, as a concept, is yet to be given a convincing content, is yet to be theorized as rigorously and sharply as it should, the possibility was always inherent in the term. Dogmatic Marxism recognized this. Thus its frustrated, panicked, rearguard attacks on postcolonial studies. It knows what might be won or lost in this battle. Thus my own imperative to make the emergence of the term worthwhile, to call into question texts that don't abide by the places they want to represent, to actually theorize the term. For a postcolonial/postempiricist Sri Lankan leftist reader cannot and should not submit to the authority of the West, of Eurocentrism.

Partha Chatterjee makes a distinction, in *Nationalist Thought and the Colonial World*, between what he calls the "thematic" and the "problematic" of "any social ideology" (terms, by the way, that he owes to Ibrahim Abu-Lughod). To Chatterjee, the thematic of an ideology "refers to an epistemological as well as ethical *system* which provides a framework of elements and rules for establishing relations between elements; the problematic . . . consists of concrete statements about *possibilities* justified by reference to the thematic."[59] If one uses these terms to examine Eurocentrism, its thematic, system, framework, or, better yet, structure would assert the existence of an absolute distinction between Europe and its other. This would be made in epistemological, empiricist, or objectivist terms. The problematic, on the other hand, would bring into play the question of value, would assert that the other is inferior on a variety of grounds—social,

political, cultural, intellectual. These terms are indispensable in conceptualizing a specifically *post*colonial response to Eurocentrism (which I
understand not as an ideology but an episteme). Such a response would
take the "post" in postcolonial seriously, substantially, as something to be
thought about, tarried over, abided by, as opposed to the kind of response
to Eurocentrism that might name and produce itself as such but that does
not do much more, really, than replicate the structure of Eurocentrism. A
recent statement of such a position has been made by Robert Young, who
argues, sounding very much like Lazarus, that

> postcolonial critique is . . . a form of activist writing that looks back to
> the political commitment of the anticolonial liberation movements and
> draws its inspiration from them, while recognizing that they often oper-
> ated under conditions very different from those that exist in the present.
> Its orientation will change according to the political priorities of the mo-
> ment, but its source in the revolutionary activism of the past gives it a
> constant basis and inspiration: it too is dedicated to changing those who
> were formerly the objects of history into history's new subjects.[60]

Activism, again! This seeks, as Adam Sitze argues in relation to Benita
Parry, to save postcoloniality by destroying it.[61] For this project, of "looking back," of making objects into subjects, as Young himself implies, is
best named anticolonial. Postcoloniality, it seems to me, simply cannot be
the same thing, do the same thing, just under a different name, for to do
so would be quite meaningless. Postcoloniality should not look back but
must, if you like, go forward. If there's still a need to be anticolonial, so
be it. Indeed, being consistent, Young actually suggests that such work be
carried out under the rubric "tricontinentalism," looking back to "the great
Havana Tricontinental of 1966, which initiated the first global alliance
of the peoples of the three continents against imperialism."[62] However,
if there's still some purchase to be gained from postcoloniality, if one is
convinced it can still do some work, and imperative work at that, for this
disciplinary—or antidisciplinary—moment, then it must be theorized
differently. This task is intellectual, not activist; interventionary, not interpretive. So, in search of inspiration, to give the term actual substance,
to go forward rather than look back, I turn first to Fanon, then Chatterjee
and Spivak.

One can, of course, read Fanon, as Lazarus does, as operating within
the thematic of nationalism (which is also that of Eurocentrism), of accepting the distinction between Europe and the rest, of working ultimately within Enlightenment humanism, seeking to recast it rather than reject

it, but that would be a most unimaginative and rather predictable reading. For as Homi Bhabha and others have persuasively pointed out, struggling within the text is another Fanon, one that could be termed proto-postempiricist.[63] Fanon, in other words, must be read symptomatically. At the end of the first part of "On National Culture," he insists that there are three "fundamental tasks" before those who would oppose colonialism: "the liberation of the national territory; a continual struggle against colonialism in its new forms; and an obstinate refusal to enter the charmed circle of mutual admiration at the summit."[64] The implication here is hard to miss, even if many readers of Fanon have missed it: colonialism, clearly understood as something that exceeds a political or economic relation of dominance, is said *not* to come to an end with national liberation; it takes new forms thereafter (which might make Fanon, too, a disavower of decolonization!). These "new forms," of intellectual or epistemic dominance, perhaps even epistemic violence, which postcolonial studies have done so much to reveal and contest, are what must be resisted, unremittingly, after national liberation. If, then, the first task identified by Fanon, national liberation, could be termed *anti*colonial, the second, very different from the first, might take the name *post*colonial for the simple reason that, in Fanon's formulation, it happens after the end of a certain stage in the colonial project, because it also wants to acknowledge, to avow, that a certain kind of colonialism is over, even if another remains to be dealt with. Fanon, at least in my reading, insists on the distinction. But what do we make of his third charge, to not "enter the charmed circle of mutual admiration at the summit"? What might that statement mean? Does it offer further substance to Fanon's understanding of postcoloniality, a term he did not have available to him? Yes, if it is read in the context of his injunction, in the memorable conclusion to *The Wretched of the Earth*, to not seek to follow Europe, to leave it behind, perhaps even throw it into that by-now-overcrowded trash heap of history—because postcoloniality has better things to do:

> Let us waste no time in . . . nauseating mimicry . . . Leave this Europe . . .
> European techniques and . . . style ought no longer to tempt us . . . Let
> us not pay tribute to Europe by creating states, institutions, and societies
> which draw their inspiration from her . . . We do not want to catch up with
> anyone. What we want is to go forward . . . We must seek the response
> elsewhere than in Europe.[65]

Europe, it is crucial to notice, does not emerge here as just a geographic entity; it is also a matter of "style" and "techniques," a place of possible intellectual, ideological, institutional inspiration—in other words, an epistemic space.[66] One that must be left behind! Fanon is absolutely clear about it: Europe should not be seen as a source of inspiration, should not be imitated. How else can one read the very last sentence of that text, which begins with an exhortation to violence against colonialism: "For Europe, for ourselves, and for humanity, comrades, we must turn over a new leaf, *we must work out new concepts*, and try to set afoot a new man."[67] New concepts! The very text that famously and insistently begins with a call to violence as the only means of finishing, destroying colonialism ends with a call for new concepts. (Gunasinghe's text, of course, resonates with this, is, in a sense, its offspring.) Surely, where this argument leads, the more productive way to read Fanon in this disciplinary moment, since he does not see Europe geographically but epistemologically, is to see him as a critic of the very ground of Eurocentrism: the Enlightenment. If the old European concepts were adequate, why on earth does Fanon call for new ones? In my terms, he is arguing for finishing the critique of Eurocentrism.[68] For to seek to enter the charmed circle is to seek to make objects subject, to be inspired by Europe and want to relativize it, be its equal, have a seat at the table or the United Nations, as the case might be—the position of Dipesh Chakrabarty. But this, implies Fanon, is the project of anticolonial nationalism. It is a necessary stage the would-be postcolonial has to pass through, but only a stage, not one she should seek to dwell in for too long, or abide by, because that would still keep Europe in place as the global epistemological dominant.

It is precisely here that Chatterjee's terms—produced in the course, one might remind the reader, of an analysis of Indian nationalism—become indispensable to clarify what is at stake in the distinction between post- and anticolonial. If one finds the terms "thematic" and "problematic" a useful way of grasping the structural logic of Eurocentrism, one would also realize that, purely *logically*, three—and only three—possible responses are available to this structure by the other of Eurocentrism. The first is to accept both the thematic and the problematic of Eurocentrism, to accept, in other words, that the colony is both different and inferior to the West. This could be termed a colonial response to colonialism. The second is to accept the thematic of Eurocentrism, to agree that the native and the West are different but invert the problematic and insist that the native is not inferior but equal (or, for that matter, superior). This, Chatterjee argues powerfully, persuasively, is/was the structural logic of anticolonial nationalism and is why I seek to name this position, even when it may not be explicitly nationalist, anticolonial. In Chatterjee's terms, this position

"reasons within a framework of knowledge whose representational structure corresponds to the very structure of power nationalist thought seeks
to repudiate."[69] In my terms, it demands equality, subjectivity, a seat at the
table. But, structurally, such a response, such a strategy, cannot contribute
to, and in fact does not seek, the dismantling or demise of Eurocentrism—
as Fanon recognized, if intuitively, it only desires its relativizing, or, to
use a term currently very fashionable in a certain tendency within postcolonial studies, its provincializing. For, to "provincialize" Europe is not
to seek to get beyond it but simply to find for it a new place, to reduce
its dominance, to turn it from the global dominant into a "province," a
localized space, something implicitly equal to every other such space.[70]
Indeed, Chakrabarty is quite emphatic that "provincializing Europe is not
a project of rejecting or discarding European thought . . . [which] is at
once both indispensable and inadequate."[71] That is to say, he holds the
Enlightenment adequate for some tasks, not so for others. His own work
seeks to supplement the inadequacy, not put the system itself into question. Thus he characterizes his project as being about "a gesture of inversion. Let us . . . read 'plenitude' and 'creativity' where . . . [Eurocentrism]
made us read 'lack' and 'inadequacy.'"[72] To do this, of course, is to be within the thematic of Eurocentrism and merely invert the problematic, to
seek to make the object subject, to be within, broadly speaking, the problematic of anticolonial nationalism (which makes Chakrabarty share more
with Lazarus than they both realize). Indeed, Chakrabarty is a deeply
nostalgic, profoundly—but not simplemindedly—nationalist thinker, who
yearns for an India untouched by colonialism (for, perhaps, even a Hindu
India).[73] To hold this position today, as Madhava Prasad argues in another
context, is effectively to produce surrender (to Eurocentrism) as resistance.[74] My position, then, has nothing in common with Chakrabarty's.
I seek, ultimately, to dismantle the category "Europe", he merely wants to
provincialize, localize, humble it.

At the risk of digressing again, this is the most appropriate place to
discuss Spivak's position, often simply misunderstood, perhaps even deliberately misread, on what she calls "information retrieval": "Reporting
on, or better still, participating in, antisexist work among women of color
or women in class oppression in the First World or the Third World is
undeniably on the agenda. We should also welcome all the information
retrieval in these silenced areas that is taking place in anthropology, political science, history, and sociology."[75] Spivak, it would appear, directly
contradicts the argument being made here—an argument that draws its
inspiration from her own work, indeed this same essay!—and even (hor-

ror of horrors) supports anthropology. That is how this passage has been read by many, including Lazarus, who nevertheless complains that "Spivak almost invariably fails to live up to her own injunction . . . In her own work . . . the deconstructive interrogation of subalternity is given precedence over the radical historiographical account of 'native agency.'"[76] But of course. To hold that a rigorous deconstructionist critic might ever indulge in the production of historical accounts, radical or otherwise, is to profoundly misunderstand deconstruction. And Lazarus would have proved to be a better reader if, instead of only citing those two sentences, he had gone on to read the third, where Spivak actually explains why she cannot indulge in the production of such history: "the assumption and construction of a consciousness or subject sustains such work and will, in the long run, cohere with the work of imperialist subject-constitution, mingling epistemic violence with the advancement of learning and civilization."[77] Admittedly, Spivak might have been better understood if she didn't appear to contradict herself.[78] For this sounds like strategic essentialism all over again: one cannot, really, and one certainly should not, support something in the short term, put it on the agenda, if one knows its long-term consequences are disabling. But Spivak's position, when read carefully, is another way of saying that the postcolonial cannot work within empiricism and should not seek, as a response to being objectified by Eurocentrism, simply to make herself subject. For that would be to remain within empiricism and the episteme of Eurocentrism.

Which is the third possibility implicit in Chatterjee. It is not put to work or examined by him; indeed, one might say, to borrow a phrase, that Chatterjee is blind to the consequences of his own insight, but it is available to the careful reader: to *think beyond both the thematic and the problematic of Eurocentrism*.[79] That is to say, while this might seem to present itself as an "original" argument about postcoloniality, it cannot be the case. Not only is my position impossible without Chatterjee; reading, in the sense I understand it, cannot produce originality. In my reading, then, if the "post" in "postcolonial" is to have any substance, if it is not to be collapsed into anticolonial, this surely must be the only substance it could have. Or, to paraphrase Derrida, postcoloniality might then mean to put into question the system that produced the distinction between Europe and its others, the West and the rest, in the first place (something Chakrabarty is allergic to doing), and everything else that comes as an epistemological consequence. This, you will not be surprised to hear, is why I have been arguing all along that postcoloniality and postempiricism are allies, accomplices, partners in crime.[80] Thus it follows that part of the task of postcoloniality, allied with postempiricism, is finishing the critique, from within, of the intellectual legacy of the Enlightenment. Dogmatic Marxism, of course, cannot countenance this, for that would amount to conceding its leadership, its authority. Lazarus, for instance, endorses "fully . . . the indispensability of enlightenment rationality to any adequate conception of social freedom,"[81] and yet he calls himself anti-Eurocentric—repressing the little detail that it was in the name of the very same Enlightenment and reason that colonialism happened!

If postcoloniality, then, means—in my reading, now, not Chatterjee's—the project of working toward getting beyond the thematic (and problematic) of Eurocentrism, it must entail the critique of the Enlightenment, the epistemological ground of Eurocentrism. This is why postempiricism, which started this project, is its indispensable accomplice and comrade. It entails the critique of anthropology, understood not just in the narrow disciplinary sense, à la Spencer, but as a way of knowing also to be found in critics like Lazarus, a way of knowing that cannot function without the distinction between West and rest, without insisting on speaking for this rest, taking its place, seeking to maintain it as forever object. It must also entail the critique of nationalism that, even if heroic in its anticolonial phase, is to postcoloniality, quite apart from being a structure in dominance, an inadequate response to Eurocentrism because it accepts its thematic, does not put it into question, let alone seek to get beyond it. Thus postcoloniality cannot, really, find any sustaining intellectual inspiration in those national liberation movements. After *Subaltern Studies*, after Fanon, after Guha, Chatterjee, and Spivak, so doing is impossible. To say this, however, is not to "disavow" those movements but to point out their limit. Indeed, one might say of them what Paul Ricoeur said of Hegel:

> We no longer think in the way Hegel did, but after Hegel. For what readers
> of Hegel, once they have been seduced by the power of [his] thought . . .
> do not feel the abandoning of this philosophy as . . . a wound that . . . will
> not be healed? For such readers, if they are not to give into the weaknesses
> of nostalgia, we must wish the courage of the work of mourning.[82]

I might note in passing that nobody committed to postcoloniality could possibly be seduced by Hegel. But my point is that, to the postcolonial, the object—the episteme that structured anticolonial nationalist thought—must be read as lost, not in a historical sense but in that it has been subject to a searching critique. We may wish to mourn the failure of anticolonial nationalism, to complain that it wasn't adequate to its task—because it could not be. We may wish it were, but we must have the courage to admit its limit. And we should not forget, to say this one last time: if the "post" and the "colonial" in postcoloniality are to be taken seriously, if the term itself is to be (re)conceptualized, then it should be the name of the project that takes as its task finishing the critique of Eurocentrism—concept by concept, thought by thought.

2

Majority Rules:

Reading a Sinhalese Nationalist History

If we argue in a liberal way we must say: the majority decides, the minority submits.

—Lenin, *The Socialist Revolution and the Renegade Kautsky*

A Complex Conflict

Crushed culturally and politically for some four and a half long centuries by three Christian Western powers (Portugal, Holland, Britain), attacked incessantly by Tamils (Hindus from southern India) in the even longer centuries before colonialism; in short, subjugated, dispossessed, victimized, and wounded by history itself, the Sinhalese Buddhist majority in Sri Lanka, a world-historically unique people, is simply trying, according to its autobiography, to redress the balance, heal those injuries, correct those wrongs, attempting to finally live in peace and security in the postcolonial period. All it seeks is nothing more, or less, than to enjoy the universally recognized rights and privileges of a majority; all it has done since independence is exercise this privilege within a democratic framework—this privilege of a majority that is not just democratic but *democracy*. Sri

Lanka would be at peace today if only the Tamils, fighting for a separate state, demanding extravagant rights a minority is not entitled to, recognized and accepted this. A straightforward-enough story, one of whose chief advocates, within the academy, has been Kingsley Muthumani de Silva. Through his relentless intellectual production, which has consistently abided by Sri Lanka, de Silva has not only written many chapters of this autobiography, as it were, but in so doing also drafted a formidable petition for such hegemony,[1] one made even more authoritative by its disciplinary allegiance, history. An effective leftist academic response to Sri Lanka, intervention within its terrain, or plea for peace—I might even say *any* leftist petition for peace in Sri Lanka—must not just oppose but come to terms with de Silva's positions, demands, justifications and (narrative) strategies. It must come to terms, that is, with the claim that Sinhalese history—the oppressive past—justifies Sinhalese (nationalist) politics— hegemonizing the present. Out of such conviction, I read in this chapter de Silva's recent product, *Reaping the Whirlwind: Ethnic Conflict, Ethnic Politics in Sri Lanka*, a fairly straightforward instance of empiricist history.

But, it must be stressed, this particular text is adopted for analysis not as a consequence of its novelty or (only) its Sinhalese nationalist politics or because I consider the text dominant or even representative (of either his intellectual production or the autobiography of Sinhalese nationalism). Deeming a text (or position) representative, holding its content metonymic or typical of several others, reckoning in other words that one is somehow equivalent to and can therefore take the place of many, emphasizing or privileging the general (a routine happening within social science and literary criticism derived from social science) must be a hazardous if not suspect exercise to the postempiricist/postcolonial reader. To the postempiricist, such a position can only make the representative claim about a text—in other words, produce generality from specificity— by denying difference, suppressing singularity.[2] To the postcolonial, representation—speaking for or taking the place of the other—also rehearses an all-too-familiar colonial logic, one that I hold it the task of this critical persuasion to quite determinedly oppose, as argued in the previous chapter. Rather, *the text appropriates me* because it rhymes with Sinhalese nationalism, because I have to address it in order to abide by Sri Lanka. In so doing, it also allows me to address, apart from the more specifically "Sri Lankan" concerns, three other broad and broadly related sets of questions that animate this study. The first set, upon which the emphasis falls in this chapter, concerns history as writing, which is the work or, better yet, "operation" (de Certeau) of history; more particularly in the latter regard, it concerns the nexus between history and politics. *Reaping the Whirlwind* may legitimize the Sinhalese nationalist account of Sri Lanka but, and these are two of the three most important claims advanced by the text, *it produces itself as a work of unbiased disciplinary history, and, more contentiously, it asserts that history—understood as a faithful, unbiased representation of past events—determines the present, or politics.* Paradoxically, for the second claim to be persuasive, de Silva must convince his reader of the first, that his arguments are apolitical, disinterested, the product of his disciplinary allegiance alone. If de Silva were to admit that they were indeed subjective, then the past's claim upon the present, Sinhalese nationalism's justification of its right to hegemony, would—or at least could—turn out to be the contention of an interested author, rather than the inevitable consequence of objective history, and would therefore be suspect, unpersuasive, open to doubt. That is to say, de Silva's thesis—that history determines politics—hinges on the claim that *Reaping the Whirlwind* is disciplinary history, only disciplinary history, and nothing but untainted disciplinary history. Consequently, I spend most of this chapter investigating this claim, reading the text closely to see how it operates. I will examine whether it is, on the one hand, coherent or de-constitutes itself, and, on the other hand, whether it is always already inter-disciplinary, in fact indelibly marked by other knowledges, disciplines, and, of course, an interest—the demand of politics. Reading *Reaping the Whirlwind*, then, enables me to pose the question whether (closely) reading works of history may indeed compel the deauthorization of the discipline.

In this context, it is crucial to notice that *Reaping the Whirlwind* is a sig-nificant revision of some of de Silva's earlier positions on Sri Lanka, es-pecially those produced in *Managing Ethnic Tensions in Multi-Ethnic Societies*. *Managing Ethnic Tensions* does not produce the ancient Sri Lankan past as an incessant series of attacks on the Sinhalese by the Tamils, and the Sinhalese there are not deemed the victims of historical injury. *Reaping the Whirlwind*, in contrast, produces the Sinhalese as victims and, in so doing, rhymes more harmoniously with the more popular strand of Sinhalese na-tionalist history. Such a drastic revision enables, indeed demands, consid-eration of the question of the operation of history. For, if history can be so easily and so radically rewritten, and by the same writer at that, what does that tell us about the facts? In the conclusion of this chapter, I address that and the other questions raised by this revision, its content, determina-tions, the narrative moment it produces, and the consequences thereof for those concerned with conceptualizing peace in Sri Lanka—in rela-tion to the different narrative moment produced by *Reaping the Whirlwind*. This narrative moment or conjuncture I would characterize, *upon reading the latter text*, as a pessimistic Sri Lankan present, in contradistinction not necessarily to an optimistic past but to a less pessimistic conjuncture that *Managing Ethnic Tensions* produces. (Both, of course, see Sri Lanka, produce this moment, from a Sinhalese nationalist perspective.) I stress the importance of reading here to make the claim that the "moment" of the text is not something to be identified by accessing information outside it. Rather, as Mowitt might remind us here, "the text *engages* its moment," and thus its contours are accessible to the careful reader.[3] Since *Reaping the Whirlwind* is published twelve years after *Managing Ethnic Tensions*, twelve years in which this perspective will hold that many things have changed drastically in Sri Lanka, the calendar-driven disciplinary historian, and the historicist literary critic, would find *Reaping the Whirlwind* occupying a different *historical* moment from the earlier text. However, I prefer to see *Reaping the Whirlwind* as the product of, and producing, a different *narrative* moment, both within de Silva's own attempts to come to terms with Sri Lanka and in the relation of his intellectual production to Sinhalese nationalist discourse. I characterize the moment as a narrative one in order to emphasize that it is not a changed empirical reality that is at stake here or that the deployment of a new and improved (historian's) method for representing or analyzing the same old reality has produced a better, and thus different, account of it; de Silva does not make such claims. Rather, he simply narrates, without apology, a different *structured story* about the "same" Sri Lankan past in the two texts. The difference is signified by their very titles: the first book is about "tensions," mere worries—something "managed" without great difficulty, not the cause for much pessimism; the other, is about battle, an outright "conflict"—one compared to the might and dangerousness of a whirlwind, a drastic and dramatic fact of nature beyond the capacity of human agency to manage or subdue. Revisiting the "same" set of "past" events as *Managing Ethnic Tensions*, then, *Reaping the Whirlwind* revises them, produces them as portending great pessimism about the immediate future of Sri Lanka, thus raising questions about the persuasiveness of de Silva's characterization, in *Reaping the Whirlwind*, of the nexus between history and politics, and more fundamental questions about the operation of history itself. The second set of questions, partly following from the above, concern the relation between reading in a postempiricist fashion and politics; whether, indeed, there might be such a relation. While I leave discussion of this to later chapters, it should be pointed out here that without a close reading of de Silva, especially his arguments about democracy, the symptomatic reading of Jeyaratnam Wilson produced in the next chapter would not be possible. There, I rethink what might be termed a minority perspective and the ethics of nationalism, which in turn enables my gesture toward a subsequent critique of democracy from such a perspective, which is at the heart of the political implications, the relevance if you like, the putting to work of the ethical, of this study. The third set concern history and postcoloniality: in revising the account of the Sri Lankan past to be found in *Managing Ethnic Tensions*, *Reaping the Whirlwind* produces itself as a work of *anti*colonial history.

In the very first page of the Preface of *Reaping the Whirlwind*, after naming the Sri Lankan "ethnic conflict" as his object of study, de Silva foregrounds his disciplinary allegiance and training, explains his understanding of its significance. This narrative unit is of critical importance to the text, something underlined by its placement even before the narrative, a move that, of course, seeks to determine the reading that follows:

> My approach to the problems analyzed in this book is historical. I make no apology for that. I am by training a historian specializing in the problems of modern and contemporary South Asia. Moreover, as the conflicts in the Balkans and the Caucasus regions remind us, ethnic and religious conflicts have a complex history, and one can neither understand them nor devise strategies and tactics to resolve or manage them without a grasp of the historical background. (De Silva 1998, ix)

The unit begins subjectively then becomes objective; its voice shifts from the first person to the third. The three opening sentences of the unit, being in the first person, suggest that the text might be shaped by what could be called, provisionally, a *personal* "level." They convey autobiographical information and certify de Silva's expertise and intellectual convictions. The information itself may not be of much concern to the reader, but she is made to notice it. What narrative function does this perform? Why is this information relevant? What suspicions of the reader might it seek to allay? What kind of (implied) reader might contest the text's claims without it? *Reaping the Whirlwind* is quite evidently disciplinary history of the most conventional sort. It passes, as it were, the Hayden White test: it is a narrative of (Sri Lankan) events with a single central subject, an identifiable narrative voice, and a clearly demarcated beginning (in the precolonial past), middle (in the colonial period), and end (in the postcolonial present).[4] It gives closure to its story and distinguishes definitively between past and present—the clearest signifier of a work of history. Why, then, must de Silva's being an academic, a trained historian, be on record? Surely any literate reader will notice it? The statement—

and this cannot be emphasized too much—is necessary because it *autho-rizes the narrative that follows;* its placement, too, in the Preface, before the narrative proper, emphasizes that it seeks to determine the reading of the narrative: *Reaping the Whirlwind* is disciplinary history, a true and verifi-able account of Sri Lankan events produced by a trained professional, as opposed to political propaganda pronounced by a Sinhalese nationalist ideologue. Indeed, de Silva, in an extremely careful choice of phrase, pro-duces his subject position, in the Preface, as that of a "concerned witness." That is to say, he does care, he is concerned about Sri Lanka—unlike, say, a Spencer—but his text must be understood as the product not of the concerned citizen or national, subject positions that might imply cathexis or an emotional or political bias, but of a neutral observer, the witness, a scholar who sees, understands and, most crucially, can, like someone called before the judge and jury in a courtroom, *attest* to the objectivity and veracity of the narrative that is to follow—thus my contention that the entire narrative hinges on its claim to impartiality, to be the pure, un-tainted product of disciplinary history. The mere assertion of objectivity, of course, does not guarantee it—and Althusser might interject here that "the 'subject' plays not the part it believes it is playing, but the part which is assigned to it."[5] But what the reader must notice, right now, is that the narrative wouldn't be possible, at least not in its present form, without this particular disciplinary allegiance. She must also realize that de Silva understands Sri Lanka historically not simply because of his training; to hold so would be to find him the kind of scholar who merely seeks in his writing to justify that training. Rather, he treats the country thus be-cause without history one cannot understand "complex" conflicts; even the Balkans—especially the Balkans—attest to that. The claim is apodic-tic ("incontrovertible"): only a (trained) historian, or at the very least a history-competent person, can accurately comprehend the complexity of the Sri Lankan ethnic conflict. If the reader suspected otherwise, she would be wrong. This is an audacious move, and its truth or falsehood does not concern me. Rather, I hold that the task of the reader when con-fronted with such a claim is to determine whether the text keeps its prom-ise and demonstrates the historicity of the conflict and also to situate the significance of such claims, to ask what work they perform for the text, to ask whether it is untainted history or whether the text's disciplinary level is overdetermined by another.

After providing this personal information and without warning, indeed with the aid of a weak conjunction ("moreover"), which signals that the analogy itself is feeble, the narrative unit shifts from the individual story to a global one, in which not only is its cardinal claim announced but, and perhaps more importantly, the consequences thereof are drawn. Let's revisit its two initial clauses: "as the conflicts in the Balkans and the Caucasus regions remind us, ethnic and religious conflicts have a complex history." In the first, it is the conflicts that speak; the conflicts themselves—not de Silva as their professional analyst—inform the reader that they have a complex history. It is an exemplary instance of the "referential illusion," where "the historian claims to let the referent speak for itself."[6] This suggests, taken together with de Silva's own prior attestation, that *Reaping the Whirlwind* is shaped by another level, a *disciplinary* one. Since the referent itself speaks in that unit, no evidence need be adduced—and none is—to buttress the assertion; it too is apodictic; the reader will not, cannot dispute it, despite the weak conjunction. Like de Silva's attestation of his own training, the conflicts themselves attest to their complexity. The reader should pause at this word, since it is deployed constantly, perhaps even excessively, by the historian, so much so that an F. R. Leavis might find in it an instance of adjectival insistence! My purpose in drawing attention to it is not to dispute that Sri Lanka could be understood as complex; that, after all, is a matter of perspective. Wilson—who, by the way, has called de Silva the "leading [Sinhalese] historian of the present day"—does not comprehend Sri Lanka as complex. Rather, I want to make two preliminary observations about this usage: that its reader must, again, determine whether de Silva actually demonstrates Sri Lanka's complexity, as opposed to merely asserting it, and that the term functions within his narrative as an "indice," to take another term from Barthes. The term is "integrational" not "distributional" in function; it helps summarize the text's design; it is not descriptive but metaphoric; it demands elucidation rather than conveys meaning. "Complex," in other words, is not an innocent term faithful to the reality it seeks to describe but an instance of what I have called de Silva's subtle narrative strategy.

To get back to the Balkans: why make the analogy—and weakly, at that? The resort to analogy, of course, suggests that *Reaping the Whirlwind* might be shaped by another level, a *narratological* one. But why this particular comparison? Why gesture toward (Eastern) Europe in a petition on, and perhaps addressed to, Sri Lanka? For Sri Lanka to be properly comprehended, must it be referred to Europe as a place of authoritative knowledge? What, precisely, is the work done by the Balkan conflicts for de Silva's plot? The comparison is, obviously, Eurocentric; it is yet another instantiation, perhaps, of Dipesh Chakrabarty's thesis that Europe is the subject of Third World histories.[7] But this Eurocentrism is of a routine kind that need only be dog-eared. *Reaping the Whirlwind* also compares Sri Lanka to places in Asia. By drawing our attention to an apparently complicated problem, and one apparently accepted as such, in a part of the world far away, the analogy—in a move that could be comprehended as characteristic not just of history but of social science—implies the same for Sri Lanka, produces identity out of mere relation, makes Sri Lanka a case, an instance of a generalizable condition. The country might appear, to Western discourse on the ethnic conflict, to be a fairly straightforward instance of the oppression of a minority (the Tamils) by a majority (the Sinhalese); Wilson—Tamil nationalism—certainly produces it in those terms. But de Silva insists otherwise: "The current ethnic conflict in Sri Lanka is a *much more complex business than a simple straightforward confrontation* between a once well-entrenched minority—the Sri Lankan Tamils—and a now powerful but still insecure majority—the Sinhalese" (de Silva 1998, 12; emphasis added). The rhetoric of that narrative unit, at the risk of stating the obvious, suggests that it is written against those—like Watson, Daniel, and Spencer—who see the ethnic conflict as a straightforward one or in binary terms. This makes it necessary to examine again, and at slightly greater length than in the previous chapter, an instance of Western discourse on Sri Lanka. So doing will help properly situate the text within the terrain in which it intervenes and, perhaps more importantly, which shapes it quite fundamentally. For, while this text may not explicitly direct its petition to the West, while it might appear to be an intervention within a purely Sri Lankan debate, it does address the West in some narrative units—it complains, for instance, about how Western academics understand Sri Lanka; it distinguishes, in other words, between Sri Lankan and Western academic production. A careful reading will also demonstrate that not just its claims but the very structure of its narrative is determined by a powerful, authoritative account already in place. Western discourse, in other words, is an authoritative strand of the network of texts that shape *Reaping the Whirlwind*, thus making it, in Partha Chatterjee's very precise sense, derivative: "different . . . yet . . . dominated by another."[8] Or, in my terms, *Reaping the Whirlwind* is inside the West; no instance of disciplinary knowledge production can be otherwise.

Human-rights discourse has made many pronouncements regarding Sri Lanka. What follows, as was Watson in the previous chapter, is randomly selected from my bookshelf, the "Background" section of a 1987 report of the U.S.-based Asia Watch. This, too, cannot be considered a representative text; human-rights discourse is not univocal. (Indeed this report differs in many respects from the "International Commission of

Jurists" read later.) The Asia Watch narrative begins with Sri Lankan "independence in 1948." This may appear self-evident, obvious, even indisputable. When else could the story begin? But such a move signifies to the informed or patient reader that Asia Watch does not find the conflict to have a past in colonialism or even before and that, contra de Silva, you may not need history to understand, solve, or manage the problem, which is purely a postcolonial one:

> The post-independence cycle of claims began [in 1956] when Prime Minister Bandaranaike's government made 'Sinhalese Only' rather than English the national language, the knowledge of which was required for employment and advancement in the civil service. Its Sinhalese supporters saw this as justice for a suppressed majority . . . the Tamils felt that the act threatened their existence in the country. (12)

The rhetoric of this report presents itself as balanced; two perspectives are given narrative time, without the rival "claims" being evaluated. Nevertheless, the significance of the unit is clear: the conflict began with an act of the Sinhalese ("Prime Minister Bandaranaike's government"), an act understood by its advocates as justice for these same Sinhalese, while the Tamils felt it threatened their very existence. Equity for one side signified potential genocide for the other. To cite just one more instance from the same report, this time on what it considers the "events that turned civil disturbance into civil war": "On July 23, 1983, Tamil militants ambushed a patrol of soldiers near Jaffna, killing thirteen. In the days that followed, anti-Tamil rioting by Sinhalese mobs paralyzed Colombo and other areas of the south, ultimately claiming hundreds of lives, mostly Tamil, and leaving Tamil neighborhoods and businesses in ruins."[9] Again, notice the attempt at balance: a Tamil deed is presented before a Sinhalese, suggesting a relation of causation, a "cycle of violence," as the report titles itself. But it should be evident by now that, while this account, like Watson's and Spencer's, comprehends the country in binary terms, it produces the Tamils as victims and the Sinhalese as villains. Sri Lanka, here, is clearly seen as a "straightforward conflict" between a majority and a minority. The reader would also notice that Sinhalese and Tamils are, in a certain sense, not essentialized: the narrative unit distinguishes between Tamil "militants" (who "ambush"—a military term—"soldiers") and Tamil civilians (against whom Sinhalese "mobs" "riot"—a word that suggests organized but nonmilitary mayhem). To repeat, despite its striving for balance, there is no actual symmetry in this description of an event considered originary of the country's "civil war" or postcolonial misery. First event: (thirteen) Sinhalese fighters are killed by Tamil fighters; second: Sinhalese civilians kill (hundreds of) Tamil civilians—while, the report continues, the (Sinhalese) police watched without intervening. Despite the care of its phrasing, to an essentialist perspective like de Silva's, the Sinhalese would emerge here as the villain of the story. De Silva finding Sri Lanka complex, in its politics and especially its history, his unapologetic insistence on beginning his account well before independence, must be read not so much as a response to Asia Watch, to this particular text, but as a product of this epistemological moment, in which a discourse has emerged and taken hold in the West about the Sri Lankan ethnic conflict, a discourse that encompasses both academic (i.e. Spencer, Daniel, and Watson) and other intellectual production on Sri Lanka, one that is, and this is the point that must be stressed, authorized by the moral high ground assumed by Western liberal/human-rights discourse. *Reaping the Whirlwind* must be read as a response to, if not a rebuttal of, Western discourse on Sri Lanka, with the West's binary understanding of the conflict, its villainization of only one party, and its refusal to see the conflict as having a protracted colonial and precolonial past. *Reaping the Whirlwind*, that is, addresses itself to the West, which in turn suggests that it might be shaped by an anti-Western, or better yet an anti-imperialist or *anticolonial* level. It also reinforces my claim that "complex" is an indice: to be properly apprehended, it must be (con)textualized; its significance does not lie in being descriptive but in being a rejoinder to the Western human rights (and also, as will be evident later, the Tamil nationalist) accounts of Sri Lanka. In so doing, and this cannot be emphasized too much, *Reaping the Whirlwind* is an acknowledgment of the dominance of the West as an epistemological space, of its establishment of the terms, disciplinary and otherwise, within which anti- and postcolonial intellectual production must situate, comprehend, narrate, and explain itself, and of its demarcation of the contours of what I have termed a narrative moment. To put this differently, *Reaping the Whirlwind* is an acknowledgment of the continuing force of that discourse Edward Said called, in a text that forever transformed our understanding of the world, "Orientalism," and what now, to capture the phenomenon that exceeds the Orient, is better termed Eurocentrism. For the question does arise: why does Sinhalese nationalist discourse feel accountable? Why does it have to address itself to, state its case against the West? Hegemonic Western nationalisms are not so called into account. During the 2004 U.S. election that made George W. Bush president, for instance, the United States was not accused by the world— a few snide remarks by Fidel Castro notwithstanding—of suppressing its minorities or disenfranchising African-American voters. But Sinhalese nationalism must explain itself; it has no other choice.

De Silva's narrative subtlety, his truly incredible politico-intellectual dexterity, is also in evidence in that unit, which makes a move that appears incontrovertible, a matter of course—the seemingly routine historicism of yoking the past to the present. This, of course, is the task of conventional disciplinary history, as laid down in one of the discipline's dominant prescriptive texts, Edward Hallett Carr's *What Is History?*: "The function of the historian is neither to love the past nor to emancipate himself from the past, but to master and understand it as the key to the understanding of the present."[10] If distinguishing between the past and the present is a cardinal element of historicism, de Silva takes the injunction one step further than Carr, who only wants his "disciples" to understand the past in order to understand the present. De Silva implies that because the past is complex, so must be the present; that the past, while different from the present, is also alike; and—the extra step—that if the present is complex, then any solutions to the Sri Lankan ethnic conflict cannot be conceived in simple or binary terms but must, of course, take this complexity into account. That move, that yoking, insists—but oh so discreetly—that history will not just inform the understanding of the present; in complex countries it must actually determine politics: "one can neither understand them [these conflicts] nor devise strategies and tactics to resolve or manage them without a grasp of the historical background." The argument has moved from disciplinary activity to something else, from understanding the present through the past (history) to intervening within it (politics). In that last assertion, the reader will also notice, the identity of the speaker shifts in midsentence: in its first two clauses it is the conflict itself, ethnic conflict as such perhaps; the speaker thereafter is de Silva—but not quite the historian, since he cannot, qua historian, strictly make a political claim.[11] This distinction will be returned to. But it suggests that the text might also have a *political* level, which cannot be reduced to the disciplinary. The subtlety of the rhetoric lies here, in making a contestable claim apodictically, in passing the political as the disciplinary, for—while it may be a received academic prejudice—it is by no means self-evident that the past determines the present. Which brings me to the following, perhaps predictable, questions that inevitably confront not only my reading of de Silva, but also this study: Does history determine politics? How is a claim of this kind to be settled? Conceptually, by turning to theory, to the (French) critique of history? By considering the specific argument made by this particular text and checking them against the record? Or by working with the specific *and* the conceptual?

In the rest of this chapter, keeping those questions in the front of my mind, I consider *Reaping the Whirlwind* as an intervention into the Sri Lankan debate, as a text that speaks to the debate that is Sri Lanka, that abides by the place, and that needs to be unraveled, situated, contemplated—in a word, *read*—before it is opposed. Therefore, what follows, since the text will be eventually opposed, but not dismissed, cannot be an "innocent" reading, to borrow a term from Althusser. It is, one might say, an "interested" one, an interventionary one. I do not confront the text without baggage or purpose. It does not, however, follow from this that my reading, what I "find" in the text, is determined exclusively by my own questions and concerns, political and intellectual convictions, those sedimentations or inheritances. Turning to Althusser, and that remarkable exposition of Marx, *Reading Capital*, might help clarify this. In Althusserian terms, what I attempt in this chapter is a *"symptomatic"* reading: "producing, in the precise sense of the word, which seems to signify making manifest what is latent, but which really means *transforming . . . something which in a sense already exists*."[12] Or, as he puts it elsewhere in the opening chapter, such a reading "divulges the undivulged," demonstrates that the text is *other* than it is. De Silva produces *Reaping the Whirlwind* as simply and exclusively a work of disciplinary history, a faithful interpretation of the facts unmarked by anything but a disciplinary allegiance. It is an account not a petition, a document without politics, a document whose political consequences may emerge from its narrativization of history but cannot be conflated with it, or at the very least an account of Sri Lankan history that should not and cannot be considered a petition on behalf of Sinhalese nationalism. In my reading—and the bulk of this chapter is devoted to establishing this—the text is both history *and* politics. More accurately, it emerges transformed, as shaped by what I have been calling many "levels" (as opposed to just the one claimed by de Silva).

I focus here on demonstrating the impress of four of these levels on the text: a disciplinary, a narratological, an anticolonial, and an abiding. (I argue later that the "personal" and "political" levels referred to above are best understood as elements of one, the need for identifying that was discussed in the previous chapter, the abiding.) If a text, if transforming that which already exists, can be termed, after Barthes, a "productivity," as a meeting of the reader and the written, then noticing its levels, divulging the undivulged, can only be the product of this particular encounter.[13] Another reader, with different baggage, could find more or fewer levels in *Reaping the Whirlwind*, could even deem that it has none. This chapter, then, attempts to show *that* these levels shape or help determine the text, that in their interweaving, or articulation, is produced a forceful, formidable petition—or component of a petition—on behalf of Sinhalese nationalism, that, if you like, the text is always already interdisciplinary; and to show *how* the levels are so woven, or the relations of "articulation, displacement and torsion" between these levels.[14] To say this is not to suggest that all four levels are homogenous, in any manner but the conceptual, or that they shape the text equally. *Reaping the Whirlwind* might turn out to be overdetermined—the term "articulation," at least in the Althusserian sense, suggests exactly that—by one level.

What follows, then, might be characterized as being compelled to address, quite apart from the broader questions outlined above, a number of particular ones: How does *Reaping the Whirlwind* address or abide by Sri Lanka? In what ways, exactly, does it differ from anthropology or Western/Eurocentric discourse? Could it escape its clutches? How does it conceptualize the question of peace? What are the specific conditions it deems necessary for the establishment of such peace? What narrative strategies does it deploy to secure this conception? More particularly: How is its story emplotted? How does it treat its actants? Does it grant all of them equal narrative time, or does it privilege the perspective of one? Is it unbiased disciplinary history or a petition on behalf of Sinhalese nationalism? Which actants, Sri Lankan and otherwise, does it identify as helping with peace and which as hindering it? Why does it insist that history must determine politics or play a role in the establishment of peace? How should the postempiricist reader, persuaded by the French critique of history, respond to the work done by history for de Silva's argument? What labor does analogy perform for this emplotment? Can history— and social science, more generally—work without analogy (which itself can only work by a certain confusion of arithmetic and geometry)? How should the postempiricist reader respond to the deployment of analogy by history/social science?[15] Can this reader have a position on analogy as such? What does de Silva's revision of his own positions teach this reader about the work or operation of history? What follows if his text does not turn out to be rigorously historical? Does one deem it just bad history and so dismiss it, as the discipline might encourage, or could other conclusions be reached? And the question I find most unsettling, given my own impulse, after more than a decade spent thinking about the question of peace in Sri Lanka, spent simply opposing the likes of de Silva: Should the leftist desire, is it in her interest, to accept a continuing role in a *peaceful* Sri Lanka for Sinhalese nationalism—a politics that is hegemonic at best, genocidal at worst, and which therefore could be characterized as embodying the very antithesis of peace? Is Sinhalese nationalism compatible with peace? In other words, the bottom-line question, as it were, is: To what end does the leftist oppose Sinhalese nationalism? With a view to eliminating it, to marginalizing it, or to some position in between? Would it be naively and irresponsibly utopian to prefer the first alternative, to wish Sinhalese nationalism away? Would it be extreme, mirroring one's opposition, to wish such a consummation devoutly? In all sincerity, can a leftist, or any ethical subject for that matter, advocate compromise with what must be characterized as a genocidal nationalism?

Actants: Two Plus Two Plus One

The reader of de Silva will quickly notice that he does not often take the risk of making what would be called, at least in the terms of social science, purely descriptive statements. Take, for instance, his summation of the country: "The island has one of the most complex plural societies in any part of the world: three important ethnic groups, and as many as four of the world's major religions" (1998, 7). This narrative unit, though brief, is a fine instance of a cardinal element of de Silva's perspective, its verticality: some ethnic groups are more "important" to this text than others and some (world) religions "major," greater, principal—a claim that can only be made if some other religions are deemed minor. Indeed, a compulsion to hierarchize suffuses the entire text. But what requires pause in that unit is the assertion that it is not the conflict alone that can be considered— the indice recurs—"complex," so can the country itself. A geographically informed reader might point out that a country constituted by three ethnic and four religious groups is far from unique; that if these are the terms through which one wants to think or to graph the social, then many, if not most, members of the United Nations, not just Bosnia, would be analogous to Sri Lanka. But de Silva disagrees; he produces the country as complex, disturbs an otherwise descriptive statement with an evaluative adjective, and thus imposes interpretation upon the reader. This text cannot risk leaving the task of making meaning with the reader.

Like any narrative, *Reaping the Whirlwind* has actants: the "three important ethnic groups" identified above. The first presented is the Sinhalese:

who constitute the majority of the population, have two segments, one from the south-western parts of the country—the area subjected to colonial rule since the mid-16th century—and the Kandyans, descendents of the subjects of the . . . last of the Sinhalese kingdoms, a kingdom with a

long record of successful resistance to a succession of colonial powers . . .
Sri Lankan scholars generally believe that the Sinhalese originally came to
the island over 2,500 years ago from Northern India . . .

The Sinhalese today constitute just short of three-quarters of the
island's peoples, while the Sinhalese Buddhists are just over two-thirds of
it. Yet the Sinhalese Buddhists often tend to emphasize their minority status vis-à-vis the Tamils by linking the latter's ethnic affinity to the Tamils
of southern India. Sri Lanka's location off the coast of South India, and
specially its close proximity to Tamilnadu, separated by a shallow and
narrow stretch of sea, serves to accentuate this sense of a minority status
among the Sinhalese. (8)

The assumption here is that the Sinhalese are a cohesive, unmarked whole.
That an "ethnic group" could be considered otherwise—in other words,
taking on board the critique of essentialism—is incomprehensible to this
perspective. The reader is also very quickly informed that the Sinhalese
actant is the major, or "majority," which is the first qualifier applied to it
and consequently of cardinal significance. This term, too, may appear to
be purely descriptive, a simple reflection of a fact of number; that, certainly, is how it would appear not only to history but to social science;
nevertheless, it too must be seen as indicial, of immense metaphoric consequence, its polysemy utterly indispensable to de Silva's entire thesis.
While the implications of this statement can only be addressed later, it
should be noticed now that seeing the country as composed of a majority and minorities, as structured hierarchically, is another instance of de
Silva's right-wing perspective. The description then takes an unexpectedly anti-essentialist turn, describing the Sinhalese group as not necessarily
homogenous or a unity; it is marked, has "two segments," a southwestern
and a Kandyan. But this division is effectively denied in the very next sentence, when the unity of the actant is carefully reproduced: the segmentation of Sinhalese identity is recent, a matter of a few hundred years during
colonialism; its unity is much older, can even be considered ancient, and
can therefore only be displaced, not destroyed, by colonialism.[16]

This detail is not incidental: the disciplinary level, which can be seen
at work here producing Sri Lanka through the conventional categories
of history, is woven with the political and anticolonial. The seemingly
descriptive narrative unit that appears to draw upon geography alone
makes a political claim too: while one segment of the Sinhalese may have
a lengthy history of being colonized, the other does not. The Kandyans,
unlike their southwestern kin, have "a *long record* of successful resistance to

a succession of colonial powers." The Sinhalese, in other words, may have a colonized segment, but they also have a heroic one that resisted colonialism for centuries. This is a matter of record, to which the disciplinary historian can attest—remember, de Silva is a trained historian—and which the reader can access without great difficulty. The Sinhalese, de Silva wants his reader to understand, are in some sense still anticolonial— or at least see the postcolonial conjuncture as such. They haven't been able to erase the memory of those injuries caused by colonialism; and adding insult to this injury is (Western) human-rights discourse, a product of the same places that once colonized them, which refuses to see the validity of the Sinhalese argument. Thus my identifying an *anticolonial* level to the text (as opposed to an anti-Western or anti-imperialist). Western discourse might consider them the villains of Sri Lanka, but they are the real heroes. They fought the real villains for a long time. That is the function of that ostensibly descriptive statement about resisting colonialism; it, too, is an indice as much as it is informative.

The narrative then introduces number, or arithmetic, which strengthens the claim that the Sinhalese are the majority—they form a whopping three-quarters of the country's population. Here, too, weavings in level are crucial to the establishment of the arguments being advanced. The first sentence of that narrative unit, about population, is presented objectively; its level is disciplinary. So is the second, but it also contains a slight distancing: "Yet the Sinhalese Buddhists often tend to emphasize their minority status vis-à-vis the Tamils by linking the latter's ethnic affinity to the Tamils of southern India." The Sinhalese are indeed the majority in Sri Lanka, states the historian affirmatively (the facts, or rather the figures, demonstrate that); nevertheless—"yet"—they also produce themselves as a minority, by "linking" the Sri Lankan Tamils with those in India. The distancing allows the historian to re-present the claim, which is a political one, but not identify with it entirely, because it is not (social) scientific, because the discipline usually counts and classifies numbers like these within the contours of a country, or more properly, a state. Besides, it is the Sinhalese who are identified as the agent of the "linking," not the Tamils. Thus, while the Sinhalese feeling of being a minority maybe objectively false, it is without doubt a perception—the appropriateness of using this term will be evident soon—something that the historian must admit to the record, however reluctantly.[17] We will return to this bemusing claim on the part of an avowed majority to also be considered a minority; it is crucial to the text's production of hegemonic Sinhalese nationalism as an ethical project.

The relation between the Sinhalese and Buddhism, glossed over in that prior narrative unit, has to be explained, and the text does so with some care:

> [The Sinhalese] sense of ethnic distinctiveness is identified through religion—Theravada Buddhism—and language—Sinhalese. They take pride in the fact that Buddhism thrives in Sri Lanka while it has practically disappeared in its original home, India. Their language . . . has its roots in classical Indian languages, but it is now a distinctly Sri Lankan language, and one that is not spoken anywhere else. (8)

Sinhalese ethnicity is characterized by language and religion, which begs the question: How does one categorize those Sinhalese, the difference between three-quarters and two-thirds of the Sri Lankan population, implied above to be non-Buddhist? Sinhalese but somehow nonethnic? Perhaps even nonauthentic? Are they atheists, agnostics, or practitioners of another religion? De Silva elides these questions, even though addressing them would help him further establish his claim that Sri Lanka is a complex country. The attentive reader might begin to suspect that elision, or, better yet, silencing, is a cardinal element of his narrative strategy. She will also realize that the Sinhalese Buddhists are not only the majority in Sri Lanka, they are also a proud people, not just preserving a religion that has disappeared from the country of its origin but making it thrive, and they are a peerless people, too, presumably without an "ethnic affinity" to any other people, anywhere. Most significantly, they speak an ancient language, one related to the classical Indian languages—which would make it Indo-Aryan, perhaps?—but which today stands apart from all the others in the world. The plot, or rather the actant, has thickened: the Sinhalese are not only a good (anticolonial) people; they are also unique, ancient, classical.

The next actant presented, logically enough given that the numbers according to the census are second to the Sinhalese, are the Tamils. Such logic, as noticed before, is generalizing, essentialist. It is also taxonomic—characterized not just by a commitment to classification but also to hierarchy or verticality: the Sinhalese are presented before the Tamils because their numbers are greater. This finding of significance and value arithmetically, a routine move in social science and by no means an innocent one, serves to situate the Tamils in relation to the Sinhalese, to narratively minoritize them, to comprehend the story of the Tamils, as a Sri Lankan actant, not on its own terms but by comparing it to the majority:

Among the Tamils, there are two distinct groups, the Sri Lankan or Jaffna Tamils, whose origins go back well over 1,500 years, and the Indian Tamils, whose forebears were brought to the island by British planters . . . The two Tamil groups do not have much in common except their language. Both groups are mainly Hindu, but their distinctive geographical locations and the rigors of the Hindu caste system have generally kept them apart, the bulk of the plantation workers being regarded as "low" caste by the . . . Jaffna Tamil elite. Again, there is also the "class" element, the Indian Tamils being, in the main, plantation workers. (9)

The reader is not told what characterizes Tamil ethnicity, or what makes them ethnically distinct, although they do have a language and religion "in common." What percentage of the Sri Lankan populace is Tamil is not stated, either; but then it doesn't matter—it must be less than a quarter. Unlike the Sinhalese, who are merely segmented, the Tamils comprise "two distinct groups" with "not . . . much in common"—a remark one is compelled to term incoherent since they share the same elements, language and religion, that de Silva finds characterizes Sinhalese ethnicity. Unlike the Sinhalese, who "Sri Lankan scholars generally believe . . . originally came to the island over 2,500 years ago," the Jaffna Tamils "go back [merely] . . . 1,500 years."[18] Of course the two actants are not explicitly compared, but the reader must do so and is guided by the narrative in that direction; in other words, this narrative unit can be read as an instance of parataxis ("the placing of propositions or clauses one after another, without indicating . . . the relation—of co-ordination or subordination—between them" [OED]). It does not simply present the "facts" about different groups in sequence, the narrative information is also ordered, and interpretation is thrust upon the reader. The Sinhalese presence in Sri Lanka is to be compared to the Tamil: when done, it is found to be longer, and by a whole millennium. Arithmetic, again, determines significance and value: older is deeper—that being, as it were, the missing link; an older presence would sink deeper roots. This makes the Sinhalese claim to Sri Lanka more organic than the Tamil, a conclusion that coincides with that of Sinhalese nationalist discourse—even if not buttressed by the record—as does the fact that these Tamils have an "ethnic affinity" to other Tamils not residing in Sri Lanka. The Tamils, that is, are not authentically Sri Lankan. (The Sinhalese are from India, too, but their longer presence in Sri Lanka, presumably, makes them genuinely native.) In making these claims, albeit implicitly, the text subordinates, further minoritizes the Tamils. That actant is minor not only in number but also in (Sri Lankan) history. Other (catalytic, not cardinal) points of comparison should also be noted: the Tamils are classed, and have a caste system, but no such possibility is raised in relation to the Sinhalese—even though anthropology might insist otherwise about caste, and Marxism might about class. More significantly, the Tamils do not have a group, or even a segment, that resisted colonialism; indeed, one of the two Tamil groups arrived in the country as a direct consequence, perhaps even as a beneficiary, of the British. Is something rotten, the reader must wonder, about the Tamils?

Given their lesser numbers and the taxonomic worldview, the Muslims are introduced into the narrative, as they should be, after the Tamils. This is coherent, if vertical, logic (and verticality, hierarchization, at the risk of stating the obvious, is a fundamental element of right-wing thought.) What the text has to say about the Muslims, at least initially, is brief:

> The Muslims in Sri Lanka regard themselves as, and are treated as, a distinct "ethnic" group even though most of them are Tamil-speaking. They are closely integrated into the country's political system through the national political parties. Their rivalry with the Tamils is a long-standing one, and has frequently erupted into violence . . . they have been strongly opposed to the establishment of a separate Tamil state. (11)

Muslim ethnicity, presumably, is characterized by religion alone. They speak Tamil, but this does not appear to be an element constitutive of their identity. This actant—the identification of parataxis demands comparison with the two others—is apparently not segmented.[19] The Muslims also do not appear to have an origin, or, if they do, it is not significant enough to get narrative time. The patient reader might speculate that this is because the Muslims, at least according to de Silva's narrative, don't make a political claim to any part of the territory of Sri Lanka. So the question of length of residence does not arise to the disciplinary historian, even though consistency might suggest otherwise. Whether the Muslims might have an ethnic or some other affinity with an extra-Lankan group is also elided, which should signify to the reader that the narrative structure of this text is not coherent: the same questions are not asked of each of its actants; they are not described through the same categories. What does signify to de Silva is that the Muslims are integrated into the political system—making them, to take a term from another debate, something like a model minority. It is also important to de Silva to notice what he calls their "rivalry," often violent, not with the majority Sinhalese but with the Tamils. This is unexpected, certainly to the implied reader of *Reaping the Whirlwind*.

That reader was tacitly identified quite early in the narrative. Given de Silva's assumption that the reader of this work would know that the Balkan conflict is complex, the implied reader of *Reaping the Whirlwind* has to be familiar with Western discourse on ethnic conflict. This, of course, would not be the only characteristic of such a reader; but my contention is that, within this discourse, and Asia Watch is conveniently cited as an exemplary instance, minorities have quarrels with majorities, not other minorities. However, the Muslims, despite being "closely integrated into the country's political system," have a quarrel or rivalry with the Tamils—who, recall, never resisted colonialism and cannot be considered anticolonial. The reader's suspicions about these Tamils must now grow stronger.

But I should pause here and consider further the question of the implied reader of this text. It has been noticed that *Reaping the Whirlwind* addresses the West. If, as stated before, disciplinarity can be considered a "Western" mode of knowing, or organizing and authorizing knowledge, then by proclaiming the text's intellectual procedures as disciplinary, by asserting that it follows the protocols of its discipline, de Silva in a very precise sense writes from inside the West, because his text is dominated and determined by it. If so much is implicit, *Reaping the Whirlwind* also explicitly addresses the West and distinguishes between Western and Sri Lankan knowledge production. That it seeks to rebut the human-rights argument against Sri Lanka discussed before is evident throughout the text. In one narrative unit, denying Tamil claims to be discriminated against with regard to university admissions, de Silva states: "There were also distinguished scholars *based in the West* who also helped perpetuate these misleading claims through their own writings" (172; emphasis added); the names cited are Virginia Leary and Stanley Tambiah ("the distinguished Sri Lankan–born American anthropologist"). In criticizing their positions, de Silva isn't just being a good academic taking into account other points of view (for he does not cite alternative views consistently); rather, he *has* to rebut Leary and Tambiah—because, as he sees them, they are based in this powerful West. Or, one might say, the West emerges as powerful, authoritative, in this text because its account is that which has to be rebutted. The "misleading claims" of dozens of oppositional intellectuals publishing in Sri Lanka, academic and activist, leftist, liberal, and Tamil nationalist, who don't so much echo these sentiments as, perhaps, begin them, which then return authoritatively under the names Leary and Tambiah, can be silenced; *Reaping the Whirlwind* hardly ever cites Sri Lankan intellectuals who hold opposing positions. But not silenced is the work of Leary, Tambiah and, later in the narrative, "well-known U.S. political scientists such as Donald

Horowitz, Myron Weiner and Thomas Sowell [who] would cite the Sri Lanka example prominently in their studies on ethnic conflict" (136).[20] De Silva, in other words, cannot avoid a powerful, authoritative, Western account already in place in which the Sinhalese is the villain of the story. For his reading of Sri Lanka to be persuasive, these other *Western* readings must be demonstrably incorrect, and demonstrated to be so. In this context, the early assertion of his disciplinary training takes an added significance: *Reaping the Whirlwind* is to be read as the product of a professional academic, not of an ideologue. It is a disciplinary rebuttal of the Tamil nationalist and leftist accounts of Sri Lanka, yes, but most of all of the Western accounts. Its imperative to respond to the latter, and this claim will be elaborated later, constitutes an indispensable element of this text's anticolonial level. Put differently, while *Reaping the Whirlwind* abides by Sri Lanka from a position of authority or even dominance—it speaks, after all, from a majoritarian perspective—it is, as said before, dominated by the West.

To return to the actants: these, then, are the three cardinal players in the Sri Lankan story according to Kingsley de Silva. One: the Sinhalese—anticolonial, ancient in origin, world-historically unique, major. Two: the Tamils—recent in origin, derivative of India (not unique to Sri Lanka), collaborators with colonialism, minor. Three: the Muslims—without origin, allies of the Sinhalese, rivals of the Tamils, also minor.[21] Put differently, *de Silva finds no Sri Lankans in Sri Lanka.* The only forms of subjectivity he sees in the country are those constituted by ethnicity (as opposed to citizenship). We will return to this cardinal element of his perspective. But the country, clearly, looks complex: it has Sinhalese and Sinhalese Buddhists, two groups of Tamils and, to further complicate matters, another ethnic group, the Muslims. Christians are yet to enter the stage but will do so eventually (though not as actant). The reader has not been told exactly who is fighting whom, but she must surely be informed of the enmity between the Sinhalese and the Tamils; to make matters worse—as is only to be expected in a complex conflict—the Tamils and the Muslims also have a rivalry. However, as it turns out, those are not the only players. The reader of this text will notice the stamp of another that, within de Silva's schema, might also be considered actant—not another ethnic group this time, or an individual, or even another country, but something that, nevertheless, has an autonomous influence on Sri Lankan events: history. De Silva introduces it as a category entitled to its own narrative space in the very first chapter of *Reaping the Whirlwind*, not long after the descriptions of the ethnic groups discussed above:

In Sri Lanka the past is a powerful presence and often carries with it painful memories of invading armies, battles lost, cities destroyed, temples and palaces pillaged and kingdoms subverted. Ethnic consciousness in combination with nationalism raises expectations of restoring some of the glories of the past . . . and in the process, creating a new society upon ancient foundations. Attempts to restore the past often involve an obsessive concern about securing a redress of ancient grievances; in many such instances *the past is an incubus* which not only dominates the present, but carries with it the added danger of jeopardizing the possibility of establishing a stable political structure for the new society of the future. (19; emphasis added)

This is, of course, both an empiricist and a historicist conception of the past, not as a writing or narrative but as an object existing independently of the historian, which it is his disciplinary obligation to recall, and as one that is distinct from but bound to the present. If that much is consistent with Carr and with A. J. Greimas's formulation of the temporal illusion, respectively, the past also emerges here as an actant in the present, unconstrained by other actants. Even if it is "ethnic consciousness in combination with nationalism" that works upon it in the present, that seeks to make it return to the present rather than remain past, its *presence* is "powerful," independent of such consciousness. Powerful but suffering, like the Sinhalese, the past "carries painful memories," it is injured itself, seeks redress, and, as an object to de Silva, has its own subjectivity and agency, in relation to another object (a time—the writer's present—understood as different from it). Thus it, too, can be characterized as actant. Greimas and Courtes will help clarify this: "An actant can be thought of as that which accomplishes or undergoes an act, independently of all other determinations . . . The concept has the advantage of replacing, especially in literary semiotics, the term of character . . . since it applies not only to human beings but also to animals, objects, or concepts."[22] De Silva's ethnic groups are players on the Sri Lankan stage: they do things; if you like, they have agency. The same with history—synonymous with the past; it does things, plenty of work, and cardinal work, for de Silva's narrative. In other words, the narrative function of history in *Reaping the Whirlwind* is similar to the narrative function of the other actants identified above, the ethnic groups. So it must be considered separately as an actant— understood now as a performative, not a constative, category.

One more element can be noticed in the production of history in that narrative unit: it is an "incubus," so powerful it can "jeopardize" the present, not to mention make the future nightmarish. This is an intense statement from a historian about his object of study. How is the reader to comprehend it? Considering this question, perhaps somewhat redundant here since it was discussed in the previous chapter, will enable me to clarify further why I find the term "abiding" indispensable. This, in turn, would be easier to establish if I refer to another relatively recent academic work on Sinhalese history, one *not* randomly selected from my bookshelf: Steven Kemper's *The Presence of the Past*. As its title suggests, it addresses the same kinds of questions that bother—indeed give bad dreams to— de Silva. Here are the first lines of the Preface: "This book . . . attempts to explain how the past weighs on present-day affairs in one South Asian society. My interest in the Sri Lankan past derived from my concern for a society that has descended into terrorism, civil unrest, and social despair" (ix). Here, too, the past is understood within the logic of historicism, as distinct from, and having the capacity to act upon, the present. But the relevant point is this: like Watson and Spencer, Kemper, a professor of anthropology somewhere in the United States, is true to the protocols of his discipline identified in the last chapter; he produces himself as an outsider, as external to the society he investigates, to the object of his study. If he weren't, if he were inside it, he wouldn't have to explain his "interest" in Sri Lanka. He is concerned about it, for sure, like any good liberal, but he isn't a part of the terrorism, civil unrest, and social despair. To him, Sri Lanka is just "a society," a case—which by definition is not singular but one of many—of civil unrest. De Silva, recall, also understands Sri Lanka as a case, but, unlike Kemper, he cannot be read as outside his text—his political commitments bring him back into it. It was noticed earlier that he calls himself a "witness" to Sri Lankan events; this would be consistent with Kemper. But the reading I am trying to establish in this chapter is that de Silva emerges in his text, despite his claims to the contrary, as more than just an academic or witness. The past matters to him disciplinarily, of course, but it also matters extradisciplinarily: *it can actually jeopardize his present*. Kemper's interest, however, is merely academic; the Sri Lankan past cannot jeopardize what emerges, implicitly, as *his* present—presumably the same as Daniel's, Watson's, and Spencer's—to be identified, not in cartographic but political terms, as a place outside violence, terrorism, and despair. This is why the claims made by de Silva within a disciplinary level are constantly woven with another level not to be found in anthropological texts like those of Kemper. Here is Kemper again on what, within the terms of social science, would be understood as the same phenomenon described by de Silva (the past as an incubus):

What interests me are the constraints that make some views of the past more serviceable than others . . . [For instance] the capacity of some pasts to evoke pathos, specifically those that, having linked past to present, go on to make a distinction of this order—the present is continuous with the past, but the past was better than the present, or the present is an even more desperate time than the past, although the hostility of today's ethnic neighbor was a problem even then.[23]

Unlike de Silva, Kemper is consistently disciplinary; he understands the past empirically and within the logic of historicism; strong terms like "incubus" do not suffuse this text. As I have already contended, much is at stake in characterizing this difference, between the arguments of the Sri Lankan historian (plus something else) and the U.S. anthropologist—not as such but in terms of their stakes, in terms of how their texts produce their investment in their object of study.

One option, as discussed in the previous chapter, is to point out the obvious: de Silva is a citizen of Sri Lanka, Kemper is not; the stakes cannot be the same for the two of them. But citizenship, which implies a certain relation to the state, is an ultimately inadequate notion to capture this difference. It also cannot encompass the work of a noncitizen like David Scott, mentioned before, which does not place Sri Lanka in an object position to the investigating subject.[24] Thus my resort to "abiding by." It is an indispensable term that enables both a characterization of de Silva's text and of how it differs from those of Spencer and Daniel. Indeed, I would go so far as to state that the texts themselves demand the term, and the distinction it implies. Yes, de Silva writes disciplinary history; not only does he insist upon that, his arguments follow its protocols (if inconsistently, incoherently). But, by its inability to keep the concerns produced by a personal/political level from infecting that of the disciple, it thereby does much more than just witness the Sri Lankan present; it stands by, abides by, the country, dwells within its debates, endures its intricacies. Kemper's work simply doesn't, since it cannot be produced without distance from Sri Lanka, from Lankan social unrest (or was it despair); it cannot proceed without establishing such a distance, producing itself as written from outside; it speaks *of* and *for* Sri Lanka and so commits the cardinal and irremediable sin of anthropology—sees the country as purely an object and represents it to the authoritative epistemological space of the West. In contrast, by standing by it (after the anthropologist has left, as it were), by its concern not only with understanding the conflict, but devising "strategies and tactics to resolve or manage" it, de Silva's work displays a *commitment* to Sri Lanka. This commitment is to be understood as both intellectual and political. The implied reader of *Reaping the Whirlwind*, then, is not only the Western (liberal); de Silva (also) intervenes within a Sri Lankan debate. One might say, to repeat a point made in the last chapter, that Sri Lanka, to *Reaping the Whirlwind*, emerges as simultaneously object (of study), to which it is in the relation of subject, and subject (of intervention), to which it is in the relation of, to stretch a concept in the interests of a neat parallel, object.

Emplotment: Injured Majority, Privileged Minority

Reaping the Whirlwind's summary of the ethnic conflict—the conditions inhibiting peace, if not those that produce peace as a problem in the first place—in Sri Lanka comes soon after its identification of its actants. It will be predictable but also surprising to the reader of this study—who would expect an explanation, however brief, of why the conflict can be understood as complex. The narrative unit cited earlier needs to be reproduced now at some length:

> The current ethnic conflict in Sri Lanka is a *much more complex business than a simple straightforward confrontation* between a once well-entrenched minority—the Sri Lankan Tamils—and a now powerful but still insecure majority—the Sinhalese . . . [who] are not the only players in this intricate political drama even though . . . they play the principal roles. There are two conflicting *perceptions* of these conflicts. Most Sinhalese believe that the Tamil minority has enjoyed a privileged position under British rule and that the balance has of necessity to shift in favor of the Sinhalese majority. The Sri Lankan Tamil minority is an achievement-oriented, industrious group who still continue to enjoy high status in society, considerable influence in the economy, a significant if diminishing role in the bureaucracy and is well placed in all levels of the education system. The Tamils for their part would claim that they are now a harassed minority, the victims of frequent acts of communal violence and of calculated acts and policies of discrimination directed at them. Nevertheless, they could hardly be described as a beleaguered minority, the victims of regular episodes of violence—though violence had admittedly been frequent enough in recent times—given the impassioned ferocity with which sections of them have fought against the Sinhalese-dominated security forces, and the frequent attacks of Tamil terrorist groups, against the civilian population—Sinhalese in the main. This is quite apart from the eth-

nic cleansing they have indulged in at the expense mainly of the Muslim population . . . Most of the Tamil fears and their sense of insecurity stem from the belief that they have lost the advantageous position they enjoyed under British rule . . . in brief, a classic case of a sense of relative deprivation. (12; emphasis added)

The human-rights summary of what goes by the name of the ethnic conflict would go something like this: the Sinhalese have discriminated against the Tamils since independence. The Tamil nationalist summary would prefer a stronger verb: oppression, say, perhaps even genocide (and its narrative would begin in the late-colonial period). The anthropological summary would be straightforward: ethnic violence. De Silva's understanding of the complexity of Sri Lankan politics, or of why the conflict can be read as complex, as noticed before, is partly a response to the simplification of the first two, the comprehension of the conflict in binary terms, and implicitly rebuts the latter. But complexity, surprisingly enough, is not demonstrated in this narrative unit, even though it is proclaimed. Despite asserting that the Sinhalese and the Tamils are not the only players in the intricate Lankan drama, after insisting early in the narrative that the ethnic conflict is not a "straightforward confrontation" between two actants—one major, one minor—but takes place between four, de Silva proceeds to further narratively minoritize the two other actants—the Muslims and UpCountry Tamils—which he himself identified, earlier, as equal players in the drama, because, he states, their "roles" are less than "principal." So he banishes these two actants from the generality of his narrative; he does grant their situations specific attention in two discrete chapters, but this, of course, only structurally reinforces their narrative minoritization and makes it even more difficult for the reader to accept his claim that the Sri Lankan conflict is complex. A coherent narrative, in contrast, would allow (more or less) equal narrative time to all four identified actants regardless of their numbers. De Silva, however, can only identify and grant such time to two "principal" perceptions of the conflict: one Sinhalese, one Tamil; the perceptions of the two other actants are not recounted, even though so doing would not just complicate the picture, but buttress his reading of Sri Lanka as a complex, Balkan-like conflict *because* it has several players that enable several perceptions. Simply reversing the reading of human-rights discourse and making the majority the "real" victims of the story might make it different but does not make it complex—at least not within de Silva's own terms.

Nevertheless, the historian's description of the Tamils appears to gain depth in this unit, certainly compared to the actant's first appearance within the narrative; he seems, at the very least, to be balanced, to present not only the Sinhalese but also the Tamil perception of the story. But does his rhetoric correspond to its appearance? Is there narrative balance, actually? The Tamils claim harassment. To evaluate this claim, a professional historian, following as it were standard disciplinary procedure, would have cited what he considered a representative Tamil argument, or many such arguments, and evaluated it/them. But de Silva does not; he silences scholarship that self-consciously advocates a Tamil perception. Despite this, he does appear to consider, to take seriously, and so to investigate these claims of oppression. He finds them, upon inspection, barely tenable. The Tamils not only claim harassment but have been the victim of frequent episodes of violence; that is undeniable. However, some of them are "terrorists" who attack Sinhalese civilians. In addition, "sections" of them—terrorists? civilians? why is the reader uninformed?—have fought the Sinhalese security forces with "impassioned ferocity." The reader has noticed, before, de Silva's essentialist understanding of what he calls ethnic groups—indeed, that passage is a classic case of essentialism—from which it follows that he will also comprehend them metonymically. The reader must appreciate the cardinal significance of metonymy to this perspective: the part can represent the whole. Some Tamils may have been attacked by Sinhalese (civilians? terrorists? the military?), but sections of them have attacked the Sinhalese in turn, ferociously, like tigers perhaps, so one cannot term them beleaguered, not even if it is Tamil civilians who have been attacked and Tamil militants who've done the attacking, which might make the former victim (object) and the latter agent (subject). Those distinctions, made by human-rights discourse and the left, are incomprehensible to de Silva's discourse, in which a Tamil is a Tamil is a Tamil. To the essentialist perspective, ethnic subjectivity cannot be marked. Besides, these same Tamils who claim harassment are actually (still) privileged: they may no longer be as "well entrenched" as they used to be; nevertheless, they continue to enjoy high status in society, influence in the economy and the like; their deprivation is merely relative. They continue to enjoy social and economic privilege and so, he implies later in the narrative, cannot complain about political subordination.

Of course, the Tamils have lost some of this privilege in the post-colonial period. They are somewhat insecure today, but theirs—and this statement is iterated throughout the narrative—is a purely relative loss, a consequence of their special treatment by the British during colonialism. Two claims utterly critical to de Silva's petition are advanced in this statement, one most subtly: the Tamils didn't resist colonialism (or at least the British) because they didn't have to; they were its beneficiaries, perhaps even its collaborators. The second, following from the first, rewrites the Western and Tamil nationalist story, in which the Tamil is the victim of postcolonial Sri Lanka. The attentive reader will realize, now, why it is so important to de Silva's plot, or rather emplotment,[25] to begin his story in the precolonial past; he cannot but do so. When their story is compre-hended in a long historical frame, the Sinhalese can be produced as not aggressors but victims, especially in a postcolonial disciplinary moment, merely redressing the balance in the postcolonial period, seeking repara-tion for a historical injury. In so doing, the Sinhalese can also be pro-duced as having a grievance, making a complaint, and insisting upon the recognition of a wrong during colonialism that has to be righted in the postcolonial period. The Sinhalese are the victims in this story: they were injured by history; they are entitled to heal those wounds, right those wrongs; *that* is the real story of Sri Lanka. In so emplotting it, in—as will be seen—so revising his earlier account of the Sri Lankan past, lies the significance of the text's anticolonial level. By now, *Reaping the Whirlwind's* implied reader is no doubt supposed to have lost her sympathy for the Tamils, to be utterly suspicious of their calling themselves a beleaguered minority. Not only are they not victims, they are actually terrorists and attack other minorities. Strikingly enough, their treatment of the Muslims—and the Tamils as a whole are found responsible for this—is called "ethnic cleansing." The implied reader of *Reaping the Whirlwind* will easily follow the analogy, since that term emerged to describe the Balkans: the Tamils are like the Serbs—terrorists, butchers en masse of innocent civilians, people without legitimate grievances who should probably be prosecuted for war crimes.

De Silva terms the Sinhalese insecure in that narrative unit but doesn't explain why. Perhaps because of "the burden of historical memories" they carry, which, he finds, "is the essential starting point for an analysis of the issues that divide the people of Sri Lanka." This privileging of history, and of the Sinhalese perspective exclusively, is actually a conclusion, not a beginning; but let's continue with his description of this burden. It takes the argument from colonial to precolonial history:

> There is, first of all, the Sinhalese *sense* of historical destiny, of a *small and embattled people* who have preserved Theravada Buddhism when it was obliterated in India under a Hindu revivalist tide . . . Linked to this is their *perception* of the Tamils as a traditional "national" enemy against whom they

have fought at various times over two thousand years of a common history. There is also the *perception* of southern India as the source of scores of invasions of the heartland of ancient Sri Lanka.[26]

Equally important is the historical *memory* of a long . . . and successful *record* of retaining national independence in the face of western invaders . . . Meantime, the short-lived Tamil kingdom of Jaffna had been crushed by the Portuguese after some early resistance . . . Thereafter, there is no *record* of Tamil resistance to western rule comparable to that of the Sinhalese. (20; emphasis added)

It should be pointed out here that *Managing Ethnic Tensions*'s discussion of the Tamils differs significantly from this; it does not see them as "a traditional enemy." But, now, to "good," "unique," and "insecure" can be added "embattled," or "injured." The reader must, by this stage, feel sympathetic toward the Sinhalese, very sympathetic indeed. They are victims of history, colonial and precolonial. Several other (catalytic) details must also be noticed about that narrative unit: the Sinhalese are a small people—a claim that reinforces the one made earlier about a minority complex— but nevertheless have a sense of historical destiny, since they preserved Buddhism, destroyed in India by the Hindus. In that other narrative unit analyzed previously, Buddhism was described as having "disappeared" in India. Here, it is found to have been "obliterated," wiped out; here, too, the agent of this vile deed is identified: the Hindus. This insinuates paratactically (subtly) that the Tamils—"mainly Hindu," recall—share responsibility for this destruction, this barbarity, which, perhaps, might explain Sinhalese Buddhist insecurity. They speak a unique language "that is not spoken anywhere else." They live in a country with Hindus, a group against whom they have fought throughout history. It was Hindus who, once upon a time, obliterated their religion—albeit in another country. And though a minority in Sri Lanka, the attentive reader would recall that these Hindus have an "ethnic affinity" with those other Hindus (Tamils) in that other country across a shallow and narrow stretch of sea in nearby south India. Exactly how many Hindu Tamils live in India is not stated; nevertheless, the implied reader of *Reaping the Whirlwind* would know that India has a, well, somewhat substantial population. Wouldn't you feel insecure if you were Sinhalese under these circumstances?

But the cardinal terms, those that require pause in that narrative unit, are "sense," "perception," "memory," and "record." Why does the narrative require them? What work do they do for a historian of de Silva's perspective? The Sinhalese are the preservers of Theravada Buddhism. This may be a burden, but it has been predetermined by history itself; or, at least, this is the "sense" of the Sinhalese. Another element of the burden is two "perceptions": first, of the Tamils as a historical enemy that invaded their country—and caused, perhaps, those "battles lost, cities destroyed, temples and palaces pillaged and kingdoms subverted" encountered before—and second, of southern India as the "source" of these invasions that led to the battles lost, et cetera—invasions, not insignificantly, of the *heart* of Sinhalese country, its very core. So, while the Sinhalese and Tamils have a "common history," it is not the consequence of common being, as that phrase might suggest, but of common antagonism. The Tamils have attacked the Sinhalese throughout history, ancient history, just like—you guessed it—the colonial powers, the Portuguese, the Dutch, and the British, in recent history. The significance of the Sinhalese "memory" of successfully resisting colonialism—the significance of another element of the anticolonial level—can now be clarified: paratactically, it equates the Tamils with colonialism. So can the significance of historicizing the conflict be clarified: it enables the production of the Sinhalese as the victims of the Sri Lankan story from an ancient time to a modern; they may be the majority of the population, but they are also an embattled and injured one, constantly at the receiving end of invasions, losing their temples, palaces, and other monuments of their culture. Beginning the story in 1948, as in the Asia Watch account, would not allow this; and taking it back to just the colonial period would be inadequate, since it is necessary to draw an analogy between the Tamil invasions and colonialism. My point, though, is not that the Sri Lankan conflict doesn't have a long history. To make that claim would be to situate my own argument within a positivist problematic. Rather, my concern is to ask, with de Certeau, of the work performed by history for the emplotment of *Reaping the Whirlwind*. If history is understood not as a faithful account of real events but as an authoritative story, then one must ask how does this (revised) story help or hinder *Reaping the Whirlwind*'s nationalism? When that question is posed to this narrative unit, the disciplinary and anticolonial levels can be seen working together to produce the Sinhalese claim to injury in the past and to authorize its petition for hegemony in the present; to, in other words, connect history and politics. Wouldn't you, after all, be sympathetic to the claims of the victims of history—as so many postcolonial historians have asked you to be?

It is, consequently, to be expected that when the question of anticolonialism is asked of the Tamils, no "record" is discovered of that actant having been so. This is yet another instance of de Silva's subtlety: he appears to present both sides of the argument, but the reader will notice that the Sinhalese are entitled to make their case through sense, perception, and memory. My point is not that de Silva doesn't present the facts here or that perception and memory should not be the concern of the historian, though, of course, these are not categories deployed by conventional disciplinary history. Rather, unlike the Sinhalese, the Tamils are evaluated in disciplinary terms, with reference to the record. The Tamil actant cannot sense, remember, or perceive—it must prove. A similar move is made a little earlier in the narrative:

> This tendency to seek a restoration of an *imagined past* is not confined to the . . . Sinhalese. In Sri Lanka it has affected the Tamil minority as well, and forms the basis of their claims of a "traditional homeland," the successor as they see it of the short-lived Jaffna kingdom of old. But the historical evidence the Tamil advocates of a "traditional homeland" provide in support of their claims is so flimsy that only "true believers" can accept them. (18; emphasis added)

Here, the reader will notice, is the past as actant: imagined or otherwise, it has the capacity to intervene within the Tamil, and therefore the Sri Lankan, present. Here, once again, a Tamil contention—and a most cardinal one to Tamil nationalism, the "traditional homeland," in which a historical claim is staked to a part of Sri Lankan territory—is dismissed as having no factual basis; there is no evidence, no record to buttress it; it is deemed "imagined." At best, the Jaffna kingdom was "short-lived"; unlike, of course, those Sinhalese kingdoms. The other implication here is that the territory thereafter was not predominantly Tamil. How could it be? There must have been concentrations of Muslims for them to be ethnically cleansed in the postcolonial period. Subtlety again: points cardinal to de Silva's argument are not clearly stated but have to be deduced.

The reader would by now have guessed where I am going with this: de Silva does not ask whether the Sinhalese senses, perceptions, and memories are supported by a record, whether they are buttressed by evidence. One way of understanding this is to call him biased—because the Sinhalese nationalist claim wouldn't stand up to such rigorous disciplinary scrutiny. Greimas might find in the narrative structure a lack of coherence; and my deployment of the term should now be clarified. To Greimas, coherence is "understood in terms of the unending recurrence, throughout a given discourse, of the same group of categories by which one might justify a given instance of paradigmatic organization," characterized by "a 'common denominator' that will buttress the entire discourse."[27] There isn't a categorical common denominator at work in *Reaping the Whirlwind*; if so, the Tamils would be entitled to make claims through the same categories as the Sinhalese—belief, sense, memory, and perception—or else the Sinhalese recourse to such terms would also be evaluated with reference to the record. The careful reader will also see here the weaving together of the text's levels; this time, however, the one overdetermines the other. De Silva evaluates Tamil claims within the protocols of the disciplinary level (the record); Sinhalese claims, in contrast, are evaluated differently—he abides by them. Why do the levels, here, work against each other? Is this simply to be considered incoherent, bad history, or is there something else at work? My conclusion is that what is coherent about *Reaping the Whirlwind*, what integrates the text, its common denominator, is not its disciplinary rigor or the use of a consistent set of categories but its politics, its commitment to abiding by Sri Lanka from a determinedly, self-consciously hegemonic Sinhalese nationalist perspective.

In this regard, it is crucial for my purposes, given the importance of the question of revision, to compare *Reaping the Whirlwind* with *Managing Ethnic Tensions*'s approach to the record, to pose the question of coherence to that prior text. In *Managing Ethnic Tensions*, too, the Sinhalese are produced as having a "sense" of being a small and embattled people, a "perception" of the Tamils as "the traditional national enemy" and "of southern India as the source from which scores of invasions of the heartland of ancient Sri Lanka were launched." But de Silva does not stop there; he finds, rather, that "to accept the Sinhalese perception of themselves as a minority facing a massive and implacable phalanx is to *ignore several facts* of Sri Lankan politics" (1986, 362; emphasis added). The two most salient of these "facts" are that those Tamils living outside the northeast, in the Sinhalese dominated parts of the country, do not necessarily subscribe to northeastern politics, whether federalist or separatist, and that the group that *Reaping the Whirlwind* effectively forgets, the "Indian Tamils have strong political links with the . . . governing party." To cite this narrative unit is not to contend that *Managing Ethnic Tensions* isn't complicit with Sinhalese nationalism, but it is important to notice that the prior text does not comprehend the Tamils in essentialist terms. Not only do the Tamils, in *Managing Ethnic Tensions*, have *three* distinct groups, but the politics of all three do not coincide. That is to say, the Sinhalese nationalism in *Managing Ethnic Tensions* is nuanced differently than in *Reaping the Whirlwind*, which aligns itself quite categorically with it. Here, Sinhalese perceptions are checked against the record *and deemed incorrect;* the nationalist position is explicitly critiqued, kept at some distance. This never happens in *Reaping the Whirlwind*, which is why I consider *Managing Ethnic Tensions* the product and producer of a different *narrative* moment. It addresses the "same" happenings but emplots them very differently. The consequences of this for my reading of *Reaping the Whirlwind* will be addressed in the conclusion of this chapter. It is necessary, now, to return to the narrative, having examined *Reaping the Whirlwind*'s discussion of precolonial history, to move to the colonial.

The period does not gain as much narrative time in *Reaping the Whirlwind* as it does in his previous work, including *Managing Ethnic Tensions*. This is unexpected, given the critical importance of Sinhalese anticolonialism to *Reaping the Whirlwind*'s plot. To take a term from Gerard Genette, what occurs here is "ellipsis" (narrative acceleration):[28] despite its avowed conviction about the importance of history—the past—to understanding the present, despite its entire thesis being predicated upon the historicity of its argument, *Reaping the Whirlwind* is more anxious to discuss the (postcolonial) present than the past. It rushes through, summarizes its production of the past in order to arrive at the present; most of the narrative is a treatment of postcolonial events. *Reaping the Whirlwind* allows hardly any narrative time to the ancient past (even though the Sinhalese, according to *Report of the Sinhala Commision*, have a recorded history of some 2,500 years); it invokes this past, but—unlike *Managing Ethnic Tensions*—doesn't narrativize it, doesn't present any detail. It allows just one chapter to the colonial period, covering some four hundred and fifty years, but the years 1951–1977, 1977–1983, and 1983–1990, respectively, get a chapter each. The narrative emphasis, then, is not just on the postcolonial period but on the years after 1977 (the governments, mainly, of Junius Richard Jayewardene).[29] This signifies what is at stake in this work, which presents itself as historical and even constitutes the past as an actant in the present: it is the postcolonial "present" that *Reaping the Whirlwind* seeks to narrate—and legitimize—from a Sinhalese nationalist perspective. Is this another instance of narrative incoherence? Given his own insistence that one needs to be familiar with Sri Lankan history to understand the conflict, shouldn't the precolonial period get at least a chapter of its own? Ideally, yes. However, it is also important to notice that, to de Silva, the significance of the past lies not so much in its pastness but in its presence, its capacity as an actant to intervene in the present. Besides, it is possible to read him as proceeding on the assumption that the precolonial record is not contested, at least not by this text's implied Western reader. This is not to imply that it isn't contested by others; I have referred previously to the work of R. A. L. H. Gunawardana. But it has already been noted that de Silva silences oppositional Sri Lankan intellectual production, while responding to the West's, and that he cannot allow the seamlessness of its argument to be contradicted, however momentarily, by the citation of dissenting positions. As for human-rights discourse, if Asia Watch did not see a historicity to the conflict, Virginia Leary, in the report de Silva cites, concedes the Sinhalese nationalist past. In what would be the first of many substantial human-rights reports on Sri Lanka, written in this instance for the Geneva-based International Commission of Jurists, she stated: "The present racial tension between the Sinhalese and Tamil populations in Sri Lanka has deep historical roots, dating back to the first century A.D. . . . The Sinhalese population of Sri Lanka has historically considered the Tamils as invaders."[30] If that much is consistent with de Silva, or at least the de Silva of *Reaping the Whirlwind*, Leary nevertheless refuses to see the Sinhalese as injured and seeking reparation, refuses to accept this past as an alibi for the present—and charges the Sinhalese with being discriminatory. Since it is Western discourse that determines his emphasis, de Silva will only have to mobilize the past briefly. Asia Watch, as it were, has to be rebutted. However, given Leary, given, more correctly, the polyvocality of human-rights discourse, de Silva can afford to be summary in his account of the colonial period, as well as selective— he can choose to narrate only those events that will enhance the Sinhalese claim to loss, to injury.

Consequently, on the question of colonialism, the emphasis in *Reaping the Whirlwind* falls exclusively on religion—apart, that is, from the question of resisting colonialism, of being anticolonial. Significantly enough, however, that heroic Kandyan story gets no serious narrative time, despite the existence of that "long record." The struggle for decolonization, self-determination, and representative government are barely mentioned, despite an appearance in the very opening of the narrative: "Sri Lanka . . . was referred to as the 'model' colony in the early years of independence . . . where an eminently sensible national leadership has preferred a negotiated transfer of power, in contrast to the Indian model. Indeed, the leadership had decided to follow the conventional, if unglamorous, constitutional evolution of the 'settlement' colonies of Canada, Australia and New Zealand into independent states" (5). The Kandyans might have resisted colonialism, but *Reaping the Whirlwind* has no mention of any Sinhalese doing so after 1815.[31] It appears from the above unit that the Sinhalese didn't resist the British at all after that—unlike, the reader is told, the Indians. De Silva might find these Sinhalese leaders eminently sensible. But, surely, this does not make our heroes sound very heroic, does it? It actually makes them seem like those collaborative Tamils the text villainizes. For, after all, they would not have been deemed model colonials if they actively resisted colonialism. Not surprisingly, this statement, appearing at the beginning of the narrative, isn't returned to thereafter. The possibility that the Sinhalese collaborated with and benefited from colonialism is a question this text cannot consider; if it did, there would be no balance to redress, no wound to heal, no hegemony to justify in the postcolonial period. Of course, a more populist historian could concede that the Sinhalese elite collaborated, but the masses did not. But de Silva's essentialism precludes such a move.

If the record "suggests" that the Sinhalese collaborated with colonialism, something Wilson takes great care to establish, then silencing it and emphasizing religion would allow de Silva to keep insisting that the Sinhalese are the aggrieved party, the victim. The narrative, Genette might remind one at this point, is "iterative": the same story is repeated, is emplotted, of the colonial Sinhalese past as it was of the precolonial. Thus *Reaping the Whirlwind* summarizes "the religious intolerance that came to Sri Lanka with the Portuguese . . . leaving behind a memory of temples destroyed, temple properties confiscated and turned over to the church" (70), et cetera. The Dutch, who followed the Portuguese, continued the practice, left further memories of destruction and pillage. The British, in contrast, were "more latitudinarian." When they defeated the Kandyan kingdom in 1815, they even agreed to "protect Buddhism, its bhikkus, places of worship and the properties of the temples" (72). But this was short-lived; they reversed policy in the 1840s, after which "the Buddhists in Sri Lanka began . . . a decades-long agitation for a restoration of this link" (73). Does this count as resisting colonialism? Should it be understood as collaboration? The question is irrelevant because "Most colonial administrators . . . did not understand that Sri Lankan Buddhism had no central organization that could either formally appoint heads of viharas, or . . . [recognize] the property rights of viharas and devales" (75). Why didn't our heroes establish organizations for themselves? Why did they want Westerners, non-Buddhists, to do so? De Silva does not attend to this question. Neither does he even bother to wonder if Hinduism, Hindu temples and property were also the target of colonialism. So doing might be good disciplinary practice; it would certainly be coherent; but, quite apart from signifying, again, the lack of a "common denominator," so doing might lead to the admission that the Sinhalese Buddhists were not the only group victimized by colonialism.[32] This, of course, would vitiate the emplotment of the narrative, or, at least, its anticolonial element. So de Silva simply concludes his discussion of the colonial period by stating that the British were insensitive to the Sinhalese Buddhist requests, that our heroes did not find redress until after decolonization, in the years following 1956. Silencing, clearly, is an indispensable element of de Silva's narrative structure; it has the appearance of balance, but this does not survive the scrutiny of the attentive reader.

Pierre Macherey has argued that the "speech of the book comes from a certain silence," that "what the work *cannot say* is [as] important" as what it does say, and that "it is this silence which . . . informs us of the precise conditions for the appearance of an utterance."[33] If silence is the condition of appearance of any text, then what exactly does de Silva silence? It has been noted that, to *Reaping the Whirlwind*, while Sri Lankan society, history, and the ethnic conflict are all complex, this complexity gets reduced to the actions and perceptions of just two cardinal actants, one Sinhalese, one Tamil. This text, to repeat and rephrase an earlier reading, effectively silences, or better yet minoritizes, what it terms the Muslim and UpCountry Tamil perception; it also silences a potential actant that is not named as such, the (Sinhalese) Catholic. The Sinhalese Buddhist is evidently the only legitimate perception to *Reaping the Whirlwind*; or, rather, the Sinhalese nationalist story is the one the text legitimizes. But it does not do so just by narrating the Sinhalese perception alone but rather by shuttling between it and the Tamil perception, by villainizing the latter by not discussing it through the same terms and categories used to discuss the former, in short, by making the narrative incoherent. Reading de Silva through Greimas, Macherey (and Propp) suggests that legitimizing the Sinhalese story *requires* effectively silencing the Tamil, a silencing—minoritizing is a more exact term here, since he places significance in number—I find subtle since, rather than just ignore or suppress the Tamil perspective, as he does the Catholic, *Reaping the Whirlwind* actually presents it and grants it narrative time, albeit in terms designed to delegitimize it. In this context, another, more profound aspect of the narrative's silencing can also be appreciated: its refusal to cite the other side, as it were, of the story. While de Silva mentions David Horowitz, Thomas Sowell, and Myron Weiner, their work is never actually cited; Leary and Tambiah are cited only when they can be easily rebutted; Sri Lankan liberals, leftists, and Tamil nationalists are barely cited at all. De Silva, in other words, will not let oppositional voices into his narrative. He does tell some kind of Tamil story, but only after translating it into his Sinhalese nationalist voice. That I would identify politics at work here should be by now obvious. But it should also be clear that it is not politics alone that produces this narrative: paying attention to its form, structure, and rhetoric reveals the impress of a narratological level intimately abetting its politics.

In his account of Sri Lankan colonial and precolonial history, then, de Silva produces the Sinhalese as injured, as the victim. The Tamil is the aggressor in the precolonial period and, under colonialism, collaborator with the British, and so aggressor or oppressor by analogy. The story of postcolonial Sri Lanka, given that the majority now rules the country, cannot of course be emplotted thus. The Sinhalese, with control of the state, cannot continue to be produced as mere victims, at least not persuasively. The plot has to turn, and it does. Before discussing that, it is necessary to pause a moment here and address the question of emplotment. I want to emphasize that the plot of a history, or more correctly its emplotment, is the result of the disciplinary, narratological, and abiding levels working together. "Events" cannot be understood as narrativizing themselves in the form of a finished story; to hold so would be to work within the terms of the referential illusion, of empiricism. Rather, they must be seen as strung together, connected, *narrativized*. As Hayden White might remind one here, "events are *made* into a story by the suppression or subordination of certain of them and the highlighting of others."[34] One does not have to accept all of White's categories, or his humanism, to take his point that the plot of a work of history is made or produced; one does not, after all, have to understand the "making" of history as an agential activity. If, as de Certeau reminds one, an element of the operation of history is place, understood nonempirically, then what one might say of *Reaping the Whirlwind* is that its emplotment is indeed the product of place—a polyvocal place it inhabits called Sinhalese nationalism. "The historiographical institution is inscribed within a complex that permits only one kind of production for it and prohibits others. Such is the double function of the place. It makes possible certain researches through the fact of common conjunctures and problematics. But it makes others impossible."[35] Thus, *Reaping the Whirlwind*'s emplotment will produce the Sri Lankan story as one of Sinhalese victimization because it is enabled by the same "institutional" place (which, in turn, disables, censors, or silences a Tamil nationalist emplotment of the Sri Lankan story). In my terms, and maybe this should have been made clear much earlier, this working together of the levels makes it possible for the reader, only once she has read the text and not before, to identify an entity called Sinhalese nationalist history, which is constituted by a combination of levels: the historical (disciplinary) level, the level of story (narratological), and of course the political level of a certain claim upon a place called Sri Lanka (abiding).

In the postcolonial period, de Silva produces the Sinhalese as using their newly won control of the state to attempt to heal those historical wounds, to live finally in peace and security. But, in so doing, it does not behave like an insensitive majority. It is accommodating of the demands and concerns of the minorities; indeed, it is the minorities, the Tamils in particular, who are aggressive, if not excessive, in their demands upon the Sri Lankan state. This can be seen in *Reaping the Whirlwind*'s treatment of the language question, the first postcolonial happening given significant narrative time by the text. These are cardinal moments in the autobiographies of both Tamil and Sinhalese nationalisms—and Asia Watch, the reader will remember, found the "post-independence cycle of claims" to begin then. De Silva therefore has to consider this moment at some length, and he grants the question an entire chapter. To him, the new prime minister, Solomon West Ridgeway Dias Bandaranaike, came "to power [in 1956] . . . through a successful exploitation of a wave of Sinhalese-Buddhist emotion" and the promise of "language reform." Bandaranaike, states de Silva, wanted to replace English with Sinhalese as the official language of the country—which both the Tamil nationalist and human-rights accounts identify as an originary event in the story of the ethnic conflict. This attempt is endorsed by *Reaping the Whirlwind* because it "gave a sense of dignity to the common people and fortified their self-respect" (27), the dignity and self-respect, of course, *of the Sinhalese* that was allegedly lost during the colonial period. Now, with decolonization, the healing process can begin. It is important to notice here that the Sinhalese are still victims; the plot is consistent. But, now, with decolonization, they are not mere victims; they are beginning to heal those ancient wounds—with, however, no malice to the Tamils, their old enemy. To de Silva, Bandaranaike also wanted to "balance"—a term we've encountered before and to which we'll have to return—the interests of the minorities, in keeping with an agreement reached in 1944 between Sinhalese and Tamil politicians. (The reader might remember that Asia Watch did not find Bandaranaike balanced or concerned about the minorities; neither does Leary. Human-rights discourse is very clear on who is the villain of the story.) That agreement did not foresee the Tamil language being allowed a statutory status equal to the Sinhalese, but it would be allowed something resembling equality, administratively, in the Tamil majority parts of the country. However, Bandaranaike was prevented from implementing the agreement by a "formidable combination of bhikku activists and 'Sinhalese Only' ideologues acting in unison" (51).[36] The cardinal point to notice here is that de Silva distinguishes between two variants of Sinhalese nationalism: he produces what one might term bourgeois or hegemonic Sinhalese nationalism (of Bandaranaike and parliamentarians) as prepared to be accommodating to the Tamils; it is the more radical or extreme variant (of activists and ideologues) that is not. (In making the distinction, de Silva distances his text, if subtly, from the position of the extreme.) But it was the extreme that triumphed; as a result,

> On the post-independence controversies over the language issue, the Tamils started with the moral advantage accruing to an aggrieved party . . . Had the Sinhalese leadership . . . not forced the pace of language change . . . they may well have ensured the primacy of their language on a much more solid basis . . . Quite apart from the natural advantage accruing to Sinhalese as the language of over two-thirds of the population, there was the powerful attraction of economic necessity . . . As it was the objective of 'Sinhalese Only' has been pursued at the cost of conceding to the Tamils all the advantages of proclaiming to a sympathetic world that they, as a minority, have suffered greatly. (68)

The claims in this narrative unit show the abiding level at work; and I am constrained to label it remarkable, truly astounding. De Silva's objection to what goes by the name "Sinhalese Only" is not made on ethical grounds—that it could be understood as discriminatory or oppressive of the Tamils, as a leftist might argue. Rather, his objection is purely tactical: it was done in undue haste, which enabled the Tamils to produce their position to the "sympathetic world" as that of victim, to lay claim to an injury. This outside world, of course, is Western discourse, which, as has been seen, accepted the Tamil claim to victimhood. Thus de Silva's anger at extremist Sinhalese nationalism for being tactically inept. He has no ethical objection to the "primacy" of the Sinhalese language in Sri Lanka, finding that such dominance would have occurred anyway, in the "natural" course of events, as a consequence of demographic fact, economic necessity, and the working of democracy, where the majority will have its way. Inhabiting positions like this, of course, is what enables de Silva's account to be characterized as advocating, but subtly, the hegemony of Sinhalese nationalism in Sri Lanka, if hegemony is understood, after Ranajit Guha's persuasive recasting of Gramsci, as a relation of dominance where the element of persuasion "outweighs" that of coercion.[37] For, to de Silva, it is important that the Tamils accept their minority status and accept it as "natural," inevitable, a product not of politics—which can always be contested—but of nature—which cannot. De Silva wants the Tamil to accept their status as, in a word, apodictic, so they would not want to, because they would not comprehend their status in such terms, present themselves as injured and seek the sympathy of the West.

Buttressing this argument requires producing the Sinhalese as not dominating but accommodating, as concerned about the sensibility of the Tamils. Bandaranaike, as has been noted, is produced as such by de Silva. Two of de Silva's later chapters (5 and 6) narrate in great detail the many attempts of other Sinhalese governments—particularly that of Junius Richard Jayewardene from 1977 to 1989—to "balance" the interests of the Tamil minority. Reading the detail of these chapters is not relevant to the present study; it is enough to note that he presents the language question as essentially being solved by Jayewardene. This, of course, makes the Sinhalese accommodating; they are the majority and entitled to have their way in a democracy but were still prepared to make concessions to the Tamils. Despite this, these ungrateful Tamils continued agitating in the 1980s for a separate state. De Silva concludes, from his own reading of those many conferences, negotiations, diplomatic encounters, and so on, that the failure of the Sinhalese and the Tamil to reach an accommodation in these years, on the question of some kind of autonomy for the Tamils, is a consequence of Tamil intransigence:

> In situations of prolonged ethnic conflict fashioning an outcome that is intermediate between victory and defeat for one of the combatants becomes extraordinarily difficult . . . Conflict resolution requires an outcome that has something for everyone. Parties to the conflict cannot expect to give up their claims without some compensation, and this implies a willingness to compromise on at least some of the underlying issues. The LTTE . . . has never shown any readiness to compromise. (246)

The narrative voice here, of course, is no longer disciplinary but straightforwardly political. Thus, also, my calling the narrative moment produced by this text pessimistic: blaming the Tamils and their extravagant demands for the conflict, it doesn't see a "readiness to compromise" on the part of those Tamils. Consequently, the ethnic conflict can have no quick resolution. This conclusion is drawn not from a consideration of the Sri Lankan instance alone but from "situations of prolonged ethnic conflict." De Silva makes a general claim here, based on his study of the Balkans, Malaysia, and so on. Sri Lanka, the student of civil war and of modern history determines, is doomed to "reap the whirlwind" of ethnic conflict for years to come. De Silva's position on peace is also most clearly enunciated here: the obstacle to peace in Sri Lanka is not the Sinhalese, not the deeds of the postcolonial Sinhalese state, not the majoritarian

Sinhalese nationalist desire for hegemony—as opposed to equality for the ethnic groups—but the extravagant demands of the Tamils. Sinhalese governments—and, to the metonymic perspective, government and ethnic group are interchangeable—were routinely willing "to compromise on at least some of the underlying issues"; the Tamils were not. In this narrative unit, the blame for failure falls upon the Liberation Tigers of Tamil Eelam (LTTE), which, to this text, dominates Tamil politics from the 1980s. The same claim is made, in the course of the narrative, of other political organizations the text identifies as the LTTE's predecessors—the Federal Party (FP) in the 1950s and 1960s and the Tamil United Liberation Front (TULF) in the 1970s. The difference between the parliamentary FP/TULF and the "terrorist" LTTE lies less in demand than method: the former agitated nonviolently to maintain Tamil privilege within a single Sri Lankan state, wanting equality of status for its language and devolution of power to an autonomous Tamil-majority region; the latter are violent terrorists wanting not just autonomy but their own state. The difference, ultimately, is only a matter of degree. Both the FP/TULF and the LTTE want to maintain Tamil privilege. The Tamil, whether parliamentarian or terrorist, is the villain of this story.

This may sound like a gross simplification of a detailed, though not necessarily "complex," plot. Surely history does not have villains and heroes? Surely it is more nuanced than that? Some history, perhaps, but not *Reaping the Whirlwind*. Greimas and Courtes, again, will help us understand why. They find the villain in Russian folktales to have, in Propp's reading of them,

> the essential function of establishing the lack and thereby setting off what Propp calls the narrative's "movement" . . . Parallel to the tests realized by the hero, there is another story, that of the anti-subject, the villain . . . the narrative thus introduces two trajectories that are opposite and complementary (as in a closed value system where what is given to one person is done so at the expense of another . . .).[38]

De Silva's history, of course, isn't a Russian folktale, but Propp's analysis can be put to work to unearth the not-very-complicated structure of *Reaping the Whirlwind*'s narrative, or, more exactly, to follow an element of its movement. De Silva does tell two stories (he, of course, calls them perceptions), but one is clearly subordinated to the other. The Tamils, to this text, are a group without a very long presence in Sri Lanka, one that has attacked the Sinhalese throughout history and later collaborated with colonialism, earning itself privileged status in the process. They are a minority that refuses to accept the consequences of being minor, produces itself as victim, and makes extravagant demands on the post-colonial state—demands buttressed initially by civil disobedience, later by ferocious terrorism and ethnic cleansing. The Sinhalese is everything the Tamil is not: a world-historically unique ethnic group; a majority with a longer presence in the country; the victim of Tamil invasions and Portuguese, Dutch, and British colonialism; the real injured party, the real victim of history trying to redress the balance, trying to find reparation for the injuries of (colonial and precolonial) history in the postcolonial period. The Sinhalese are a majority that, despite being the victim of history, is benevolent, accommodating of the demands of the Tamil (and other minorities), and desiring to produce a balanced polity.

The narratological level, of course, does not work alone here; it is woven with the others: *Reaping the Whirlwind* moves, or is emplotted, as a shuttle between the perceptions of its two principal actants, perceptions that are both opposed to each other and complementary—but not equal. The Sinhalese perception, or story, cannot be told without the Tamil, but the story of the hero also has to be legitimized and this cannot happen without delegitimizing, or narratively minoritizing, that of the villain. No story with a plot structured as a contest between two implacable antagonists can present them both as heroes or give them balanced treatment; this was noted even in human-rights discourse, which has no political stake in Sri Lanka, in the sense that it does not abide by it, does not call for political reforms. The Tamil thus emerges in *Reaping the Whirlwind* as indeed the lack. It demands what it does not have: equality, majority status, the station of the Sinhalese. This extravagant, inequitable—and, as will be seen, ultimately antidemocratic—demand, the refusal of the minority to be a minority, to accept the facts of number, which after all are natural, apodictic, is the pivot around which de Silva's narrative turns. If that is the impress of the narratological, the text's other levels can be seen shaping it here, too: the production of the Sinhalese as hero and Tamil as villain is cardinal to *Reaping the Whirlwind*'s political claims, to its petition for Sinhalese hegemony; in the production of this narrative historically, in its being structured as a conflict between hero and villain from ancient times to the present, can be seen the mark of the disciplinary level; in its rebutting the human-rights account, that of the anticolonial. Thus, then, my reading of this text: it cannot be understood as a pure and untainted work of disciplinary history.

Narratology also helps explain another element of the text's disciplinary level. In a profoundly compelling formulation, Greimas contends that history cannot account for what he terms "synchronic diversity."[39] In other words, a work of disciplinary history cannot narrate complexity, understood in de Silva's sense as a diversity of perceptions or, more accurately, stories. A work of disciplinary history can only narrate/emplot one story, from *one perspective;* or rather, it can only produce the perspective of one subject in any one narrative, because it must have, as White argues, a single central subject and an identifiable narrative voice. To put this differently, and in more obvious terms, a work of disciplinary history cannot relate, in the same narrative, stories that would not complement or supplement one other but would contradict one another. My point, of course, is not that all histories simplify. Rather, when faced with two (or more) competing or contradictory accounts of the "same" events, the disciplinary historian must adjudicate between them, must *select,* as Carr would enjoin, which account is more persuasive—and then narrativize it. Thus history must *suppress,* as White reminds the reader, inconvenient evidence and alternative accounts, minoritize them. Or, to cite de Certeau, every historical text manifests "a political will to manage conflicts and to regulate them from a single point of view"(1988, 92). The disciplinary and narratological levels of the text, then, show the reader that de Silva simply cannot narrate synchronic diversity, cannot present the conflict as complex. This does not constitute an indictment of his book as bad history, for what de Certeau, Greimas, and White all argue is that the discipline itself cannot and will not allow it. Disciplinary history, in other words, cannot be complex, in the very precise sense that—and I don't want to be misread on this—however complicated or detailed the story might appear, however many subplots it might have, and even if its footnotes outdistance its narrative, it can't tell more than one story and still remain disciplinary history. It does not follow from this that de Silva must actually hero-ize the Sinhalese and villainize the Tamil; he could always do the converse (if he weren't within Sinhalese nationalism). But it does explain why he can only narrate one story, why the others must be delegitimized or minoritized.

After language in the 1950s and 1960s, it was over education policy—admission to the university—that hero and villain fought in the 1970s. I do not need to rehearse that discussion; it has the same structural logic as de Silva's treatment of language. The Sinhalese seek to heal a wound caused by colonialism; the Tamils complain about discrimination; the Sinhalese accommodate the Tamil demands. The Sinhalese might take some time to do this, their heroism may not be perfect, they may make tactical blunders, but they will eventually accommodate the Tamils. To de Silva, language and education are the two issues that caused Tamil political dissension in the postcolonial period. However, they were resolved by the early 1980s by, it is stressed, the Jayewardene government. Nevertheless, *Reaping the Whirlwind* finds Tamil politics turning violently separatist in this same time. This, of course, presents the narrative with a problem. If their grievances were actually addressed, why did the Tamils turn separatist? Leary blames the Sinhalese: the "communal violence against the Tamils by the Sinhalese population coupled with the measures relating to language, religion, education, and government service resulted in a pervasive sense of insecurity among Tamils . . . and eventually the adoption . . . of a policy of . . . the creation of a separate state of Tamil Eelam" (Leary 1984, 74). Wilson, as will be seen in the next chapter, makes a similar argument, with a longer narrative of oppression. The two main issues that drove Tamil politics were the question of representation in the legislature in the colonial period and that of regional autonomy in the postcolonial. *Reaping the Whirlwind* simply ignores, silences these questions. Given his commitment to the Sinhalese story, and to rebutting human-rights discourse, de Silva cannot blame his heroes. He must acknowledge state violence against the Tamils, of course, but finds it legitimate, downplays its significance, produces it as cause without effect: Tamil separatism is not a response to the acts of the state but a product of something else. Indeed, with tremendous ingenuity, de Silva advances two explanations for the rise of separatism, both of which have nothing to do with Sinhalese actions or politics. The first:

> Where an ethnic or (religious) minority is concentrated in a region or regions of a country, and where in addition it constitutes the overwhelming majority of the population there, as is the case with the Tamils of the Jaffna peninsula . . . geography and demography combine to provide an ideal breeding ground for a separatist movement. Ethnic cohesion and a heightened sense of ethnic identity, important ingredients for the emergence of separatist sentiment, had existed in Jaffna since the mid-1950s. (150)

The mere concentration of a population in a place, especially if its numbers dominate that place, will lead to separatist sentiment, inevitably, almost as a fact of nature. Notice the rhetoric: "geography and demography" mate and "breed" separatists. It is abetted by "ethnic cohesion." Significantly enough, politics, the actions of the Sinhalese state, the demands and desires of Tamil nationalism, are not an element of this story. Naturally, then, the Sinhalese cannot be a contributor to this turn in Tamil politics, cannot be blamed for provoking separatism.

However, despite the threat of separatism in the 1980s, despite the nonsensical basis of the Tamil claim to a homeland, the Sinhalese have been willing to grant them some sort of autonomy. Or, at least, such is the claim advanced about the Jayewardene government, which established District Development Councils in 1981. Autonomy is not a justifiable Tamil demand; language and education alone are the Tamil grievances this text recognizes as having legitimacy. Establishing these Councils, then, is yet another example of Sinhalese benevolence. To *Reaping the Whirlwind*, this moment is pivotal: "by the middle of 1982 it seemed as though the establishment of the District Development Councils had yielded the political results expected from them," ethnic peace. The Councils, in other words, should have solved the ethnic conflict. But, the narrative continues, "it was not a durable peace, for violence continued to take its toll either in clashes between separatist groups and the police and security forces, or in the fratricidal conflicts among the fragmented separatist groups themselves" (187). In this narrative unit, "violence" emerges as an actant; it took its toll. But the attentive reader would notice that, once again, it is the Tamil who is produced as the obstacle to peace, as fighting meaninglessly. The Sinhalese, as always, are accommodating; they gave the Tamils autonomy—but the ungrateful bastards continued their purposeless violence. The Tamil, indeed, is produced as "fratricidal," someone who turns against his own brother. Is it surprising, therefore, that such an actant will make extravagant, crazy demands, for a separate state, for instance, based on an argument without the slightest basis in fact, that a part of the country is their "traditional homeland"? Of course not. Rather, it might even be expected that such an actant would be quite literally crazy, perhaps suffer from some psychological disorder, even a complex.

Which brings me to *Reaping the Whirlwind*'s second explanation for the continuation of separatism in the 1980s: *the Tamils have a "majority complex."* In the concluding chapter of the text, having given the reader every possible piece of evidence about the extravagant, ungrateful Tamil, de Silva finally reveals why he doesn't find the Sri Lankan ethnic conflict to be "a simple straightforward confrontation between a once well-entrenched minority . . . and a now powerful but still insecure majority." It is because it is actually a conflict between "a majority with a minority complex, and a minority with a . . . majority complex" (304). Once again, the rhetoric appears balanced; de Silva does not appear to find just one actant suffering from delusion; both of them have complexes (which makes the conflict, if not complex, at least about complexes!). But, once again, the attentive reader would know what sense to make of this. The "minority complex" of the Sinhalese is buttressed by the facts of number. Not only are they actually a minority in a larger South Asian context, speaking a language that is world-historically unique, and so on, but those hordes of other Tamils in southern India, whose ancestors attacked these same Sinhalese throughout history, whose coreligionists obliterated Buddhism, are just a shallow and narrow sea away. The Tamils, in contrast, are a minority in Sri Lanka. They may have once had a kingdom in the northeast, but that was centuries ago; and, anyway, it did not produce a traditional homeland. Nothing—not their history, numbers, or their treatment by the accommodating Sinhalese—authorizes them to make any claims to special status. Rather than entertain delusions of being major, they should learn to accept the facts of number, be happy that the Sinhalese are a benevolent majority, not trying to obliterate them but, rather, giving in to their demands wherever possible, trying so hard in the 1980s and 1990s to legislate some form of provincial autonomy even though the scheme for district autonomy was more than adequate—and was destroyed by fratricidal Tamil violence in the first place.

Given this final element in de Silva's petition for Sinhalese hegemony, the third most important claim advanced by the text, the claim that Sinhalese hegemony is ethical, can now be presented. Though produced in an earlier narrative unit, on the consequences of the events following 1956, its significance is best appreciated here. While situated early in the narrative, it is actually the conclusion of *Reaping the Whirlwind*'s plot:

> Firstly, the concept of a multi-ethnic polity ceased to be politically viable [after 1956] . . . The emphasis on Sri Lanka as a Sinhalese-Buddhist polity carried an emotional popular appeal, compared with which a multi-ethnic polity was no more than a sterile abstraction. Secondly, the justification for this . . . laid stress on a *democratic sanction deriving its validity from the clear numerical superiority* of the Sinhalese-speaking group. (25; emphasis added)

Again, the rhetoric of the unit signifies the most. Of cardinal significance here is that, for the first time in the text, the term "democratic" is used to describe the project of Sinhalese nationalism. Another indice, it is the foundation of de Silva's entire production of Sri Lanka, the cement of his plot. The events of 1956, the events that Asia Watch believes began the conflict, are understood by *Reaping the Whirlwind* as democratic, and democracy itself, as synonymous with majority rule, is understood as a matter of finding significance and value in number. Such a resolution of the plot cannot by now surprise the attentive reader, given de Silva's belief in the "natural" victory of the majority and in the triumph of the facts of number over time. The equation of democracy and majority rule does tremendous explanatory work for this text: it clarifies, for instance, why the Western critique of Sri Lanka is simply incorrect, why the Tamil claim to oppression ultimately lacks an ethical basis (because the minority must know its place), why Sinhalese nationalist dominance must be understood not only as healing a wound or redressing an imbalance but as a democratic and profoundly ethical happening, if not as the most profoundly ethico-political happening Western liberalism can authorize. Alexis Tocqueville might be usefully cited here: he understood the ethical foundation of democracy, based on his examination of the U.S. case, to be the belief that "the interest of the greater number should be preferred to that of those who are fewer."[40] (The resonance of this position with the workings of social science should be noticed now and will be returned to.) De Silva doesn't actually cite any Western theorist of democracy; he doesn't really have to. The implication of his argument, given that it seeks to rebut the Western account of Sri Lanka, is unmistakable. Making the desires of the majority the law of the land is an ethical, a democratic happening. That is common knowledge. The (Tamil) minority has no right, no basis, to complain about this on principle; it happens all over the world—as everybody knows. And the Tamil minority has no right to complain in this instance because the majority—even if the West is ignorant of this—has actually been quite benevolent toward it. In making such a move, one might say that *Reaping the Whirlwind*, and with it Sinhalese nationalist discourse, seeks to hoist Western liberalism with its own petard.

In so doing, it also rebuts the anthropological account of Sri Lanka, of which Daniel has been taken to be exemplary. The problem of peace, as emplotted in *Reaping the Whirlwind*, has very little to do with violence, which is seen by the text as just a symptom of something else. Thus the "riots" of July 1983, pivotal in the anthropological narrative, are not seen to be of great significance here: "a terrorist ambush which killed 13 soldiers in Jaffna on 23 July led first to army reprisals there and subsequently to the worst outbreak of ethnic violence since 1958 . . . The worst affected area was the city of Colombo and its suburbs" (189). The "violence," here, has no agent; it simply breaks out. Indeed it is a response to an act of terrorism, so is almost justified. The point is that it did not alter the course of Sri Lankan history, as both anthropology and human rights contend. This is consistent with de Silva's nationalism for two reasons. He cannot, of course, produce the Sinhalese as villains; thus he must narratively de-emphasize the importance of 1983. But when the country is viewed in a historical frame, when all those broken Sinhalese temples and so on are taken into account, the riots of 1983 become just another instance of violence in the long history of the country, a history in which the Sinhalese have suffered much more than the Tamils. Thus the crucial significance of the disciplinary level to *Reaping the Whirlwind*. To Daniel, whom, like Tambiah, de Silva might also dismiss as a "distinguished Sri Lankan–born American anthropologist," the problem, or the object that becomes visible when he sees Sri Lanka, is only the events of the last few years, which he captures, as does the *New York Times*, through the signifier of violence. Peace, in this understanding, would be the absence of violence. To de Silva, the problem—and *Reaping the Whirlwind* has absolutely no uncertainty regarding this—is about the *democratic* rights and privileges of a majority, one that has been victimized by history and is misunderstood and misrepresented by the same West that once colonized it. He writes, one might say, from the security of knowing his place, his rights, his privileges. In this understanding, peace will only break out in Sri Lanka when the Tamils accept the incontrovertible facts of number and come to terms with their status as a minority—which nothing can change. Thus my claim that when the inhabitant of the West and of Sri Lanka see the country they produce very different objects: where Daniel sees two major ethnic groups battling each other violently, de Silva sees—without any incomprehension—a minority refusing to accept majority rule, behaving antidemocratically, and making extravagant demands. Thus the cortical significance to my entire study of identifying an abiding level to the texts I read, because, by making a different object emerge when I read Sri Lanka, it enables the reconceptualization, from a minority perspective, of the questions of peace and democracy. But so doing will have to wait until the next chapter, where reading a Tamil nationalist text after a Sinhalese nationalist one produces the need to rethink such a perspective, suggests what the contours of a minority perspective will look like. Besides, I am not done with the narratological level of *Reaping the Whirlwind* yet.

Analogy: The Identitarian Illusion

Reaping the Whirlwind's emplotment, then, could be summarized thus: the Sinhalese, the majority in Sri Lanka, are the victims of verifiable historical injury at the hands of the Portuguese, Dutch, and British for centuries during colonialism, and before that for even longer centuries by (Indian) Tamils, which are the contemporary Sri Lankan minority. Given this past, Sinhalese actions in the present, after colonialism, like establishing Sinhalese as the sole official language of the country, cannot be considered discriminatory or oppressive. Rather, they are therapeutic, intended to heal the wounds of history, and, more importantly, they are democratic. All the Sinhalese have done since independence is exercise the right of the majority to hegemony, despite which, and despite their accommodative treatment of the minorities, their willingness to dilute their power, their demonstrated disposition to balance their interests with that of the other ethnic groups, they are considered the villains of Sri Lanka, not only by the Tamils but also by Western human-rights practitioners, the heirs of colonialism, who call themselves democrats but don't really understand democracy. However, the facts, when properly interpreted, when placed within a historical frame—without which you can't really understand the country—corroborate beyond doubt that the Sinhalese are the authentic, indisputable heroes of this story. History itself proves that the Sinhalese are correct. Thus the indispensability of the disciplinary level to de Silva's statements, claims, and conclusions, although a close reading demonstrates that these claims are ultimately shaped not by the disciplinary but the abiding level, that the latter overdetermines the former. Such a reading also showed that, while *Reaping the Whirlwind* keeps one promise, the argument that history is necessary to understand Sri Lanka, even if it fails to narrativize the ancient part of that story, it does not deliver on another. Despite the avowed desire early in the narrative to produce the ethnic conflict as complex, it emerges in *Reaping the Whirlwind* as a fairly straightforward struggle between its two cardinal actants, the Sinhalese and Tamils, and them alone, over status, power, and position in the country. The other ethnic groups, even though identified as actants by the text, are not granted cardinal status; their stories are not told; they do not count because they are small minorities, not "principal" players.

The structure of *Reaping the Whirlwind*'s plot was identified as "iterative," in Genette's terms: "events considered only in terms of their analogy."[41] Sri Lankan history is emplotted in *Reaping the Whirlwind* as a repetition of the same event, the Sinhalese victimized, over colonial and precolonial centuries (and recovering from victimization, healing the wounds of colonialism, in the few postcolonial decades). To history of the de Silva variety—and the claim would probably hold for social science more generally—analogy is not a literary trope but a self-evident mode of argumentation indispensable and foundational to its ability to make truth claims. It should be stressed that, by "analogy," I do not only mean the comparison of one object to another, for instance, "ethnic conflict" in Sri Lanka and Rwanda. The generality characteristic of social science, placing one and one together and manufacturing two objects (and so on) and producing arguments using these objects as self-evident, countable categories, can also be understood as grounded upon analogy in the robust sense. So it could be asserted, at least from the postempiricist perspective I am advocating, that history's, if not the social sciences' reliance on generality, number, statistics, without which it/they cannot make authoritative statements or produce knowledge, is a reliance, from a literary perspective, on analogy. Even Daniel, the reader might remember from the last chapter, interviewed twenty Sinhalese before coming to any conclusions about their "disposition"; one or two would simply not have been enough. The individual or the singular does not signify to social science; it cannot count. The point here is not that the recourse to analogy, as such, is somehow flawed or wrong. Rather, in literature, any deployment of analogy maintains the difference between the two (or more) objects being compared. When love, to cite the banal cliché, is likened to a red rose, even the most naive reader would not make the mistake of conflating the two, of seeing them as somehow the same. In social science, in contrast, analogy works to produce identity out of difference. Two Sinhalese would always be Sinhalese, comprehended only in terms of what they ostensibly share, to that perspective, which must repress difference in order to make statements, produce knowledge.

But another, more philosophical argument about the reliance on arithmetic in social science can and must be made: one and one do not make two, at least not always. Does this sound absurd, unnecessarily contentious? My authority here is Gottlob Frege. He argued in *The Foundations of Arithmetic* that "no two objects are *ever* completely identical."[42] That is to say, to take off from his argument, the *assumption*—and it is not a fact but an assumption—that one plus one equals two is necessary for mathematics. Such an assumption, so long as it remains within arithmetic, is politically harmless, for its objects are purely abstract; they do not have a social dimension. But addition outside that discipline, addition in the social sciences, addition that in my terms produces identity out of difference, has very different consequences since its objects are also different. For a start, addition in the social sciences is impossible without analogy: the production, the presumption or illusion of identity between "similar" objects. Take, for instance, the statement, "There are two Sinhalese in the room." If the two subjects referred to have been successfully interpellated as Sinhalese, there would be nothing wrong or incorrect about that statement. There is no Archimedean space from which to make such a claim. However, it does not follow that the statement is necessarily true. The two subjects could also be identified in a variety of different ways: in terms of their gender, or sexuality, or age, or birthplace, or whatever. That is to say, they could be produced as identical or as different. It depends entirely on the perspective being advocated. That which emphasizes the singular would see difference; social science would find identity. To social science, of course, its perspective would also be true, verifiable, and indeed self-evident. The postempiricist reader, though, would insist that it is the position of a perspective—an authoritative one, yes; the dominant one in our disciplinary moment—that has naturalized its statements as self-evidently true, but of a perspective nevertheless. That is to say, de Silva's assumption, which is not open to question, that all "Sinhalese" have one and only one identity and can be counted together is not a self-evident fact but an assumption authorized by social science (in collusion with nationalism and institutions of the state, like the census).

Any number of texts can be deployed to instantiate social science's inability to work without analogy; and I would only have to reach, once again randomly, for something on my bookshelf. But, for my purposes, Donald Horowitz's *Ethnic Groups in Conflict* becomes the most appropriate since it is cited by de Silva as villainizing Sri Lanka. Horowitz's text is of truly staggering breadth, a product of the kind of arrogance only political science—the discipline that emerged with the Cold War, intimately bound to U.S. imperialism, which has had an impeccable career producing knowledge abetting such imperialism—can exhibit: a study of "ethnic conflict" in virtually all of postcolonial Asia and Africa, the adjective *postcolonial* being understood both historically and geographically. Writing in 1985, he presents his argument as lagging behind the event. Ethnic conflict itself has been proliferating since decolonization; more than ten million have been killed in these African and Asian countries as a consequence of such conflict; but its study by political science has been inadequate to its object. (This is the same disciplinary moment, the reader might remember from Jeganathan in the previous chapter, that anthropology intervened globally to explain such conflict.) His book makes the case, indeed it pleads, for the establishment of ethnic conflict as an autonomous and credible object of study:

> What has emerged is a plethora of more or less parochial material on ethnic conflict in scores of countries. What has not yet emerged is a comprehensive set of generalizations that fits the material and into which new material can be fitted . . . We no longer lack basic data on ethnic conflict. We lack explanation . . . There is, in the main, too much knowledge and not enough understanding.[43]

One can almost touch the anxiety evident in this eloquent plea for generalization (analogy); without it "data" would be parochial, limited, even meaningless. The method of political—if not social—science, which undergirds this argument, is clearly evident: generality is imperative to get beyond knowledge to understanding, beyond parochiality and provinciality to the production, actually, of pigeonholes—a "comprehensive set of generalizations that fits the material and into which new material can be fitted." Specificity is deemed parochial, is avowedly anathematic to this perspective, which, the attentive reader will notice, is quite comfortable with soothsaying: one of its goals is to predict the future. If the kind of disciplinary activity Horowitz advocates produces good generalizations, "new material," ethnic conflict yet to happen, will "fit" into this predetermined scheme. Undoubtedly. This perspective isn't hindered by the slightest hesitancy nor dogged by the slightest doubt that—provided it gets its act together—it couldn't forecast what is to come. Which, of course, raises an obvious question: if this were the case, if good generalizations are those that will "fit" the future, then wouldn't the actual study of such conflicts become redundant—after an examination of two or three examples? Wouldn't we understand others even before they happen? This, in turn, begs another question: can this kind of vacuous theorizing account for new knowledge, the production of new generalizations?

Contrary to political science, indeed in this instance to social science, postempiricist literary criticism would insist, as implied above, that generality is a form of analogy and that analogy, if an unavoidable structural element of language, is nevertheless a mode of argumentation that must be resorted to with circumspection, caution. The difference it suppresses, when it occurs outside arithmetic, must be scrutinized with great care.[44] Let me explain the significance of this position for my argument by citing, very briefly, Paul de Man's conclusion to his reading of Rousseau's treatment of number: "for Rousseau . . . number is par excellence the concept that hides ontic difference under an illusion of identity."[45] The point to take from here, apart from the usually forgotten notion that number is not a self-evident fact but a *concept*, is not that one and one don't make two but that one may not always equal one, either. It is not that all claims to identity are false but that every claim to identity—the production of sameness through the self-evident, "disinterested" logic of arithmetic—suppresses difference. One way of characterizing the work of arithmetic, in social science that cannot make any claims without resorting to generality, is that it negates difference. To illustrate again: take two hypothetical Sri Lankans interpellated, this time, as Tamils. Let's assume one is blind but the son of rich parents, able to significantly overcome his disability; the other is a poor, pregnant peasant woman who does not want another child but cannot afford an abortion. The postempiricist (feminist) reader would call attention not only to the similarity but also to the difference between the two; she would not, here, automatically see one and one as making two Tamils. To Tamil nationalism, however, they would appear the same—as just plain unmarked Tamil. Nationalism, of course, is not social science; but for it to do this work—producing identity from difference—it must have some epistemological basis, if not authority. Social science, insofar as it finds significance in number, counting, provides this basis, authorizes this move, enables the categorizing, counting, and cataloging of population, and the production of sameness; or, at least, it legitimizes the logic of arithmetic.[46] To say this is not to argue that the postempiricist reader would deny these two fictional constructs their Tamilness but that she would insist upon a different emphasis; she would insist, in Jean-Luc Nancy's formulation, that all Tamils—not to mention Sinhalese, Muslims, Burghers, and Malays—are "singular plural."[47] Or, perhaps more clearly, she would hold that the subjectivity of these two constructs are not identical but rhyme, that they must be understood as a mixture of sameness *and* difference.

Reaping the Whirlwind's deployment of analogy provides an excellent instantiation of the consequences of not just the text's reliance on this trope but perhaps even of the discipline's. To de Silva, the Sinhalese demand for redress and hegemony, for hegemony as redress, is legitimate not only for historical reasons; its democratic basis has also been conceded by two Sri Lankan minorities, the Muslims and Sinhalese Catholics, and in these analogous instances, the narrative implies paratactically, can be read the fate of the Tamils. Before discussing the latter, it must be noticed that, much more significantly, analogy also enables the former argument, that past oppression justifies the present domination (of others). Without analogy, these two happenings would not be comparable. In other words, de Silva's central thesis, the pivot on which his whole text turns, that history (past injuries) determines politics, is impossible without analogy. As Nietzsche powerfully insists, such thinking is based upon "the idea that every injury has its *equivalent* which can be paid in compensation, if only through the *pain* of the person who injures."[48] *Reaping the Whirlwind* doesn't acknowledge much Tamil suffering in the postcolonial present, for that would make the Sinhalese the oppressor and not the victim, but it does acknowledge relative Tamil deprivation—clearly to be understood as retribution for, and thus in a sense equivalent to, Sinhalese suffering in the past. The same holds for Sinhalese pleasure in the present—hegemony, uninhibited majority rule—which also emerges in the text as in a sense equivalent to suffering in the past. Because they suffered in the past, the Sinhalese have the right to enjoy the present. The Sinhalese must enjoy an analogous or equivalent dominance of the present *and* see their injurers, the Tamils, suffer in the present for that past suffering to be mitigated or ameliorated, for the historical wounds to be healed, for the therapy to work. These claims upon and about the past and the present may not appear very similar, but their logic, what enables them to be advanced at all, is one of equivalence or analogy. *Reaping the Whirlwind*'s emplotment, then, relies fundamentally on analogy in both its senses—as iteration and as equivalence.

As stated above, *Reaping the Whirlwind* also sees, in the present of the Muslim and the Sinhalese Christian, the future of the Tamil. The autobiographies of these two groups may differ markedly, but, being Sri Lankan minorities, *Reaping the Whirlwind*, following the protocols of social science, sees them as *one*, or the same, and thus comparable. The Muslims, de Silva argues often, have benefited substantially from Sinhalese hegemony and accommodativeness. For instance, after the Tamils were granted devolution, those District Development Councils discussed in the previous section, by Junius Richard Jayewardene,

> There were some misgivings among the Muslims about the creation of these District Development Councils . . . Since [they] were seen as primarily a response to Tamil pressures, the balance was adjusted to the advantage of the Muslims . . . by the creation of a Department of Muslim Religious and Cultural Affairs placed under the senior Muslim member of the Cabinet. This was as good an example of a political establishment engaged in calibrating the machinery of democracy to secure a *tolerable* balance of interests as we are *ever* likely to find in a plural society. (177; emphasis added)

The Sinhalese, here, are perfect; we are not likely to find such accommodativeness on the part of any majority, anywhere in the world, or at least in any plural society. Not now. Not *ever*. An incredible statement. A dismissal out of hand of the Tamil nationalist and human-rights critique. But that unit will also repay closer attention. What, to de Silva, have these Sinhalese actually done? First, they legislated autonomy for the Tamils. Investigating how these councils actually performed, whether they were adequately funded, if they delivered the goods as it were, however, is of no concern; the fact of legislation is evidence of Sinhalese benignness.

Second, since this could be interpreted as unfairly favoring one minority, to balance the desires of another (the Muslims), a cabinet department was established to look after Muslim religious and cultural affairs. What this department actually did, once again, is not investigated. Those things don't matter. The fact of its establishment, again, is adequate evidence of Sinhalese benignness. The attentive reader would have noticed two asymmetries here: the question of balancing the interests of the other minorities identified by *Reaping the Whirlwind* is not raised, and that, while the Tamils are "given" something political, the Muslims are given something—in de Silva's own terms—religious and cultural. Do the Muslims have any political demands of their own? What were their "misgivings" about the District Councils? Can those misgivings be deemed political? Why are they not addressed? On the other hand, if the Muslims have no political demands, can that actant be coherently compared with the Tamils? Is this analogy persuasive? Doesn't "balance," here, imply equivalence but sound iniquitous? And which perspective finds this balance "tolerable" in the first place? The Muslim? The Tamil? Or only the Sinhalese nationalist? These questions are not addressed by the text. Silencing, again, enables de Silva to make the Muslim not an actant but an analogy, for its narrative function is hard to miss. The Muslims are not invoked as an element of the story demanding consideration on its own, as an ethnic group with its own concerns, history, demands, and insecurities, or as an actant that complicates the plot. The narratological level, here, works with the abiding to inform the West that the Sinhalese are indeed accommodative and to inform the Tamils that, if they integrated themselves into the political system, rather than making extravagant demands and asserting themselves through ferocious violence, their interests too would be "balanced."

The Sinhalese Christians, when finally admitted to the story, serve a similar narrative function. Like the Tamils, this actant (which, like the Muslims, is also not quite an actant) was privileged under colonialism. Consequently, once Sinhalese Buddhist nationalism began to organize and assert itself, demand the legitimate rights of the majority, "religious strife in the form of tensions and conflict between Buddhists and Christians—in particular . . . the Roman Catholics" broke out; indeed, this became "one of the most divisive factors in Sri Lankan public life for about 80 years or so beginning in the last quarter of the 19th century" (304). But, despite the tensions *and* conflict, this "ceased to be a contentious issue in politics since the early 1970s." As a matter of fact, "by the end of the 1960s the Roman Catholics had reconciled themselves to a more limited role . . . in Sri Lankan public life" (304). That is virtually all the text has to say about the Sinhalese Catholic. The "tensions and conflict" between the Buddhists and Catholics do not receive much narrative time in *Reaping the Whirlwind*, even though they caused "one of the most divisive factors in Sri Lankan public life for about 80 years." A Sinhalese Catholic "perception" must logically exist but, unlike the Muslim, it isn't even seen as actant by *Reaping the Whirlwind*; and it is no doubt unnecessary, by now, to identify incoherence, the silencing or the lack of synchronic diversity, here. The work done by the Catholic for the plot is very clear: like the Muslim, it serves as example. The Sinhalese Catholics may not have always been a model minority, they may even have once had exaggerated claims to special status, like you know who, but they learned the value of transforming their ambitions. This actant once had a significant "role in Sri Lankan public life" but eventually accepted a limited or insignificant one. Or, to be precise, the Catholics "reconciled" themselves, a term that suggests a reluctant and unhappy act, if not a coerced one, to public insignificance. The Catholics, that is, learned the proper place of the minor—insignificance—and acceded to it; they conceded the right of the majority to hegemony. If two minorities were persuaded and/or coerced into accepting Sinhalese Buddhist hegemony, this implies paratactically, so can—and will—the third, even if it might take the Sinhalese eighty years to "reconcile" the Tamils to their status. This, by the way, is another reason why I characterize the conjuncture, or narrative moment, *Reaping the Whirlwind* produces as pessimistic: given the intransigence and obduracy of the LTTE, noted earlier, there's no reason to hope that the ethnic conflict will be solved any time soon. It will be solved eventually; the behavior of the Muslims and Catholics demonstrate that—analogy provides some reason for hope—but such resolution is unlikely to happen quickly.

In the context of the plot's reliance on analogy, in its implication that in the past of two (hegemonized) minorities can be read the future of the intransigent other, the unexpectedly optimistic conclusion of an otherwise pessimistic narrative becomes comprehensible. These are the two very last sentences of *Reaping the Whirlwind*: "In most instances of prolonged ethnic strife, pragmatism and compromise combine to thwart even the most obdurate champions of a struggle to the bitter end to compel a settlement even when there seemed no hope of one. Time, it would appear, is not merely a great healer, but an ally of governments in their struggle against separatists" (332). Sri Lanka may look hopeless now, like Bosnia, and no solution to the conflict seems likely in the present, but time is on the side of the Sinhalese. Analogy—"most instances of prolonged ethnic strife"— demonstrates that even "the most obdurate champions of a struggle to the

bitter end," presumably the uncompromising LTTE, with its absurd arguments about being discriminated against, its extravagant insistence upon
a separate state, based upon the even more absurd claim to a "traditional
Tamil homeland," will be compelled to accept this. Separatism will never
work. (Although, of course, a Tamil nationalist would no doubt counter
analogy with analogy, by referring to Pakistan, Bangladesh, Eritrea, East
Timor, perhaps even the Balkans. Examples abound on either side of this
debate; this is not a question empiricism can settle.) If military means fail
to defeat the LTTE, they would be thwarted by time itself. The narrator
and evaluator of time, history, which is the other player in the conflict
and actant in this narrative, proves the validity of this comparison with
the example of the Sinhalese Catholic: that group wanted privileges minorities are not entitled to and fought hard to maintain them; like the
Tamil, it caused tensions *and* conflict, but, eventually, it learned its lesson
and accepted, if reluctantly, that the majority has the right to rule and set
the rules. This signifies that, ultimately, the Sinhalese will win the battle
against their historical enemy, too; they "persuaded" the Muslims and
Catholics to concede; they will persuade the Tamils.

   The example of Sri Lankan minorities alone doesn't convince de Silva
that the Sinhalese will triumph. The Sri Lankan Tamil instance is analogous to happenings in other countries. Significantly enough, though, long
before the conclusion, the Balkan analogy has decreased in importance to
the text. De Silva turns, instead, to help consolidate his case to another
country, this time in Asia, Malaysia. If Bosnia is *Reaping the Whirlwind*'s early
example of Sri Lanka's pessimistic present, Malaysia is a reason for optimism, the text's late example of what its peaceful future should resemble:

> There are many reasons for the relatively peaceful operation of the
> Malaysian political system. Among the most important of these is the
> existence of a pragmatic political bargain between the principal ethnic
> groups in the country, Malays and the Chinese. This bargain is more im-
> plicit than explicit but it acts as a powerful restraining influence on both.
> Its basic principle is that the Malays would treat the Chinese economic
> interests as the engine of the national economy, and agree to absorb the
> young Chinese into the political system while the Chinese . . . would ac-
> cept Malay political dominance and an increasing share for the Malays in
> the economy in return. (298)

The objectivity of this narrative unit, its disciplinary level, must be noticed.
Its essentialist production of Malaysia, of course, cannot by now surprise
the reader of de Silva; this reader would also, given her familiarity with

Western discourse on ethnic conflict, presumably know that the Malays are counted as the majority in that country. She will also notice the recurrence of a binarized logic: de Silva's Malaysia must have more than two ethnic groups, since only the Malays and Chinese are termed "principal" actants, a usage that implies the existence of nonprincipal actants, but those others are—surprise, surprise—silenced by this text. The question as to whether Malaysia is a "complex" country is also not addressed; but, then, it would only be the most naive of readers who would by now expect coherence from de Silva. His cardinal claim is that Malaysia has been peaceful—unlike Sri Lanka—because the principal minority in that country has been pragmatic, has accepted its status as minor, lesser, and subordinate, in short, because the Chinese minority is successfully hegemonized by the Malay majority. In not resisting this, the Chinese enabled what to de Silva is a "balanced" polity: "something for everyone." In the Sri Lankan instance, this would translate into, as argued earlier in the narrative, a "reconciliation of the legitimate interests of the Sinhalese Buddhist majority and those of the minority" (82). In the Malaysian case, one party, the minority, accepted political weakness in return for which, states de Silva, it was allowed to maintain economic strength; the other, the majority, ruled as is its legitimate right—and indeed set the rules. The implications of this for the Tamils is almost transparently clear. Like the Chinese, the Tamils are produced as economically privileged. Nowhere in *Reaping the Whirlwind* is it suggested that such Tamil privilege is undeserved, inappropriate, or should be threatened. Indeed, it is the ultimate proof of Sinhalese benevolence: if they were truly genocidal, they would have destroyed, or at least diminished, Tamil economic advantages decades ago. Accept it, implies *Reaping the Whirlwind*'s Malaysian analogy, accept also the legitimate right of the majority to rule, renounce your extravagant claims, grow out of your majority complex and you Tamils can live in peace, security, and prosperity in a Sinhalese-dominated Sri Lanka.

The comparison of Sri Lanka and Malaysia can, of course, be contested empirically. It could quite easily be pointed out, by even a mediocre undergraduate, provided she was willing to labor in the library, that Sri Lankan Tamil history and Malaysian Chinese history are very different; and it is no doubt worthy of note that, despite being a historian by training, despite the crucial significance of the analogy to his thesis, de Silva does not narrate any Malaysian history. But the attentive reader of *Reaping the Whirlwind* would notice that the analogy deconstitutes itself; it trips, as it were, over its own feet. De Silva actually admits to a fundamental difference of the Malaysian Chinese case from the Sri Lankan Tamil:

"While the minorities in Malaysia are much larger numerically than in Sri Lanka there is no large territory with a Chinese or non-Malay majority . . . In short there is no territorial base to encourage aspirations to separatism" (299). This is consistent with de Silva's thesis on the causes of separatism, noted before, which does not identify discrimination/ oppression by the majority as one cause; but, of course, it works against his analogy. Malaysia, it appears from de Silva's own narrative, is quite different from Sri Lanka. This is a startling declaration: it certainly allows the conclusion that the Chinese may have accepted Malay hegemony, to work within de Silva's terms, not because they were pragmatists or realists or liked the bargain they were offered but only because they did not have the territorial base to turn separatist. Speculation, however, is beside the point here. For it does not follow from de Silva's admission—or any other "facts" that might prove Malaysian difference—that the two instances cannot be compared. Pineapples and oranges, after all, are both sweet and might, despite their apparent differences, indeed be fruitfully compared. Rather, the comparison of Sri Lanka and Malaysia signifies, to the postempiricist reader, to reiterate the point, that one doesn't always equal one, that analogy is possible only by the suppression of difference. Even Horowitz, that tireless crusader against parochialism, concedes as much: "Comparability does not imply perfect identity or even very close similarity, but rather a restricted range of difference."[49]

How does the postempiricist/postcolonial reader react to this admission, not only by de Silva, but also by a canonical text on ethnic conflict, that a foundational element of its ability to produce knowledge and make truth claims, appears upon inspection to be based on what must be deemed a fiction, the fiction of analogy, the illusion of identity, based upon the suppression of difference? What might constitute a proper response to this? Should she reconsider, therefore, the viability of the categories, claims, and classifications of history, political science—if not of social science (and literary criticism grounded upon such social science)? In this regard, most cardinal to the present study would be the category "ethnic group"; the ethnic group, or any like grouping, any such collectivity, as should be evident by now, is the product of analogy: it produces subjects, who could always be seen as different and as the same. What, she might therefore want to ask, is the work done by analogy/generality for the operation not just of history or social science but for our notions of community? These questions, which will (also) inform the following chapters of this study, are best dealt with in its conclusion, after reading the literary texts. Before ending this section, it is only necessary to make it clear that my critique is not of analogy itself, which would actually be a quite absurd thing to do; rather, it is of the erasure of difference when this literary trope is deployed too quickly and unselfconsciously to produce generality. And, to reiterate, not only does de Silva's resort to analogy in *Reaping the Whirlwind* suppress difference, the difference narrated by his own text, but it hasn't actually advanced his own argument or buttressed his claims: the iterative emplotment of the past wasn't persuasive because the ancient part of that past wasn't narrated, because the text relies on silencing to emplot its own detail in such a manner. The Balkan analogy isn't consistently deployed throughout the text; it disappears when inconvenient, to be replaced by another, the Malaysian/Chinese, which by the narrative's own admission does not compare very well with the Sri Lankan/Tamil. Neither, upon consideration, do the cases of the Sri Lankan minorities: when the detail is attended to, the Muslim and Sinhalese Christian cases, whose narrative function is to serve as warning to the Tamil, read very differently from the story of the Tamil, the resistant/oppressed group. In so doing, once again, *Reaping the Whirlwind* deconstitutes itself.

Conclusion

Before closing this chapter by examining the significance of de Silva's revisions of some crucial positions he held before, it would be useful to consolidate my argument. I have contended here that, despite de Silva's protestations to the contrary, *Reaping the Whirlwind* cannot be read as the product, exclusively, of the discipline of history. It is undoubtedly a work of history but not exclusively so. The symptomatic reading demonstrated, I trust, that the text is other than it is, that it's also limited by the structural constraints of the narrative form as it works within the discipline, marked by de Silva's imperative to rebut the Western human-rights account of postcolonial Sri Lanka, and profoundly contoured, if not overdetermined, by its politics, its essentialist perspective, and its commitment to a certain conception of the Sri Lankan future, one in which the Sinhalese majority, as a matter of democratic right, and a consequence of a historical injury and consequent grievance, enjoys hegemony over the other, minor ethnic groups; it is marked, in other words, by the way it abides by Sri Lanka. (This, of course, is another way of saying this text is shaped by levels other than the disciplinary, that, in the strict sense, it is interdisciplinary.) Such a conceptualization and narrativization of a peaceful Sri Lankan future rests on three related grounds. The first could be termed democratic/universalist and political: a form of government, whose rules are known worldwide and is known in this post-Soviet conjuncture as the most ethical form of government, that *Reaping the Whirlwind* understands as one in which the majority has both the right to rule and to set the rules by which a country shall function. The second could be termed historical or specific (as opposed to a universal): the Sinhalese are the victims of historical injury at the hands of their ancient enemy, the Tamils, and as a consequence of colonialism; healing these ancient wounds, in a democratic manner of course, also requires their hegemony over the rest of the country. The past, in other words, both justifies and determines the present. The third, which could be called narratological, is the text's reliance not on the facts, as it were, but on literary devices, like analogy and silencing, to secure its emplotment, disciplinary arguments, and of course its political positions.

The second position, that history governs politics, betrays the impress of what I have been calling the abiding level. Identifying a narratological level to the text enables the reader to recognize exactly how these two other levels work, sometimes together, sometimes displacing the other, to produce this petition for Sinhalese nationalist hegemony. De Silva seeks, he says, to produce the Sri Lankan as a complex conflict, as the story of four actants, but a work of disciplinary history can only narrate the story of one central actant. Thus discipline and politics coincide to villainize the Tamil, effectively silence the other minorities, and produce a narrative, albeit an incoherent one, in which the perspective of the Sinhalese (nationalist), identified as the majority, emerges as the one true, heroic account of the Sri Lankan conflict. Since the story of the majority is the story of Sri Lanka, and since the past determines the present, de Silva's understanding of what a peaceful Sri Lankan future would look like, its conceptualization of peace, can be summarized in two words: majority rules. Two Sri Lankan minorities have accepted these rules, accepted the consequences of being minor, and thus contribute to peace. The Tamils, however, insist on seeing themselves as major too, as actually having rights equal to the Sinhalese. This extravagant, preposterous position, this irrational refusal to accept the facts of number, this astounding rejection of democracy, indeed this mental complex, this psychological disease, is the primary reason for the absence of peace in Sri Lanka. Human-rights discourse may acknowledge, if not authorize, the Tamil version of postcolonial Sri Lankan history as the correct one, may endorse the Tamil claim to equality. However, in so doing it not only reveals its ignorance of Sri Lankan history but of the very rules of democracy and, to nobody's surprise, also reveals its support for its old buddies, its collaborators during colonialism.

Which brings me to my claim, made early in this chapter, that this text is anticolonial or shaped by a level that is better termed anticolonial, rather than anti-Western or anti-imperialist. This, in turn, requires addressing the question of revision. It was noticed early in this chapter that *Managing Ethnic Tensions*, de Silva's prior account of the ethnic conflict, does not see the Tamil as "the traditional national enemy" or southern India "as the source from which scores of invasions of the heartland of ancient Sri Lanka were launched." *Managing Ethnic Tensions* admits such to be the Sinhalese perception but adds, in a most significant departure from *Reaping the Whirlwind*, that the perception doesn't stand the scrutiny of the record. To the prior text, from "the early centuries of its recorded history, i.e., for over 2,000 years, the island of Sri Lanka has had a poly-ethnic society; its main component elements . . . the Sinhalese and Tamils . . . have a *common Indian origin*" (7; emphasis added). *Reaping the Whirlwind*, it will be remembered, did not find such commonality between the Sinhalese and Tamils. Indeed, it found no commonality at all except in enmity; it consistently and insistently emphasized the differences, the clashes, the conflicts between the two actants. *Managing Ethnic Tensions*, too, finds the "dominant core of the Sri Lankan state system" to be Sinhalese; so much of its perspective is consistent with *Reaping the Whirlwind*. But, by naming its understanding of the Sri Lankan past polyethnic, *Managing Ethnic Tensions* admits what it calls "a distinctive Tamil element" to the history of the country. The Tamils, that is, are not written out of Sri Lankan history (as foreign). In a later narrative unit, de Silva explains what exactly he understands by polyethnic: "a conception which emphasizes harmony and a spirit of live and let live" (1986, 12). This is contrasted with a "plural society . . . in which tension between ethnic or other distinctive groups is a main feature." The difference between this account and *Reaping the Whirlwind* couldn't be more stark, more astonishing. The latter text, as has been noticed, does not discuss the past in any detail; rather it summarized it, and in that summary of ancient Sri Lankan history, did not find any commonality, any harmony, any "spirit of live and let live," between Sinhalese and Tamil: to *Reaping the Whirlwind*, the Tamil is simply, and always already, the historical enemy of the Sinhalese. *Managing Ethnic Tensions*, in contrast, makes what appears to be an extra effort to emphasize ethnic "harmony" and peaceful coexistence. It even distances itself from that foundational text of popular Sinhala history, the *Mahawamsa*, when narrating by far the most controversial, and contested, story to be found in Sri Lankan history books, that of the Sinhalese king popularly known as Dutugemunu:[50]

The long . . . campaign waged by Dutthagamini . . . a Sinhalese prince, which culminated in the defeat of Elara is the central theme of the later chapters of the *Mahawamsa* and is developed there into a mythic confrontation between the Sinhalese and Tamils. It is a powerful myth, part cultural, part political which has had a profound influence in shaping popular perceptions of the past and of the role of the Tamils in Sri Lankan history as the single most powerful and persistent threat confronting the Sinhalese. But the historical evidence we have suggests that there were large reserves of support for Elara among the Sinhalese, and that Dutthagamini . . . had to face the resistance of other Sinhalese rivals. (11)

This story, which has had a "profound influence in shaping popular [Sinhalese] perceptions . . . of the role of the Tamils in Sri Lankan history" is called a "myth." In de Silva's terms—he is, recall, a conventional historian—a myth is something unverifiable and therefore untrue, a perception incompatible with disciplinary history. *Managing Ethnic Tensions*, in other words, distances itself from the dominant/popular strain of Sinhalese nationalist discourse. That text is shaped more coherently by the disciplinary level than *Reaping the Whirlwind*. The battle between Dutugemunu and Elara, then, is not to be seen as one between the Sinhalese and Tamils; that is the fabrication of the *Mahawamsa*—which to *Managing Ethnic Tensions* sought to produce the Tamils as the historical enemy of the Sinhalese. If *Reaping the Whirlwind*'s relation to Sinhalese nationalist history—which is not to be conflated with politics—can be characterized as subtle alignment, *Managing Ethnic Tensions*'s, therefore, could be considered demystificatory; it actually challenges the text held most sacred by popular nationalism. One more quotation, from the prior text's summation of the Sri Lankan past, will help make this difference between the texts absolutely clear:

> Until the first quarter of the twentieth century a vast forest belt separated the Sinhalese from the Tamils of the north and the east; but they were not totally isolated from each other, nor was there a break in the economic and social relations between them. Just as real as the historic rivalry if not enmity between the two peoples were the long periods of relatively harmonious social relations, during which the remarkable resilience of the cultural and religious bonds . . . which they had in common was repeatedly demonstrated. (14)

What should be noticed in this narrative unit is that *Managing Ethnic Tensions* does not constitute a complete break with *Reaping the Whirlwind*: it mentions the "historic rivalry" between the Sinhalese and the Tamils.

But *Managing Ethnic Tensions* also mentions "long periods of . . . harmony" between the two groups. Significantly enough, a stated reason for this harmony is that they had *common* religious and cultural bonds, whereas, of course, *Reaping the Whirlwind* sees Buddhism and Hinduism as fundamentally different, if not opposed, religions with a history of enmity—the former having been obliterated by the latter (albeit in India). *Reaping the Whirlwind* revises this story of commonality to one of straightforward animosity between the two, erasing any mention of religious or cultural compatibility or peaceful "economic and social" interaction. It also completely erases Elara from its narrative, giving that "powerful myth" absolutely no attention. How does one account for these quite startling revisions, or silencings, produced as they are without any mention of new evidence about this past or the application of a new method? What do they signify? Why are they relevant to my reading of *Reaping the Whirlwind*?

Before addressing those questions, it is necessary to consider *Managing Ethnic Tensions*'s account of two other cardinal elements of *Reaping the Whirlwind*'s narrative of the Sri Lankan past: colonialism and the majority complex of the Tamils. To examine the latter first, here, too, *Managing Ethnic Tensions* differs quite radically from the later text. The relevant unit should be quoted at some length:

> In the last decade of the nineteenth century and in the early years of the twentieth there was, as we have seen, a remarkable contrast between Tamils and the Sinhalese in their political attitudes: the former were far ahead in political consciousness and receptivity to nationalist ideas then emerging in the Indian subcontinent . . . During this period they did not regard themselves as a minority, but aspired to equality with the Sinhalese as one of two majority groups in the island as indeed their enfranchised segment was under the restricted franchise then prevailing. This state of affairs was too good to last. In democratic politics . . . numbers were inevitably a decisive factor. Soon numbers began to count and when that happened . . . the artificiality of the "two majority communities" concept was easily exposed. (1986, 59)

It is important to notice, as David Scott has pointed out about this same unit, that "de Silva does not consider that it is number (in my terms, analogy) that produces the majority/minority distinction in the first place. That the Sinhalas constitute a 'majority' and the Tamils a 'minority' and that this is a significant fact for political representation is . . . self-evident to de Silva's historical narrative."[51] Scott himself, surprisingly enough, does not consider that de Silva's arguments might be overdetermined by his politics; but I am driving at a different point. De Silva claims here that the Tamils were actually the first to embrace nationalism, by definition an anticolonial politics, in Sri Lanka. Not only is this silenced in *Reaping the Whirlwind*, but in that text the Tamils are produced, if implicitly, as collaborators with colonialism (which, of course, they cannot be if they were in fact nationalist leaders). The other point, and one of critical significance to this entire study, is that, at the turn of the century, the Tamils were also considered a majority or major community; there were *two major communities* in Sri Lanka. In other words, the term "majority" or "major" signified two very different things then and now (with the Donoughmore Commission's reforms constituting the moment of the break). It did not simply reflect, as it were, the quantum of bodies on the ground. The significance of this for the critique of democracy will be addressed in the conclusion of this study. What needs mention here, of course, is that the alleged "majority complex" of the Tamils, *Reaping the Whirlwind*'s ultimate insult and rebuttal of the Tamil nationalist petition, does not sound so ridiculous in the light of this statement, also disappeared in *Reaping the Whirlwind*.

With regard to colonialism, *Managing Ethnic Tensions* finds it an "interlude" in the Sri Lankan story, a mere pause, without the determining role within the Sri Lankan present it is allowed by *Reaping the Whirlwind*. Consequently, the Kandyan Sinhalese are not presented in the prior text as being great resisters of colonialism. This is easily comprehensible. If colonialism was just an interlude in Sri Lankan history, then resisting it cannot be of cardinal significance. Of the fate of Buddhism in this period, it is stated that the religion "suffered greatly under Portuguese rule": but "so for that matter did Hinduism and Islam" (1986, 17). In short, and this cannot be stressed too much, a radically different role is scripted for the colonial (and precolonial) Sri Lankan past, both in and of itself, and in relation to the Sri Lankan present, in *Managing Ethnic Tensions* than it is in *Reaping the Whirlwind*. This is not to imply that *Managing Ethnic Tensions* doesn't justify Sinhalese hegemony in postcolonial Sri Lanka. It does, but on grounds that do not invoke the injuries and grievances of the past to legitimize its case. To *Managing Ethnic Tensions*, Sinhalese hegemony in Sri Lanka is justified upon one ground alone: the democratic, that the majority, being greater in number, enjoys this right by definition. On this level, the arguments of the two texts coincide. Why, then, does the later text need to revise the past, both colonial and precolonial? Why does it (need to) produce the Sinhalese as hero and victim, as injured—and so insistently—in order to buttress its claims? What might this revision signify about the text's politics? And what might it tell the postempiricist reader of the operation of history? Why does de Silva need to align his understanding of the Sri Lankan past so much closer to the account of dominant/popular Sinhalese nationalist history? That so doing reinforces the petition for hegemony would by now go without saying. But could this revision in de Silva's account of the Sri Lankan story be determined by another level? Why does the disciplinary level, in the later text, appear to be not just overdetermined but eventually almost displaced by the Sinhalese nationalist?

It is, I think, no coincidence that *Reaping the Whirlwind*—an avowed work of disciplinary history—produces the Sinhalese as the victims of colonialism in the disciplinary moment of the emergence of postcolonial studies, a moment or conjuncture in which it has become academically legitimate, at least within a certain strand of the field, to continue to produce those who endured colonialism as victims, to continue to remind the world of the fact of colonialism. But too much could be made of this, and I do not seek to blame this text on postcolonial studies, though a certain tendency within the field, or subfield, certainly helps legitimize it. Nevertheless, works like *Reaping the Whirlwind* should serve as a warning to those, like Lazarus, who position themselves on the postcolonial left and are inclined to think of an uninflected anticolonialism, which passes itself as an anti-imperialism, as an acceptable "oppositional" politics today. The production of victimhood and injury in the past may not only serve to justify but to take attention away from an oppressive politics in the present, to recast or recode oppression in the present in entirely different terms, as therapy. De Silva, after all, does not see Sinhalese nationalism as in any way oppressive, but it should now be evident, I hope, why I term this level anticolonial and not anti-Western or anti-imperialist: for one thing, it is nationalist—and nationalism, as argued in the Introduction, thinks within the thematic of Eurocentrism and is therefore anticolonial (not postcolonial); for another, it is the experience of colonialism that is invoked by *Reaping the Whirlwind*, revising *Managing Ethnic Tensions*, in order to produce the Sinhalese as the hero/victim of the Sri Lankan story. Calling this level anti-Western would not be entirely inaccurate, since *Reaping the Whirlwind* implicitly binds colonialism with Western human-rights discourse, since it blames scholars "based in the West" for essentially spreading falsehoods about the Sinhalese. But the ethical force of de Silva's claims to victimhood is not grounded or secured by his being anti-Western, inasmuch as the West is understood as an epistemological space and not a cartographic one; rather, it is grounded by his deployment of colonialism in his production of his hero as anticolonial and of his victim as victimized by colonialism and its collaborators.

That alone does not explain *Reaping the Whirlwind*'s politics or de Silva's incredible alterations of his own positions from his prior work. Unlike *Managing Ethnic Tensions, Reaping the Whirlwind* is produced in a conjuncture in which Sinhalese nationalism faced two accounts of postcolonial Sri Lankan history, both of which identified it as the villain of the story: the Tamil nationalist account, as with *Managing Ethnic Tensions*, and, in addition, the powerful and authoritative Western liberal/human-rights account. In the absence of the latter, Tamil nationalist claims could have been ignored, as Sinhalese nationalism did with disdain in its early postindependence career. But the powerful human-rights discourse legitimized and endorsed the Tamil nationalist account of the ethnic conflict, recognized the Tamil as the victim, and authorized its demands—which *Reaping the Whirlwind* found to be extravagant—as just. Faced with this, *Reaping the Whirlwind* had to revise, renarrativize, the story told of Sri Lanka in *Managing Ethnic Tensions*. It could no longer assert the democratic right of the majority to hegemonize the minority because, to human-rights discourse, minority ethnic groups have rights, too. This discourse does not recognize democracy, at least outside the West, as the uninhibited hegemony of the majority. With this authoritative presence, with the West setting the very terms of the debate, Sinhalese nationalism could either submit and renounce its claim to hegemony, or it could renarrativize its story. Given that human-rights discourse sees the Tamil as victim and Sinhalese as villain, such a renarrativization could either reverse these terms (option one) or produce Sri Lanka in very different terms—as, for instance, complex (option two). De Silva desires, he says, to see Sri Lanka as complex, to see the conflict as composed of more than two antagonists. However, he not only does not do this, he cannot do this; he cannot tell the story of more than one actant from more than one perspective and still produce disciplinary history, for history does not enable the narration of synchronic diversity. But de Silva the Sinhalese nationalist abiding by Sri Lanka must produce *disciplinary* history in order to buttress, if not justify, the Sinhalese claim to hegemony in postcolonial Sri Lanka. So, option one gets selected (by default, as it were): the perspectives of the other ethnic groups identified as actants by *Reaping the Whirlwind*—the Muslim and the UpCountry Tamil—are minoritized, and that of the Tamil is villainized, as is that of the ancestor of human-rights discourse, the colonial West. Given this revision, the Sinhalese can emerge as the heroes of the story, imperfect perhaps, but willing to admit to their imperfections and to work to overcome them, like all true heroes.

However, as for the existence of a prior and very different argument in *Managing Ethnic Tensions*, in which the Sinhalese are not heroes nor the Tamils villains, de Silva must silence it, revise it, in order to continue to produce the Sinhalese as heroes or, more accurately, as hero-victims, as unsung heroes because they are the real victims. The logic at work here isn't difficult to decipher. Since, to de Silva, the past determines the present, a "poly-ethnic society" in the past would suggest the possibility of a polyethnic, harmonious Sri Lanka in the present or future. Thus my contention that the conjuncture or narrative moment *Managing Ethnic Tensions* produces is less pessimistic than that of the later text. It sees the possibility of some accommodation between the Sinhalese and the Tamils, albeit structured upon Sinhalese nationalist hegemony. In contrast, the conjuncture or Sri Lankan present produced by *Reaping the Whirlwind* is hopeless: it is one compared to a whirlwind, a force that produces not harmony but destruction. For this position to be maintained, disciplinary coherence demands that *Managing Ethnic Tensions*'s past be forgotten. Here, paradoxically enough, the disciplinary level overdetermines the disciplinary. Or, perhaps, it should suggest that the writing of history is as much about forgetting as it about remembering, as much about silencing as it is about narrating, as much about repressing as it is about recording, that, in short, history is not the faithful recapture of past events but a narrative, a structured story that doesn't represent the past so much as serve the interests of the present.

This, in itself, is not a controversial formulation, although the discipline is not in the habit of acknowledging it. Even its more allegedly radical disciples cannot let go of some notion of objectivity, of the empirically verifiable.[52] Take, for instance, the position of that historian who has insisted perhaps more than anybody else in the U.S. academy about the "literary" element of history writing, Hayden White: "How a given historical situation is to be configured depends on the historian's subtlety in matching up a specific plot structure with the set of historical events that he wishes to endow with a meaning of a particular kind. This is essentially a literary, that is to say fiction-making, operation."[53] Quite apart from his very schematic thinking, White's reduction of the literary to "fiction-making," a position dismissive of reading and, actually, that branch of narratology inspired by semiotics, must also be objected to. But what has to be noticed about this argument is that it contains absolutely no critique of the discipline, that it is grounded upon the empirical: a distinction between "a given historical situation," or "set of historical events," and their subsequent narration. My position, of course, is that this distinction is untenable and that both the French critique of history (theoretical or the conceptual) that inspires this study and closely reading de Silva (the specific) reinforce/demand such a conclusion. For what de Silva's revisions also suggest is that the past is not simply an event (which can be recaptured in its integrity) but its writing and, perhaps, nothing much more than writing, however authoritative such writing might be in this age, as Foucault reminds us, of history. If the "same" historian can narrativize the "same" events very differently at two different conjunctures, without new evidence or method, then the past might turn out to be, at least in this instance, nothing more than the present seeking to legitimize itself, nothing more than the "fiction," as de Certeau puts it, of the present. In other words, it is not the Sri Lankan past that determines the present, as de Silva confidently asserts, but *the present that determines the past*. De Silva's understanding of the present, and even of the future, determines his narration of the past; his politics determines his history—which is *not* another way of saying that history is not a faithful account of past events. I can, at the end of my reading of de Silva, be a little more precise: disciplinary history may turn out to be not much more than a structured story told about a putative object identified as the past in order not to produce knowledge of that past but to justify a petition about the present.

If this is the case, if history is a story, only a story, however authoritative, then it follows that the past, as an objectively existent entity, cannot and does not determine the present. Rather, the discipline of history operates by suggesting that the past has such a determining effect. If the past doesn't determine the present, of course, then it follows that history cannot be understood as a roadblock to peace in Sri Lanka, as de Silva contends. The historical injuries he reproduces, the desire for hegemony he codes as therapy, can—indeed must—then be seen as nothing more, or less, than a Sinhalese nationalist alibi for dominating or hegemonizing other Sri Lankans. And, consequently, that almighty discipline, history, can be seen as just a way of authorizing stories about something categorized as the past; history is a story or narrative that, upon close inspection, actually deconstitutes itself, thus enabling one of this study's overall goals: deauthorizing the discipline, negating its authoritative claim upon the present, and exposing its pretensions—in short, taking the mystery out of history. If that is the case, I also hope it is now clear why, after this reading, *Reaping the Whirlwind* must be comprehended as a majoritarian, exclusivist, hierarchical, hegemonic, and incoherent statement on behalf of Sinhalese nationalism; it is a "democratic" argument that, like social science, locates value in number, an alleged work of history and nothing but history that is inerasably shaped by many other knowledges or levels, an unapologetic and unaccounted-for revision of previous contradictory positions; in short, it is a petition for Sinhalese nationalist dominance of Sri Lanka and not the purely disciplinary history it produces itself as being. This, therefore, is why I contend that its demands must be opposed by the leftist.

3

Minority Matters:

Reading a Tamil Nationalist History

They masquerade as physicians, while in fact they... administer a poison...
—Friedrich Nietzsche, "On the Utility
and Liability of History for Life"

Compelled by Conscience

The autobiography of Tamil nationalism produces the transformations in its political demands—beginning with enhanced legislative representation and constitutional protection from discrimination by the Sinhalese Buddhist majority, and disregard from British officialdom in the late colonial period, through a federal polity for Sri Lanka soon after independence, to Tamil insistence that only an autonomous, sovereign, majority-Tamil state can bring peace to its people—as a reluctant, purely defensive response to the Sinhalese nationalist demand for hegemony, a prolonged series of broken Sinhalese promises to end seeking such hegemony, and consistently and escalatingly aggressive, if not genocidal, Sinhalese oppression. The Tamils, in this story, are not proactive but reactive, not a minority, which is how they are seen by antagonistic Sinhalese nationalism and even sympathetic Western human-rights discourse, but a nation: they have their own language, culture, territory, and characteristics that make them distinct from other Sri Lankan groups in the present. Equally, if not more importantly, they had an independent kingdom in northern Sri Lanka for centuries; that is, even their past is distinct from that of other Sri Lankan groups. This Tamil kingdom was never conquered by a Sinhalese king but only by a colonial power, the Portuguese, who administered its people separately from the Sinhalese, as did their successors, the Dutch. Only the British, some centuries after the Portuguese, forcibly united the Sinhalese and the Tamils—these otherwise discrete, distinct peoples, cultures, and parts of the country—into one administrative, therefore socio-political but not cultural or national, unit. At the moment of decolonization, 1948, the Tamils were forced by the British to live together with the Sinhalese, despite never having done so, or having had to do so, in the past and despite their fears of Sinhalese dominance, fears justified by the behavior of the Sinhalese elite in the years before decolonization. Nevertheless the Tamils were reasonable and willing to live in common, provided that such common life was based upon equality and nondiscrimination, which had to be constitutionally guaranteed. The Sinhalese rejected this, wanting to hegemonize the Tamils instead. So, after many failed attempts at reconciliation, at (re)negotiating the Sri Lankan political contract from one that enables domination to one that guarantees equality and gives the Tamils a stake in a common country, and after many broken Sinhalese promises, the Tamils reluctantly arrived in the 1970s at separation as the only way to save themselves from political insignificance, perhaps even physical elimination. All they ask, now, is to exercise the right of every nation: that of self-determination. Again, a fairly straightforward story, which, arguably, no academic effort has propagated with greater determination than that of Alfred Jeyaratnam Wilson. His early intellectual production strongly echoed the Sinhalese nationalist perspective on Sri Lanka (something almost impossible to picture today).[1] After what one might call his conversion into a champion of Tamil nationalism, his recent work to advance the Tamil cause, if not as relentless as de Silva, is at least as tenacious, and seems to be inspired by all the zeal of the convert.[2] A leftist intervention into the Sri Lankan debate will find Wilson's history, his petition for a separate Tamil-majority state, his chapter in the autobiography of Tamil nationalism, at the very least a convenient counterpoint to the work of de Silva.[3]

So, in this chapter, I read Wilson's most considered statement on what he calls, tamely and strangely enough, "the Sinhalese-Tamil dispute," *The*

Break-Up of Sri Lanka. The title signifies, of course, that—like de Silva, Daniel, and so on—Wilson has an essentialist understanding of identity. The Tamils, to this perspective, are a cohesive group, the cohesiveness of which is not open to interrogation. As the reader of this study would also expect, I don't consider *The Break-Up of Sri Lanka* a text representative of Tamil nationalism; I see it, like *Reaping the Whirlwind*'s relation to Sinhalese nationalism, as singular, as rhyming with it. Reading this work of history allows me to address concerns, similar to the previous chapter's, about the past and the present and the past in the present, about how (Tamil) nationalist history works, about the operation of history. But demonstrating that this text, too, is shaped by many levels, that it is incoherent and cannot narrate synchronic diversity, or that it finds analogy—the identitarian illusion—indispensable to its emplotment and politics will not gain too much attention; making such arguments in any detail would, quite simply, be redundant. Rather, my focus in this chapter will be on three other sets of issues. Reading Wilson—and I presume I don't need to state here that, like *Reaping the Whirlwind,* this text is better seen as having thrust itself upon me, rather than having been chosen—allows me to further elaborate my reading of de Silva, since Sinhalese nationalism cannot be fully comprehended without reference to its counterpart. Doing so also enables me, more importantly, to interrupt de Silva's story, his assertive and self-confident account of Sri Lanka unhindered by the slightest doubt about its claims, to supplement its elisions and silences and demonstrate that its emplotment is not a matter of record but a narrative strategy—one whose every claim, almost, is contested by the Tamil nationalist account of Sri Lanka—and, of course, to confront its politics. Reading *The Break-Up of Sri Lanka,* therefore, enables me provisionally to complete my scrutiny of histories of the Sri Lankan "ethnic conflict," which Western discourse identifies, as does Sinhalese nationalism, as a battle between just two parties, the Sinhalese and its Tamil counterpart, over the present and the past, over politics and history. It allows me to continue the conversation—or perhaps the confrontation—between them that I seek to stage in these pages. Such a confrontation allows me, a Sri Lankan leftist—this is the first of the issues to be foregrounded in this chapter—not to disinterestedly counter one account with another or to present both sides of the story and leave it to the reader to judge which account is the more persuasive. Claiming to speak from the left, of course, suggests that I do not see myself as occupying an uncommitted, Archimedean space. Rather, it enables me to *evaluate the adequacy of Tamil nationalism as a response to Sinhalese nationalism.* Sinhalese nationalism, as seen in the last chapter, has an exclusivist, hegemonic, and oppressive understanding of peace. It accepts Sri Lankan distinction, to work within the Adornean formulation, but it doesn't foresee an end to domination; indeed, it is predicated on Sinhalese domination of the other groups. Tamil nationalism, in response, produces itself and its promise as a medicine, as liberatory, as the only hope for a people made politically insignificant, unable to control their own affairs, and who face military oppression tantamount to genocide at the hands of the Sri Lankan state (though Wilson does not advance the last claim). In other words, the current project of Tamil nationalism, separatism, produces itself as being as much an ethical as a political enterprise. The leftist must, therefore, examine these ethical claims as well as the politics and ask if this promise to those whom it identifies as its "nationals" is kept, if this cure can be accepted as working and workable within the (exclusivist) terms offered by Tamil nationalism, as well as the more inclusive ones of the left;[4] the leftist must ask whether, in Nietzsche's terms, the medicine is an effective antidote or whether it turns out to be, as it were, a poison, whether Tamil nationalism is best grasped as, in a word, pharmakonic.

Wilson informs his reader *before* the beginning of the narrative proper, in a significant move that therefore seeks to determine the reading to follow, that his arguments are not only shaped by a disciplinary level, they are also informed, explicitly, by an ethical one: "I have tried to treat my subject in consonance with my academic calling *and my conscience*" (vi, emphasis added). This, of course, is where *The Break-Up of Sri Lanka* differs, and very considerably so, from *Reaping the Whirlwind*. De Silva produces the Sinhalese as injured, as carrying a historical grievance, as the real victim of the Sri Lankan story, but his claim to be ethical is implicit, shaped by the anticolonial level, and is an instance of his text's subtlety. De Silva's text must be read, especially against Western, liberal, human-rights discourse, to be noticed. Wilson's claim to be ethical is explicit, resolute, and an instance of his text's certainty that, being oppressed, the Tamils occupy the moral high ground; they are indisputably the victims of the Sri Lankan story. Wilson's certainty is asserted in his Preface itself where he affirms that, as he "kept reading with horror the operations by [the Sri Lankan] security forces," he realized he "could no longer be a *silent witness*" (v, emphasis added) to those events. At this level, the contrast between Wilson and de Silva couldn't be clearer: to de Silva the Tamils have no legitimate grievance—they did once, but those issues were resolved in the 1980s—and he thus sees the actions of the security forces as justifiable and necessary, the inevitable and proper response of the state—of any state—to the extravagant demands and dastardly deeds of terrorists; more crucially, he produces his subject-position as that of a mere witness to Sri Lankan events, as a disciplinary practitioner, albeit an unavoidably concerned one. While my reading demonstrated, I trust, that the text's political commitments overdetermine the disciplinary level in *Reaping the Whirlwind*, it is not a claim the narrative itself makes. Wilson, in contrast, rejects the subject-position of mere witness, and it is quite uncanny that his choice of term resonates with de Silva, even if he rejects that position. For Wilson is (refreshingly) explicit about, in my terms, the abiding/ethical levels of his text—which are clearly twisted together—overdetermining the disciplinary; he's explicit about, if you like, his ethical and political commitments. The witness, here, is not an adequate subject-position, being someone who knows, not sees: Wilson is at a distance from the "operations of the security forces," which he comes to know about secondhand, by reading, not by actually being there or seeing. Witnessing is also, in this understanding, a position that imposes a certain "silence" or limitation upon that subject, who can merely attest to knowledge, like any conventional disciplinary practitioner (de Silva?), without evaluating it. However, learning about these atrocities, Wilson feels obliged, compelled by his conscience, not to keep quiet; he feels an ethical imperative to propagate such knowledge, and by doing so he exceeds the subject-position of a mere witness or disciplinary practitioner; by doing so, *The Break-Up of Sri Lanka* abides by Sri Lanka (and gains my readerly sympathy). In admitting this, *The Break-Up of Sri Lanka* acknowledges the definitive impress of the abiding and ethical levels on its claims. Unlike de Silva, then, Wilson produces his subject-position as an academic or disciple *and* an abider; he may be domiciled outside Sri Lanka, but his response to the oppression of the Tamils cannot be that of the outsider. That is to say, *The Break-Up of Sri Lanka*, even if published in the West, is not just a part of Western discourse on Sri Lanka; its object is not to inform the West about it or to objectify the country but to intervene in a Sri Lankan debate. This enables me to effectively confront the one text, *Reaping the Whirlwind*, with the other, *The Break-Up of Sri Lanka*; they not only interrupt each other over this question of peace from "opposing" ends of the debate, they also abide by Sri Lanka, seek to get involved with its present, and change its future.

The second set of issues important to my study addressed in this chapter concerns revisionist history. As stated before, *The Break-Up of Sri Lanka* authorizes itself, legitimizes its petition for a separate Tamil-majority state in northeastern Sri Lanka by producing its arguments as sanctioned by two facts: that of oppression and broken Sinhalese promises in the colonial past and postcolonial present and that of difference dating back to the precolonial past—by, that is, the discipline of history. The uncanny mirroring of de Silva's *Reaping the Whirlwind* has already been noticed; Wilson too foregrounds his disciplinary allegiance in the Preface to *The Break-Up of Sri Lanka*: the book is the product not only of his conscience but also of his "academic calling," which is specified: "I have presented the facts in a historical frame of reference." Obviously, then, *The Break-Up of Sri Lanka* is shaped by a disciplinary level; if it weren't a work of (Tamil nationalist) history, if it didn't produce itself as a straightforward, empiricist account of the facts, if it didn't pass the Hayden White test, it wouldn't fall within the net of this study. The terrain of history, the same disciplinary ground that Sinhalese nationalism insists justifies its positions and politics, must be the terrain on which Wilson rebuts that petition for hegemony/dominance. Given the appropriation of the terrain and authority of history by Sinhalese nationalism and that that nationalism justifies and legitimizes its claims to dominate the present by reference to injuries and grievances from the past, given that Tamil nationalism holds the same position about the past determining the present, and given also the authority of history in modernity, Wilson cannot but challenge de Silva's account, renarrate the story of Sri Lanka, in order to effectively authorize his own petition for Tamil autonomy. For Wilson's petition to be persuasive, it must demonstrate that the Sinhalese nationalist account and claims, historical and political (the historical account that seeks to legitimize political claims) are incorrect. The Tamil nationalist perspective cannot be right without the Sinhalese nationalist perspective being wrong. Chatterjee's description of the challenges facing a different nationalism, the anticolonial, can be usefully cited here: "nationalist thinking is necessarily a struggle with an entire body of systematic knowledge, a struggle that is political at the same time that it is intellectual. Its politics impels it to open up that framework of knowledge which presumes to dominate it, to dispel that framework, to subvert its authority."[5] The Sinhalese nationalist perspective must be wrong, then, not only as a political or ideological position that is simply to be opposed but must be demonstrably wrong within the rigorous protocols of disciplinary history. Tamil nationalism's politics compels it to challenge the political and the intellectual positions of Sinhalese nationalism. The political and intellectual claims of the former or, in my terms, the disciplinary and abiding levels, cannot be dissociated (except of course for analytic purposes). Tamil nationalism, that is, cannot seek to legitimize its petition for separation by only making arguments about the present, by pointing to the fact of discrimination or oppression, or by, in short, laying claim to the ethical and political; it must also have, or it feels an inescapable imperative to have, an alternative, persuasive, *verifiable* account of the history of Sri Lanka. And not just for its own sake or because it, too, like *Reaping the Whirlwind*, holds that the past determines the present. The point is that, without being buttressed by the disciplinary, the ethical level of *The Break-Up of Sri Lanka* would lose much of its force, for what the ethical argument demonstrates, the only work it can do, is that the Tamils are oppressed; I say "only" because the political consequences of this claim are limited: it might entitle the Tamils to the sympathy of human-rights discourse and a wider world, it might even entitle them to recompense that might take the form of constitutional tinkering stretching to some version of federalism, but not necessarily to self-determination, separation. In order to assert the latter, the Tamils have to prove themselves a nation. And the criterion here is discreteness not only in the present but, perhaps more importantly, in the past. For, as all students of nationalism know, without a long and discrete past, the nationness, as it were, of a group of people is incomplete. Without producing a history for itself, the political project of nationalism cannot proceed, which is another way of saying that this text does not abide by Sri Lanka in the same way as de Silva's. *Reaping the Whirlwind* is produced from within the dominant/majoritarian perspective; it proceeds from the certainty that it is correct—thus it need not make its ethico-political claims explicitly; it knows its place and is secure in that knowledge. Tamil nationalist history, on the other hand, does not have this luxury. It has much more work to do; it is contestatory as much as it is confident in its rhetoric (which is not to say, of course, that it is uncertain of its claims). If *Reaping the Whirlwind*, then, abides by Sri Lanka with all the self-confidence of being the dominant or majoritarian account of its history, *The Break-Up of Sri Lanka* does so as a minor or dominated one. Insofar as it produces itself as a nation and not a minority, it too knows its place—or, rather, what its place should be; thus the confidence, the certainty underlying many of Wilson's statements. But, insofar as it also admits to being a nation without a state, to being a minority in another's state, it should be understood as, in a sense, without place, as searching for a secure place from which to speak; thus the contestatory aspect of its rhetoric.

Making one nationalist history interrupt another also enables posing again the question, raised in the previous chapter and cortical to the Sri Lankan debate, of the relation between history and politics. Crucially significant in this context, of course, is that both de Silva and Wilson hold that the past—understood within the terms of the referential or retro-spective illusion—determines the present. However, reading both texts carefully shows that forgetting, elision, and revision are indispensable to their projects. Both de Silva and Wilson rewrite the past and elide or disappear positions they held previously in order to make their account of that past compatible with their understanding of and, more crucially, commitments to the present. What reading de Silva's *Reaping the Whirlwind* against his earlier *Managing Ethnic Tensions* and reading *The Break-Up of Sri Lanka* against an earlier Wilson text divulges, to put it crudely, is that *when the presents of de Silva and Wilson change, so do their pasts.* For each writer, the past has an amazing malleability, an incredible dexterity, a fantastic ability to get reconstituted (renarrativized) according to the demands of a changing present. This should be impossible within a historicist perspec-tive, to which by definition the past has already happened and therefore cannot change (unless new evidence is discovered of it or a new method is invented to examine it). Despite this, Wilson, in a move that stretches credibility to its limits, actually reverses himself and assumes positions in *The Break-Up of Sri Lanka* radically opposed to those he previously held and thus enables me to advance my own claim that history can and must be deauthorized. Take, for instance, Wilson's summary of events in post-colonial Sri Lanka in a prior work, *Politics in Sri Lanka, 1947–1973,* a book whose dustjacket, unbelievably enough, reproduces without irony just one (large) image—the armed (and dangerous) Sinhalese lion that domi-nates the Sri Lankan flag:

> The Buddhist ethos and a continuing process of modernization even up
> to present times have contributed in no small measure to generate that
> tolerance and accommodation which are so necessary for the satisfactory
> functioning of parliamentary government . . . Compromise and middle-
> path solutions . . . have in fact been the guidelines of Sri Lanka's political
> development since the beginning of the twentieth century. (1)

This doesn't, you might think, sound very different from Kingsley de Silva! The Sinhalese Buddhists in this account are tolerant, prepared to compromise, do not govern from the extreme but seek accommodation, reconciliation, and the middle path and have behaved thus from the first moment that the British allowed the natives some voice in government at the beginning of the twentieth century. Parliamentary rule is deemed here to have functioned satisfactorily—not perfectly, but nevertheless satisfactorily—in postcolonial Sri Lanka. In *The Break-Up of Sri Lanka,* however, not only is the Buddhist ethos characterized antonymically as oppressive and the Sinhalese elite accused of being consistently intolerant, uncompromising, and prone to breaking its pledges (in the rare instances it made any) from the beginning of that same twentieth century, but the Sri Lankan past, dating back to colonialism, is rewritten in such a way as to seamlessly produce this new present, one in which parliamentary government has manifestly failed, in which Tamil politics has been forced to resort to extraparliamentary activities since the late 1950s, and in which Sri Lanka since the late 1980s has "already [been] split into two entities" (v) in spirit if not in fact, psychologically though not yet territorially.

Such outright reversals in position—"revision" is an inadequate term for this—not only makes it easier for a reader like myself to contend, with de Certeau, that the past is the fiction of the present but also to take what I consider to be the logical—and necessary, given the impasse facing Sri Lanka—next step, to seek to deauthorize history. If history is able to endlessly revise its account of the past, not in the light of allegedly new "evidence" of that past or the invention of new methods to treat it but purely in order to justify the writer's present and politics, then surely the authority of the discipline itself must be, if not very suspect, at least open to question and questioning. Consequently, in this chapter, I am able to examine the issue of revision, history as an operation, and the literariness of the discipline at somewhat greater length and depth than in the previous one. Taken together, then, the argument of the two chapters leads toward the conclusion that history cannot be understood as a true account or faithful representation of past events but as writing, a literary activity, a story—not fable or fiction, in the common senses of those terms, but a powerful, structured story—that seeks not to represent or reconstruct a past but to authorize a present; if it weren't, the forgetting of previous positions in the almost cavalier, certainly unapologetic, fashion of de Silva and Wilson would not—could not—occur. This, in turn, raises the possibility that history may not necessarily determine politics or be bound to the question of peace or, at the very least, not be bound in quite the way suggested by nationalism. Additionally, to repeat a statement made in the previous chapter, closely reading works of history, which can be shown to "deconstitute" themselves, might suggest that deauthorizing history, paradoxically enough, is a project that history itself appears to compel upon its informed, attentive, rhetorically sensitive readers.

The third set of issues raised in this chapter concerns scrutinizing representative democracy from a minority perspective (I say "raised" because these issues are not discussed at a sufficient length—that would take a study of its own). Wilson himself doesn't examine democracy as a problem for the minority; unlike in de Silva's *Reaping the Whirlwind*, the term occurs infrequently in Wilson's text. Nevertheless, the problem of democracy, democracy as a problem for the left/ist, and not just in the context of peace in Sri Lanka, arises as a consequence of my reading his narrative; most compellingly, it arises upon reading it after *Reaping the Whirlwind*, arises as a consequence of the Tamil nationalist critique of Sinhalese nationalism. It raises itself as a consequence of what I call the minority critique of majoritarianism as such. Since Wilson doesn't address these questions in any systematic or theoretical manner, since his exclusive concern is the predicament of the Tamils, this chapter too must be understood as a symptomatic reading. It seeks to "read the illegible," to answer a question that is not posed by the text, to produce an answer—a second text if you like—"articulated with the lapses in the first."[6] Wilson cannot pose this question because it lies outside his problematic. His argument is structured—one might even say straitjacketed—by the logic of nationalism; all he can see, as an alternative to one exclusivist politics, is another; more inclusive possibilities, leftist or even liberal, are not contemplated, not even raised by the text. *The Break-Up of Sri Lanka* simply seeks to rebut the narrative, claims, and contentions of one nationalism, the Sinhalese, from the perspective of another, the Tamil. Committed as he is to telling that story, justifying the claims and legitimizing demands of the Tamil, which his own text admits to being exclusivist, he cannot see where his argument leads, that the very movement of his narrative might suggest quite different, productive, and enabling conclusions from the ones he reaches. As opposed to the Tamil separatist, *The Break-Up of Sri Lanka* leads the symptomatic/postcolonial leftist reader elsewhere, to perhaps the most important question addressed by this study; it leads her to question, from a minority perspective, nothing less than the promise and possibilities of democracy, for so long the definition of her dreams and desires, for too long understood as synonymous with peace, and not just in Sri Lanka. Indeed, *The Break-Up of Sri Lanka*'s narrativization of the Tamil response to Sinhalese nationalist majoritarianism enables a rethinking of what is understood by a minority perspective. I will argue, through my symptomatic reading of Wilson, that a minority is no longer usefully thought of empirically, numerically and relationally, or analogically (as it is by social science and the dictionary) as a cohesive group of subjects lesser in number to another; it is more usefully thought of conceptually, as *a place from where one reads, a perspective and position that is opposed to finding significance and value in number*, a position that, therefore, emphasizes the singular. The leftist response to the question of peace in Sri Lanka must work through this perspective for it to be truly innovative, to be a new response to the question of peace, rather than being a repetition of the tired old clichés of political science and constitutional law.

In this chapter, then, I address the following questions: What is the basis of the critique of Sinhalese nationalism produced by *The Break-Up of Sri Lanka*? Is the narrative essentially politico-ethical in its emphasis, overdetermined by the abiding level, or are the other levels, including the historical and narratological equally important to it? What is the work of the disciplinary level in this text? Is history asked to do the same work for both nationalisms or do their deployments of it differ? Which of these histories, which account of the Sri Lankan past, is more persuasive: the Sinhalese nationalist or the Tamil? By what criteria does the postempiricist reader make such an evaluation? Can she in the first place? Equally important given his drastic reversals of previous positions, is Wilson's claim to be producing pure disciplinary history in *The Break-Up of Sri Lanka* convincing to the postempiricist reader? If not, and given the finding of *Reaping the Whirlwind* as incoherent, does this lead such a reader toward a critique of the authority of history itself? What exactly might such a critique entail? What would be its consequences? Then: is separatist Tamil nationalism an enabling alternative, from a leftist perspective, to the view of a peaceful Sri Lanka produced by majoritarian Sinhalese nationalism discussed in the previous chapter, to Sinhalese nationalism's exclusivist notion of community? Or does separatist Tamil nationalism emerge as also majoritarian and exclusivist in structure? Does it, in short, provide a useful basis for reconceptualizing peace in Sri Lanka that the leftist could support? If not, does a symptomatic reading of Wilson (after de Silva) enable such a reconceptualization of the keywords, as it were, of this study? Does it enable a broadening of the questions the Sri Lankan debate must address so that the question of peace is discussed in a more enabling, less restrictive fashion, one that not only brings into consideration Muslim and UpCountry Tamil perspectives but also asks the question of democracy?

Emplotment: Promises, Promises

Reaping the Whirlwind, as noted in the previous chapter, sees the ethnic conflict as a battle between essentially two actants, two ethnic groups, the Sinhalese and Tamils; individual members of the groups are of secondary importance to its plot and perspective. *The Break-Up of Sri Lanka* also has a binarized understanding of what it terms the "Sinhalese-Tamil dispute";

it does not—cannot, given its commitment to Tamil nationalism—find the conflict "complex" even in name but, in a significant difference from *Reaping the Whirlwind*, produces it and sees Sri Lankan events largely as a consequence of the deeds of individual subjects, of *representative* individual members of the Sinhalese and Tamil elite and of the British colonial administration.[7] That is to say, this text's actants are not so much ethnic groups as they are (metonymic) individuals.[8] These individuals act for a variety of reasons, are inspired by diverse motives; things happen in this story because the people who act, or with the capacity to act, are good, bad, or weak, majoritarian, myopic, or misguided, et cetera, et cetera, et cetera. However, a close reading demonstrates that most of these actants, especially the Sinhalese, do not have effective agency; they appear to be bound by a script written for them. More importantly, the narrative emphasis in *The Break-Up of Sri Lanka*, its engine as it were, is ultimately its plot and not its actants; the narrative is compelled by the things that happen, not by the people who make them happen. This, of course, is only to be expected in a petition of this kind: the imperative of *The Break-Up of Sri Lanka* is to demonstrate the fact of Tamil oppression and Sinhalese betrayal, not so much the (deliberate, majoritarian) complicity of individual Sinhalese leaders or the (inadvertent, misguided) complicity of British colonial rulers with such oppression or even of the resistance—sometimes heroic and farsighted, sometimes uninspired and myopic—of Tamil leaders to it (although *The Break-Up of Sri Lanka*, as will be seen, has a strong judgmental subtext; or, more precisely, making judgments upon the behavior of individual actants is a strong element of this text's ethical level). Consequently, it is the emplotment of this narrative that will determine my own emphasis in this chapter; a separate section on its actants is unnecessary. Nevertheless, it will be impossible not to grant Wilson's individual actants, given that they are interwoven with the plot, their actions narrated sometimes in elaborate and luxurious detail, and that they are understood to be representative of their ethnic groups, more attention than is perhaps necessary or desirable in a study such as mine; the texture of his narrative makes it unavoidable.

The Break-Up of Sri Lanka's narrative begins in the early nineteenth century, with British colonialism. Does this suggest that it, too, is shaped by an anticolonial level? Yes, but not simply because it discusses colonialism, even if not in a fashion that resembles *Reaping the Whirlwind. The Break-Up of Sri Lanka*'s account of colonialism does not produce any victims, though it finds the Sinhalese—and not the Tamils—to be the collaborators in a perhaps predictable reversal of the Sinhalese nationalist account. In my reading, this signifies the impress of the anticolonial level: *The Break-Up of Sri Lanka*, that is, is the consequence of the distinguished career of anti-colonialism and the product of the conjuncture of postcolonial studies. It can take for granted that collaborating with colonialism is self-evidently wrong. If its narrative begins in the nineteenth century, its story, as implied before, is begun much earlier, with "historically-established invasions of Ceylon from the Dravidian kingdoms of South India" (26). The disciplinary level can be seen at work in that statement: these invasions have been "established," documented, proved by the discipline of history; they are a matter of record. But, as with *Reaping the Whirlwind*, the precolonial past isn't granted much narrative time in *The Break-Up of Sri Lanka*; the units in which that story is told are all instances of ellipsis and serve just one purpose: to enable that disciplinary argument, to which end Wilson cites, when convenient, both nationalist historians like de Silva and anti-Sinhalese nationalists like Gunawardana to establish his case for "a *tradition*, interrupted at times, of a separate kingdom of the Tamils of Ceylon" (30, emphasis added). One must pause at the term "tradition": it signifies that the Tamil kingdom was not a mere accident, a chance or incidental happening, but something more lasting and recognized. Ultimately, however, it is not this "tradition" but the colonial past, indeed just the British colonial past, that interests Wilson, that has to be renarrated, and at some length, to buttress his petition. *The Break-Up of Sri Lanka* does not have to expend much effort to establish the existence of a Tamil kingdom in Sri Lanka or a centuries-long Tamil presence in the country. Even if popular Sinhalese history disputes this, academic Sinhalese history concedes it. As was seen in the previous chapter, de Silva admits to such a presence, indeed, finds it uncontroversial. This is not to imply that the significance of this past can be underestimated; without a history, as stated before, any group's claim to nationhood is incomplete. But, once a historical presence is demonstrated, the narrative can move to the more contested terrain, to the battlefield over what happened during British colonialism in the early nineteenth century and to the narrative's substantial concern, the ethical claim: the fact of Tamil oppression.

The crucial event in Wilson's account, the beginning of Sri Lanka's current misery—the past that determines the present—occurs in 1831, when "the [British] Governor . . . was issued with a commission which for the first time brought the island under a single unified legislature" (3), when the Sinhalese and Tamils, that is, were made a part of one political unit and were forced to live together for the first time in their history. Within Genette's terms, the narrative units telling the story during British colonialism are instances of "summary": the time of the story exceeds that of the narrative; events are recounted as sparely, as summarily as possible, without much detail. Also in 1831 came "the Colebrooke-Cameron Report . . . [which] recommended a tighter degree of centralization" (3) of the administration of the country. In the years following these reforms, there were "notable changes in the economic landscape" and "strides in education"; a plantation-dominated economy took shape; the spread of the railway resulted in the whole country being connected; an indigenous elite began to emerge. This, in turn, "promoted the growth of religious revivalism among the majority Sinhalese Buddhists and the minority Hindus and Muslims. A natural consequence of this multifarious mix of ethnically and religiously divided groups was the emergence of cross-cutting synthetic nationalist umbrella organizations" (5). Why religious revivals should "naturally" lead to nationalist movements is not explained, but that need not concern the reader too much. The point is that, for a brief period in the late nineteenth and early twentieth centuries, these "umbrella organizations" worked with each other. There was some communal amity, or, rather, cooperation, between the Sinhalese and Tamil (and Muslim) elites. Wilson endorses such cooperation, codes it as "consociationalism," a crucial term in his argument, the opposite of broken promises. This conjuncture, of consociationalism, is the only positive moment between the two groups identified in the story. And it is a tremendous signifier of the hierarchical, right-wing allegiance of the text that, to Wilson, a "studied attempt at 'consociationalism' between the elites of the two major ethnic groups"—and notice the binary understanding of the Sri Lankan dispute present in every little crevice of the text—"could have prevented the friction that lay ahead" (16). There is no sympathy in this text for subaltern politics. If the elites cooperated, Sri Lanka wouldn't have gotten into the mess it did; but the Sinhalese upper classes wanted things entirely their own way. (And the rest, within this logic, is history . . .)

The Tamil hero in this part of the narrative is Ponnambalam Ramanathan, elected to represent the Sri Lankan elite, the "Educated Ceylonese" as they were then categorized, in the legislature in 1911, and reelected in 1917; on both occasions not only with elite Tamil but also with considerable elite Sinhalese backing. So cordial were the relations between the two groups of elites at this moment that Ramanathan acquired, "in the latter part of his second term, the leadership of the Unofficial Members" in the legislature; consequently, he even "committed his support to the Sinhalese Buddhists during the Sinhalese Buddhist-Muslim riots of 1915" (57), rather than support the victims, the Muslims, which Wilson suggests was a mistake. The other dominant Tamil politician in the late colonial period, the other cardinal Tamil actant identified by the narrative in this brief conjuncture of consociationalism, is Ramanathan's brother, Ponnambalam Arunachalam. One of the "founding fathers of the Ceylon National Congress" in 1919, he too worked toward understanding and consensus between the Sinhalese and Tamil elites. But, as would later happen with his brother, his attempts at consociationalism resulted in failure. The Sinhalese leaders promised to support Arunachalam's most insistent request, "for adequate representation for the Tamils . . . in the legislature . . . [But the] pledge was broken, as in many other instances later in the century" (58). The postempiricist reader will insist on identifying the narratological level as being at work here: slipping in interpretation, connecting events that could be seen otherwise, producing a continuous and continuing narrative, producing commonality and comparability (in a word, analogy) from events that could also be understood as discrete and different, effectively creating a story of broken Sinhalese promises. Effectively, that is, *emplotting* the story into one of broken Sinhalese promises. For continuity/narrativity is not inherent to an event; one "broken promise" does not anticipate another; indeed one may not, upon close consideration, even resemble another. Like *Reaping the Whirlwind*, then, *The Break-Up of Sri Lanka*, too, is an instance of an "iterative" narrative: "events considered only in terms of their analogy." Like de Silva's (Sinhalese) nationalist history, analogy proves to be essential to the emplotment of Wilson's history, too.

Following this unmet pledge, the story continues, Arunachalam left the Congress in 1921, "condemning it as . . . [an organization] 'representing mainly a section of the Sinhalese'" (8). Wilson argues that the well-meaning but naive Ponnambalam brothers were used (by the cunning, majoritarian Senanayake brothers, one of whom, Don Stephen, would become the first prime minister of Sri Lanka): "There is little doubt that the [Ponnambalam] brothers were flattered by the leadership roles assigned to them, little knowing that when the Sinhalese reformists no longer needed them, they would be edged off the political stage" (11). Ramanathan's disenchantment with the Sinhalese elite took place a good decade after his brother's; it is dated to the prospect of universal adult franchise, following what goes by the name of the Donoughmore Reforms in 1931, which among other things recommended that the right to vote in Sri Lanka be granted to all persons over twenty-one. Ramanathan opposed "the extension of the franchise recommended by the Donoughmore Commission, because he knew that universal franchise would mean the institutionalization of a Sinhalese territorial majority which . . . would be detrimental to the interests of the Ceylon Tamils" (10). Instead, the Tamil leader wanted the franchise restricted to those with "property and educational qualifications." He, too, failed to prevail and ended his cooperation with the Sinhalese. It should be emphasized here, since this is a subject that will be returned to, that the issue over which both the Ponnambalam brothers are said to have broken with their Sinhalese counterparts is that of *representation* (in the legislature). Arunachalam fought for "adequate" representation for the Tamils even before the Donoughmore reforms. This implies that the Tamil elite considered their numbers in the legislature inadequate or insignificant virtually from the very moment the British allowed the natives some voice in government. Their numbers in the legislature may have been an accurate representation of their numbers on the ground, as it were, but that did not translate into giving them an effective voice in the making of legislative decisions, that is, making them politically significant. His brother's arguments suggest that, with the franchise being extended, or democratized, the Tamil situation worsened. After Donoughmore, says Wilson, Ramanathan's politics turned exclusivist; the one Tamil leader who most represented the possibilities of consociationalism in "his last years . . . reverted to the role of defender of the Ceylon Tamil interests" (57). Ramanathan, in this account an opponent of extending the franchise from the elite to the larger population, does not, of course, sound like a democrat. Significantly enough, though, Wilson does not reach that conclusion, call him that name. Or, rather, "anti-democrat" would be one way of comprehending Ramanathan's position. Another way, the possibility of which I am raising in this chapter by reading Wilson symptomatically and by reading *The Break-Up of Sri Lanka* after *Reaping the Whirlwind*, is that the Tamil dilemma, the elite Tamil response to democratization (within colonialism), the Tamil nationalist response to the Sinhalese nationalist understanding of democracy as majority rule (an argument developed with some care by de Silva), perhaps even the minority response to democracy as such, might suggest to the postempiricist/postcolonial leftist reader that democracy, when scrutinized from a minority perspective, turns out to be hostile to peace (with peace, of course, not understood as the absence of war). For, reading Wilson/Ramanathan—they are impossible to separate in that unit—symptomatically leads one to the consider the possibility that the Tamil complaint, though not of course phrased in these terms, is not only against a particular act or two of the colonial state; implicit in the specific complaint is another, against democracy as such. Or, rather, the informed, symptomatic reader can see what is not visible to

Wilson. Ramanathan "knew," says Wilson, that extending the franchise, or democracy, would "institutionalize," systematize, and provide a structure for the minoritization of the Tamils. Arunachalam presumably "knew" this too. His demand for enhanced representation is surely an argument against minoritization, against being unable to count or matter in the legislature. Yes, the complaints of the Ponnambalam brothers were only about the potential institutionalized insignificance of those who shared their subject-position or were members of their ethnic group, the Tamils. Wilson does not contend that either even attempted to represent or make alliances with the other minorities. But, lying hidden in that complaint, visible to the Althusserian "informed gaze," is an argument about the fate of any minority under a governmental system based on territorial representation and majority rule, under, in a word, democracy: that it would be reduced to structural insignificance. At moments like this, Wilson seems to glimpse, to place his finger on, the structural problem at stake here; but disposed as he is to a predetermined response to that problem, he cannot follow through on his own intuition. The possibility that the question of peace in Sri Lanka can be conceptualized as not something peculiar to just the Sinhalese and Tamils, or to allegedly analogous ethnic/nationalist disputes elsewhere, but that it might be "connected" (cf. Gupta and Ferguson 1997) to a much larger question of democracy itself consistently evades his grasp even though he appears to be so close to it.

My questioning of democracy, it should be stressed, derives from and rhymes with that made by David Scott in chapter 7 of his *Refashioning Futures*, which I discuss at some length in the Conclusion. To Scott, the Donoughmore reforms "sought to reshape that emerging modern order" in Sri Lanka, inaugurated by the earlier Colebrooke-Cameron reforms of the nineteenth century, "through the scope of an explicitly democratic reason" (165); they enabled, unsurprisingly to Scott, Sinhalese majoritarian rule. In Wilson's account, "the Donoughmore Commissioners tended to look the other way on the problems caused by multiethnicity" (1988, 13). They did realize that the country was "not homogenous"; however, they responded to this problem not by respecting heterogeneity but by trying to produce ways of eliminating it. Wilson does not, retrospectively, oppose the extension of the franchise in 1931 but argues that its majoritarian consequences could have been avoided if the commissioners had instituted some constitutional safeguards for the minorities. Liberalism, in this argument, could have reformed—or better yet, saved—itself, but, paradoxically enough, only if it acted in a decidedly illiberal fashion: the commissioners could, for instance, have heeded the advice of a former British governor of Ceylon, William Manning, who is only a catalytic actant in this narrative but one of the few good, farsighted colonialists identified by Wilson. Indeed, Manning is produced as a proto-consociationalist, who had "expressed the view in a dispatch to the Secretary of State [in 1922] that the ethnic composition of the legislature should be such that 'no single community can impose its will upon the other communities'" (7). But, rather than heed the advice of a Manning, the commissioners were determined to justify the colonial enterprise, to make Ceylon a modern nation modeled on the West, to produce (unmarked) Ceylonese nationalists out of Sinhalese, Tamil, and Muslim communalists. Wilson, however, holds that such an identity never came into being; the minorities (or rather their leaders) were committed to it—indeed, they would have been condemned to remaining minoritized if they hadn't been—but not so the Sinhalese, who always put their interests first. So Wilson deems Ceylonese nationalist "a term without validity" (57). This might suggest that the term "Ceylon," too, should be without much validity to Wilson, especially since it is undeniably a colonial coinage and imposition, but he insists upon deploying it in place of "Sri Lanka":

> I have used "Ceylon" advisedly because that is how the country was called for well over 150 years before Sri Lanka was unilaterally introduced into the vocabulary of international usage in 1972; this was done without the consent of the principal minority, the Tamils, the community to which I belong. *Sri Lanka* is used in the title to convey to readers evidence of the disintegration of the polity under its new name. (v)

Several elements of this unit deserve notice. For a start, it must be pointed out that Wilson expressed no objections of any kind to "Sri Lanka" in the title and body of his previous work, *Politics in Sri Lanka*. Second, while I share the Tamil nationalist objection to "Sri Lanka," I continue to use the term, albeit under erasure, and I wonder whether Wilson's alternative, "Ceylon," does not betray a certain nostalgia for colonialism, for a time when the Tamils were not oppressed and a neutral, disinterested arbiter existed—if only in the abstract—to adjudicate their dispute with the Sinhalese. After all, to a Tamil nationalist, the Tamil word for Sri Lanka, "Ilankai," is also available. Why is it not deployed? It might also be pointed out that the same objections Wilson has to "Sri Lanka" could be used against "Ceylon": it, too, "was unilaterally introduced into the vocabulary of international usage"—albeit by the British—without the consent of native opinion. But the reader would not, by now, be surprised at finding narrative incoherence in *The Break-Up of Sri Lanka*. She might, indeed, wonder if it is not a constitutive element of nationalist history. My final comment on this unit has to do with Wilson's substantive—actual?—concern in *The Break-Up of Sri Lanka*. The narrative pays occasional attention to the problems and predicaments of the other minorities—Muslims, UpCountry Tamils, Burghers—but Wilson's objection to "Sri Lanka," the rhetorically sensitive reader would have noticed, is not made on the grounds that the country's name was changed without consulting minorities but that this was done "without the consent" of just the Tamils—in his understanding the *"principal* minority" of the country, the only one that counts. *The Break-Up of Sri Lanka's* avowed concern may be the "break-up" of *Sri Lanka*, but the story this text narrates, the perspective it seeks to legitimize, the petition it supports, is exclusively that of the Tamil nationalist. In so doing, like *Reaping the Whirlwind*, it silences and minoritizes the perspectives of the other ethnic groups, finds some perspectives to be more important than others, and shows its perspective to be hierarchical—which, as argued in the previous chapter, is a constitutive element of right-wing thought. Like *Reaping the Whirlwind*, then, *The Break-Up of Sri Lanka* also looks increasingly like a right-wing text.

The minoritization of the other actants can be seen throughout the narrative. Take, for instance, *The Break-Up of Sri Lanka's* discussion of what it considers the Muslim objection to the Donoughmore reforms. Wilson cites a speech by T. B. Jayah, "the virtual leader of Muslim political opinion," that is apparently critical of the Ceylon National Congress, but the—almost meaningless—quotation doesn't tell the reader exactly why Jayah was opposed to the changes.[9] Indeed the function of that narrative unit is hard to decipher. Wilson, in his summary description of the Muslims, calls them "the solicited minority." This, of course, sees the Muslim from an external perspective, rather than in the terms of what (elite) Muslim opinion might have to say for or about itself, which is how *The Break-Up of Sri Lanka* sees the Tamils and often the Sinhalese; that is, a discrete Muslim perspective is denied or silenced by this text, which is another way that *The Break-Up of Sri Lanka* resonates with *Reaping the Whirlwind*. The relevant narrative unit, the text's summary of the Muslims, repays close attention:

> Both Sinhalese and Tamils seek their [the Muslims] support on political issues. Although they are mostly Tamil-speaking and have empathy for the Tamil political situation, they do not align themselves with the Tamils. This is because they (1) are interspersed among both Sinhalese and Tamils, (2) do not wish to be a minority within a minority (as in a

separate Tamil homeland), and (3) are in competition with Tamils and Sinhalese, more sharply with the Tamils because most of them are Tamil-speakers. The Muslims are also used by the Sinhalese leadership to divide the Tamil-speaking entity. (34)

This unit is an excellent instance both of narrative incoherence and of Wilson's inability to deal with the specificity of the Muslim. The Muslims, here, both "have empathy" for the Tamils *and* compete with them (for what?) "because most of them are Tamil-speakers." Why does speaking the same language result in competition? More importantly, if the Muslims are a distinct, discrete group, which Wilson acknowledges here and elsewhere in the text, by what logic can they be produced as a part of a "Tamil-speaking entity"? If the Muslims and Tamils are not just discrete but competitors, if the Muslims are not aligned politically with the Tamils, despite the empathy, if, that is, the Muslims and Tamils do not have common interests, what holds this entity together? If the Sri Lankan "dispute" is between the Sinhalese and "Ceylon Tamils," as *The Break-Up of Sri Lanka* consistently asserts, what role does this other actant, this "Tamil-speaking entity," play in the dispute, if any at all? If the Muslims don't support Tamil separatism because they do not want to be minoritized, then to what extent, really, do they "empathize" with the Tamils? And, finally, if the Muslims are or can be "used" by the Sinhalese, does this mean that they don't have interests of their own? If this is the case, how can the Muslims be "competitors" with the Tamils, or be a part of that linguistic entity? Wilson does not address these crucial questions. Such significant elisions, taken with his deployment of the phrase, "Tamil-speaking entity," signifies, on the one hand, to his complicity with a hegemonic tendency within Tamil nationalism that has attempted, consistently throughout its career, to incorporate the Muslim within its project by positing the notion of a "Tamil-speaking people." This notion denies Muslim specificity and, as Karthigesu Sivathamby and others have pointed out, is one that Muslim politics has consistently rejected.[10] On the other hand, and this point is of greater significance to my study as a whole, this narrative unit shows a crucial silencing on the part of Wilson that was also noticed in de Silva's narrative: to phrase it differently, *both* Sinhalese and Tamil nationalisms, which produce the Sri Lankan conflict (or dispute or whatever) in binary terms, *cannot come to terms with the specificity of the Muslim.*[11] The consequences of this for the leftist, for the nonexclusivist thinking peace in Sri Lanka, will be discussed in the next two chapters. Let's, for now, return to Wilson's narrative.

The Donoughmore commissioners didn't only recommend an extension of the franchise as a panacea for the country's communalism, they
had other suggestions that took into account the lack of a unified national
consciousness or Ceylonese identity. They proposed that meetings of the
Sri Lankan legislature be held not only in Colombo but in Kandy and
Jaffna as well, so as to help integrate the Kandyan Sinhalese and Jaffna
Tamils into the polity. This could, in Wilson's opinion, "have helped miti-
gate the island's later ills" (15), but such sessions were never held. The
commissioners also wanted to encourage cooperation rather than seek
to (re)produce in Sri Lanka a British-style party system with a government and opposition, a system that might have encouraged confrontation between the communities. So they disallowed political parties and
divided the legislature not into government and opposition, or majority
and minority, but into "seven executive committees . . . designed for the
purpose of providing some opportunities for minority ethnic representatives to secure election to . . . the Board of Ministers" (15). Nevertheless,
to Wilson, the "Sinhalese leadership . . . evinced no willingness to share
power with the minority ethnic groups" (15). Two members of minority
groups managed to be elected to the first board of ministers in 1931—one
Muslim and one UpCountry Tamil—but they "did not agree with all
the demands presented by their Sinhalese colleagues" (67). This lack of
cooperation or refusal to compromise with the majority would have its
consequences: five years later, after the next election to the legislature,
Don Stephen Senanayake, the future prime minister, got his act together
and engineered the numbers in every single executive committee such
that each of them could elect a Sinhalese minister; every single committee
proceeded to do so. Consequently, the minority members of parliament
became effectively insignificant—they had no voice in the cabinet. The
Donoughmore executive committee system, Wilson concludes, was unable to prevent the majority from asserting itself. This should suggest to
Wilson (it certainly does to me) that the problem facing the Tamils was
representative democracy itself, a system that finds significance in, and
places value upon, number. It should suggest that if the guiding, structuring principle of a system of government is majority rule then a minority
cannot prevent the majority from ruling and that the system, as a system,
cannot actually make the minority matter, however many safeguards it
may institute, because *the system itself is structured in order to enable the majority
to rule.* But all Wilson can see is the particular: yet another evil act of the
Sinhalese. Incidentally, this instance—not, after all, a broken promise—
works against the emplotment of *The Break-Up of Sri Lanka.* Wilson, how-

ever, only concludes from it that, even before independence, the Sinhalese elite signified its intention to dominate Sri Lanka. But I hope the reader is beginning to notice why I contend that, within the specific Tamil nationalist complaint against the Sinhalese, another more general argument about democracy can be discerned by the symptomatic reader.

The Tamil response to what came to be called the "Pan-Sinhala Board of Ministers" is, predictably enough in Wilson's account, greater insecurity about what decolonization might entail—especially since it looked increasingly imminent. They had a new leader now, G. G. Ponnambalam, "the dominating figure in Tamil politics in this phase . . . a skilful criminal lawyer . . . a debater without equal . . . and a flamboyant personality" (Wilson 1988, 61). This, actually, is faint praise; to Wilson, Ponnambalam is simply flamboyant, a lawyer rather than a politician, and not credited with being a good tactician, strategist, or thinker of any kind. From the perspective of my study, though, Ponnambalam's response to Senanayake's chauvinistic shenanigans must be considered brilliantly innovative: it took the form of a demand for "fifty-fifty" or equal numbers in the legislature for the representatives of the Sinhalese and the minorities.[12] This way, he argued, the non-Sinhalese would not be dominated in parliament, whereas under a system of straightforward territorial representation they have been and would continue to be, since their numbers simply wouldn't count. A political scientist might point out, in response to this or the other Ponnambalams, that enhanced representation alone wouldn't have solved the problems facing the Tamils; the majority could, for instance, always work in coalition with the representatives of one minority against those of the others. Indeed, the British governor at the time, Andrew Caldecott, had that exact response to the fifty-fifty proposal, says Wilson. However, the workability of the scheme is not my concern. The point I am interested in developing is that, in my symptomatic reading, Ponnambalam's proposal emerges as an implicit critique, from a minority perspective, of the consequences of territorial representation. Instead of seeing the Sinhalese, Tamils, Muslims, and others through the logic of arithmetic, as things to be counted, as entities whose value lies purely in their number, as—in a word—quantity, he sees them through what I have been calling the logic of geometry, or quality. Or, at least, one might read him, against the grain of Wilson's argument, as trying to do so. For, having to formulate his demands, having indeed to think within the strictures of parliamentary democracy, Ponnambalam cannot entirely avoid the trap of number. But the symptomatic reader will realize that the genius of his proposal lies in its visualization of the majority and minorities somewhat outside the restrictive logic of number. For, what "fifty-fifty" insists on is that both be seen as equal, as, therefore, neither major or minor. Even if unable to think completely outside number (fifty-fifty), Ponnambalam nevertheless complains about the tyranny of the majority: *representative democracy transforms quantity* (the majority is the greater number) *into quality* (what the majority does is right); he complains, that is, about a system that places significance, and value, in number.

Wilson, of course, cannot see this. He does, as stated before, come close, even arguing that "the Westminster-style democratic system . . . in the final instance depends on the counting of numbers" (32). But he cannot follow through on his own insight. Emplotted as it is toward an inevitable conclusion, broken promises leading to separation, his narrative cannot consider alternative understandings of the problems raised by Sri Lanka. But, given my reading of his treatment of Ramanathan, Arunachalam, and especially Ponnambalam, of the Sri Lankan Tamil response to Sinhalese nationalism, which I see as an argument about the minority predicament as such, I am now in a position to rethink what I have been calling the minority perspective. It should not, I submit, be understood either relationally or numerically; it should not be seen as the perspective of a group that is the "smaller number or part; a number which is less than half the whole number . . . a small group of people separated from the rest of the community by a difference in race, religion, language, etc." (*minority* in the *OED*),[13] for Wilson's discussion of the three Ponnambalams does not lead to such a conclusion. They are not depicted as accepting the facts of number or their minority status, as prepared to submit to the will of the majority. If they were, then they must be seen as understanding minority in numerical terms. Rather, it is the political consequence of number that they constantly draw attention to. What appears to de Silva and Sinhalese nationalism as simple, straightforward, self-evident numerical *facts* are exposed, in their arguments, their demands, their pleas, as *political positions*. They are said to have insisted, over and over again, that numerical insignificance must not and cannot be translated, as it were, into political insignificance (as happens in a system of representative democracy), which makes their position one that is opposed to representative territorial democracy, opposed to a system that places significance on number. Thus my claim: *a minority perspective is best understood not numerically or relationally, not as that of a smaller and cohesive entity that can be counted, in relation to another that is larger, but as one opposed to the placing of significance and value in number as such—one that, to phrase this differently, refuses to know its place.*

Several things follow from this, including, perhaps most predictably, another strand of the critique of identity politics. Identity, as argued in the previous chapter, is based on the proposition that objects that could always be seen as different are seen as identical, are grouped together and counted. Such counting is epistemologically grounded on arithmetic, or analogy, from a literary perspective. So, the minority perspective would be opposed to groups produced by such logic. From this it follows that the ally of the minority perspective would be the singular. This would make social science, which as seen in the last chapter cannot work without placing significance in number, the adversary of the minority perspective as I am advancing it in this study. (It should perhaps be stressed here, to avert any misunderstanding, that I do not argue that social science is opposed to sociological minorities.) I develop these claims and put this perspective to work in the next chapter, when reading Sivanandan's novel and Macintyre's play, both of which can be understood as working within the logic of geometry, as stressing the singular. But I more fully expand these lines of thought and their consequences only in the conclusion to this study; their usefulness is best made apparent there, where I argue that this rethinking could be more fruitful than other conceptions of minority, leading to a questioning of democracy itself. Right now, I should return to Wilson's narrative.

By the criteria of Arend Lijphart, whom Wilson cites, "fifty-fifty" sounds like a proposal consistent with consociationalist principles. One of the more important elements of this power-sharing scheme, as identified by Lijphart, is "mutual veto": a structured system in which the representatives of the "minority" will be able to veto legislation the representatives of the majority alone desire. The whole point of asking for equal representation, of course, is to be able have such a veto, at least structurally. Wilson, however, who cannot evaluate any act of Ponnambalam positively and is also committed to a separatist perspective on Sri Lankan history, does not read the scheme thus. But, the reader will notice, representation is to Wilson the pivot around which the "Sinhalese-Tamil dispute" revolved during colonialism; it was raised by the Ponnambalam brothers early in the twentieth century and by another Ponnambalam (no relation) later. If accepted, G. G. Ponnambalam argued, his proposal would prevent a pan-Sinhalese ministry happening again; consequently, it would make the Tamils feel more secure. The colonial office had at this stage asked the new British governor, Caldecott, to investigate if any modifications were required to the Donoughmore reforms. Ponnambalam, with the Ceylon Tamils behind him, campaigned for this radical revision of the representational system on the grounds that the Sinhalese had demonstrated themselves to be majoritarian and not willing to share power, that the Tamils should not be seen as paranoid or communal or antimodern but as having good reason to be suspicious of Senanayake and his allies, and that the Tamils were feeling increasingly insecure. In Wilson's account, the reader will notice, it is the Tamils and not the Sinhalese, the minority and not the majority, that are insecure. The Sinhalese leaders, in turn, resorted to a story de Silva has made the reader familiar with: they "justified their actions by claiming that they were endeavoring to redress an imbalance suffered . . . due to oppression by colonizing powers" (Wilson 1988, 16). The Tamils might feel insecure, but they are wrong; what is actually happening in Sri Lanka, at this moment anticipating decolonization, is that the Sinhalese are about to reclaim their rightful title to their country. The Tamils have nothing to worry about. This, I should point out, is one of those narrative units in which Wilson actually depicts the Sinhalese perspective in terms that are not dismissive or inconsistent, which even a de Silva cannot quarrel with. Unlike de Silva, who never sees the Tamil perspective, or the Muslim or UpCountry Tamil perspective for that matter, through anything but a Sinhalese nationalist lens, Wilson occasionally does produce the Sinhalese (but never the Muslim or UpCountry Tamil) thus. This does not amount to a narration of synchronic diversity—the Tamil is always the privileged perspective—but it does signify a difference between his text and de Silva's.

Caldecott, whom Wilson deems an "unimaginative governor," did not find anything alarming in the actions of Senanayake and his Sinhalese allies and "declared his total opposition to . . . [Ponnambalam's] demand" (17). To the liberal colonial imagination, of course, Ponnambalam must have appeared a communalist, if not a primordialist. Undeterred, however, as the prospect of independence loomed, Ponnambalam continued with his campaign for fifty-fifty. In Wilson's account,

> he became heir to the tradition of the unsuccessful Ceylon Tamil agitation of the 1920s; but he lacked the foresight to seize upon federalist or secessionist solutions as the way out for the Ceylon Tamils. He cannot be wholly blamed because he was in various ways captive to the numerous Ceylon Tamils with vested interests in the Sinhalese provinces, in particular those who with time came to be referred to derogatorily as the Colombo Tamils. (62)

Significantly enough, Ponnambalam and the Colombo Tamils—and not the Sinhalese—are blamed here for the Tamil leader's lack of success. Their "vested interests in the Sinhalese provinces," it is suggested, prevented, at least for a time, a more effective politics in opposition to the hegemonic ambitions of an increasingly assertive Sinhalese nationalism. That unit is more important than it might appear at first glance: it signifies how deeply *The Break-Up of Sri Lanka* is embedded within Tamil nationalist discourse. Ponnambalam "lacked the foresight to seize upon federalist or secessionist solutions as the way out for the Ceylon Tamils." That is to say, the *only* "way out" of or solution to the predicament of the Tamil that *The Break-Up of Sri Lanka* can conceive is a polity distinct from the Sinhalese. This, of course, is a separatist/nationalist position; and it makes Wilson, not just Caldecott, seem unimaginative! Ponnambalam, after all, produced an amazingly imaginative scheme. The narrative unit also allows the reader to locate the narrative moment of *The Break-Up of Sri Lanka*, something that should perhaps have been addressed sooner: it is the product of, and produces, a conjuncture in which Tamil nationalism has figured its "way out," or the end to its problems—separation from the Sinhalese. It is a conjuncture, therefore, in which Tamil nationalism, as a politico-ethico-intellectual project, can finally be called, after many years of failed negotiations with the Sinhalese state that produced nothing but broken pledges and pessimism about its future, at peace with itself and optimistic, not in the chronological sense of an imminent end to the oppression but in a logical sense of a moment in which, now in its separatist phase, it foresees or predicts a conclusion, and a happy one at that, to its long struggle. It is a moment in which Tamil nationalism has resolved, at least in theory, its contradictions not only with its oppressor, the Sinhalese nation-state, but also, as my reading will show, with its own people.[14] This conjuncture is "happy" because it sees its fate as self-determined, as opposed to being determined by, dependent upon, concessions—like federalism—begged on bended knee from the more powerful Sinhalese nationalist Sri Lankan state.

For a brief time, Ponnambalam succeeded in rallying the minority representatives around the fifty-fifty demand, which had now been amended to contain a proposal for a balanced executive branch as well as legislature. The representatives included Jayah and Arunachalam Mahadeva, son of Ponnambalam Arunachalam. Mahadeva, however, defected from the minority cause when offered a place on the board of ministers in 1942. Why did the Sinhalese hegemonists suddenly and unexpectedly become accommodative? Why didn't they maintain the exclusively Sinhalese composition of the board by electing another Sinhalese? Wilson, significantly, turns to a Sinhalese politician for an answer: "Sir John Kotelawala (prime minister, 1953–56) in an interview with this writer, said that the Pan-Sinhalese Ministry wished to diversify its ranks to signify to Britain that its members were not bent on monopolizing power for the Sinhalese"

(65). The Sinhalese, that is, were not really concerned about the minorities; they merely wished to engage in a public-relations exercise with the British, to send them a signal. This conclusion is made even stronger by the fact that, within Wilson's protocols, it is not reached by him but rather made "objective" by being advanced by a leading member of the Sinhalese elite, a former prime minister no less. Once on the board, Mahadeva, one might say, followed his father's footsteps: he tried "constructive engagement with his Sinhalese counterparts" on the question of representation. The Sinhalese wanted a fairly straightforward system of territorial representation, one that would guarantee their majority in any legislature. Mahadeva, although having abandoned his commitment to balanced representation, insisted on some weightage for the minorities. The issue of representation, again, is the terrain on which the Sinhalese and Tamils fight. Mahadeva, as the reader no doubt expects by now, like his father and uncle before him, also failed to convince his Sinhalese counterparts to listen to the fears of the Tamils; consociationalism failed again (though the reader will notice that no promises were broken this time). But Mahadeva's inability to produce results had a cost: Wilson concludes that Mahadeva "had to pay the price" for being deemed by the Tamils a "'traitor' in the demand for fifty-fifty" (69). He lost his seat in the next election, in 1947. Wilson's rhetoric here, despite the attempt to distance itself from the term "traitor," by its very mention, of course, signifies that he shares what he considers to be the popular Tamil judgment of Mahadeva; put differently, the judgmental element of the ethical level of *The Break-Up of Sri Lanka* asserts itself here and shapes this narrative unit.

The 1947 election was the result of a new constitution enacted for Sri Lanka following yet another set of colonial recommendations, known once again after the head of the commission that recommended them, as the Soulbury. Like Caldecott, this commission also rejected Ponnambalam's demand for balanced representation, looking "on it as the reimposition of communal representation in a rigid form" (70). Colonialism, despite the pan-Sinhala ministry, and an increasingly insecure minority vocal about this insecurity, was still determined to produce Ceylonese nationalists out of communalists; or, at least, that was its story. Wilson thus concludes that Ponnambalam's lack of success could be attributed to the fact that he "was fighting against heavy odds" (72). Nevertheless, Wilson also accuses the Tamil leader of being "maladroit" and failing "to provide innovative leadership" (72). Incoherence again: if the odds were stacked against Ponnambalam, then it should follow that no amount of "innovative" leadership or adroitness on his part could have succeeded in changing the course of events; but this point, while it must be noticed, since it is a contradiction in this perspective, which cannot consistently arbitrate the nexus it produces between individual agency and social forces, need not be labored. If Ponnambalam's demands were rejected by the colonial authorities, he himself was not by the Tamil people. During the 1947 election, he challenged Mahadeva, now a Senanayake ally, directly. He: "moved from his safe seat in Point Pedro to contest the premier seat in the Jaffna peninsula . . . in opposition to Mahadeva . . . and won a convincing majority" (69). This should suggest, within Wilson's own terms, that Ponnambalam, whether "captive" to Colombo Tamil "vested interests" or not, had considerable popular support in Jaffna; he wasn't, after all, elected from Colombo. To the historicist perspective, this should suggest that the Tamil voter at this moment was quite happy with nonfederalist or secessionist solutions. But Wilson is simply unable to evaluate Ponnambalam positively.[15] Despite informing his reader of Ponnambalam's electoral success, Wilson produces "fifty-fifty" as nothing more than a negotiating card and even states that, following the election in which Ponnambalam's party, the Tamil Congress (TC), won seven of the nine seats it contested in the northeast, Ponnambalam petitioned the colonial office that the Tamil people had rejected the "Soulbury Constitution" and "'in the absence of a satisfactory alternative' . . . should be granted the right of self-determination" (73). This sounds like the terminology of someone prepared to consider, or at least threaten, some form of autonomy/secession for the Tamils. It certainly contradicts that earlier statement that the TC leader lacked foresight. But Wilson judges Ponnambalam's entire record on his subsequent decision, upon independence, to join Senanayake's cabinet.

This was opposed by Ponnambalam's deputy, S. J. V. Chelvanayakam, "a man of unquestioned integrity and with an impeccable record" (76), the one who, of all the cardinal Tamil actants identified by this text, will dominate the rest of the narrative.[16] The Soulbury commissioners had recommended certain constitutional safeguards, which were enacted, prohibiting the passage of legislation deemed discriminatory of the minorities, but Chelvanayakam held that the Tamils, rather than worry about preventing prejudice in the future, had, as a matter of greater urgency, many problems to deal with in the present:

> the future of the Indian Tamils, the question of the official languages of Ceylon and the ending of state-aided colonization of the traditional homelands of the Tamil-speaking people, and indeed a national flag for

independent Ceylon . . . [It] was Chelvanayakam's contention that these should be satisfactorily resolved before the Tamil Congress could decide whether or not it should join the Senanayake government. (75)

It is very important to notice here that, except for the language question, de Silva does not recognize the other issues mentioned as a substantial source of any conflict between the Sinhalese and Tamils; he is, as stated before, able to assert that Tamil grievances have been settled only by disappearing these other concerns raised by Wilson/Chelvanayakam, concerns that, Wilson argues, were never satisfactorily resolved. As for Ponnambalam, he joined the government anyway, against his deputy's entreaties, arguing that he could best raise these issues, help his community, now after independence and in the absence of a colonial arbiter, from within the government. He advocated a new strategy of "responsive co-operation." Unimpressed, indeed deeply suspicious by now of Ponnambalam, increasingly disillusioned by the Sinhalese leadership, Chelvanayakam left the Congress and inaugurated a new party, the Federal Party (FP). Senanayake, in turn and as should be expected, did not keep his promises to Ponnambalam regarding the issues of pressing concern to the Tamils. Despite this, the TC leader maintained his alliance with Senanayake. Consequently Ponnambalam, again as the reader might expect given the example of Mahadeva, given the possibility that even *The Break-Up of Sri Lanka*'s subplots might be iterative, "paid dearly" for betraying the Tamils: in a few years, the Tamil leader's Congress would be eclipsed by Chelvanayakam's Federal Party.[17] Wilson's narrative strategy is by now becoming evident: it is iterative; wherever possible, it considers events in terms of analogy, produces identity out of discreteness, which leads him, as noticed before, to make conclusions that don't always fit. By what logic, after all, can Ponnambalam be blamed for Senanayake's broken promises? If it is the latter who broke his word, surely it should be the latter who receives narrative condemnation? But Wilson reserves his scorn for Ponnambalam and is not content to reproduce only his own evaluation of the TC leader. Given his relationship to Chelvanayakam, Wilson's opinion might not be deemed objective, so he introduces into the narrative the "verdict of political scientists and others" on the TC leader, which is characterized as "harsh though accurate" (75).[18] Betraying the Tamils, to this nationalist perspective, is something that history, as writing, must condemn.

However, Wilson's rhetoric isn't as condemnatory of the Sinhalese leaders. The cardinal Sinhalese actant whose deeds around the moment of decolonization are identified as contributing the most to the subsequent "break-up" of Sri Lanka is Senanayake, whom the text takes some care to produce both as a Sinhalese majoritarian or chauvinist and as a onetime "rebel" turned "conservative collaborator of the British" (78). Of significance here is not only his role in engineering the "Pan-Sinhala Board of Ministers" and his refusal to address minority fears about representation; the reader is also exposed to every piece of evidence that might damn the Sinhalese leader. Thus she is informed that Senanayake, with his brother Francis Richard, "started the *Sinhala Maha Sabhas* (the Great Sinhalese People's Association) in the Sinhalese villages" (9) in 1919. All that is said about this organization, which does not find mention in many Sri Lankan history books, is that it "supported Buddhist candidates as against Christians in elections"; its popularity or actual impact on Sri Lankan politics is not discussed. Senanayake's collaboration with the British is narrated in much greater detail, especially his negotiations with the British state in the 1940s to allow it to maintain military bases in postcolonial Sri Lanka in exchange for independence and his cooperation "with the British in the war effort while a great number of Indians in the neighboring subcontinent were imprisoned for their opposition" (92). Such detail is best comprehended in the light of the Sinhala nationalist claim, echoed in *Reaping the Whirlwind,* that the Tamils benefited from their collaboration with colonialism: it seeks to interrupt that argument, contest and reverse it, to produce the Sinhalese instead as the true collaborators, as the running dogs of the British. Analogy, or the narratological level, the reader would have noticed again, is slipped in here to abet the abiding/anticolonial: the comparison with the Indian anticolonial resistance is not strictly relevant to Wilson's particular claim in this unit; Sri Lankan and Indian political organizations, as de Silva could very well point out, were not allied, not working together on some common anticolonial program. It does serve, though, to add insult to insult.

Wilson also, predictably enough, details how Senanayake misled governor after British governor about his real intentions regarding the minorities—that he would respect their concerns—all the while plotting something else. Upon independence, however, Senanayake soon unveiled his true majoritarian colors. One of his first acts as prime minister was to disenfranchise the UpCountry Tamils: "At one stroke of the legislative pen nearly half the Tamil population of the island (i.e. the Indian Tamils) lost all their seven seats in the House of Representatives, and in fourteen other electorates they lost their ability to influence the outcome" (35), an act that Wilson deems broke an unwritten "compact on representation"

(37) between the two elites. Senanayake followed this by legislation depriving the UpCountry Tamils of their Sri Lankan citizenship.[19] Both deeds were justified on the grounds that these Tamils, even if many had been working in the plantations for decades, for generations if you like, could not be deemed to have a commitment to Sri Lanka since they or their parents or their grandparents were born in India. Senanayake in this account is produced as executing a well-conceived plan to further minoritize the Tamils by reducing their numbers in the legislature. The new prime minister's next act against the minorities affected not the "Indian" but the "Ceylon Tamils"; he

> set in motion the process of land settlement in the areas traditionally and politically recognized as the 'traditional homeland of the Tamil-speaking people' . . . Sinhalese from the densely populated southwest quadrant of the island were settled in the newly organized "colonization schemes" . . . Consequently, some traditional Tamil constituencies have had significant increases in their number of Sinhalese voters. (37)

Senanayake, in other words, while guaranteeing both the British and the Tamils before independence that he was sensitive to their demands and respected their most pressing concern, weighted representation in the legislature, acted promptly after independence in the opposite direction, reducing the number of Tamils who could be elected to parliament, thus reducing the capacity of the Tamil elite to influence government policy. (It should be noted in passing that this issue, which has been at the heart of Tamil politics, is never discussed by de Silva in *Reaping the Whirlwind*.) Wilson concludes from all this evidence, going back to the beginning of the twentieth century, that "the *impolitic* actions of Don Stephen Senanayake *awoke* Tamil nationalism" (38, emphasis added). From the early twentieth century, the time of the Ponnambalam brothers, to the moment of independence, the leaders of the Tamil people had tried to convince the Sinhalese leaders that a parliamentary system based on territorial representation was unsuited for Sri Lanka, that a different kind of governmental regime had to be created for the country, and that a special mechanism had to be devised to grant the minorities greater representation than their numbers allowed. From the perspective of the symptomatic reader, the complaint is that democracy of the Western kind, based on territorial representation, on finding significance in number, not simply made the minorities insignificant but structurally constituted them as minor and therefore effectively unimportant; to put it crudely, democracy actually enabled the insignificance of the minority. But not only did the Sinhalese elite not concede to greater minority representation in the period before independence—though taking care to make some noise for the benefit of the British—upon independence, they began actively to reduce Tamil representation, Tamil power, in parliament. The Tamils, remember, were always a nation; to be consistent with Wilson's metaphor, one presumes that this nation was dormant during colonialism. Senanayake's blows disturbed its slumber, opened its eyes. After detailing this story, Wilson concludes, somewhat redundantly, that the first Sri Lankan prime minister "was a Sinhalese and not a Ceylonese" (73): if the term "Ceylonese nationalist" is one without validity, of course, Senanayake could not have been otherwise. Deeming his actions "impolitic" is a surprisingly mild choice of adjective, given Wilson's claim that they virtually produced Tamil nationalism. We will return to this judgment of Senanayake. But the argument to be noticed in Wilson's evaluation of Senanayake is his identification of cause: Sinhalese indifference—it hasn't become aggression yet—produces Tamil nationalism. The Tamils were reasonable, prepared to compromise, even though they hadn't lived with the Sinhalese before British colonialism; two generations of their leaders tried to make the Sinhalese hear their case during colonialism, when all they asked for was weighted representation. The Sinhalese elite, however, led by Senanayake, was adamant, unyielding, majoritarian; they insisted on having their own way. Whenever they conceded to the demands of the Tamil elite, whenever they made promises, they broke them.

Ponnambalam, having joined Senanayake's government, had effectively become a party to these moves against his own people. His deputy Chelvanayakam—the man of integrity—who opposed these moves, felt he had no alternative but to leave Ponnambalam's Congress and establish a different organization, one with a radically new demand that changed the face of Sri Lankan politics. At this stage of his narrative, Wilson reaches a general conclusion about the growth and intensification of ethnic conflict. Being a unit of some significance, especially since this text doesn't often make general claims, it must be cited fully:

> There is an unstated law—that of escalation of demands when reconciliation between ethnic groups is delayed. The majority ethnic group's response is generally negative. If the minority ethnic groups show solidarity and inhabit contiguous territory, it becomes difficult to resist their demands. The better course then is to effect a compromise on the demands, but the general trend has been to deny concessions . . . These demands take the form of separately carved-out communal electorates,

and a measure of autonomy within a unitary or federal set-up. If these two fail, there is civil disobedience and non-violent non-cooperation from the minority ethnic leaders and their followers. If that strategy still fails to bring results, the politicized younger groups in the minority ethnic groups take up arms . . . The stages are usually of this pattern. The Indian leadership was a case in point. Timely concessions to the Muslim leaders could have avoided the creation of Pakistan. And Pakistan could in like manner have avoided the creation of Bangladesh. (39)

Analogy, the production of sameness out of difference, again demonstrates itself to be indispensable to the emplotment of this narrative. Although I'd suspect that a conventional Indian or Pakistani historian, an Ayesha Jalal for instance, might respond to this unit dismissively, arguing that "civil disobedience and non-violent non-cooperation" or, later, "politicized younger groups in the minority ethnic groups taking up arms," were not parts of the story—or record—of the Muslim Congress's agitation for Pakistan, and indeed that this is an untenable encapsulation of events before the creation of Pakistan.[20] But then, the work of analogy in social science, as argued in the previous chapter, is to produce the illusion of identity; the comparisons it makes cannot be expected to survive close inspection; or, to be more precise, the "events" compared can always be narrated or read differently by other social scientists. Besides, my argument about this unit does not concern the invalidity of analogy—which would be an absurd argument to make—but rather two other points. The first concerns the inability of *The Break-Up of Sri Lanka*, too, to narrate synchronic diversity: Wilson does not effectively present the Sinhalese nationalist perspective on its own terms, nor does he discuss in any depth the Sinhalese argument that the majority has the right to rule, and set the rules, and thus negate minority demands. He can ultimately tell only one story, the Tamil one, and that, too, from a nationalist perspective. Second, he cannot rest his case, the justification of the "escalation" of Tamil nationalist demands in response to Sinhalese "negativeness," until they became separatist, purely on the basis of the Sri Lankan example, on the fact that the Sri Lankan Tamils are oppressed by the Sinhalese. The ethical level, here, needs the disciplinary and narratological to buttress its case: it needs generality; the apparently self-evident example of two other countries in the neighboring subcontinent makes it easier for Wilson to advance his own argument that the Tamil situation in Sri Lanka has reached the point of no return, of separation, of demanding sovereignty. Gesturing toward Pakistan and Bangladesh, both states that were created out of other states and therefore successful instances of separat-ism, makes the Tamil instance both comprehensible and separation seem more plausible, persuasive, indeed possible. The response, here, if not to de Silva, is certainly to Sinhalese nationalist discourse: separatism is not produced as an extravagant demand, as the latter tends to characterize it, or even a unique happening. Indeed, this happening is granted the status of a "law," the mutation of analogy into identity, into a general principle that a Daniel Horowitz would approve of, which can predict the course of relations between *any* majority and minority. Evaluated on its own, the possibility of a separate Tamil state might sound remote, but if it hap-pened before—and in neighboring countries, at that—then it can happen again. If separatism is so general that it can be termed a law (and the pas-sive voice works to enable this) then the chances are that it *will* happen again. Like with *Reaping the Whirlwind*, analogy—a fundamental element of social science's ability to make arguments—here provides reassurance of how the plot will be resolved; the disciplinary and narratological levels work together to aid the inhabitant.

After Ponnambalam, the demands made of the Sri Lankan state by Tamil nationalism changed or, as Wilson phrases it, they "escalated." The change from "fifty-fifty" to federalism, or from representation to autono-my, need not be seen as an "escalation." Indeed, it can be comprehended as its opposite: Tamil politics did not now desire to influence the actions of the state as a whole, which it could have done with equal representa-tion in parliament, but only affect a part of it. So doing, however, would not be consistent with Wilson's "general law," with his emplotment of this story as changing Tamil demands as a consequence of consistent and ris-ing Sinhalese neglect and oppression, of blaming the Sinhalese, of iden-tifying them, in a strange denial of agency, as the cause of movement in Tamil politics. Thus, this story continues, with the emergence and then dominance of the Federal Party, Tamil (nationalist) politics moved away from the question of representation in the Sri Lankan legislature to an em-phasis on regional autonomy, from, if you like, conceiving of the Tamils as a minority to conceiving of them as a nation. The point now was not to figure out a governmental mechanism that allowed working with the Sinhalese but something that enabled a structured and secure, if amicable, distance. Autonomy, the reader might recall, was not a subject that occu-pied much of *Reaping the Whirlwind*'s narrative time: if it had, it would have conceded some legitimacy to Tamil claims about continuing discrimina-tion and would also simply disable de Silva's resolution of his plot, where-in he sees the Tamils eventually accepting Sinhalese hegemony. Thus de

Silva insists that the two cardinal issues that defined the ethnic conflict are language and education. Those are important issues to *The Break-Up of Sri Lanka*, too, but—and this cannot be stressed enough—those issues it emphasizes, and which take up the most narrative time in Wilson's text, are (weighted) representation during colonialism, then autonomy/separation in the postcolonial period. And it is the latter, the question of autonomy, that dominates the text and gets the most narrative time. Representation was a significant issue "because the Tamil voting strength in the house can, on occasion, block the passing of a measure if there is disagreement between the two [Sinhalese] parties" (36). Under a territorial system, given that no less than half the "Ceylon Tamil" population of the country lived outside the northeast, their numbers were too dispersed to elect Tamil representatives. With weighted representation this problem could be solved and Tamil politics could not only be more secure about looking after its interests, it could influence the entire Sri Lankan legislative agenda (which would, in turn, give it greater certainty about being able to secure its own interests). With weighted representation, if properly secured, a minority would not necessarily be minoritized; it may remain small in number, but this would not get translated into political significance. However, all attempts to achieve this failed, after which the focus of Tamil politics changed to a regional or protoseparatist emphasis; the demand "escalated"; Ponnambalam, the responsive co-operator, was replaced by Chelvanayakam, the federalist. Or, at least, that is the conclusion Wilson draws from his story. He can do so, however, only by forgetting some of his own evidence, for, actually, it was not Senanayake and his cabal who wrote the rules by which postcolonial Sri Lankan politics was to function, it was British colonialism—Wilson names, in particular, Donoughmore, Caldecott, and Soulbury. Even if these colonialists are produced as listening to Senanayake over Ponnambalam, seeing Sri Lanka in Sinhalese/majoritarian terms, they are also shown to have their own agency, to believe in democracy, to desire to produce Ceylonese nationalists out of subjects they perceived as communalists. Given Wilson's desire to rewrite the story in binary terms, however, with a straightforward oppressor and victim, colonialism cannot be granted a formative or determinate role in producing the conditions that enabled the subsequent conflict. My contention here is not that colonialism must be held responsible for producing the conflict, although it is possible to understand its role as constitutive; rather, my point is that Wilson cannot account for all of his evidence. He can only produce the Sri Lankan "dispute" in binary terms by effectively writing colonialism out of his plot, even if it is an integral component of his narrative. Put differently, the dominant element of *The Break-Up of Sri Lanka*'s anticolonial level is the argument that the Sinhalese and not the Tamils collaborated with colonialism; in return for this collaboration the Sinhalese were allowed, by the British, who wrote the country's constitution, to rule the country at independence. But, somehow, this does not amount to a contribution to the conflict. Wilson does not, or cannot, indict the British. In units like this, where the evidence is not sufficiently accounted for, where the emplotment does not adequately represent the story, the text deconstitutes itself.

The Federal Party was inaugurated a mere year and a half after Sri Lankan independence; it only took so long, that is, for the visionary Chelvanayakam to determine that Senanayake's majoritarianism or Sinhalese nationalism demanded a different response than Ponnambalam's "responsive co-operation"; that, in opposition to the unsuccessful strategy of cooperation or consociationalism between the elites, organization of the people might be necessary; and that Tamil demands had to be escalated. In telling the postcolonial story, the pace of the narrative slows down. Most of its units, while still summary, have elements of scene and contain much greater detail, including information that appears insignificant, if not irrelevant. For instance, the reader is told that, at the party's first convention,

> The Ceylon Tamils were *reminded* of their historic past as a separate kingdom till its conquest by the Portuguese in 1619, and that they, the Tamils, satisfied the test of nationhood on account of their "ancient" and "glorious historical past," their distinctiveness from the Sinhalese as a linguistic entity, and "their territorial habitation of definite areas which constitute over one-third of this island." (100, emphasis added)

What does the rhetorically sensitive reader, one compelled by the critique of history, make of the statement—not only in relation to its "original" assertion by the FP but in Wilson's iteration—that the Tamils had to be *"reminded* of their historic past" and that they "satisfied the test of nationhood"? (The criteria here, one might notice in passing, are language, history, and territory.) How, why, were these cardinal facts forgotten by the Tamil people? Presumably, they were forgotten in the course of the colonial encounter, beginning with the Portuguese, when it was Tamil subjugation and not past glories that defined their everyday life. But the rhetoric of the unit actually implies that history isn't simply a record, for "record" suggests a permanent inscription. However, even if it is contended that records do get lost sometimes, in at least this one instance, surely, the timing of the (re)discovery tells the reader something else, something quite significant about the operation of history. For in this instance it is incontrovertibly resurrected, by a political organization, not for disciplinary purposes but for avowedly political ones. If the FP had not sought to mobilize the Tamil people and make them start thinking of themselves not as a minority but as a nation—once dormant but now wide awake—if a political party, that is, did not have a substantial stake in invoking Tamil history, remembering or rediscovering it would not only serve no purpose, it may never have taken place. Without the demand of postcolonial politics, Wilson's text suggests (against the grain of its own narrative), Tamil history may well have remained forgotten, as it was during colonialism. History, once more, is seen to serve the interests of politics and the past to be the production, if not the fiction, of the present.

Although distinct and awake, the Tamil nation did not desire at the beginning of decolonization to separate itself completely from the Sinhalese. Rather, in its very first resolution passed in that same first convention, the Federal Party, in this argument having a metonymic relation to the nation, called

> attention to Canada, India, Switzerland and the Soviet Union as successful "multinational and multilinguistic states" which had solved their complex "problems" by the establishment of a federal system of government; it therefore stressed "the Tamil people's unchallengeable title to nationhood and proclaims their right to political autonomy and federal union with the Sinhalese." (22)

Analogy at work again: the examples of other countries provide inspiration and justification for the Tamil petition. But what is to be noticed about Wilson's narrative in this unit is the rhetoric, no longer that of a minority seeking, or begging, for concessions from the majority but of one nation demanding equal relations with another. Unlike Ponnambalam, Chelvanayakam was not about bargaining for anything; rather, he demanded the recognition of the rights of *all* Ceylon Tamils. His stance is to be seen, most significantly given the emphasis of this chapter on evaluating the ethical claims of Tamil nationalism, in his response to the predicament of the "Colombo Tamils" (I prefer, again to make visible a somewhat different object, the more inclusive term "southern Tamils"): "the enterprising Tamils," as Wilson now describes them,

> who have migrated to the seven Sinhalese provinces, developing a vested interest in staying there . . . The federal solution was a way of reconciling

the claims of the well-to-do Tamils in the seven Sinhalese provinces and the Ceylon Tamils living in their traditional homelands in the north and east. (83)

In other words, Chelvanayakam could have espoused outright separatism, "but gnawing at . . . [his] conscience all the while was fear for the fate of the Tamils in the seven Sinhalese provinces." These same Tamils were earlier deemed, in the context of Ponnambalam, only to have "vested interests" with the oppressive Sinhalese; indeed, "Colombo Tamil" is described in that narrative unit as a term of derogation. Now, in the context of Chelvanayakam, these Tamils are presented more positively as "enterprising." (What, I wonder in passing, does this make the Tamils who did not leave the northeast?) Federalism, says Wilson, allowed Chelvanayakam to emphasize his base, the "strongholds in the north and east" where the FP's "political strength lay"—given, one might add, a system of territorial representation that effectively disenfranchised southern Tamils who constituted their subjectivity as Tamil—without entirely sacrificing these other Tamils to the majoritarian ambitions of the Sinhalese. I must not just notice but stress here, and somewhat emphatically, the impress of the ethical level: Tamil nationalism is produced in this unit as a self-consciously ethical enterprise. Chelvanayakam, the reader is told, was concerned about *all* the Tamils in Sri Lanka, or, at least, all the "Ceylon Tamils." The electoral system may have enabled his party to represent only those in the northeast, but this man of integrity was not about to betray any section of the Tamil people. (However, the question of the UpCountry Tamils, most of whom reside and labor in the plantations, as Sivanandan will remind the reader in the next chapter, is not raised here.) So, at this conjuncture, the moment of decolonization, federalism is preferred to separatism, sovereignty. In Wilson's account, of course, federalism is the logical next step in the "escalation" of Tamil demands. Given the way this narrative is emplotted, in terms of that "unstated law," separatism, the ultimate escalation, would require many more broken promises, or perhaps much greater oppression, than the Tamils had yet experienced. It is a sacrifice that the attentive reader could anticipate.

That would, of course, take some years to happen, although the narrative expects it. Consequently, the FP began organizing itself. But the party did not enjoy an immediate rapport with the Tamil voter. It was unsuccessful in the first elections it contested, in 1952; even Chelvanayakam could not win his seat, despite his integrity. However, four years later, in 1956, the FP would triumphantly assert its leadership of the Tamil people, effectively crushing Ponnambalam's Congress. The reader might remember from the previous chapter that the critical issue at this election, which made S. W. R. D. Bandaranaike prime minister, was language. To de Silva, establishing Sinhalese as the sole official language of the country was a matter not only of the democratic right of the majority but of asserting the national pride of the Sinhalese masses, a necessary first step in healing the wounds of colonialism. Wilson, as might be expected, sees this issue very differently, producing it as yet another broken Sinhalese promise. Wilson's view involves connecting events from two very different moments. In 1943, during colonialism, J. R. Jayewardene, who would become president of Sri Lanka in 1978, proposed making Sinhalese the official language of the country (this motion, says Wilson, would not be binding on a future legislature). The parliament, in considering Jayewardene's exclusivist resolution, made it inclusive, amended it so that both Sinhalese and Tamil would replace English as the official languages of the country at decolonization. In supporting the amendment, Bandaranaike is cited by Wilson as an inclusivist, as calling it "necessary to bring about . . . confidence among the various communities." Wilson concludes from the passage of this resolution that, at the moment of decolonization, there was a "compact" on language like the one on representation, an understanding between the two elites "to recognize the two languages as official" (40). Other issues may have remained unsolved, but on language at least consociationalism was working. However, upon his election as prime minister in 1956, Bandaranaike, the onetime inclusivist, made Sinhalese the exclusive official language of the country. "Thus in 1956, to the despair of those Tamils who had trusted in the reliability of the Sinhalese elite, Sinhalese was enacted as the one and only official language throughout the island" (41). This statement, too, must be deemed incoherent, for, to this point in the narrative in instance after instance related by Wilson, the Sinhalese elite have done nothing but prove themselves unreliable. What else could be expected of them? On the other hand, by refusing to be critical of a Tamil elite that should have known better, the statement does signify emplotment at work: the Tamil elite must continue to believe (naively?) in the reliability of the Sinhalese, despite the mounting evidence, in order that this story can be emplotted as one of unending broken promises. Subsequently, Wilson continues, legislation was passed—in 1958, 1965, 1972, and 1978—to enhance the status of the Tamil language. These are the events de Silva points to in order to buttress his claim that the language issue was solved. But Wilson—and this must be seen as an interruption of de Silva—considers these bills a "dead letter"; their provisions, he says, were unimplemented. What matters to him is not the passage of legislation but whether or not it actually worked. Besides, "they were events after the fact and failed to repair the damaged relationship between the two communities"; consequently, the "forces of history that had been set in motion . . . [produced] an aggressive Tamil nationalism" (41, 45).

This aggression took the form of civil disobedience. Escalation again: at decolonization, the impolitic actions of Senanayake merely awoke the Tamil nation; now, eight years later, with Bandaranaike effectively granting the Tamil language lesser status than the Sinhalese, this nation, wide awake, had gotten out of bed, or mat, and was becoming active, aggressive. Unlike the charismatic Ponnambalam, whose strength was his oratory and whose politics were parliamentary, Chelvanayakam was a visionary and an organizer, inspired by Gandhi, unafraid to consider extraparliamentary agitation (as long as it stayed nonviolent). He had built "a network of local organizations . . . in the villages" (102) in preparation for "a campaign of non-violent direct action" (111), against the increasingly majoritarian government, if this were ever to become necessary. But it didn't for a while. Given the insistence with which the FP pressed its case, in July 1957, Bandaranaike and Chelvanayakam reached and signed an agreement, known as the B-C Pact, in which Bandaranaike conceded, if not exactly federalism, then significant autonomy. Regional councils were to be created in Sri Lanka, giving the Tamils control over their own affairs. In addition, the agreement promised that the status of the Tamil language was to be strengthened by legislation; the alterations of the population ratios in eastern Sri Lanka by colonization would cease. What happened next takes no guesswork, even of the most uninspired kind. As the reader should by now expect, Bandaranaike did not keep his promise: "inter-ethnic tensions and agitation organized by . . . the United National Party, and opposition from elements within the governing party led to the Pact being abrogated" (110). Bandaranaike himself, the reader will note, is not blamed; only the UNP, other members of Bandaranaike's party, and "inter-ethnic tensions" are blamed. Chelvanayakam and his allies tried hard to persuade the prime minister to change his mind, to keep his word, but failed. Finally, convinced they had no alternative, the FP used its network of local organizations and launched a nonviolent campaign of protest on 25 May 1958. "On that day and the three days following, there was widespread violence against Ceylon Tamils resident in the Sinhalese areas" (111).

This bland sentence, unexpectedly and incredibly enough, is the only statement made by *The Break-Up of Sri Lanka* about the "riots" of 1958.

Other Tamil nationalist histories of Sri Lanka, other chapters in the autobiography of Tamil nationalism, like that of Satchi Ponnambalam, connect
this to the "riots" of 1977, 1981, and 1983, thus producing the Sinhalese as
genocidal and justifying the Tamil argument for separation.[21] Why does
Wilson not take this predictable route? If the ethical level avowedly overdetermines the disciplinary in this account, if it is Sinhalese oppression
that leads to escalating Tamil demands, how might deemphasizing the
first organized attack on Tamil life and property, narratively suppressing or perhaps even hiding what, within Tamil nationalist discourse, is
deemed the most unconscionable act of Sinhalese oppression to that date,
be explained? Contemplating this confronts the reader with the question of the ethics of nationalism. It also shows Wilson to be in quite significant disagreement with the autobiography of Tamil nationalism in its
dominant manifestation, its LTTE edition. An LTTE pamphlet published
soon after July 1983 describes 1958 with very emotive rhetoric; it calls
the attacks on Tamils a "great betrayal . . . by the Sinhalese national bourgeoisie . . . [It] blew up all hopes of national harmony . . . This communal
fury that ravaged the island stained the pages of Ceylon's history with
blood. The horror and savagery perpetrated against the innocent Tamils
are indescribable."[22] In the LTTE account, "all hope" of national reconciliation was lost after 1958, just a decade after Sri Lankan independence;
indeed, any such possibility was not just lost but "blown up," or smashed
to little pieces by the fury and savagery of the Sinhala nation-state. Given
the LTTE's remarkable success since at blowing things up themselves,
this choice of phrase now seems perversely, and tragically, ironic. In its
context, of course, it is apt, abetting its contention that Sinhalese violence can only be met with Tamil counterviolence. Thus the LTTE locat-
ing the rupture between what it calls the two nations in an originary act
of Sinhalese violence makes both logical and political sense: the LTTE
document is a manifesto; it sought to mobilize the Tamils away from the
bourgeois political leadership and so must deploy such rhetoric.[23]

But Wilson does not locate the parting of ways between the Sinhalese
and the Tamils so early or in an act of violence. To him the year of the
break is 1976, and the act, again predictably enough, of the Tamil elite:
the TULF's formal call for separation in May of that year. Numerous
things took place between 1958 and 1976 to warrant this call, with the
FP experiencing—yes I know you are beginning to get bored with this—
more broken Sinhalese promises. All of them need not be reproduced here.
The most significant such event took place in 1965, when Chelvanayakam
made a deal with Senanayake's son, Dudley, who was prime minister at

the time. Similar in many respects to the agreement with Bandaranaike, except that this promised district and not regional autonomy, the D-C Pact, as it was called, was also not implemented.[24] Chelvanayakam was by now most suspicious of the Sinhalese leadership, so,

> At the time the Pact was signed . . . [he] asked Senanayake how certain he could be that he would honor his word. Senanayake replied that he had been thirty years in politics, that he had never gone back on any of his promises, and that it would be the same in the present case. But now, faced with a threatened revolt inside his own ranks, the Prime Minister invited the leaders of the F.P. and explained his difficulties to them. He offered to resign . . . [Instead] the F.P. leaders said . . . they would withdraw from his government and give it qualified support while in Opposition. (126)

The purpose of this narrative unit, this little detail, is to point out that even a Sinhalese leader who never broke his promises—presumably to the Sinhalese people—would do so to the Tamils. If a Sinhalese leader who kept his word to the Sinhalese for thirty whole years would let down the Tamils, could they trust anyone? Is the reader surprised that a parting of the ways is becoming inevitable? Despite this detail, despite Senanayake the son's pledge breaking (in his father's footsteps?), a leading member of the FP actually remained in the cabinet for three whole years afterward. Given this, one might think that Chelvanayakam, too, had to "pay dearly" for his collaboration with the perfidious Sinhalese. Surely, to the social science perspective within which Wilson writes, this must sound like an iteration of Ponnambalam's "responsive co-operation"? In which case, like Ponnambalam, surely Chelvanayakam should take the blame for the Sinhalese leader's actions? But no; Wilson does not reach such a conclusion, and, the reader is told, the Tamil voter stayed loyal to the Federal Party.

Then, in 1970, Bandaranaike's widow, Sirima, replaced Dudley Senanayake and, under her tenure, things got steadily worse. I will reproduce here just a few of the instances mentioned by Wilson. In 1971, "a system of standardization of marks was introduced for admissions to the universities . . . obviously directed against Tamil-medium students."[25] In 1972, a new constitution was enacted for the country, which "entrenched" the status of the Sinhalese language, gave the Buddhist religion special constitutional recognition, consequent to which the name of the country was changed (without, of course, the consent of the principal minority). The FP submitted its own draft federal constitution for consideration to Bandaranaike, but she ignored its concerns, refused even to consider them. The party thereafter boycotted the proceedings of the body that was drafting the constitution. Consequently, states Wilson, as at the moment of decolonization when the Tamils rejected the Soulbury constitution, the Tamils could not be considered a party to the new, post-1972 Sri Lankan social contract. And then, in 1974, came the final blow: "All these unpopular actions were brought to a head when there was a clash between the police and the public at the International Tamil Research Conference held in Jaffna in 1974; nine Tamils died and several were injured" (130). This narrative unit, by the way, is brilliantly deceptive. It suggests that the police killed those nine Tamils; but a careful reading will show that it is only a suggestion: "there was a clash between the police and the public . . . [and] nine Tamils died." The reader is not told exactly how they died, whether, indeed, the police killed them or the deaths were the consequence of some kind of accident.

Having experienced all these acts of oppression, between "1970 and 1977, a serious and well-established political party, which had consistently stood for the unity of Ceylon as a single island sovereign state, sensed a change in the mood of Tamil public opinion, and moved away from its previous stand for a united Ceylon . . . Mrs. Bandaranaike . . . was the catalyst of the concept of a separate Tamil state" (86). The emplotment here is consistent, blaming the Sinhalese for changes in Tamil political demands; but one notices again the denial of agency. The FP is not proactive but reactive; it is indeed responding to a change in Tamil opinion, but, more importantly, the response is to the actions of Sirima Bandaranaike, that is, the actions of the Sinhalese leadership. If Don Shelton Senanayake was called impolitic, Sirima Bandaranaike is deemed "catalytic." Without her, one is presumably meant to believe, there might never have been the transformation, in 1976, of the Federal Party into the Tamil United Liberation Front nor that ultimate "escalation" in Tamil demands, the call for separation. Nevertheless the question arises: given that, in this story, the Sinhalese elite always breaks its promises, how else could Bandaranaike be expected to behave? If the script, in other words, was already composed, if the individual Sinhalese actants of this text do not have effective agency, if they cannot walk out of the script that has been written for them, by what logic can they be blamed for their actions? But we need not pause too long on the question of narrative incoherence; after all, that is only to be expected by now of (nationalist) history.

The reader would have noticed that, of all the events narrated here, only two—the 1958 "riots" and the deaths in 1974—could be deemed acts of violence. Additionally, as has already been pointed out, these two events are narratively condensed instances of ellipsis (as described by

Genette); they get just a sentence each. Even the 1974 deaths, which were pivotal, brought things "to a head." How and why this precipitated a crisis Wilson does not explain. Given the emplotment of *The Break-Up of Sri Lanka*, the weight of the narrative has to fall on the many stories of broken promises. These become even more pronounced in the postcolonial period, which Wilson says he had virtual "first-hand" knowledge of given the intimacy of his access to Chelvanayakam. The second half of the text contains many instances of "scene," narrated in substantial detail, further emphasizing the relative insignificance to the emplotment of this text of what the dominant element within the autobiography Tamil nationalism deems genocidal violence. This difference can be noticed by reading a narrative unit that contributes very little, if anything at all, to *The Break-Up of Sri Lanka*'s plot, an account of a meeting between Senanayake and Chelvanayakam, an instance of summary, not scene:

> The new minority Prime Minister, Dudley Senanayake (he functioned from 20 March to 21 July 1960), wished for a meeting with Chelvanayakam, and this took place at the residence of a common friend, Sir Edward Jayetileke. I am the only survivor of those who met on that occasion . . . Senanayake requested support from Chelvanayakam, pledging that his government would do nothing prejudicial to the interests of the Tamil people. Chelvanayakam replied . . . that his party would consider supporting Senanayake only if its minimum demand—basically, the implementation of the Bandaranaike-Chelvanayakam Pact—were met. The new Prime Minister agreed to consider the matter. Chelvanayakam informed me of what passed. The Prime Minister explained that he could not do what had been requested of him because the basis of his campaign had been his declared opposition to the Pact. The discussions thus came to nothing. (121)[26]

In the context of the truly impressive quantum of detail Wilson gathers in support of his petition, this little incident sounds trivial. "Nothing," after all, came out if it. Why, then, is that unit in the narrative at all? If it does not contribute to the story, what narrative function might it perform? And what does one make of the detail within the detail—the information that this meeting took place at "the residence of a common friend, Sir Edward Jayetileke"? Jayetileke is not even of catalytic significance to the narrative; he contributes nothing at all to the plot and very little to the story (except to suggest that the Tamil nationalist Chelvanayakam had Sinhalese friends). Nothing of any importance happened as a consequence of the meeting taking place in Jayetileke's house. It could have happened anywhere, in anybody's house, or on Galle Face Green for that matter; the result, one assumes, would have been the same—nothing. Why, then, is the reader given such "futile" (in Barthes's sense) detail? Why is there such "narrative luxury . . . thereby increasing the cost of narrative information"?[27] The work of such detail, Barthes might remind one here, is to signify the real, to produce its effect: this is how things really happened. More importantly, in so doing, the narrative detail attests to the veracity of its narrator. To put this crudely: if Wilson knows even such trivial little things, if he has gone so far as to get right the little facts about where meetings took place, even though the whereness of the meetings is irrelevant, then his access to and reporting of the more central events must be correct, must, indeed, be incontrovertible. That is to say, if he is the kind of historian who gets the little details right and has access to all this information, everything else he says, about happenings where he wasn't present or wasn't a witness to, must also be true. He must have checked and rechecked his sources, must have dusted off and perused every file in the archive, must have interviewed every possible source and her second cousin, and perhaps even attended to the voices of people many miles from Jaffna before reaching his conclusions. Such copious detail, in short, seeks to establish Wilson's narrative as the true and authentic account of the "Sinhalese-Tamil dispute." Implicitly, of course, this detail consigns de Silva's text to that celebrated and no doubt overflowing trashcan of history.

In Genette's terminology, that narrative unit of the meeting that came to nothing would be an instance of "summary"; but, interestingly enough, it is closer to "scene" than summary proper. Summary is a narrative unit in which the time of the plot exceeds that of the story, in which narrative information is condensed. In scene, the time of the story and that of the narrative coincide.[28] Instances of scene, of course, are more likely to be found in fiction in units containing dialogue, particularly those that deploy the literary trope of realism. The narrativization of history does not proceed in quite such a fashion; the discourse of history seeks, generally, to summarize events, not to reproduce them in all their luxurious detail (though Barthes would remind us again, here, that history must, however occasionally, narrate detail in order to produce the effect of the real). The rhetorically sensitive reader will notice that *The Break-Up of Sri Lanka* departs from what might be called this norm: although the early part of its narrative, the moment of the Ponnambalam brothers, is mostly summary with occasional moments or units of ellipsis, about a third of the way into its story, the narrative slowly drifts toward being dominated by scene. Its description of events in the postcolonial period integrates ample detail, as noticed in the narrative unit above, and the closer the story comes to the narrator's present, the more the narrative is bedecked with detail, the more its units are scene and not summary. Not incidentally, this shift from summary to scene makes *The Break-Up of Sri Lanka* both resemble and differ from *Reaping the Whirlwind*. De Silva's narrative is predominantly summary, but its narrative emphasis, as discussed in the previous chapter, is on the present, as is Wilson's. What this signifies, of course, is that it is the present that these two nationalist texts fight over. Yes, they invoke the past, and sometimes even narrativize it. They have to; their petitions cannot be persuasive without history. But the stress, the very movement of the narrative, signifies that the object of both the texts is not to make an argument or tell a story about the past but to intervene in the present, into a debate that indeed constitutes the present, and only consequently to (re)produce the past.

The Tamil nationalist present Wilson's text produces, as stated at the beginning of this chapter, is one in which Sri Lanka is effectively broken into two. It is broken, the narratological level allows the reader to notice, not just as a consequence of recent, postcolonial Sinhalese violence against the Tamils, violence with a history of just forty or so years, but as a consequence of a much longer history dating back to colonialism, a history of broken promises one hundred years old. The adroitness of this move has to be appreciated, for it enables the narrative to resolve a fundamental problem it faces in its petition for separation. If Tamil separatism is a response to (recent) Sinhalese attempts at genocide, then it could be argued—as it has been, by Western liberal discourse—that an end to Sinhalese violence, or peace in Sri Lanka, must be accompanied by an end to separatism. A United Nations peacekeeping force or similar object can, at least in the abstract, guarantee the end of Sinhalese violence. If, however, the story is a longer one, the case for separatism and separation becomes stronger. If the Sinhalese keep breaking promises, if indeed the inability to keep its word is a constitutive element of the Sinhalese national character, or at least that of its elite, then an end to violence alone cannot end the "dispute" between the Sinhalese and the Tamils, for the only thing that the Tamil knows for certain about the Sinhalese elite, after more than a century of attempts at national reconciliation, is that it will keep making promises and keep breaking them, something the modern history of Sri Lanka demonstrates, indubitably. This is why the Tamil people, albeit with great reluctance, arrived at separation as the solution to this problem. This solution was not inevitable; things could always have been different. On the other hand, the facts seem to show that the behavior of the Sinhalese could not have been otherwise.

As said before, then, when Wilson's present changes so does his past; more precisely, when his political commitments shift, history—incredibly enough—renarrates itself to seamlessly produce this new and different present as a result of the "objective" consequences of an entirely new past. (His political commitments, and the reader may need no reminder, are to be divined from his text, not from some outside source.) This shifting of the past, of course, raises some fundamental questions about the operation of history, about its writing, and about whether it can be understood, as Wilson wants the reader to understand it, as a faithful account of what really happened or whether it is, in de Certeau's precise sense, the fiction of the present. In order to address these questions, in this section of the chapter, I examine some cardinal units in Wilson's previous text, *Politics in Sri Lanka*, in light of my reading of *The Break-Up of Sri Lanka*, to notice exactly how Wilson's account of the Sri Lankan past has changed in the latter. I do not need here to compare every unit of *The Break-Up of Sri Lanka* with a corresponding one in *Politics in Sri Lanka* to exhaustively treat the earlier narrative. Rather, looking at how a few of the "same" cardinal actants and events of the later text are depicted in the earlier is adequate to notice how exactly it abides by Sri Lanka and how it differs from *The Break-Up of Sri Lanka*. This, in turn, will enable me to consider two questions central to the study. The first concerns the revision and the authority of history and asks whether, if it can be rewritten with such a cavalier disregard for previous positions, history's authoritative claims upon the past, and more crucially the present, need not be submitted to serious and skeptical scrutiny. The second asks whether history can adjudicate the dispute between Sinhalese and Tamil nationalisms, whether, that is, the discipline can do the work the nationalisms ask of it, or if the question of peace must be addressed on an altogether different epistemological terrain.

The reader might remember that *Politics in Sri Lanka*, published in 1974, found Sinhalese Buddhists tolerant and accommodating. In *The Break-Up of Sri Lanka*, as was just seen, they are the exact opposite—intolerant, if not oppressive of the Tamils, makers of many promises they can only be relied upon to disregard. In *Politics in Sri Lanka*, the possibility of Sri Lanka "breaking up" barely merits attention; the Tamils do have some complaints against the Sinhalese, but the text anticipates them being resolved; violent "communal strife" is an exceptional happening in an otherwise peaceful and harmonious story. Sri Lanka, here, is an exemplary Third World country. Thus, *Politics in Sri Lanka*'s narrative can begin on a self-congratulatory note:

Sri Lanka was the model British crown colony that made the transition from dependence to sovereign status without rancor or violence . . . Whereas, in other societies, communal and religious strife have become endemic and more the rule, in Sri Lanka these have, with one or two exceptions . . . been kept within the bounds of constitutional agitation, and on occasion extra-parliamentary but non-violent protests. (1)

The first thing to notice about this unit is its production of Sri Lanka as a "model" colony and then a model postcolonial democracy—the narrative of political science in the pre-1983 conjuncture. The second is that this sounds very much like de Silva: while communal relations are not perfect in Sri Lanka, while there is strife between the two groups, parliamentary institutions are seen as nevertheless working. The Sinhalese Buddhists are tolerant, and this tolerance is the ethos within which Sri Lankan politics operates. The unit from *Politics in Sri Lanka* quoted earlier follows the above: "The Buddhist ethos and a continuing process of modernization even up to present times have contributed in no small measure to generate that tolerance and accommodation which are so necessary for the satisfactory functioning of parliamentary government." Due solely to the accommodative, compromising Buddhist ethos, there has been no violence—or even something as mild as rancor, for that matter. The communal problem—a matter of strife, after all, nothing very serious—will sort itself out sooner rather than later, unlike in other Third World countries, where such problems are endemic. Given such a reading of "communal" relations, *Politics in Sri Lanka* can display the Sinhalese nationalist symbol that dominates the Sri Lankan flag, the armed lion, on its book jacket as representative and commanding the allegiance of all Sri Lankans. It sees no problem, no unresolvable lack of fit between the politics and projects of the majority and the minorities. If it is less than wildly optimistic—though far from pessimistic—about the Sri Lankan future, it is only, incredibly enough, because the minority is responsible for raising alarm. For a start, the Tamils themselves are communal: "until 1956, Ceylon Tamils in positions of authority tended to prefer their compatriots in the matter of public service appointments and promotions" (Wilson 1979, 47). This has been the charge of popular Sinhalese nationalism, that Tamils in the state bureaucracy would employ only other Tamils, thus discriminating against the Sinhalese. Incidentally, this charge has never been documented in a way persuasive to social science; de Silva, for instance, does not reproduce the claim in his work. But it is a crucial signifier of *Politics in Sri Lanka's* alliance with Sinhalese nationalism that it reproduces the allegation without any supporting evidence. Indeed, in units that sound just plain astounding, given the positions held in *The Break-Up of Sri Lanka*, the earlier text strains hard to blame the Tamils for their problems:

> Sections of the Ceylon Tamil intelligentsia look on the average educated Sinhalese as being lazy and foolish. Such an extravagant and self-defeating communalism could not but produce, as it did after 1955, an equally intense communal reaction from sections of the Sinhalese intelligentsia. The deterioration of Sinhalese-Tamil relations in the years after 1956 can be largely attributed to this fact. (47)

Events after 1955, most particularly the changes in language policy and the 1958 "riots," are blamed explicitly on Tamil politics and attitudes. The Tamil "intelligentsia" patronized the Sinhalese, considered them slothful and stupid. Wilson, the careful reader will note, does not actually dissent from this opinion; he does, however, insist that it is not just communalist but—in a choice of term that resonates with de Silva—extravagantly, superabundantly so. Everyday or routine communalism might have gone unnoticed by him and the Sinhalese; the extravagant version, on the other hand, must produce a reaction, and it did. The tolerant Sinhalese, purely as a response to the Tamils, began to assert themselves. In other words, the subsequent "deterioration of Sinhalese-Tamil relations" could have been avoided if not for Tamil communalism. In *The Break-Up of Sri Lanka*, as seen above, Tamil politics is produced as defensive, as a reaction to Sinhalese actions. A similar emplotment is to be found in the LTTE's manifesto and in Satchi Ponnambalam's *Tamil Liberation Struggle*; that is why the texts rhyme, why they can be considered chapters in the autobiography of Tamil nationalism. *Politics in Sri Lanka*'s emplotment, however, is exactly opposite; it is Tamil communalism that causes the problems for the Tamils. Sinhalese communalism is described as intense, yes, but it is also a "reaction" to the Tamil. The difference between how the two texts understand the causes of Sri Lanka's "communal" problem, then, couldn't be greater or more astounding.

A similar difference can be seen in how those Tamils identified by *The Break-Up of Sri Lanka* as cardinal actants are characterized by *Politics in Sri Lanka*. Ponnambalam Ramanathan is not mentioned once, not even once, in the earlier text, despite dominating the first part of the narrative of *The Break-Up of Sri Lanka*, where he is depicted as virtually anticipating Tamil separatism. As for his brother, the following unit contains the text's single reference to him:

In 1915 the Ceylon Tamil leadership supported the Sinhalese in the Sinhalese Buddhist–Muslim riots. During 1917–19, leaders of both groups co-operated in inaugurating the Ceylon National Congress and it was a prominent Ceylon Tamil, Sir Ponnambalam Arunachalam, whom the Congress elected as its first president. Thereafter, however, differences arose over the question of ratios in communal representation between the different groups . . . The Sinhalese leadership was becoming increasingly antagonistic to the communal principle. Up to this time . . . the Ceylon Tamils often regarded themselves and the Sinhalese as the two major communities in the country, while referring to the other groups as minorities. This notion continues to die hard even to the present day and is part of the reason for the Ceylon Tamil minority not being able to adjust itself to the rapid political changes that have been taking place since 1931. (48)

Nineteen thirty-one was the date of the Donoughmore reforms—the extension of the franchise and the end to communal representation—which Ramanathan opposed. But the crucial point to note here is that Wilson blames the Tamils—in a position that, again, resonates strongly with de Silva—for not "adjusting" themselves to the political realities of postcolonial Sri Lanka, for not accepting the facts of number, for not accepting what they clearly and self-evidently are: a minority. Although de Silva's term, "majority complex," is not used here, once more, Wilson's depiction of Sri Lanka in *Politics in Sri Lanka* resonates with that of Sinhalese nationalism. Things were fine in the early part of the twentieth century. Following Tamil support for the Sinhalese after the "riots"—and one might notice in passing that a consideration of the Muslim perspective is deemed insignificant here—the two elites worked together to form a political organization. So cordial were their relations, in fact, that a Tamil was even elected to lead it. Then things fell apart over the question of representation. But, unlike *The Break-Up of Sri Lanka,* the Tamil perspective is not privileged here; indeed, it is deemed incorrect. To Wilson, the Tamils should have adjusted, come to terms with the changing realities, accepted the facts of number, realized that they are actually and only a minority, and not insisted upon enhanced representation. There isn't any sympathy in this text for what is called "communal" politics. The "same" events that would demand an ethical level to *The Break-Up of Sri Lanka* leave Wilson, here, unsympathetic to and critical of the Tamil response.

Like Arunachalam, G. G. Ponnambalam does not figure prominently in *Politics in Sri Lanka*, either. He, too, is discussed in just one unit:

Formed in 1944 under the charismatic leadership of G. G. Ponnambalam, the TC in the phase up to 1948 agitated for "balanced representation" in the legislature. After 1948 it allied itself with the UNP on the basis of "responsive co-operation" with the Sinhalese. Ponnambalam received a portfolio which he retained until 1953 when Sir John Kotelawala dismissed him. (163)

Like Arunachalam, Ponnambalam is incidental to the Sri Lankan story as produced by *Politics in Sri Lanka*. He agitated for a few years, then joined the government, after which he was forced out. His story is described rather than evaluated, insofar as the distinction is possible, in *The Break-Up of Sri Lanka*. Nothing he did really matters to this text, for the detail of his politics is given no narrative attention. The reader would notice that the question of representation emerges again, as in the unit on Arunachalam; the text cannot avoid or repress it. But the question is not seen as particularly valid nor discussed at any length. Why was "balanced representation" an issue? The text does not say. *Politics in Sri Lanka*, that is, recognizes the specificity of Tamil demands, but it deems them communal and cannot acknowledge their legitimacy. To do so would be to work against its emplotment as a story of a uniquely successful, though far from perfect, Third World democracy. In other words, *Politics in Sri Lanka* is an exemplary instance of the story of the country according to political science, the discipline that dominated academic knowledge production on Sri Lanka in the pre-1983 conjuncture. Sri Lanka was a "model" colony. In the postcolonial period, it followed this script, becoming an equally model Third World democracy. For such emplotment to be successful, Tamil politics—an extravagant response to just one or two instances of strife—must be depicted derogatorily as communalist, as a sideshow to the real story, as, in a word, minor. *Politics in Sri Lanka* is clearly not driven by the same ethical compulsions as *The Break-Up of Sri Lanka*.

This difference can be seen most clearly in *Politics in Sri Lanka*'s treatment of Chelvanayakam and the Federal Party: "The FP has been essentially a party of crisis leadership. In June 1956 it led the opposition to the Sinhala Only act and the action . . . caused a chain reaction of violence between Sinhalese and Tamils in sensitive areas throughout the island" (165). Satchi Ponnambalam's description of what he calls the "rampage" against the Tamils has already been noted; he is quite clear that the Tamils were the victims of the riots, not the cause. Wilson, though, actually produces these events as the consequence of an originary Tamil act—protests against the changes in language policy; more significantly, if anything, he does not see the Tamils as victims, either. Both sides are produced as agents here and are said to have attacked each other in a "chain of violence." On the pacts between the two sides not implemented by Bandaranaike and Dudley Senanayake, which get significant and detailed narrative attention in *The Break-Up of Sri Lanka, Politics in Sri Lanka* strives for a neutral rhetoric. Unlike the later text, this story is not emplotted as a series of broken Sinhalese promises; rather, the Sinhalese elite actually works toward an accommodation with its Tamil counterpart, but, as a consequence of Tamil communalism and Sinhalese extremism, these compromises have not worked out. The Sinhalese elite is never assigned any blame for these failures. Inspired no doubt by the tolerant spirit of Buddhism, they are the only Sri Lankan group identified in *Politics in Sri Lanka* as committed to compromise on the ethnic question, committed to producing a noncommunal country.

Thus it should not surprise the reader that *Politics in Sri Lanka* will produce Don Stephen Senanayake—by this logic, the person who turned the model colony into a model democracy—in the most positive of terms:

> Communal tensions were exacerbated during the period of the Donoughmore constitution (1931–47) because the Sinhalese desired further change and utilized the power they had obtained to improve the conditions of the Sinhalese electorates, while the minority groups, especially the Ceylon Tamils, felt neglected and "dominated" and at every stage demanded safeguards which, however, were construed by the Sinhalese reformers as impedimental to the path of self-government . . .
>
> There was one man who tried to stand above all this communal conflict and function as a conciliator . . . D. S. Senanayake, the leading conservative Sinhalese statesman. (13)

Senanayake is above communalism; unlike the rest of the Sinhalese leadership, he is no ordinary politician but a statesman. All other Sri Lankan politicians were committed only to their self-interest and advancing their own causes, but Senanayake was a conciliator, stood above pettiness, and tried to bring the entire country together. The man whose impolitic actions in *The Break-Up of Sri Lanka* awoke the Tamils to the fact of being discriminated against emerges here as a model for others to emulate. The reader will also notice that Wilson's rhetoric has the appearance of balance: he presents the Tamil perspective, then counters with the Sinhalese, and so appears to tell both sides of the story. But, of course, the perspective the narrative privileges is not hard to notice. The Tamils may have felt dominated, but their demands were "impedimental" to achieving independence, self-government. Indeed, Tamil communalism is produced here as dangerously reactionary; if conceded to, it might have actually prevented decolonization. Wilson doesn't call the Tamils collaborators with colonialism, but the implication is hard to miss. Once again, the resonances with Sri Lanka according to de Silva are strong, and utterly unexpected after reading *The Break-Up of Sri Lanka*. *Politics in Sri Lanka*, one might say, abides by Sri Lanka in a way that rhymes with de Silva's *Managing Ethnic Tensions* and *Reaping the Whirlwind*: it (re)produces the majoritarian perspective and accepts that minorities will be dominated by the majority.

Given a narrative thus emplotted, the following formulation—perhaps to be understood as a "general law"?—cannot be unexpected, either: "it is in the order of things for the major group to have the larger number of representatives" (45). This statement is made in the context of *Politics in Sri Lanka*'s discussion of caste among the Sinhalese, but it can also be read as Wilson's more general response to what he considers Tamil communalist demands for enhanced representation. Given the logic of democracy, the majority will have the greater number of representatives in any legislative body. That is not only fair, it is also just. Indeed, it is in the very order of "things," objects outside human agency that cannot therefore be contested, let alone changed. The minority must accept what that term signifies— minor, lesser, secondary, and insignificant status—and work within the framework provided by democracy, not become communal, make extravagant demands of the state and threaten the modular, exemplary nature of the country. Making communal demands can only lead to further strife or worse. But that is unlikely to happen because—yes, you guessed it—the Sinhalese are tolerant. This is *Politics in Sri Lanka*'s conclusion to its consideration of communal "tensions" in postcolonial Sri Lanka:

> In a plural society like that of contemporary Sri Lanka . . . a national consensus on basic social and political goals is hard to establish. . . .
>
> However, an overwhelming number of middle-class Ceylon Tamils in the north and east look towards the Sinhalese south . . . for economic gain and political preferment. This inhibits the development of a separatism. . . .
>
> The Sinhalese power elites are keenly aware of the need to maintain national unity. They have therefore not pushed Sinhalese Buddhist nationalism too hard so as to bring about the break-up of the nation itself. The Buddhist ethos of moderation acts here as a deterrent to extremism. (59)

The possibility of separatism is admitted into the narrative. Like that of representation, *Politics in Sri Lanka* cannot avoid it. Chelvanayakam, it is mentioned, has even raised the question in some of his political speeches.

But, given the emplotment of this narrative, such a possibility has to be denied. Tamil politics may be communal. Nevertheless, "an overwhelming number of middle-class Tamils," the vast majority, have political and economic commitments in the south, which will place a limit on what Chelvanayakam can do. More important, the Sinhalese elite is tolerant; Buddhists are accommodating, moderate, compromising. Such a conclusion, of course, couldn't be more different from that of *The Break-Up of Sri Lanka*, in which text Sri Lanka is already broken into two entities, psychologically if not territorially, purely as a consequence of uncompromising Sinhalese Buddhism and its desire to dominate the Tamils. How does the postempiricist reader account for such a drastic change in position? Can she? What does this change signify about the operation of history, as such?

A possible explanation, one that would be advanced by the conventional historian, is that Wilson is overtaken by events, by happenings after the publication of *Politics in Sri Lanka*, that made it no longer possible for him to be a silent witness to the oppression of the Tamils, and in the light of the new events, the past itself looks different. Such an explanation can legitimately account for the changes in his politics, his present, and for the presence of an avowedly ethical level in his later work. It cannot, however, account for the *subsequent* changes in the way he understands the past, the radically different historical narrative he produces in *The Break-Up of Sri Lanka*. For, if the past has already happened, objectively, then it cannot change from one narrativization to another. Some details, of course, always could—if new evidence is discovered or a new method devised that leads to the reevaluation of old evidence. But Wilson makes no such statements. He blithely renarrativizes the story of Sri Lanka he produced in *Politics in Sri Lanka* into a drastically different version in *The Break-Up of Sri Lanka*, without reference to the previous story, without accounting for how the past (history) could have changed with the present (politics)— just like de Silva did in *Reaping the Whirlwind*. Thus my contention, with de Certeau, that the past is the fiction of the present, that history is not the pure product of the disciplinary level but is overdetermined by the abiding. This has been seen in all four texts under scrutiny so far in this study: when their presents change, the pasts of both Wilson and de Silva change too. Their texts have also been seen to be incoherent, to rely on not disciplinary rigor but a variety of narrative strategies to advance their claims; thus my identification of a narratological level to the texts and my conclusion that, indeed, they deconstitute themselves. Therefore, from the perspective of the postempiricist reader, the authority of history becomes very dubious on two crucial counts. One, in this particular instance, I am convinced that history cannot provide a reliable account of the past and thus be a basis for settling the Sri Lankan dispute. Two, more generally and more importantly, following from both this study of Sri Lanka and from what I have been calling the French critique of history, I am convinced that history, as such, is a story about the present, not the past.

Disciplinary history would respond to this claim by arguing that de Silva and Wilson are just bad historians, that their work is not evidence of anything about the discipline itself but, rather, of individual scholarship. The postempiricist reader would reply that this is the canonical position and that, to her, just as there ain't no such thing as a "bad" novel, there ain't no such thing as bad history; there are only texts to be read—authorized as they are by different disciplines. That is to say, all texts are not to be understood as similar to this perspective. History, for instance, carries much greater authority than fiction, or journalism, in our disciplinary moment. Taking this position, it must also be stressed given the rampant confusion on this question, does not make such a literary critic a relativist. For she would not hold that all texts are "equal"; rather, some are more useful than others; still others, as argued in the Introduction, are deemed dangerous. Which implies, especially since I have situated myself as a leftist and have brought (I trust) that commitment to bear on my readings of de Silva and Wilson, that I am not and cannot be considered a relativist (to whom all positions are equally valid and who effectively has no politics). Nevertheless, for my claim to be persuasive that it is the discipline of history itself that is at stake here and not some individual instances of it, the defense of history after what it calls the postmodern critique or literary turn must be taken into account. For, like anthropology with respect to postcoloniality, history believes it has come to terms with the critique of objectivity. So I go now, briefly, to two recent and influential instances of such a defense, *Telling the Truth about History* by Joyce Appleby, Lynn Hunt, and Margaret Jacob and *Silencing the Past* by Michel-Rolph Trouillot.

The first is a response to what it sees as the postmodern challenge, which has shaken the discipline "down to its scientific and cultural foundations."[29] It is by no means an old-fashioned objectivist defense, dismissive of the critique; it admits some validity to postmodernist arguments, "embraces a healthy skepticism," but rejects the "cynicism and nihilism that has accompanied contemporary relativism." Such a position is the consequence either of straightforward duplicity or a truly astounding ignorance of the very same "postmodernist" texts they purport to have read. I say "purport" because Appleby et al. actually haven't read many of the writers they argue against; it is clear from their footnotes that they almost always rely on others' accounts of often difficult works. Quite apart from being something one tries to disabuse one's graduate students of, this practice makes their arguments simply unpersuasive, if not irresponsible. For, the postempiricists ("postmodernists" to Appleby et al.) that influenced my study—Barthes, Derrida, Spivak—are by no means relativist, nihilist, or cynical. But demonstrating ignorance of "postmodernism" is not my concern here, even though, given their ignorance, Appleby and company have much to be embarrassed about. What is at stake is whether or not their defense of history is compelling. This is their central thesis:

> We are emphasizing the human need for self-understanding through a *coherent narrative* of the past and the need for admittedly partial, objective explanations of how the past has worked . . . Rather than underlining the impossibility of total objectivity or completely satisfying causal explanations, we are highlighting the need for the *most objective possible explanations* as the only way to move forward, perhaps not on a straight line of progress into the future, but forward toward a more intellectually alive, democratic community, toward the kind of society in which we would like to live.[30]

This argument, of course, contradicts itself. Statements, or "truths," are either objective or they are not. They cannot be partly, or partially objective—a truly, I am constrained to observe, nonsensical category. But, again, my aim here is not to embarrass Appleby and company (they do that job too well themselves), for this unit does contain the intriguing claim that history is essential for democracy.

This takes democracy to be both a known entity and an uninterrogated, if not uninterrogatable, good. In contrast, I have been arguing in this chapter that, to the symptomatic reader, the Tamil nationalist critique of Sinhalese nationalism's defense of its actions as democratic signifies that (representative) democracy itself, in the form of majority rule, could be considered structurally oppressive to minorities. But that does not constitute an adequate response to Appleby et al. Indeed, by insisting that history has an explicitly political purpose—to produce democratic subjects—their position seems to constitute an acceptance of my claim that the abiding level overdetermines the disciplinary. This position, if correct, would make my critique of history somewhat less than interesting, if not redundant. If history has already conceded this point, why repeat it? What force would it carry? A lot, actually, because Appleby and company haven't really conceded the point. For one thing, they want to have it both ways. Unable to effectively counter the force of what they call the postmodern critique of objectivity, they *appear* to make a concession to subjectivism, to bias or partiality, but they ultimately come down upon the side of the empiricist, the objective, the verifiable (the "most objective possible explanations"). For another, the readings of Wilson and de Silva suggest that democracy itself is a contested concept. To de Silva, democracy sanctions majority rule and the majority setting the rules by which any country will function. His history, his position, implies that, uninflected by the abiding level, democracy has produced good democratic subjects—at least among the Sinhalese and Muslims in Sri Lanka—and should produce them among the intransigent Tamils, too, if only they would have a proper understanding of the Sri Lankan past. To Wilson, or rather to some of the Tamil politicians he discusses in *The Break-Up of Sri Lanka* (Ramanathan, Ponnambalam), democracy as majority rule cannot produce good citizens but leads to the domination and sometimes oppression of minorities, thus provoking their resistance to democracy itself. Furthermore, one must ask if there is such a thing as a "human need" for history. As the discipline itself admits, until the nineteenth century, until modernity, "humans" appear to have lived quite happily—or sadly or middlingly, but lived nevertheless—without history. So, quite apart from being an essentialist claim, how can this assertion be justified, coming as it does from historicists? Then, as my readings of de Silva and Wilson suggest, history itself is always contested. No reliable account of the Sri Lankan past can be deemed possible after reading them, unless one dismisses them as bad and partial—which the Appleby position cannot, once it concedes that all history is somewhat partial. For, after looking at the detail of those texts, how can one hold that a "most objective possible explanation" of what really happened in the country is possible? Surely even a junior undergraduate would realize that the narratives of Wilson and de Silva, incoherent in themselves, cannot be brought together to produce a coherent account of Sri Lankan history. If such is the case, then there is and can be no ground from which history—or the Applebys of the world—can claim that it can account for the present or produce good citizen-subjects, for the latter would require some consensus about the past. If the last two chapters have demonstrated anything, they have shown, I trust, that a reliable or truthful or unbiased account of the Sri Lankan past is indeed impossible. Wilson and de Silva, both more-than-competent trained historians, look at what empiricism would consider the same events and see quite different things, so much so that they cannot be deemed to be seeing the same events or objects in the first place. There is, quite simply, no way of reconciling the Sri Lanka according to de Silva with that according to Wilson, no way a little bit of one and a little bit of the other could be pickled together to produce a "partially objective" account of the past that might enable Sinhalese and Tamils to agree on enough detail so as to find enough common ground, literally and metaphorically, to live together as good Sri Lankan citizens. The two nationalist histories simply contradict each other too much, too often, and too fundamentally. Appleby and company might yearn to produce "coherent narratives," but when the story of any place contains the stories of more than one central subject—and the story of every place does—then producing *objective* narrative coherence out of such stories is out of the question and epistemologically inconceivable. This, of course, is a (theoretical) argument from Greimas, that history cannot narrate synchronic diversity; my readings of Sri Lankan histories simply bear out that claim.

Trouillot, for his part, attacking the theoretical critique of history, actually contends that "theories of history rarely examine in detail the concrete production of specific narratives . . . The heavier the burden of the concrete, the more likely it is to be bypassed by theory."[31] This, of course, is an empiricist position and, as argued in the Introduction, misunderstands the very work of theory (and, by the way, betrays an embarrassing ignorance of Barthes, Rancière, and others). One does not, to rehearse that argument quickly, need to be familiar with "real" dogs to conceptualize "dog." But a good part of the reason why I have spent so much attention on a detailed and perhaps overly lengthy reading of the narratives of de Silva and Wilson is precisely to anticipate and rebut this kind of argument. For the more closely one reads "concrete" histories—including Trouillot's—the more one finds, even in the most celebrated of instances and at times almost effortlessly, that they are incoherent, that they deconstitute themselves. To Trouillot, history, or the facts, matter because "collectivities experience the need to impose a test of credibility on certain events and narratives because it matters *to them* whether these events are true or false."[32] One has to ignore the critique of essentialism to concur with this statement. Even then, having read de Silva and Wilson closely, how on Earth does one decide, from where on Earth could one decide, which account of the Sri Lankan past is true? It no doubt matters to the nationalist Sinhalese that they are seen as the victims of the Sri Lankan story. But that precisely is why a problem—the lack of peace—exists in Sri Lanka in the first place: because their story is not acknowledged as true by others, despite their insistence and, despite this lack of acknowledgment, because the Sinhalese act as if it were true. The utter inadequacy of a position like Trouillot's is that it cannot provide any ground from which to rebut de Silva. Indeed, it would have to concede that de Silva and the Sinhalese nationalist collectivity might actually be correct, because they were the victims of colonialism and because they now need to tell their story—against the West. It would follow that Trouillot would have no basis to oppose the oppressive actions of Sinhalese nationalism. And then, paradoxically enough, he would also have to concede that the Tamil nationalist story, which completely contradicts the Sinhalese nationalist one, is also correct and true—because it matters to and is seen as true by another collectivity! Yes, Trouillot is not making an argument for the domination of a minority. But it is also the case that the theory of history undergirding his project must be considered, given the commitments of this study, utterly inadequate. For his response, alas, is a nationalist one, thus making it, given the distinction established in the Introduction, an anti-, not a postcolonial text. That is to say, Trouillot works within the thematic of Eurocentrism and, of course, empiricism and essentialism. Within his protocols, collectivities—unmarked subjects, products of analogy—think; they have agency; they exist as a self-evident fact (of nature?). The postempiricist, by contrast, would hold that they are produced as such and should be understood as interpellated subjects, marked and so on. Once again, then, with the work of Trouillot, an instance of surrender to Eurocentrism produces itself as resistance.

It is in this context, the inadequacy of the recent defense of history, that David Scott's intervention into the Sri Lankan debate over the status of history becomes important, intellectually and politically. Scott begins his argument with what he calls a "perverse question": "What if, at the end of 'The People of the Lion,' . . . that meticulously exhaustive exercise in historical reconstruction, . . . the author [R. A. L. H. Gunawardana] had written—as though tossing it all aside, or in our face—'But so what? What does this history really prove?'"[33] Gunawardana's justifiably famous and influential essay is a historicist rebuttal of the Sinhalese nationalist account of the ancient past, specifically of the argument that a Sinhalese (nationalist) identity can be seen in Sri Lanka for centuries. In demonstrating otherwise, Gunawardana isn't just content to make an exclusively academic point. He is all too aware that Sinhalese nationalism uses the past to make a claim upon the present. As Scott puts it, such a use of the past is "central to the apparatus of Sinhala ideology . . . that continuity of an inaugural and authentic community informs and indeed serves to guarantee the legitimacy of political claims in the present."[34] An instance of this was seen, in the last chapter, in de Silva (even if de Silva denied the political implications of his "objective" history). Gunawardana's response to such a position is to challenge the Sinhalese nationalist account of the past, to demonstrate that the historical evidence does not suggest a continuity of identity and that the term "Sinhala" did not come to describe a whole mass of people—as opposed to just the royalty and aristocracy—until the nineteenth century, and that nationalism, as most of its non-nationalist contemporary students are convinced and have argued in many a study, is a purely modern phenomenon: "It was during the period of colonial rule that the Sinhala consciousness underwent a radical transformation and began to assume its current form. In developing their group conscious-ness the social classes created by colonial rule drew as much on European thought as on their past traditions."[35] The implication of this position is clear, even if Gunawardana himself did not, deliberately perhaps, draw any political conclusions as a consequence of his study: if the Sinhalese nationalist argument about the past is demonstrably incorrect, then its claims upon the present—in short, hegemonizing Sri Lanka—which are explicitly grounded upon that specific account of the past, become de-monstrably invalid, untenable, and unfounded.

Gunawardana's paper, Scott notes, produced celebration in the Sri Lankan (academic) left. History, now, was clearly on the side of the non-communalists or antinationalists. Sinhalese nationalism, whose interpre-tation of the past had been proved incorrect, would have no option but to surrender its claims, not just about the past but upon the present, and would have to give up its hegemonic project and go away, hide, retire. However—surprise, surprise—this did not happen. Indeed, a few years later, K. N. O. Dharmadasa, a protégé of de Silva, replied to Gunawardana at some length, claiming that the latter had gotten his facts wrong, mis-read the evidence, ignored inconvenient details, repressed texts that contradicted him, and so on, and that, upon close and proper inspection, the facts actually proved the Sinhalese nationalist account to be correct. Unlike Gunawardana, a historian, Dharmadasa was a linguist by training and so produced himself as a far more competent reader of the ancient texts. He even contended, with a straight face, that he was an objective scholar and not interested in the political consequences of his arguments. He merely looked at the evidence, objectively, patiently, without a hid-den agenda—and came to the most academically proper conclusions. If his work actually had political implications, so be it; he would not be the one to advance them. This, argues Scott persuasively, effectively left Gunawardana with no epistemological ground to reply from. Yes, he could always say that it was Dharmadasa who actually got things wrong, marshal an army of linguists on his side, and so on. But one could then only expect that Dharmadasa would reply in kind, with different facts. To Scott, even though he produces himself as sympathetic to Gunawardana's position, the problem here is what the two scholars, although poles apart politically, have in common intellectually: they both hold "that a politics of the present can be wagered on a reconstruction of what community might have been in the past,"[36] that, in short, the past determines the present and history determines politics. But Sri Lankan history, to Scott, cannot do that because it will always be contested: a Gunawardana by a Dharmadasa or a de Silva by a Wilson. Thus my contention, with Scott, that another basis must be found for politics. Reading the Sri Lankan debate together with the French critique of history—Scott's own inspiration is Jean-Luc Nancy, not any of the writers I have mobilized—does not allow otherwise.

Scott's conclusion from the above is that history must be "dehistoricized," the story of the past disconnected from the politics of the present.[37] The commitment to peace in Sri Lanka demands nothing less than that history, in this instance, remain a purely academic exercise and make no claims on community, as he puts it. (Peace, of course, can also be conceptualized, and usually is, as a state of relations between communities.) To phrase this differently, Scott draws no theoretical conclusions about history from examining the exchange between Gunawardana and Dharmadasa. He finds, that is, no reason to quarrel with the discipline itself.[38] ("My argument is *not* that historicist conceptions of history are *always* irrelevant to the strategic problem of disarming nationalist discourse. My argument has rather to do with the question of how to gauge what kind of historiographical strategy will be most adequate to the target to be addressed.")[39] Keeping aside the question of whether history can ever be nonhistoricist, whether it can ever be conceptualized without a relation to some (notion of) community, and the implicit antitheoreticism of this position, which is grounded upon the strategic, I find Scott's to be too timid a response, both to Sri Lanka and to the career of the discipline. I think, rather, given the readings of Sinhalese and Tamil nationalist histories, which were shown to deconstitute themselves, and given also what I have been calling the French critique of history, the inevitable conclusion that stares one in the face must not be just the dehistoricizing of history but, as I have been suggesting from the beginning of this study, its de*authorizing*. If history, the discipline, is allowed to continue to have an authoritative claim upon the past, it will inevitably make a claim upon the present, which is why it needs to be deauthorized, made impossible. For history, even in the hands of its trendiest current practitioners, whether called Trouillot or Ginsberg or Chakrabarty, is predicated on the possibility of an accurate recreation, representation, or narrativization of an object called the past. To the postempiricist, such a possibility is out of the question. If this was all history did—produce stories of the past—one would not need to be very concerned about it or seek to deauthorize it. One could call the stories empiricist and proceed to ignore them, or enjoy them if well crafted, use the paper to wrap fish, or whatever. Unlike fiction, however, the stories of history don't enable such a response, because they are authoritative, taken to be true, as bearing some relationship to the real. Because, as Foucault keeps reminding one, ours is the age of history. Because the career of the discipline, which emerged with colonialism and, like anthropology, was an intimate accomplice of Eurocentrism. One only has to browse through Hegel's *Philosophy of History* to realize that.

Conclusion

It is of critical significance to this study to stress that, while Tamil nationalism, in calling for separation, may have announced a desire for a complete break between the Sinhalese and Tamil *nations*, it did not announce a call for such a break between the two *peoples*. Noticing this is not a matter of mere semantics, of quibbling over words. No postempiricist can hold such a position. Rather, it brings me to my claim that reading carefully might actually help nuance, if not influence more substantially, a leftist politics, that it might help reconceptualize the question of peace in Sri Lanka. To Wilson, the earliest instance of organized Tamil politics demanding separation, what he calls the TULF's "Pannakam Resolution," "was significant because for the first time the Ceylon Tamils had decided to sever their links with the Ceylon Tamils living outside the boundaries of the suggested new state" (Wilson 1988, 89). The rhetoric of this unit is noteworthy because it contains a slip: what is important to Wilson is that Ceylon Tamils, here, "sever their links" not with the Sinhalese—that, presumably, goes without saying—but with *other Ceylon Tamils*. Wilson calls the "severed" group, consistently throughout his narrative, "Colombo Tamils." In this unit, they are referred to as "Ceylon Tamils." What does this mistake—which may not be one—signify to the rhetorically sensitive reader? In a later statement, Wilson would reformulate this position, correct himself as it were:

> At the political level, the concept of "the Jaffna [Tamil] man" and the "Batticaloa [Tamil] man" is no longer of relevance . . . [Wilson is writing of the mid-1970s.] The two identities have realized that their merging is

essential for the protection of the Ceylon Tamil identity. In the process
it has become necessary to write off the "Colombo [read southern Tamil] man." The
"Colombo man" has one of two alternatives, either to remain in Colombo
and survive, facing all the uncertainties of an unpredictable future, or return to the homeland and start life anew.[40]

A sociologist might respond to this with the statement that emigration
was also an option to the southern Tamil, one exercised in huge numbers
to Europe, Australia, and North America, particularly after 1983. An east-
erner might insist that the singularity of what Wilson terms the Batticaloa
identity was never lost, never submerged in a pan-Tamil one. But the point
to notice is that, to Wilson, Tamil nationalism "wrote off," or excluded,
some Tamils from its project in the mid-1970s. Despite making its case
for separation from the Sri Lankan state on the grounds that it oppresses
the Tamils, all Tamils, indiscriminately, this same nationalism refuses to
include in its project, or to protect from the oppression of the Sinhalese
nationalist state, some Sri Lankan Tamils. If they are othered as "Colombo
Tamils" in the later formulation, the statement in *The Break-Up of Sri Lanka*
signifies, in my reading, a confession that Tamil nationalism is aware of its
failure to include in its project, bring under its protection, all those whom
it considers it must. If a "member" of a nation, or a subject interpellated
as such by nationalism, could be termed a national, then what Wilson is
arguing in *The Break-Up of Sri Lanka* is that the Tamil "people" who reside
in southern Sri Lanka could make themselves nationals, in my terms, only
by shifting their residence to the northeast. Otherwise, they would face
"all the uncertainties of an unpredictable future." Except that Tamil nationalism has already predicted this fate: continued oppression, perhaps
even genocide. It is this very prediction that provides the grounds and
justification for separation in the first place. Despite this, it will refuse to
protect these Tamils, categorized by Wilson as facing an uncertain fate
and by the LTTE as facing genocide.[41]

What does this say about the ethics, and the politics, of Tamil nationalism, of its adequacy as an ethical response to hegemonic, oppressive,
Sinhalese nationalism? Wilson, who has no ethical quarrel with this happening, would insist that Tamil politics, given a history of broken Sinhalese
promises and acts of oppression, had no alternative but to separate and
that the "severed" or "written off" Colombo Tamils could always shift their
residence and save themselves, could, in other words, take responsibility
for their own futures. I prefer to read this, however, as signifying a fundamental flaw in the project not only of Tamil separatism but of *all* national-

ism, not just of the postcolonial variety. Nationalism—and Neil Lazarus should know this—presumes a homogenous territory occupied by its nationals and makes its case to the world on such a basis. One could make an empiricist response to this, that such is never the case, that a north-south divide could be found even in the Maldive Islands. Or, one could turn to the very texts of nationalism that admit, upon close scrutiny, that the territory identified as belonging to the nation is not homogenous. Fanon himself famously—or was it infamously?—declared that decolonization "unifies . . . people by the radical decision to remove from it its heterogeneity."[42] Nationalism, in other words, and there really is no other way to put this, is hostile to difference; it would deny difference when it can; repress it when it can't. Thus my theoretical, not just political, hostility to it. In the Tamil instance, as we saw, the Muslims are said to form a significant component of the population of northeastern Sri Lanka—but they are denied political community on the basis of difference. Besides which, all the Tamil "people" Tamil nationalism identifies as its nationals, potential or actual, are said to not reside exclusively in this territory, either. Both these groups present problems for Tamil nationalism in its separatist moment, problems it seeks to solve by effectively expelling the southern Tamil from its project and trying to assimilate the Muslim under the category "Tamil-speaking person." If the southern Tamil refuses to migrate, Tamil nationalism will stop worrying about her, write her off. If the Muslim refuses to be interpellated, she would face minoritization (or, de Silva would insist, ethnic cleansing). It is cortical to this study to note that Wilson has no ethical quarrel with either such happening. He has, indeed, no ethical objection to minoritization as such, just to such categorization, treatment, being meted out to the Tamils and only the Tamils. I cannot think of a starker instance of the exclusiveness of nationalism, of its being a structure in dominance, of why the leftist, finding it therefore an inadequate response to Sinhalese nationalism, must be opposed to it.

In being exclusivist, Tamil nationalism rhymes with its Sinhalese counterpart. The ideal social imagined by both is predicated upon finding significance in number and would consist of a dominant majority and dominated minorities. Such a conception, of course, cannot coincide with this study's working notion of peace, if peace is understood to bring an end to domination. It was in opposition to the Sinhalese nationalist conception of the ideal Sri Lankan social, one predicated upon the domination of the minorities by the majority, that Tamil nationalism made its case. Its response was to reproduce the structural logic of domination, to think within the thematic of nationalism, if you like, merely reversing the problematic. All it desires is to make itself the dominant. Since the leftist is opposed to domination as such, my contention is that alternative forms of the social, of community, must be conceived if a truly peaceful Sri Lanka other than that offered by Tamil nationalism is to be imagined. For the latter, alas, is an inadequate response to the truly vile career of Sinhalese nationalism. While producing itself as the solution to the problem of peace, as the very definition of peace, it has only made matters worse. Within Nietzsche's metaphor, the leftist must observe that Tamil nationalism produced itself as the doctor, the cure, the good guy, but has administered a poison, a toxin, and is a killer. For this reason Tamil nationalism itself—and not some particular incarnation of it, as in the LTTE—must be opposed by the leftist.

What, to the Leftist, Is a Good Story?

Two Fictional Critiques of Nationalism

> Art is not a mirror held up to reality but a hammer with which to shape it.
> —Bertolt Brecht

Learning from Literature

First, some brutal summaries of the French critique of history that perhaps belong in a previous chapter but could also serve as an introduction to this one. To Foucault (1973), history is not the working out of an objective process that the discipline merely reflects but the ground of, that which enables, the modern episteme. Take for instance, biology, a historical discipline if there ever was one: since its object is understood to change through time, it would be impossible without this ground (arche). To Althusser (1997), radically rereading Marx, the historicist notion of time as single/homogenous and continuous is vulgar and empiricist, cannot account for difference or heterogeneity (Greimas would say it cannot narrate synchronic diversity), and so is unpersuasive. Time, too, emerged with modernity, as one of its epistemological accomplices: homogenous time, of course, works very well with the homogenous or unmarked subject of the enlightenment. To Barthes (1986), history is the effect of (realist) narrative, or the narratological level—a trick, if you like, of language—and not the real unmediatedly manifesting itself through language. Thus his critique of the "referential illusion." To Rancière (1994), history relies more on language, on literary tropes, than it is prepared to admit. The discipline can only function, pretend it reflects the real, by repressing this reliance, so it must, he insists, be understood as a poetics. It can only save itself, give itself a future, by emphasizing its poetic level. To de Certeau (1988), again, history is not the real narrating itself but an "operation," a combination of place (understood noncartographically as a matter of institutions and disciplinary questions), procedures (authorized by a discipline), and writing (the production of texts). And to Derrida (1982), history "convey[s] the motif of a final repression of difference." To say "this is how things happened" is to effectively disable other readings. Derrida, of course, also critiqued the notions of event and context. The work of these writers taken together, while not always coinciding, nevertheless denaturalizes the discipline; it becomes impossible, if one thinks through their arguments carefully and patiently, to accept the self-representation of history as an innocent—more or less—account of the real. Taken together, their work implies, to put it quite simply, that since we didn't always have history, since it is only as recent as modernity, a world without history could—and perhaps should—be imagined, too. If this study, after an examination of history's Sri Lankan career and readings of Tamil and Sinhalese nationalist histories, concludes that history cannot save us and that, to be somewhat schematic here, there is no political basis for holding so, then what I have been calling the French critique suggests that history not only cannot but should not save us and that, to the postempiricist, there is no epistemological basis for holding so.

For this critique has taken apart every single foundational category of the discipline. With regard to its object, it has asked two sets of searching questions. One: how, with any sort of epistemological rigor, can the past be distinguished from the present? When can the past, with any sense of assurance, be said to begin—or end? Some decades ago? Yesterday? At the end of this sentence? Two: why was this object, the past, not necessary before modernity? Chronicle, after all, worked very well without distinguishing past from present. With regard to its subject: the critique of the sovereign subject, to be found on the very first page of Postempiricism 101, as it were, is too well known to be rehearsed here. And, as Hayden White might remind one, narrative history cannot proceed without a central subject (whereas chronicle did not have one). Even the most radical social history simply replaces one subject, the elitist "great" individual, with another, a collective and usually oppressed or subaltern one. The notion of the subject, as such, is not put into question by social history, which makes it—like its cousin, dogmatic Marxism—politically radical but epistemologically conservative, because it works within the episteme of the enlightenment and Eurocentrism even though it may critique colonialism. In other words, social history is yet another surrender to Eurocentrism producing itself as resistance. With regard to the form of history, narrative, and its guarantee that it represents the real, the referential illusion has already been mentioned. Indeed, my commitment to postempiricism follows from this. And then there is de Certeau's powerful argument that the discipline itself emerged, in the early nineteenth century, to enable the nation (and that the nation, in turn, enabled history). Nationalism is impossible to conceive without a central subject (the nation) having a real/verifiable and continuous story through time. It follows that the critique of nationalism necessarily implies the critique of history (and vice versa). After the French critique of history, then, nobody with a commitment to postempiricism can or should, to put it crudely, take the discipline very seriously or find it enabling even for strictly political/strategic purposes. Appleby and company, as discussed in chapter 3, can only do so by effectively ignoring the fundamental epistemological questions posed above.

Where, then, does this conclusion leave the leftist committed to peace in Sri Lanka? She could, of course, turn to those other conventional alternatives, political science or constitutional law. But, as suggested in the Conclusion to this study, those disciplines are simply unimaginative, don't take any risks; indeed they take too much for granted and accept too much as known. They are as much a part of the problem, if you like, as history, even if peace, in an institutional sense, would be impossible without them. Literature, on the other hand, being unverifiable, is not so constrained. This is not to argue that, in the Sri Lankan context, literature has always been politically correct, as it were, that it has been uncontaminated by nationalism. Of course not. But, understood (to keep within that conceit) as a verb and not a noun, *some* fictional texts do offer the patient reader an alternative to history, alternative ways of conceptualizing peace—if and only if this reader is prepared to sift through them carefully, relate them to the Sri Lankan debate, see how they are produced by it and seek in turn to shape it, pay attention to the detail and not just emphasize the aesthetic and enjoy the stories or read just for the plot and character. Such alternatives don't just lie there, inherent in the text. They can be noticed, put to work, made an accomplice of the leftist only if she is prepared to read actively, perhaps even aggressively. Reading understood as intervention, as opposed to interpretation, demands this. What follows, then, are some interventionist, perhaps even instrumental, readings of two literary texts. They help me interfere with the projects of empiricism, history, and nationalism.[1]

Gayatri Spivak, as cited in the Introduction, argues that "training in literary reading is a training to learn from the singular and unverifiable." But what exactly does it mean that the literary text might be comprehended thus? What is it to learn from the singular and unverifiable? To make the case as simply as possible, to learn from the singular is not to need several instances of objects deemed analogous in order to make conclusions or find meaning; that is, it is not to place significance in number or the logic of arithmetic. That is the method—of course—of social science. Rather, it is the conviction of this study that one could put to most useful work singular narrative moments, which cannot or should not be deemed analogous but which operate, if you like, within the logic of geometry. And what of the term "singular" itself? Although more sophisticated conceptions of singularity are available, my understanding finds it synonymous with "rhyme" or, in Blake's delightful formulation, an "original derivation."[2] The term is useful because, for a start, it enables the conceptualization of a *relation of sameness and difference* between two objects *simultaneously*, as opposed to the binary logic that allows one to see two objects as either identical/similar or as different/opposed, as taking their sense against each other. In other words it implies, or at least can be productively deployed toward, a critique of essentialist understandings of identity. For, working with the singular would be to hold that no two things could be entirely identical. Singularity, then, is not and could not be synonymous with uniqueness or originality; indeed, it is categorically opposed to these notions and other allied ones like "purity" and even some of their alleged antonyms like "hybridity."[3] It follows that the concept of singularity couldn't find much purchase in social science, for, as argued in chapter 1, if social science is impossible without analogy, without emphasizing the similar at the cost of difference, and if it must find significance exclusively in number, in things it categorizes or pigeonholes together and proceeds to count, then reading with an emphasis on the singular, or even the minor, is something social science cannot do; indeed, it draws attention to things that social science must ignore in order to produce knowledge, to the limit of that way of knowing.

This point might be a little easier to establish if, rather than citing

Wilson or de Silva again, a convenient work of social science were used here to buttress the argument of the last two chapters. What follows is from a college economics textbook:

> In both the natural and social sciences, models based on simplified and idealized circumstances have found many, many, uses. Their usefulness depends on whether or not they result in models that are powerful and accurate.
>
> There are a number of important reasons why economists, like other scientists, use models. One is that the real world is so complex that it is necessary to simplify and abstract if any progress is to be made . . . The trick is to construct a model in such a way that *irrelevant and unimportant* considerations and variables are neglected . . . [4]

This whole argument turns on the natural and social sciences—as opposed, I suppose, to the humanities—being defined as useful. So, the first questions that arise in response to this, almost intuitively, are: Useful to whom or what? On what grounds is progress defined? How is the distinction made between the relevant and the irrelevant, the important and the insignificant? More significantly, though, this textual unit, when examined closely, turns out to be extraordinarily self-contradictory. Social science, here, actually admits an inability to handle complexity. This, apparently, is no big deal; because it can and will—shame where is thy blush, Hamlet might interject at this point—simplify, abridge, even idealize,[5] while in the same breath conceding that to do so is to be untrue to the real. My intuitive response to this is "wow!" The real world is complex, but social science cannot reproduce its complexity, so—and this resonates with Horowitz, as cited in chapter 1—it will simplify but still produce itself as accurate (and powerful), while knowing that such "accuracy" is untrue![6] I say again, wow! And here's the rub: in a superbly revealing choice of term, the entire enterprise is called a "trick," a ruse, a deception. The hoax is nevertheless produced as powerful and accurate. Need I add, at this point, that I rest my case?[7] In contrast to such a mode of apprehending the social, reading with an emphasis on the singular might be described, in a certain sense, as seeking to learn from that which appears, to this more powerful mode, irrelevant and unimportant. For the postcolonial knows only too well that what is often deemed irrelevant and unimportant to these disciplines is the different, the subaltern, the minority, the argument that lacks credence and significance because it is deemed to lack the force authorized by number. In short, then, usefulness, to social science, lies in quantity, the logic of arithmetic. The usefulness of reading differently—and, yes, my claim again is that reading is a practice that might well have its own uses—with an emphasis on the geometric or quality will, I hope, be made evident in the rest of this chapter.

As for the unverifiable, it means, or might be conceptualized as, the product of the imagination, not the archive or the field; it is something outside the reach of empiricism.[8] The unverifiable is a concept, then, that makes possible readings, arguments, positions—and literature makes arguments, takes positions, intervenes within the social, just not using the protocols of analytic intellectual production—that cannot be settled on the basis of true/false or verisimilitude. The unverifiable is a concept that social science, even of the interpretive kind, cannot relate to, for, as was seen with Clifford and Daniel, even the interpretive turn in anthropology cannot escape its dependence on empiricism. Rather, the unverifiable enables arguments and positions that become persuasive or, yes, useful as a consequence of the (interventionary) reader's *political and ethical judgment*, as a consequence not of an act of agency but of reading, which demands a patient and responsible relation to the written. This point might be easier to take if I cited one of my favorite literary moments. In Bapsi Sidhwa's enormously complicated and quite brilliant novel *Ice-candy-man* (published in the United States as *Cracking India*), which is, among many other things, a feminist critique of nationalism, the narrator, Lenny Sethi, meets Mohandas Karamchand Gandhi early in the narrative. She describes him as: "small, dark, shriveled, old." She had expected something else of this great leader, but he appeared "just like Hari, our gardener, except he has a disgruntled, disgusted, and irritable look."[9] Historians would insist that the first statement is verifiable, even though the fictional Lenny never met the mahatma; all that would be required for proof is a photograph or eyewitness account. There might be some debate over "shriveled," but not over the other adjectives. The fact that all those terms are relative would, of course, be ignored. The second statement, however, is outside the reach of true/false, for the existence of Hari the gardener cannot be verified. He is a fictional entity imagined by another fictional entity, the narrator. Could something be learned from this comparison, or should it be passed over as an insignificant narrative unit, an extra detail in a long and complicated novel? After all, Hari is just a catalytic actant; he does not get much narrative time. But the responsible reader must be able to account for every narrative unit, shouldn't she, even the most apparently insignificant? So, how does she decide?

By following the logic of the argument. In that unit, Gandhi is brought down to size, as it were, by Sidhwa (or is it Sethi?); the leader of an anticolonial resistance movement, one with an extraordinary presence in post-colonial studies, is compared to a mere gardener. Sounds perverse.[10] The analogy, however, is consistent and makes sense: Gandhi, too, tends land, although in his case not a small plot but a huge country, as history might point out. This would suggest, then, that the text contains some kind of critique of Gandhi, at the very least a demystification of the Indian leader, that the reader should be on the lookout for. Later in the same narrative unit this analogy becomes clearer; Gandhi's eyes are called cold, with "*ice* lurking deep beneath the hypnotic and dynamic femininity of . . . [his] non-violent exterior." This is a paratactic reference to the actant from whom the text gets its title and through whose figure and actions much of the plot is staged: the unnamed *ice*-candy-man, the Indian nationalist turned Pakistani nationalist. Toward the end of the narrative, after what nationalist history would identify as an event called partition, he abducts and rapes a "Hindu" woman in the name of (the patriarchal) nation, national honor, and revenge. By making such a reference, Sidhwa doesn't so much crudely accuse the avowedly nonviolent Gandhi of complicity with (nationalist) rape. Rather, in a move that Lazarus would disapprove, she asks the reader, who must make the connection herself between Gandhi and the Pakistani nationalist, to consider the possibility of conceptualizing nationalism itself as a profoundly and often violently heteronormative masculinist project, even when—especially when—it produces itself as nonviolent and feminized. For, the informed reader would know, and the patient reader would find out that, among other things, although Gandhi asked men to be in touch, as they say in the United States, with their feminine side, to make cloth for instance, he effectively excluded women from participating, except in the most minor of roles, in his movement. They were prohibited from having too public a role in the resistance and were denied access to the public sphere.[11] Gandhi did not, of course, condone rape, but he did understand nationalist resistance as an essentially masculine enterprise. The novel, then, precisely because it is unverifiable, can bring unlikely things together and ask the reader to consider whether Gandhi and the fictional ice-candy-man rhyme. It can ask the reader whether Indian and Pakistani nationalisms, ostensibly so different because one is famously anticolonial and the other apparently collaborationist, can be conceptualized together. There is much to be learned from this narrative unit, not just about Gandhi or the masculinity of nationalism but also about reading patiently and abiding by. For, in order to make sense of what might at first appear a trivial analogy, an insignificant narrative unit, many things must be known: the stories of Gandhi and

Jinnah, the autobiography of Indian nationalism, the critique of nationalism, feminism on nationalism, rape, and so on.

Unverifiability, then, is a structural, constitutive element of literature. Consequently, the postempiricist reader would hold that every literary text must be thus understood. However, it does not follow from this position that one learns in quite the same way from every single novel, play, or poem. What the colonial novel has to teach, for instance, would be quite different from what the postcolonial or the feminist novel might contain. Having read two colonial novels, *Heart of Darkness* and *Kim*, somewhat carefully, what I find there is not universal stories, not a journey into the darkness at the heart of every human in the Conrad novel or an innocent adventure novel in the case of *Kim*, but fictional instantiations of colonial discourse. To the theory of textuality, these are not the original works of great writers but inseparable, in content though not necessarily in form, from that larger discourse called colonial. This does not imply that these two novels and others of the same texture must, consequently, be damned and ignored by the postcolonial reader (the Achebe position, as it were). Holding so, although tempting—*Heart of Darkness* is at the top of my fantasy list of books to be burned publicly as a purely symbolic act, as is some book, any book, by de Silva—would, actually, be irresponsible. Such books demonstrate, albeit very differently, how literature could be, and often was, the accomplice of anthropology and how profoundly it helped colonialism in the project of making other. This is a relation, a dependence, an interdependence between disciplines that must be exposed at every turn by the postcolonial reader, the antidisciplinary reader, until it becomes axiomatic. Indeed, I would insist that a postcolonial reading of texts such as *Heart of Darkness* and *Kim* must be considered indispensable to any literary scholar, whose training would be inadequate, if not disingenuous, without a knowledge of the modern (that is to say the recent) and what must be termed the racist career, the colonial emergence, of her discipline.

For, if postcoloniality means finishing the critique of Eurocentrism, then it must put into question not only obviously tainted—I am tempted to say criminal—disciplines like anthropology but literature, too, which might turn out to be deeply implicated with colonialism. The term "literature" itself, as is not well enough known, is a recent emergence. The *OED*, to cite perhaps the most authoritative source, is quite clear that "literature," in the sense the discipline deploys it, did not come into use before the nineteenth century. (That is to say, whatever it was he thought he was doing, Shakespeare could not have thought, or known, that he was writ-

ing literature. For the discipline to function this knowledge must be repressed; students, whether in high or graduate school, must not be asked
to contemplate its consequences.) Which raises the cortical question:
why did the term emerge in the early nineteenth century? Why was a
new term necessary to classify and categorize, to conceptualize anew, an
old set of writings? What work did this new term do? Whose interests did
it serve? Terry Eagleton has argued, citing Matthew Arnold, that it was an
instrument in the hands of the ruling classes to interpellate the working
classes into Englishness; literature, to him, is ideology.[12] The postcolonial
reader, without quarreling too much with this formulation, even though it
contains a most crude understanding of ideology, would remind Eagleton
of Gauri Viswanathan, who has pointed out that English literature was
taught in India well before it was taught in England and that, even if the
concept was not "invented" in India, its emergence as a discipline was intimately bound to the English colonial mission to civilize the natives, to
interpellate the Indian elite into the superiority of Englishness[13] and to, in
Macaulay's infamous words, create "a class of persons Indian in blood and
color, but English in tastes, in opinions, in morals, and in intellect."[14] If she
finds Viswanathan's argument persuasive, then, any responsible literary
critic must come to terms with the compromised emergence of her discipline, its intimate entanglement with colonialism, its lack of innocence,
and, indeed, its racist career.

I say the above to make it clear that I do not see myself as writing from
some uncontaminated space, literature, against social science. I am only
too well aware of the compromised career of my own discipline. No serious postcolonial cannot be. But I would also remind the reader that I have
cast my lot with literature as a verb, not a noun, and as a postempiricist
reader of texts, not as a traditional, conventional, if not conservative critic
or interpreter of works. It is with the theory of textuality, strictly speaking opposed to the very notion of literature in the canonical sense, that a
postcolonial reader of my persuasion finds an ally. Thus the significance
of the singular and unverifiable to this study. I argued in the last two chapters that history, grounded as it is upon the empiricist, the verifiable, and
the logic of quantity, cannot settle the question of peace in Sri Lanka.
Both Wilson and de Silva present their texts as pure empiricist works
of disciplinary history untainted by other levels, but a close reading of
them demonstrated that they were deeply marked by the narratological,
anticolonial, and, most of all, abiding levels. Both de Silva and Wilson
understand history as objective and their writing as the real narrating
itself; thus they hold that history (the past) will determine politics (the

present); history will determine how the ethnic conflict must be resolved. But, although they both examine the "same" set of past events, they come to very different conclusions about them, conclusions that, amazingly enough, coincide with their politics, their commitments to the present. Besides, both nationalisms understand peace as a state of domination: of the Sinhalese over the Tamils (and others) in de Silva and of the Tamils over the Muslims (and others) in the Wilson. These positions, axiomatically, are unacceptable to the leftist, to someone opposed to domination, hierarchization, and exploitation. History, then, does not offer the leftist reader a stable intellectual ground from which to conceptualize peace.

Against Sri Lanka according to Sinhalese and Tamil nationalisms, I will argue here that literature, or reading textually, has something worthwhile to offer the leftist seeking to rethink the question of peace. But its lessons can only be drawn after reading: after reading the stories after reading de Silva and Wilson. In the rest of this chapter, I read two literary texts, or, more exactly, some singular moments in Ambalavaner Sivanandan's interesting novel *When Memory Dies* and Ernest Macintyre's brilliant play *Rasanayagam's Last Riot*. These books can, of course, be appreciated purely for their aesthetic value (or lack thereof), or they can be read as a part of a network of texts that constitute what is understood as the social, even while they contest it and even if they contest it without the kind of authority available to social science, with its privileged claim upon the real. So, once again, I must confess, or rather insist, that I did not choose these texts; they chose me. Although they, like de Silva's and Wilson's texts but in very different and singular ways, abide by Sri Lanka, they also interrupt those positions and critique the politics of identity, raise the possibility of different, nonexclusivist, participatory notions of community and of peace, of different bases for peace more promising to the leftist. The novel and the play are not, of course, political theory or constitutional law. They offer no blueprints, no manifestos, no programs. What they do is disrupt history, complicate the task of conflict management, and undermine its assumptions: for instance, that the parties or subjects to and causes of the conflict are known (just the Sinhalese and Tamils—as Daniel, de Silva, Spencer, Wilson, and Watson all agree) or that the solution is known (some kind of regional autonomy for the northeast, if not to the Tamils, something easy to frame but difficult to implement). These texts, when read carefully, patiently, responsibly, make such assumptions hard to sustain. If peace is to be understood, following Adorno, as not just "the state of distinction without domination" but also, crucially, "with the distinct participating in each other," then *When Memory Dies*, through its emphasis upon the singular, offers an excellent instantiation of it in the Sri Lankan context. Or, rather, having read Sivanandan's argument for, or instantiation or imagination of, what, for want of a better term, I must call multiethnic, nonexclusivist Sri Lankan community and having reading Sivanandan after Wilson and de Silva, it becomes evident that Adorno's understanding of peace, made in a very different context, could be useful-ly deployed in the Sri Lankan instance, if not brought to the attention of political theory, constitutional law, and conflict management. That is not, however, the only thing to be learned from this novel. It also explicitly ar-gues, in a postcolonial spirit, against history, or the verifiable, though not, strangely enough, against historicism. If the latter, to the postempiricist, is the limitation of the novel, then a moment in Macintyre's play signi-fies to the utterly debilitating function of history and historicism in re-lation to peace. The play also draws attention to some important ques-tions not discussed in the debate: those of gender and the dilemma of southern ("Colombo") Tamils. These texts, then, are "good"; they can be most usefully read by or put to work by or seen as accomplices of the postempiricist/postcolonial leftist reader seeking, through the literary, to call attention to the limitations of social science (history, political science, and constitutional law) and so to reconceptualize the question of peace in Sri Lanka. These texts not only abide by Sri Lanka, they take sides in ways most useful to the leftist reader, allow her to intervene in the Sri Lankan debate, and raise the possibility of imagining the country in new ways. They allow her to make peace seem possible, conceptually, at least.

Making Fiction History: When Memory Dies

In the course of an otherwise sympathetic and careful reading, Walter Perera categorizes *When Memory Dies*, Sivanandan's novel in three "books," as an "expatriate novel." The logic underlying this classification is straight-forward: it is written "by one who is domiciled abroad."[15] These pages have been arguing, of course, against such categorizations, based as they are on the geographic/anthropological distinction between inside and outside. And, one might add here that such effortlessly empiricist pigeon-holing of texts is deauthenticating, epistemologically unpersuasive, and doesn't explain very much about what is actually at stake—the texture of the written—if it explains anything at all. What should matter about intellectual production—and novels are intellectual products—on "Sri Lanka," or any other place for that matter, is not the "domicile" of those who produce them but the manner in which the texts themselves relate to their object. After all, many natives have produced Orientalist fiction on Sri Lanka while domiciled in the place.[16] On the other hand, some of the very few meaty novels about the country written in English, in my view at least, have been produced by those Perera would call expatriates, and *When Memory Dies* is an exemplary instance. The value to this study of this novel is that the text is not that of a native informant, of someone who, regardless of residence, writes about the country purely in order to report it to the West.[17] Sivanandan may not be domiciled in Sri Lanka, but that piece of information is not particularly relevant here because his text gets involved with its quarrels and conflicts. Indeed—insofar as a novel can do this—it intervenes explicitly, in an unabashedly partisan manner, into the Sri Lankan debate; it is resolutely leftist, rebukes and rebuts the nationalist accounts encountered in the previous chapters, imagines the possibility of alternative, nonexclusivist, anticommunalist community, weaves its story with labor history, casts its lot with the organized working class (though not, alas, with subalternity or feminism), and conceives the country not just as object but also subject. In short, while by no means a perfect text (but then, is there one?), *When Memory Dies* abides by the country. Patiently. It has taken the time and the trouble to become familiar with the place, with its questions and its struggles, without which intervention is impossible. It is a text driven by its abiding level.[18]

Book 1, *Forgotten Mornings*, is the part of the novel that concentrates my interest in this chapter, which is not really concerned with and doesn't discuss the other two books. Book 1 has three cardinal actants: S.W., a militant male Sinhalese worker in the railway; Tissa, his trade unionist nephew (both are active, in different ways, in the brewing struggle against colonialism and that for the rights of labor); and Saha, a male Tamil employee in the colonial postal service. These actants' attributes suggest that the text is shaped by two other levels: an anticolonial level, obviously, and, less obviously, an antinationalist level. (They also suggest, since there are no significant female actants, that it is probably not sympathetic to feminism.) The book is narrated by Saha's son Rajan and is most immediately "about," or presents an account of, to borrow a phrase from Kumari Jayawardena, the rise (and fall) of the labor movement in late colonial Sri Lanka (most of its events are set in the 1920s).[19] Its plot is staged around the relationships between Saha, S.W., and Tissa and, more importantly, between the latter two and A. E. Goonesinha, founder and leader, the reader is told, of Sri Lanka's first trade union, the Ceylon Labor Union. S.W. and Tissa are ultimately disillusioned by Goonesinha, so an impatient read might suggest that the book's emplotment is a familiar one to the leftist: the betrayal of the workers by its leadership. But to see it thus would be to miss its most radical purpose, for the novel also produces itself as the story of the country in the twentieth century, as the story of two Sinhalese and a Tamil who aren't to be read as representative of their "ethnic groups" but as inhabiting a singular relation to them, as told by the Tamil's son. Or, more precisely, the novel produces itself as a singular and unverifiable story—yes, Sivanandan has "read" Spivak—of a place called Sri Lanka, one of many possible stories about an entity that cannot be grasped as a whole. The narrative takes care to establish this at its very beginning, which opens with Rajan, "exiled" in England, remembering his childhood:

> My memory begins, as always, with the rain—crouched as a small boy against the great wall of the old colonial building that once housed the post office. It frightened me, the great monsoon downpour, and saddened me too, threw me back on my little boy self and its lonelinesses . . . the first feel of the sadness of a world that kept Sanji from school because he had no shoes. (5)

The entire novel, then, is analeptic: it looks back. It may, just a short while into the narrative, seem to move forward in orthodox realist fashion, but it is the product of Rajan's memory, which is—and this cannot be stressed too much—profoundly antinostalgic. When the narrator remembers Sri Lanka, he does not see something happy or pleasant, a blissful touristy paradise or a state of childhood innocence to which he desires to return. Rather, he remembers himself afraid, crouching. In the strict sense, there is no homesickness here. If nostalgia is a characteristic element of nationalism—de Silva yearns, one might say, for a peaceful, Sinhalese-dominated Sri Lanka that existed, in his account, before the Tamils first arrived in the country as invaders; Wilson yearns for a Tamil-dominated state that would replicate, in population at least, the former Tamil kingdom—then *When Memory Dies* takes a position, if only implicitly and in a manner that therefore requires patient reading and following the directions of the text, that it is antinationalist.[20] Or, if you like, an element of the novel's abiding level finds Sri Lankan nationalisms disabling.

Rajan also remembers himself, produces his first memory, as a little boy crouching against two objects, both termed "great" or overpowering: the weather and the architecture of colonialism. The common adjective brings the two together and reverses an old Orientalist trope; it is not native culture but colonialism that is associated here with nature. Rajan then recalls fear, loneliness—again, unhappy things—and what the Sri Lankan leftist reader will understand as exploitation. The reader will discover in book 2 that Sanji, a less-than-catalytic actant who occupies very few units of narrative, is the son of an UpCountry Tamil shopkeeper. When his father's business failed, the boy had to stop attending school because of dire poverty, because he couldn't afford a pair of shoes, something any bourgeois or petit-bourgeois child could take for granted. The narrative, that is, also begins with a gesture of solidarity toward the UpCountry Tamils, reminding the reader familiar with histories of the Sri Lankan ethnic conflict of their marginalization or minoritization in such accounts. De Silva, it will be recalled, does not grant their story much narrative attention. Wilson sees their plight from the "Ceylon Tamil" perspective. Here, for instance, he describes their disenfranchisement: "At one stroke of the legislative pen nearly half the Tamil population of the island (i.e. the Indian Tamils) lost all their seven seats in the House of Representatives, and in fourteen other electorates they lost their ability to influence the outcome" (Wilson 1988, 35). This act broke what Wilson terms an unwritten "compact on representation" (37) between the two elites. Prime minister Senanayake followed this by legislation depriving the UpCountry Tamils of their Sri Lankan citizenship. This piece of information is passed on in a neutral, "descriptive" tone, without the explicit impress of the ethical level. What matters to Wilson is not that some Tamils lost their citizenship, but that this deprived other "Ceylon Tamils" of legislative clout. Angrier accounts of this moment, marked by the ethical, can be found, and perhaps one should be cited:

> The Senanayake government directed its axe first against the Indian Tamils . . . The Sri Lanka Citizenship Act is unique in that it denies citizenship to a person born in the country before or after 1948 unless, at least, his father was born in or was a citizen. Citizenship is not related to one's birth in the country but the birth of one's ancestors. This crude legal formulation . . . [denied citizenship to] nearly a million men, women, and children of Indian origin, working and living in the country, and for whom Sri Lanka is their permanent home.[21]

In this account, the UpCountry Tamils were axed, brutalized, violently denied citizenship after independence despite being born in the country, despite considering it home. There are one million UpCountry Tamils, and their socio-political condition has often been described as indentured labor. It is thus no coincidence at all, indeed it is of considerable narrative significance, that *When Memory Dies* begins with a gesture of solidarity toward this group, begins with a reminder of its poverty and long career of being exploited, unheard, ignored, kept at the bottom, and even disenfran-chised.[22] There is, then, something to be learned from this singular narra-tive unit, the mention of Sanji, insignificant though it may at first appear.

Rajan goes on to say that these memories "connected" him to Sri Lanka; they made him, that is, both distinct from it and associated, allied, and complicit with it. So he wanted to tell its story:

> But there is no story to tell, no one story anyway, not since that day in
> 1505 when the fidalgo Don Laurenco de Almeida . . . landed on our shores
> and broke us from our history. No one story, with a beginning and an end,
> no story that picks up from where the past left off—only bits and shards
> of stories, and those of the people I knew, and that only in passing, my
> own parents and son, or heard tell of, for there was no staying in a place
> or in a time to gather a story whole, only an *imagined time and place*. And no
> story of the country—or, if of the country, not our story but theirs . . .
> Except that we all bore the imprint of that history, like a stigma, internal-
> ized it even, made it our own, against our will. (5; emphasis added)

The significance of this narrative unit cannot be stressed too much, for it determines the reading to follow. Its second sentence is the most impor-tant, where the very awkwardness of its phrasing, its stumbling move-ment, its lack of a predicate, should signify to the reader that a tension exists in the manner this text understands the relation—the resemblance and the difference—between history and fiction. It is the only such sen-tence in the whole of book 1. It must, therefore, be unraveled with care. The first and most obvious point is that the history of Sri Lanka was in-terrupted by colonialism, understood here as a definitive rupture which "broke" the people from this history. Effectively, this leaves Rajan with "no story [of his own] to tell," for he bears, now, the imprint, the indelible mark, the permanent impress, indeed the stigma, the stain of another. It is an imprint that is not just a mark on the surface but one that has also been "internalized" by the native subject and unwillingly made a part of him-self. After colonialism, that is, such subjectivity cannot be conceived or narrated exclusively on its own terms. Neither can the native story more generally. To the postcolonial reader, this position resonates with Fanon: "colonialism is not simply content to impose its rule upon the present and the future of a dominated country . . . [or] satisfied with simply holding a people in its grip and emptying the native's brain of all *form* and con-tent. By a kind of perverted logic, it turns to the past of the oppressed people and distorts, disfigures, and destroys it."[23] Colonialism, in this reading, is not an exclusively political phenomenon, as some naive postcolonial readers of Fanon hold. It is also, as argued in my Introduction, about "epistemic violence," the destruction of native *form*. Colonialism, to Fanon, always distorts, disfigures, and sometimes even destroys indigenous modes of thought. It does so not conspiratorially but through the authority, subtle workings, and capillary reach of science, reason, and disciplinary knowledge. After colonialism, the autochthonous terms through which natives might conceive their subjectivity, the narrative strategies—in a word, the form—through which they might tell their own story, and thus actually make it their "own," are no longer available; they have been irrevocably lost. The discipline of history, which patterns the stories of the rest of the world into a European form, as argued before, thus even erases the "past" of the colonized. In taking this position, Fanon, it is important to notice, does not hold to a purely empiricist understanding of history. If the past is what really happened, of course it cannot be destroyed; one could always return to the past and recover it—even if the effort involved is extraordinary and the resulting product incomplete. Thus the resonance of Fanon with the narrator Rajan, who claims that, after the arrival of the Portuguese, the history of Sri Lanka, understood in the same straightforward disciplinary sense as it is by de Silva and Wilson, was yoked to that of the West. Rajan wants to write it, would will it if he could, but can't. Clearly, then, *When Memory Dies* is shaped by an engagement with history or a historical/disciplinary level. In raising the question of the impossibility of writing Sri Lankan history through Western categories, the novel marks itself as postcolonial in the sense argued in the Introduction; it seeks to put into question, to some extent at least, the categories, the forms, the thematic of Eurocentrism; it, once again, distances itself from the seamless production of narrative histories by Tamil and Sinhalese nationalisms.

All this will—or should—tell the reader why, after reading nationalist histories in the last two chapters, narratives that turn out to be incoherent and determined not by the real but their inhabitant level, or politics, this study turns now not just to fiction but to this particular novel to pursue the question of reconceptualizing peace in Sri Lanka. *When Memory Dies* is not only about the impossibility—and this is not necessarily its strength—but also about the *necessity* of writing history after colonialism, or after, if you like, one loses or is disconnected from place. As de Certeau has argued, disciplinary narratives can only be produced from the security of a stable place or location (which he does not understand empirically). De Silva and Wilson produce history from such an assumption: that the Sinhalese and Tamils can be thought as bounded, cohesive, unmarked, stable—and, of course, empirical—wholes or communities, even as their very texts betray them, as their narratives' incoherence demonstrates. They write from the security of knowing their place, intellectually and politically, although to Wilson that place, in the geopolitical sense, is actually yet to be. But Rajan finds that there is nowhere from which this can be done, no place from which a story or an identity—whether named Sri Lankan or anything else—can be produced "whole." No location, in short, from which to write history. Indeed, place here is deemed to be, in a powerful and radical formulation that the impatient reader could easily miss, the *product of the imagination* ("*only* an imagined time and place"). The narrator of *When Memory Dies*, in other words, does not understand place cartographically or empirically but imaginatively. He understands it, and this cannot be stressed enough, somewhat like this study does, Sri Lanka is not something one can touch; like the long-ago rain, it only exists in his memory. It is unverifiable, unsusceptible to the logic of true/false. Thus, to someone of Rajan's persuasion, who wants to tell the story of Sri Lanka, the only possibility is to turn to fiction, the work of imagination, the account of things that never happened.

Nevertheless, *When Memory Dies* seems at first glance to be an almost transparently historical novel, in the old-fashioned socialist realist sense. It tells the story of a group of (mostly) working-class actants through time as they interweave with other actants—like Goonesinha, the labor leader, and "ordinary" workers—and events—like the general strike of 1923—that are a part of what, to the discipline of history, would be the record or verifiable.[24] Trained historians would attest that many of the events referred to in the novel "really happened," although it is necessary to note that, working as it does within labor history, many are events that elitist history (i.e. Wilson and de Silva) ignores. None of the cardinal events here, the strikes and so on, nor the actants, like Goonesinha, find a mention in the histories read in the last two chapters. And the actants deemed important to nationalism, such as Senanayake and the Ponnambalam brothers, get no narrative attention in the novel. Then, and also importantly, *When Memory Dies* is realist in narrative style. After the first few units the narrator disappears entirely from book 1. The first-person narrative voice is replaced, almost seamlessly, by the third-person voice.[25] The story appears to be telling itself, or rather, as Barthes might insist, the real appears to be narrating itself: there is a "systematic absence of any sign referring to the sender of the . . . message."[26] But one knows, and forgets at one's impatient peril, this to be a conceit. For the novel begins with precisely such a sign from the narrator; it begins by informing its reader that it is a product of the imagination, of the memory of an actant named Rajan, depicted as a Sri Lankan "exiled" in England, and a product of the impossibility of writing history after colonialism. *When Memory Dies is framed as such.* The opening unit—any opening unit of any narrative—determines the reading that follows; that is the structural function of its position in the narrative, something it cannot avoid performing. *When Memory Dies,* that is, might be read as wanting to be realist; its allegiance to a somewhat dogmatic Marxism might take it in that direction, but its commitment to postcoloniality takes it in the other. To read postempirically—as opposed to just for the plot—is to pay attention to such things. But then, you may ask, if this is the work of the imagination, why does it refer to things in the record? Why not just make everything up: actants, plot, and events? Because the novel confronts history as such; because the postcolonial novel—trying to work outside the thematic of Eurocentrism—must do so; and because this novel is also, more particularly, a leftist revision of and challenge, in the broad sense, to the accounts of Sri Lanka by Wilson and de Silva and a fictional response—not a challenge, just a response—to that of Jayawardena. By its reference to the record, the novel signifies to its reader that it is responding to and entangled with history, the discipline. Which still begs the question: why? If history is impossible after colonialism, why turn to fiction and not some other form? What specifically can fiction do that an account claiming to be authored by the real cannot?

For a start, and perhaps also most crucially, fiction can narrate synchronic diversity. Structurally, fiction is able to tell the story of more than one central subject or cardinal actant (without being incoherent). It need not privilege the perspective of just one. It can tell the story, as *When Memory Dies* does, of northern Tamils, Muslims, UpCountry Tamils, and Sinhalese. It can imagine these actants participating in each other. Fiction, as argued earlier, need not be filial to the record, to the verifiable or footnotable; it need not be constrained by the archive. For the record may not turn out, upon inspection, to be too enabling to the leftist, especially if that leftist seeks to reimagine the past in order, as Brecht suggests, to reimagine or hammer into shape possibilities implicit in the present. Paradoxically enough, this reimagining is what makes this not a historical novel but a historicist one, in a very specific and limited sense. It works within the structure of the discipline of history (and is, to that extent, not postcolonial in the sense I am advancing): it distinguishes between past and present; it accepts that the past is connected to and has a determining influence upon the present, even if that determination cannot be narrated seamlessly from any one subject-position, even if it can only be narrated discontinuously, even if the past is understood as fiction and not an account of what really happened. Like Wilson and de Silva, then, Rajan works within the presumption that the past determines the present. Where they differ is that the Rajan understands, on the one hand, that colonialism made the past unrecoverable except on terms unacceptable to the native subject, and, on the other, that what can be recovered from the remains of the record is not entirely fruitful for the leftist responding to the question of peace in Sri Lanka and trying to abide by the country. So Rajan will produce it, in an almost literal sense, as a fiction of the present. This turning to literature to reinvigorate, redeem, if not reincarnate history, this turning fiction into history as opposed to making history fiction or arguing against the necessity of history altogether (which would be intellectually more radical moves) makes *When Memory Dies* of particular interest to this study.

Saha, the narrator's father, first gets to know S.W.'s story, at least in part, not from the railwayman himself but from his wife. To Prema—whom an against-the-grain feminist reading would also find a cardinal actant—her husband is a hero. She tells Saha, a lodger in their house, of his past one day in 1922, when a group of militant railway workers gathered there to discuss strategy. The narrative describes S.W. and summarizes his activism thus:

> He was a fierce old man, with over forty years' service in the railways and still very active in union work. The rumor was that he had been one of the prime movers of the rail strike of 1912, but people remembered him for the charges of racial and religious bigotry he had laid against his employers before the Royal Commission of Inquiry the following year. Ironically, though, it was his own reference to the Commissioners as *para suddhas* (bastard whites) that had drawn the public's attention to his evidence and made him a national hero. (22)

Though narrated in the third person, seemingly objectively, this is an instance of a "bit" of a story Rajan must have "heard tell of" or put together from various sources (mostly Prema). And the unit is actually put together, if one reads it carefully, in a nonobjective voice. Though narrated in the third person, this summary is someone's perspective, not that of an "omniscient" objective narrator. To read it any other way would be not only irresponsible and in disregard to the novel's framing (as the product of Rajan's memory), it would also be to miss what the unit signifies, carefully, about the narrator's own politics. For it is suggested here that S.W. is no ordinary worker but a leader: tough and uncompromising, with the courage to confront colonialism literally face to face, for which he has become a hero. This does not, however, entirely please the narrator, and rereading that crucial statement will make clear why. "The rumor was that he had been one of the prime movers of the rail strike of 1912, *but* people remembered him for the charges of racial and religious bigotry he had laid against his employers before the Royal Commission of Inquiry the following year." S.W. was an organizer and leader of the workers. This, interestingly enough, is a rumor, not an established fact. However, what else could it be, since such activity was illegal in that colonial conjuncture? Nevertheless—*but*—he is remembered by the public, which does the work of the nation (*public* attention made him a *national* hero) for opposing colonialism and insulting the white man; whereas—and this is the work done by the conjunction *but*—he isn't remembered for organizing labor, despite the rumor that he was indeed a leader of the strike. The narrator's complaint is about national memory: it finds significance, value, in the mere fact of resisting, even insulting, the foreign ruler, not in the ground or basis of the resistance. Rajan is anticolonial; that is made clear from the very beginning of the narrative. His first memory, after all, is of being scared by colonial architecture. But he would rather that the working-class politics at play here also be appreciated by the nation. Once again, then, and in a very nuanced fashion, the text signifies the impress of its antinationalist level and distances itself from nationalism, which is deemed unsympathetic to the left. This raises the possibility that, to *When Memory Dies*, working-class politics and anticolonialism may be incompatible or that, at the very least, the text identifies a tension between the two.

In the course of that 1922 conversation, Prema tells Saha of the others gathered in the house, meeting with S.W.: "Hamban and Vadi and Marshall and that lot," leaders of the railway strike of 1912. Their names do not resonate with Saha. How could they? He is broken, disconnected from the history of his country. Prema then begins his alternative, anticolonial education—or re-education perhaps. "Marshall Appu had only just returned from forced exile . . . [T]he government had banished him into the wilds of the Eastern Province as punishment for his activities" (23). Marshall, this implies, was "banished" by the colonial authorities, chastised for his unionism by being forced to live for ten years in the "wilds" of the rural, underdeveloped, jungle and the disease-ridden, Tamil-dominated East, away from his comrades and unable to continue his activism. Like S.W., Marshall is a working-class hero. He suffered for acting upon his convictions, for agitating to improve the conditions of his coworkers. Prema's "eyes softened," the narrative states, as she spoke of him. Both narrative and narrator, then, approve of Marshall Appu. He may not be a cardinal actant and does not appear in many narrative units, but, given the narrator's commitment to recognizing, if not heroizing, labor agitation and given the narrative's approval of Prema, the reader cannot avoid this conclusion. Still, the question arises: why does he matter to this reading if he only appears in passing? Is too much being made of a little detail? But then, it has been argued here that, whether reading history or fiction, the work of the text is done by the detail. It is there that this novel's relation to history, the discipline, is to be noticed. For "Marshall Appu" is a name that can be found in the record: a "Marshall Wickremasinghe" also figures in Jayawardena's *The Rise of the Labor Movement in Sri Lanka*. In her account, he was "known as Marshall Appuhamy, a former railway workshop fitter . . . [was] the workers' leader during the 1912 strike . . . [He] had been dismissed and exiled to Batticaloa during the 1915 riots" (221).

The "1915 riots" get no mention in *When Memory Dies*, despite the fact that the novel can be read as being "about" "ethnic conflict." (There is, however, a passing reference to the "1915 massacres," but the reader is not told who was massacred, by whom, or why.) Although the object of much academic explanation, (re)narrating that "event" or investigating why it occurred is not this study's concern or interest. But, since Sivanandan's fiction clearly resonates with Jayawardena's history—the text is a tissue of citations, Barthes might remind one here—her account of it will signify much to the reader interested in figuring out the novel's relation to the record, the novel's relation to and revision of history. *The Rise of the Labor Movement in Sri Lanka* will, therefore, have to be cited at some length:

> The riots which took place in 1915 between Buddhists and a section of Muslims known as Coast Moors, and the repression that followed, form an important part of the history of the Ceylonese nationalist and labor movements. A close interweaving of religious, political and economic forces was evident during the riots. (163)

The "1915 riots" may be essential to history, it may be impossible to write the story of modern Sri Lanka without an examination of them, but not so to fiction, or, at least, to this novel. It will, for reasons the reader must consider, ignore them. The dispute began, states Jayawardena, in Kandy over the issue of whether a Buddhist procession should be allowed to play music in front of a mosque; when a colonial judge ruled against the Buddhists, they attacked Muslim targets, and the riots then spread to other parts of the country, including Colombo:

The spark that led to the rioting in Colombo was set by the railway workers of the locomotive workshops. These skilled workers who had constantly agitated about their conditions of work and had gone on strike in
1912 were the most literate, alert and militant section of the working class;
they were also readers of the Sinhalese press, which at that time was con-
ducting an aggressive campaign against Indian traders and Indian workers
in Ceylon. The Ceylonese railway workers, who feared competition from
the Indians who were poorer, . . . had manifested their hostility to Indian
immigrant labor on several occasions. (174)

In other words, however militant the working class, it was not immune
from what, within South Asianist discourse on this subject, is usually
called communalism. They found no class solidarity with Indian workers (recall that *When Memory Dies* begins with a gesture toward "Indian"
or UpCountry Tamils), seeing them instead, from a nationalist perspective, as foreign. This same sentiment—or is it a politics—appears to have
grounded their treatment of the "Coast Moors," who were also Indian "in
origin," in 1915. But Jayawardena does not find communalism in the latter
instance, even though, by her own account, the railway workers were interpellated by not only a class ideology but a nationalist one (the "aggressive" Sinhalese press). Rather, the workers were responding to increased
and artificial inflation:

It is to be noted that though there were some instances of killing, wound-
ing and assaults on Moors, and of attacks on mosques in other parts of
the country, the "mob" in Colombo was not bent on attacking the Moors
themselves, or pillaging their places of worship on religious grounds, but
rather on plundering the shops of the Moors which represented the hardships caused by profiteering and unfair trade practices. (176)

The questions arise, to remain within the protocols of empiricism and historicism, as to whether the Muslims were the only traders indulging in
"profiteering." What does the record say about why it appears that only
Muslim shops were attacked? Why did the property of the Muslims alone
come to "represent" the "hardships" of the poor? Were there no Sinhalese
traders indulging in such practices? Jayawardena does not address these
questions, and the reader would not expect a postempiricist to, either.
However, it should be pointed out that an alternative historicist reading
of 1915, from a Muslim perspective, is available.[27]
My concern, instead, is to pose this question: why, if the record suggests that the railway workers could be read as communal, does *When*

Memory Dies, which clearly resonates with the record and examines communalism, repress or revise that detail? Why give the name Marshall Appu to an actant in the first place, a proper name to be found in the record, and then narrate only some details of this actant's career that are also in the record, and repress or revise others? After all, S.W.'s name does not figure in the record. But one must pause here and ask: does Jayawardena actually find evidence—the verifiable—of Marshall Wickremasinghe's involvement with the riots? Her phrasing is careful: "the workers' leader during the 1912 strike, . . . [he] had been dismissed and exiled to Batticaloa during the 1915 riots." This does not say anything definitively about Wickremasinghe's involvement in the riots. History, actually, does not know whether he was guilty or not. It does not have enough evidence to decide. In calling one of his actants Marshall Appu, then, Sivanandan draws attention to the undecidability of the record. He also makes another move, drawing attention to its inadequacy for the present. I am not interested in arguing that Sivanandan produces a sanitized or "untrue" account of the Sinhalese working class. To do so would be to hold the novel verifiable, to read it against the record, and to work within the protocols of historicism. The novel is fiction, and those who would read it otherwise—and so doing has had a long and sometimes sophisticated career—simply misunderstand, to make the case strongly, the very nature of their object. Since the events depicted in a novel never happened, they cannot be verified or checked against "the facts," the economic base, or whatever. Cows can jump over the moon, dishes run away with spoons, in nursery rhyme or novel; nightingales can appear in the Arabian desert in poems. The task of the reader confronted with such happenings is not to say they are impossible but to read them, investigate their significance, explain their narrative logic, and learn from them if they allow one to do so. Thus, the fictional existence of an actant named "Vadi," also called "Vadivel" elsewhere in the text, signifies that, to *When Memory Dies,* early Sri Lankan working-class militancy is not limited to the Sinhalese alone but includes Tamils, even if Jayawardena does not record any recognizably Tamil names among the railway workers she identifies in her history. (She does say, though, that such identification is made difficult by the fact that "almost nothing has been recorded of the strikers.") But, to return to Marshall: my concern is with this particular instance of what might be considered the revision of disciplinary history by fiction. Where Jayawardena leaves open the possibility that her Wickremasinghe, as it were, may be implicated with the attacks on the Muslims, *When Memory Dies* rules it out. The working classes in the novel are noncommunal, and the veracity of this position cannot and should not be evaluated, disputed, or challenged, because the novel is fiction, not history, and because history is impossible after colonialism. Does this signify why, actually, history is impossible to *When Memory Dies*? Why, more particularly, fiction may be more enabling to the historicist leftist needing a noncommunal past to imagine a noncommunal Sri Lankan future? Why both time and place, history and location, are not understood by this text as real but as imagined? Why this text cannot be realist? Is this an instance of what could be learned from the unverifiable? Phrased thus, my answer would not be entirely unexpected, would even be predictable. But let's stay a little longer with the story of S.W. and Saha.

Born in Sandilipay, a "bone-dry village in the north of Ceylon," Saha was sent at a young age to Colombo to live with a relative and attend a Catholic school. There he received a colonial education that, on the one hand, took him into the bureaucracy and away from penurious village life and, on the other, alienated him from his people and their story. S.W., a worker with hardly any formal schooling, changes that. Indeed, he interpellates Saha into a more oppositional—"leftist" would be too strong a term here; Saha never becomes more than what was once called a fellow traveler—perspective. S.W. continues, somewhat didactically, the anticolonial education begun by Prema. He speaks, for instance, of the "famous Panadura debate":

> He must have been twelve at the time . . . 1873 . . . His father took him to hear it, a public debate: Christianity versus Buddhism. The Church was always doing that sort of thing, daring the Buddhist clergy to stand up for their religion in open discussion. But this one was more like a duel than a debate, with each side putting up their champion . . . De Silva was no match for Gunananda, who held up the whole Bible story to ridicule. (40)

A reference to this, too, appears in the record: "In 1873, Bhikku Migettuwatte Gunananda challenged the Rev. David de Silva . . . to a public confrontation because de Silva had condemned Buddhism as a false religion. The result was the sensational two-day debate . . . [in which] Gunananda . . . scored a resounding victory" (Jayawardena 1972, 45). Saha, as one might expect, had never heard of this defeat (if only in debate) of colonialism. He learns now, however, that its assumptions, intellectual and political, can be and had been challenged, that colonialism is not always right. S.W., finding a willing listener, interpellates the young man further, gives him books and journals, archived in a special shed in his garden, to read, attacks a system that would alienate a people from themselves: "There were rebellions going on all the time . . . But your school history books wouldn't tell you that, would they? After all, they are written by the English . . . I wonder what your children and Tissa's will do. Invent their own histories, I suppose, to suit their own purposes" (40). In an uncanny mirroring of de Silva, S.W. doesn't actually tell Saha about any of these rebellions. It is the present that this text is concerned with, too. Nevertheless, it is important to note that S.W. is the closest thing *When Memory Dies* has to a historian of Sri Lanka. He is, of course, untrained, uneducated even, in the formal sense. But he is the only actant who "remembers" the past and tries to pass it on. Inventing or fabricating history cannot be allowed, he insists; it must be preempted if possible. This generation may have been broken from their history, might be tempted therefore to fabricate it, but S.W. will try, first, to narrate the truth of what really happened with colonialism and, second, to reconnect the younger generation with this truth, connect resistance in the past with that in the present in order to produce a more enabling future. In so desiring, and in having an understanding of history as truth, S.W. appears to be an actant opposed to the narrator, who wants to produce fiction as history. S.W. will not and cannot endorse what he considers the invention of history; that is lying to his perspective. Given his cardinal significance to the narrative, does this mean that his figure is critical of the narrator's position? Yes, of course, but within the logic of the narrative, it is Rajan's position that triumphs, as it were, because S.W. fails not just as a historian to properly interpellate the next generation but also as an activist with a carefully thought-out agenda. Indeed, S.W.'s structural function as an actant in *When Memory Dies* is to fail, not completely but significantly. In staging his failure—and that of his nephew Tissa—lies what is to be learned from the story and the explanation of why this text turns to fiction to "save" history. In understanding the significance of this failure, the patient reader learns to learn from the singular and unverifiable.

S.W., it is important to note, is a successful trades unionist; he is among the first to organize labor in Sri Lanka—and, as the other books in the novel suggest, this is a "legacy" that endures. To that extent—and it is a crucially significant one to this text, given its commitment to organized labor and the working class—his story is depicted as one of success, accomplishment. What, by his own reckoning, he fails to achieve is ethnic accord within the working class, or, more exactly, a commitment to such a politics from its leadership, in this instance the figure of Goonesinha, since all the working-class actants in *When Memory Dies* are produced as noncommunal. The first such failure is produced by the text as a consequence not of any inherent such sentiment to be found within the proletariat but of the actions of the colonial administration, of "the new Governor [who] was deliberately setting the workers against each other, Tamils against Sinhalese and Sinhalese against Muslims"; consequently, "S.W. was afraid that everything he had worked for in his life was coming apart" (27). The governor in question is named Manning. The reader might remember that a governor Manning also appears in Wilson's *The Break-Up of Sri Lanka*, where he is said to have endorsed Tamil fears of Sinhalese domination, supported weighted representation for them in the legislature and tried to change colonial policy in a minority-friendly direction. Manning was among the very few colonial officials depicted as sympathetic to the Tamil perspective in *The Break-Up of Sri Lanka*. Here, he simply embodies divide-and-rule. I am not particularly concerned with the novel's depiction of Manning; it does not discuss him at any length or tell the reader whether he was successful or not in his stratagems. But it might be noted that in this instance, too, *When Memory Dies's* account of him resonates with that in *The Rise of the Labor Movement in Sri Lanka*: "Manning was more than interested in exploiting . . . the communal strife that existed" (201). In the novel, of course, he doesn't so much make use of the discord as actually create it. Anyway, my point is that S.W.'s politics aren't just prolabor and anticolonial. He also desires ethnic amity, at least within the working classes, and fights for its establishment. That is to say, Sivanandan holds, in a position that resonates with Newton Gunasinghe and Santasilan Kadirgamar, that to be leftist in Sri Lanka in a post-1983 conjuncture, which is the politico-epistemological moment the text intervenes within although the novel's events are situated earlier, is to take the ethnic conflict, or the question of peace, as seriously as one does the question of class, if not more so.

When Memory Dies stages S.W.'s fight for communal amity within labor around the figure of the railway worker Ramasamy, who is purely catalytic to the plot. He is, interestingly enough, not in the union or involved in the strike at all; indeed, he could be considered a blackleg. This is Rajan's summary of his story, presumably heard secondhand from S.W.:

> Ramasamy was an unskilled laborer, in his late forties, who did the cleaning and fetching around the factory workshop. He had been there, as man and boy, for as long as S.W. could remember, and everybody knew him to be an uncomplaining worker. During the rail strike, the bosses, casting around for someone to protect the plant from vandals, raised Ramasamy to the position of supervisor and put him in charge of the machinery. But when the strike was over and Ramasamy was returned to his previous po-

sition, he began to jib. He had watched over the machinery night and day and, when work began again, watched its every moving part with unblinking attention. It was his baby now, and no one was going to take it from him. After 35 years' service, he felt he had the right to a position of responsibility and, besides, he had started sending his youngest son to a proper English-speaking school and he needed the money. The men did not mind Ramasamy continuing to mind the machines—he did that anyway—but the bosses wanted him back where he belonged. No one, they declared, was going to profit from the strike. Ramasamy went off his head, and the department laid him off without a cent to his name. He was a coolie Indian and entitled to nothing. (80)

In my terms, Ramasamy would be an UpCountry Tamil, and what is produced here is an almost stereotypical portrait of such a "coolie": unskilled, uneducated, performing the most menial of tasks such as cleaning and fetching. He had started such work in the railway as a "boy," before becoming a teenager, and his situation never improved; he never advanced, not even after thirty-five years' service, even though he clearly acquired some skills. He was made a supervisor only temporarily, only during a strike, when other workers were unavailable. The point here is not that Ramasamy did not desire upward mobility but that, being Indian, he was not allowed it. He was, if you like, kept in his place. Despite this, he did not complain to anybody. The sketch is of meekness, utter passivity, abjectness, of one of the truly wretched of the earth, who does not complain because it wouldn't make a difference or perhaps because he has internalized his oppression so much that the possibility of complaining doesn't even occur to him. Nevertheless, it is also evident that he doesn't accept his position, that he desires upward mobility, for when the chance occurred, he promptly sent his son to "a proper English-speaking school," desiring one son at least to escape subalternity. (The gendered logic at work here should not be missed: he also had female children, who were not chosen to be so schooled.) Ramasamy isn't actually given a speaking part, the narrative doesn't depict him saying anything, but that is precisely the point: UpCountry Tamils are not represented in the debate that is Sri Lanka. Their positions are rarely if ever heard, as was seen in Wilson and de Silva and as Daniel complained, correctly. That is the narrative function of the actant Ramasamy: to signify the exploited status, and the minoritization, which is not the same thing, of the UpCountry Tamil. Paratactically, this reminds the reader of the gesture of solidarity the text began with.

When Memory Dies further develops this argument about UpCountry Tamils: Ramasamy did not join in the strike, but the other workers did not mind, did not see him as a blackleg or as siding with the bosses (though the reader is not told why). However, upon his dismissal, the workers did not care about his or his family's fate. S.W. alone attempted to get him compensated, but his efforts came to nothing. His coworkers wouldn't even sign a petition in this regard. In desperation, he asked his nephew Tissa for Goonesinha's help. S.W. had never liked or trusted the labor leader, on the grounds that he was not of the working class. Uncle and nephew had fought, often and furiously, over this question. The uncle's position was that only a worker could and should lead labor; someone else should not represent or speak for it. This resonates, of course, with my own critique of representation discussed in the Introduction: structurally, it subordinates the represented to the representer. The nephew's position is that he "is not leading them . . . [but] organizing them." S.W. did not concede the point, ever. But now, the reader is told, he felt he had no choice. When asked, Goonesinha agreed to help; in so doing, he acts, one might say, as the comrade of S.W., not as the leader or representative of labor. As a part of his strategy, he made the case public:

> He wrote to the general manager of . . . [the] Railways demanding Ramasamy's reinstatement on the basis of wrongful dismissal . . . [Then] petitioned the government, asking that 35 years of service should not go "unrecognized and unrewarded." He followed that up by going with Tissa to Ramasamy's miserable little shack in the Dematagoda slums and being photographed with his emaciated grandchildren. The next day's papers carried his eloquent indictment of the government for the horrendous conditions that government workers were forced to live in . . . [He then] brought Ramasamy's case to the attention of the public at a rally . . . The nation's cause, he proclaimed, was the workers' cause, and the Indian workers' cause, the Ceylonese workers' cause. (81)

The banality of the prose, the immense effort made to achieve the status of reportage (denotation without connotation), the attempt to sandpaper out, as it were, metaphor and the signification of language in this and virtually every other narrative unit that makes this kind of writing quite out of sync with its postcolonial moment—emblematized as it is by the work of Gabriel García Márquez, Salman Rushdie, and Assia Djebar—should not blind the reader to the care with which this argument, fictional though it may be, is formulated. All the institutions of colonialism are depicted as exploitative of labor, as unprepared to grant it concessions even liberalism might condone. Ramasamy does not matter to colonialism, despite thirty-five years of service. But he does to labor, to both its current leadership, Goonesinha, and its former, S.W. Goonesinha, although nationalist—he espoused the cause of the nation—is depicted here as nevertheless anticommunal and nonbourgeois. Organized labor equated the cause of labor with that of the nation. It also took as its mission the resolution of the contradictions between the groups that comprised the nation. It would produce unmarked "Ceylonese" nationals out of Muslims, UpCountry Tamils, northern Tamils, and Sinhalese. It might be communal in Jayawardena's account (the record), but in this unverifiable novel that is a response to that record, it seeks to unify the nation that colonialism, in a memorable phrase from one of Sivanandan's essays, "divided in order to rule what it integrated in order to exploit."[28] In Adornean terms, this novel imagines the distinct participating in each other.

Goonesinha, however, eventually breaks his promise to Ramasamy, to Tissa and, by extension, to S.W. The point, of course, is that he broke his commitment to maintain the unity of labor, to not discriminate, in this instance, between Sri Lankan and Indian. According to the narrative, the closer the relations Goonesinha established with colonialism, the more he forgot the demands of ordinary workers. The more he became their representative as opposed to their comrade and the more he spoke for them, the less he looked after their interests. *When Memory Dies*, that is, stages its critique of representation through the figure of Goonesinha. S.W. is finally told that Goonesinha cannot help because Ramasamy was a blackleg. Eventually, Ramasamy, frustrated by the long delay, unable to maintain his family given his unemployment, moves into S.W.'s house, or rather to a shed in the garden (displacing the history books). S.W. is a worker, in other words, who, almost literally in this instance, puts his money where his mouth is. He would actually inconvenience himself to fight for the rights of others. But S.W. fails to get any compensation for Ramasamy; as a consequence, S.W. stops trusting not only Goonesinha but also his once-favorite nephew, whom he virtually raised and educated. For his part, Ramasamy, unable to find an alternative in Sri Lanka, eventually returns to India with his family. This shatters the old man, completely destroys his spirit. "S.W. withdrew further into himself. In the mornings he sat in his empty shed with his memories. The books and papers he had removed to make room for Ramasamy's family were still in their boxes. In the evenings, he sat on the rocks between the railway line and the beach and looked out to sea. Sometimes he forgot to return home" (86). The "books and papers" are those S.W. used to educate Saha; they are a metonym for the alternative history of Sri Lanka. Significantly enough, they are now boxed, put away from use. They represent the failure of one generation of labor to fully interpellate the next, for Tissa was not as willing as S.W. to fight unremittingly for the unity of labor. The books have become memory: the residue or the failure, within the historicist protocols in which the reader is supposed to comprehend S.W., of history. That is all this militant worker is left with after his inability to connect with the next generation: memory, not history. For history is about connection, continuity, the past producing the present in a disciplined, rigorous manner. His life becoming hopeless and purposeless, S.W. dies not long after, leaving not much behind. His story, therefore, is something the reader must understand as a failure.

How should this act of narrative closure, of bringing an actant's story—a singular and unverifiable one—to an end, be read? (The singularity of the figure of S.W. should be obvious, but sometimes it's necessary to state the obvious. S.W.'s story is not the same, or even very similar, to Tissa's: though both are Sinhalese, the uncle is a worker first and always; the nephew is an organizer of labor who gave up his regular job when he started working for the union. S.W. could, of course, be more productively compared to Marshall; however, their stories are better read as rhyming, for it is crucial to remember that, although Marshall was exiled for a decade, S.W. was not. And, of course, Marshall's narrative function is to take the reader to the record, to signify the entanglement of this text with a disciplinary level and make the reader engage with it, something the entirely fictional figure of S.W. does not do. The singularity of these narrative accounts, that is, is to be found in the detail.) One of the first Sinhalese to organize labor from within labor, then, is unable to accept that the UpCountry Tamils, perhaps the most exploited sector of Sri Lankan labor, must be excluded from an equal stake in Sri Lankan community—a community that anticipates freedom and an end to colonialism—nor is he able to establish such community, even within labor. In staging this failure, though, the text does imagine Sri Lankan community in nonexclusive, participatory terms. Where Wilson and de Silva can only find exclusive, dominating forms of community, the novel is different. S.W. is also, as stated before, a Sri Lankan people's historian who would like to connect a generation he considers alienated from their history to this past but fails to do so. The staging of this failure suggests that history is impossible not just after but during colonialism, which leaves the colonized with no record, only memory. There are, as you might expect, some lessons to be learned from all this, fiction though it may be; there are many ways that S.W.'s story, if read patiently, could be seen as interrupting the Sri Lanka produced by Sinhalese and Tamil nationalisms, thus enabling the leftist reader to raise other possibilities about the question of peace, possibilities inaccessible to social science.

But, before getting there and before concluding this reading of *When Memory Dies*, two other narrative moments require attention: first, Tissa's disenchantment with Goonesinha—or the staging, if you will, of another chance for the labor leader to stand up for his comrades, for anticommunalism; and, second, the narrative's depiction of its female actants.

An incurable romantic, Tissa falls in love many times in the narrative, none more significantly, though, than with a Muslim woman, Soonoo. The logic of this narrative move is not hard to figure but should not be missed or passed over unnoticed: it enables the staging of Sri Lanka in truly polyethnic terms. Where de Silva sees an essentially Sinhalese country and where Wilson essentially sees two nations, Sinhalese and Tamil, Sivanandan sees four major groups inhabiting Sri Lanka, none more equal than the other (which does not make them all the same, either). *When Memory Dies*, in other words, demonstrates patience; it wants to tell many stories; it is not exclusivist. If this could be read as signifying, on the register of the ethnic, a successful or positive use of the imagination, it must also be read, on the register of gender, as not just inadequate but a failure—indeed, as something to be critiqued. All Sivanandan's women in book 1 are kept in their place. They feed, clean, nurse—in a word, serve—their men. Prema, for instance, who is produced as a perfectly intelligent subject completely sympathetic to her husband's organizing and never once complains about it, who actually begins the decolonizing of Saha's mind, is never once shown outside her house. She is produced as an intellectual and political subject but not as an agent who can or does act upon her convictions. She never once joins in a demonstration or march, never attends a political rally; she has no access, in short, to the public sphere. Her depiction is consistent with the logic of orthodox (hetero)sexism: she exists to simply and faithfully serve her husband—as, in a word, an object. So is Saha's unnamed mother:

> His mother's body . . . was wearied with incessant childbirth. There was certainly strength there. Once, he remembered, it had a bearing about it, to match that noble face; but now it just looked used up, and the burden of carrying it around had begun to shadow her eyes with pain. Sahadevan could not stand it, but at the same time he knew that it was from hardship and grief and the bearing of children that she had winnowed the stuff of her life. (17)

The sympathetic feminist reader will not necessarily be unhappy with this portrait, at least at first glance. It can be read as an acknowledgment of patriarchal norms. Saha's mother's story is said to be characterized only by difficulty and childbirth, by hardship and grief. No moments of joy or happiness are recorded. But the feminist reader cannot, ultimately, give it a sympathetic reading because she will also notice that there is no place in this text where resistance to patriarchy, or even a critique of it, is given a speaking part. If this is what she "felt" about her life, the mother does not articulate it. Whereas, of course, *When Memory Dies* aggressively depicts resistance to the exploitation of labor and to communalism. Ramasamy may not speak, but the reader is given no doubt how his story is to be understood. S.W., Saha, other actants, and, most crucially, the narrator make it quite explicit that it is to be read as a story of (brutal) exploitation at the levels of race and class. In contrast, none of the text's women actants are granted such narrative privilege. An against-the-grain reading might suggest that they are exploited, too, but the text does not guide its reader to such a conclusion. The text's particular failure to produce its women as not much more than objects, then, situates the novel firmly on one side of the sexist or phallogocentric divide.

It is to be expected, then, that the doings of its women actants, when examined from the perspective of narrative movement, would be found largely in instances of "summary" (to resort again to those terms from Genette) and not of "scene." In summary, the time of the story exceeds that of the narrative; in scene, they more or less coincide. Summary, says Genette, functions as "waiting room and liaison, with dramatic scenes whose role in the action is decisive."[29] Scene, then, could be considered the more important structural element of fiction, for in scenes the more significant things happen, actants' actions are described, dialogue reported, with the reader left to interpret them. In summary, information is passed on to the reader, somewhat straightforwardly but always in a condensed fashion. Thus, for instance, the interactions between this text's three cardinal actants, all men, are narrated in units of scene. Their stories are told in great detail. They get, in other words, much narrative time, and thereby their significance to the narrative, and not just to the plot, is reinforced. Consequently, the insignificance of the women to the narrative is reinforced by their stories being told in summary, like in the unit quoted above about Saha's mother, where her life is condensed into a few statements about grief and hardship—after which the narrative can move on. She does appear in a couple of other units: either in the kitchen, cooking food, or serving it thereafter. But those units, too, only underline her unimportance. The scenes in which the plot turns—for instance, the conversation between the school principal and Saha's father, where the decision is made to send the boy to Colombo—are not only narrated in great detail but the mother is absent from them, does not participate in the conversation or decision. Thus it cannot surprise that, in a move typical of a novel with a phallogocentric perspective on women, *When Memory Dies* takes great care to describe—to evaluate—the physical appearance of all its female actants, even though their appearance is not of much narrative consequence. Prema's face, for instance, is "ugly . . . in repose: featureless and pudgy, like the rest of her" (40). Beatrice, the woman Tissa finally marries, is "dark . . . plain . . . flat" (91). The male actants are not so evaluated; what matters about them is their ethics, politics, and actions, not their physical appearance.

So it is only to be expected that Soonoo will be attractive; she is, indeed, a "stunning" beauty. (Otherwise, why would Tissa have noticed her?) Though very young, sixteen, she is already engaged to be married to a cousin. She is seen, and initially only seen, by Tissa, outside her house, evidently a meager one, in which she dwelled with her family:

> She lived in the tenements across the road from the union offices. Of
> course they had not spoken to each other yet, but their eyes had met and
> talked many times. Even this morning, when she was putting out the rub-
> bish. In fact, this morning had been different: they had exchanged smiles.
> He had crossed the road on his way to work just in time to catch her at
> close quarters, and she had smiled, lowered her head shyly and smiled, at
> him. (42)

This appears to produce the Muslim woman as Orientalism stereotyped (and stereotypes) her: passive, shy, submissive, and betrothed young—and to a relative, a cousin, at that. Therefore, it cannot surprise that, "of course" the two hadn't talked; Muslim women are only supposed to speak with their immediate family, not with strangers. The careful reader would also have noticed that, while Soonoo is depicted as meeting Tissa's gaze, she is also depicted as not actually doing so, since she lowers her head at the same time. However, if Orientalized initially, this actant is said to become more adventurous later, having something like an affair, though not quite a relationship, with Tissa. This is how the text narrates it, choosing summary rather than scene, predictably enough, to describe it: "She gave Tissa her smiles and a fleeting kiss or two on his cheek, held his hand as for ever, and once, just once, kissed him full on his lips" (50). That unit, of course, dismisses Soonoo's story as quickly as narratively possible. Did the two ever speak? Did she love him, want to marry him? Did she approve of Tissa's organizing? Was she happy staying at home? Would she have liked to get an education, a job, join the union? Did she think about anything at all? The reader is not told, nor do the questions even arise. Soonoo's perspective, that of the Muslim woman, is not really significant to the text. She, too, is not given a speaking part. *When Memory Dies* can conceive of its male actants as subjects but not its women. Soonoo eventually breaks her engagement to her cousin, although it is not said why. Nevertheless, and most significantly, she does not marry Tissa. The narrative cannot conceive of a multiethnic heterosexual union (at least not between Sinhalese and Muslim. Rajan, the narrator, marries a Sinhalese—in book 2). And Soonoo, eventually, disappears from the novel. What happens to her is not narrated. Her story is not granted closure, which, of course, reinforces its narrative insignificance.

What, then, is Soonoo's narrative function? Why is she in the novel at all? Clearly, she is not there to raise the possibility that Muslim women could be daring, audacious, resist gendered norms, or even be (proto)feminist. That would have been a radical move, but the text does not work or think along those lines. The argument that Soonoo's portrait is "accurate," that Muslim women were not daring in this time, cannot hold here because this is fiction, in which anything can be imagined. Besides, as noticed before, the novel's portraits of its workers are inconsistent with the record. My point is this: significance in *When Memory Dies* is to be found in the doings of its male actants. Almost exclusively. Soonoo's figure serves a purely catalytic function in the narrative: to introduce her brother, Sultan, the crucial Muslim actant in this text. Unlike his sister, Sultan is not shy. Tissa befriends him initially as a way of getting to his sister, but he is not of purely instrumental use; Tissa also gives him English lessons. Here, too, Sivanandan's refusal to question gender norms must be noticed. Educating the Muslim woman is not an option to this text. Does Soonoo speak English? If not, would she like to learn? The reader will never know. She is, can only be, an object, the object of romance, of heterosexual male desire. The male, of course, is entirely different. Sultan is not only educated by Tissa, he is also interpellated into trade unionism. He is seen as capable of politics, of resistance, of using his intellect. Eventually, he becomes, if not quite an activist, at least an assistant to the union; he holds, like Ramasamy, a somewhat subalternized position but is, again like the UpCountry Tamil, a tireless worker. He and Tissa meet frequently in the course of the romance/teaching/work, so the two establish a close relationship. Indeed, Sultan even reciprocates

Tissa's generosity, teaching him to speak Tamil in return for those English lessons and, perhaps more importantly, feeding him buryani from time to time (more importantly because I often wonder whether Muslims' remarkably extensive, not to mention quite superb, cuisine—the other ethnicities don't have anything even approximating one—may not eventually turn out to be the Muslims' most potentially enduring contribution to peace—understood, do not forget, as the distinct participating in each other). The relationship, though friendly, is not one of equality: the boy consistently refers to his elder—or perhaps his boss—as "Mr Tissa."

Then, after some years, comes another strike organized by Goonesinha, which brings book 1 of *When Memory Dies* to a close. By this point in the narrative, his union had been transformed into a fully fledged political party: the Ceylon Labor Party. This change was inspired by the British example, following a visit of British Laborite politicians to the country. As a consequence, the leader had even gained some international recognition, establishing a permanent relationship with a section of the British left, following which he is invited to a "Commonwealth Labor conference" in England. Goonesinha attends this meeting with Tissa, by now an important figure within the union, the leader's close confidant. After the visit, the novel's staging of Goonesinha's eventual betrayal of his workers, his collaboration with colonialism, is clearly anticipated. He begins to think, one might say, within the thematic of Eurocentrism. At the conference, the Indian delegation is said to have walked out because the British Labor Party "wouldn't support their demand for immediate independence." Saha, the narrator's father, asks Tissa why the Ceylonese delegation did not follow suit, support the Indians. Because, he is told, the Indians are "mixed up with the Communists." The narrative does not endorse this as a response, suggesting clearly that a gesture of anticolonial solidarity should have been made by Goonesinha, whether or not he was sympathetic to communism (which he obviously wasn't, although for reasons unnarrativized). By not so doing, the labor leader is produced as beginning to be seduced by power and recognition, beginning to succumb to colonialism and to betray labor. That is, he begins to turn from being their comrade, someone who acts or speaks with them and who abides by them, into being their representative, someone who speaks for them. Goonesinha is turning into someone who not just takes their place or is their substitute, but someone whom they must defer to—because, in part, he is different from them, being their leader.

The book 1 ends with another portrayal of betrayal, making the emplotment of Goonesinha's story iterative. Led by the leader, the tramcar

drivers strike. The police attempt to break it up, but fail. Having successfully organized labor over the years, Goonesinha is able now to bring it
out in strength to support the driver, and the tramcar company eventually backs down. Saha, traveling outside Colombo, hears all this in letters
from Tissa. When he gets back to the city, he discovers that Goonesinha,
on his way to talks to settle the strike, was beaten up that very day by the
police. Wanting to help, he then "jumped into a rickshaw and directed the
man to the offices of the Labor Union" (109). One should pause at this
statement, which at first glance might appear insignificant, purely catalytic in function, merely providing detail and local color, as something
that could be ignored. After all, of what possible significance could it be,
to the plot or its politics, how Saha actually got to Tissa's office one day
in Colombo? But it is in the detail—Barthes's narrative luxury—that the
alliances and interests of the text emerge most clearly; in the detail, the
text cannot hide. Just as much as the detail signifies *When Memory Dies*'s
sexism, the patient reader—who knows a thing or two about rickshaws as
a mode of transportation—would find, here, an instance of what must be
termed the text's resistance to, if not repression of, subalternity. In a rickshaw, as I remember from some picturesque postcards my grandfather
once gave me and told me not to lose because the vehicles would soon
go out of existence, one man transports another (man or woman) by pull-
ing him or her. My point is not that the exploitation of labor is less easy
to ignore when almost excruciatingly visible, as in the case of the rickshaw puller, as opposed to when hidden behind the walls of the factory
but that only certain forms of labor are visible as exploitation to *When
Memory Dies*. The text's commitment to organized labor is evident—and
exemplary. However, the rickshaw puller, not proletarian in the dogmatic
Marxist sense, is not seen or produced as belonging in an allied category.
Unlike S.W., Tissa, Marshall, and company, there is not only no need for
this actant to be given a speaking part; unlike Ramasamy, there is no need
for narrative attention to be granted to his labor, either, no place, that is,
from within the text from which his predicament could be read. As stated
before, even if Ramasamy did not speak resistance, the reading of his narrative function was made clear by other actants. Not so with the rickshaw puller. It is presented as the most natural thing in the world for Saha
to jump into a rickshaw and travel. Just as much as, after Prema's death,
it is also natural that he would run "the house with the help of an old
servant woman" (86). This woman actant, too, does not speak, is never
even named, and the text, predictably enough, does not provide a space
from which her predicament could be read. If expected from a bourgeois

novel, this is surprising from a leftist one. Woman's labor cannot be recognized as labor, as exploited labor, by this text; like nature, perhaps, it is something that just happens, not something the narrator or narrative need tarry over or abide by.

This, of course, is consistent with the novel's perspective on women. In book 1, at any rate, the women actants are objects either of male romance or male exploitation (the latter understanding requiring an against-the-grain reading); they are, that is, only objects. But how can the "servant woman" be categorized together with the rickshaw puller? What makes them comparable? The notion of subalternity. At the risk of digressing, let me take this opportunity to point out a symptomatic element of the text and to make an argument about the continuing usefulness of the term "subaltern." It emerged, it is often forgotten today, to supplement a lack in orthodox or dogmatic or inflexible Marxism, which only recognizes forms of exploitation authorized by its (Eurocentric) canon. Such Marxism, to Ranajit Guha, did not and could not capture the complexity of the South Asian social, which he found quite different from that of industrialized Europe.[30] The term "subaltern" became necessary—or, rather, some new term became necessary—because of this inadequacy. Not being hostile to Marxism, *Subaltern Studies* went searching for such a term within the Marxist canon—and found one in that creative thinker, Gramsci. Not being entirely satisfied with Marxism, or Gramsci, they had to recast the term, use it catachrestically. So they did. This was not, it should be stressed, a move inspired by the desire to be trendy, to be new or different for its own sake, or, as Dirlik might allege, to gain visibility in the West (the first few volumes in the series, it is often forgotten, were published exclusively in India, by scholars mostly "domiciled," as Walter Perera might put it, there). Confronted by how they understood the South Asian social, wanting to abide by it rather than report it to the West, the scholars and activists behind *Subaltern Studies* had no choice but to produce a "new" term. The category wasn't new in the sense of "original." But that is a part of the constitutive predicament of postcoloniality; it cannot simply walk out of the West, or Eurocentrism. It is dependent upon those categories—even while it seeks to question them, if not put into question the system that produced them. My reading of *When Memory Dies*, I hope, further demonstrates the necessity of the term: why it was coined and why it continues to be useful. For, if dogmatic Marxism—and *When Memory Dies* emerges, now, as such a text, at least at one level—cannot recognize the servant woman and rickshaw puller as requiring narrative attention, postcoloniality cannot ignore them, either.[31]

Since postcoloniality's task is, as argued in the Introduction, to "finish" the critique of Eurocentrism, it must point out that a (perhaps) "European" but non-Eurocentric category, subaltern, emerged precisely in order to capture the difference signified by rickshaw pullers and servants, a difference of significance to postcoloniality and one that dogmatic Marxism would categorize, dismissively, as "lumpen." To say so is not to seek to "blame" the author, Sivanandan, for some lapse or bad politics but simply to point to a limitation of the text. Yes, it helps in reconceptualizing the question of peace in Sri Lanka. It draws attention to things nationalist history has missed, must miss. But that does not make it perfect. No single text, of course, could be. Thus the necessity to read more than one piece of literature in this chapter. My point is simply this: the responsible leftist reader, while learning what she can from a novel, cannot afford to ignore its weaknesses, either. Otherwise, she risks producing literature as an uncritically privileged space opposed to social science.

To return, then, to the novel and the strike. Saha gets to Tissa's office to find that Goonesinha has not been beaten very badly. Nevertheless, the many workers gathered there, angered, move in a crowd toward the nearby police station, Sultan in the front shouting, "Kill the police!" (This scene, significantly enough, is narrated in considerable detail.) The police, in response, shoot at the gathering, killing the boy and some others. Before the crowd can express their fury, though, Goonesinha appears:

> [A] voice came over the loudspeaker. "Friends," it began, and the crowd stood still. Tissa looked up and saw his Chief standing on the top step above him, beside a white man in a white suit, with braid and buttons, and a plumed white hat on his head.
>
> "Friends," the velvet voice had put aside the loudspeaker. "The strike is over. The Colonial Secretary and I have come to an agreement." (111)

It is the white man, of course, the colonial secretary, who is wearing the white suit—or is it? A slight ambiguity exists in the phrasing to suggest it could be Goonesinha himself. Either way, though, Goonesinha's association with colonial power has now become complete. One of his workers, one of his most tireless organizers, has just been killed by the police, unnecessarily, but the leader does not protest this murder. He does not even lament it. Rather, with the fresh corpse lying literally in front of him, in the arms of one of his closest aides, he announces an agreement with colonialism. Something that should have provoked a rupture with colonialism—the murder of a worker—is ignored by Goonesinha. This astounds Tissa, completely shatters his spirit and what was produced in the early narrative units of *When Memory Dies* as his unbreakable faith in Goonesinha. He had called the police "bastards" earlier in the narrative unit, when Sultan was killed. He calls Goonesinha one now, effectively equating the labor leader and the repressive colonial state. With this narrative unit, book 1 ends. In the next, Rajan's story, where Tissa is a purely catalytic actant and where he appears in very few units of the narrative, it is revealed that he left the union after this incident (and eventually joined another political party, a more mainstream or bourgeois one).

Of the three cardinal actants in book 1 of *When Memory Dies*—S.W., Tissa, and Saha—only the first two, the Sinhalese men, are of pivotal significance. The plot of the novel is staged around their actions. Nothing that Saha does matters very much or changes anything of great consequence in the novel. While book 1 appears to be his story, as told by his son, it is superseded as the narrative progresses by that of S.W. and Tissa, who dominate the early part of the novel. Saha's relative narrative insignificance mirrors his political insignificance. From the perspective of the text's politics, it is important to notice that, despite being persuaded by the arguments of S.W. and Tissa of the need to organize labor and oppose colonialism, he remains, even prospers, in the colonial bureaucracy; resistance is not his thing. What is to be learned from book 1 resides, mainly, in the story of the two Sinhalese workers. How, then, is their story to be read, situated, made an accomplice of the leftist? Both of them, uncompromisingly committed to the working class, were obviously betrayed by its leadership. If the figure of S.W. is to be read as an argument for the organization of labor by labor, against representation, against speaking for the substitution of working-class labor leaders by nonworkers, it is one that ultimately fails. For Goonesinha, a nonworker, assumes such leadership by the end of the narrative—in the course of which the significance of the workers themselves decreases: S.W. and his comrades fought the early battles, did the early organizing, led the early strikes; S.W. himself dominates the early to middle parts of the narrative; but Goonesinha gains narrative prominence in the later units, where the workers themselves have only minor roles. If the figure of Tissa is to be read as an argument for the organization of labor by those committed to labor, it ultimately fails, too, for Goonesinha allies himself with colonialism by the end of the narrative—at the cost of labor. It is in fact possible to read the conclusion of book 1 as suggesting that the nephew comes around to the position of the uncle, that labor must learn to lead itself, not be led by outsiders, who cannot ultimately be trusted, who will inevitably betray it. The conclusion of book 1 can, furthermore, be read as suggesting that labor must not let itself be represented or spoken for, and it may amount, in a proper postcolonial spirit, to an argument against representation as such.

But *When Memory Dies* isn't only a fictional account, a renarrativization, a reading if you like, of the rise and fall of the labor movement in Sri Lanka. It also imagines the possibility and stages the failure of what, for want of a better phrase, I have been calling multiethnic Sri Lankan community. S.W., a Sinhalese, is effectively a surrogate father to Saha, a Tamil, and Prema a surrogate mother. They instruct him, interpellate him into Sri Lankanness, move him away from his colonial education; they make his sensibility, if not his politics, anticolonial. In the course of this education, the three also establish strong emotional bonds. S.W., for instance, once obtains a fake medical certificate so that Saha, otherwise without leave, could visit his dying mother. And Saha, it must not be forgotten, reciprocates the treatment he receives from them: he looks after S.W. (with the help of that servant) when Prema dies. Through this relationship, it is critical to notice, is staged not only the possibility but the success of Sinhalese-Tamil or nonexclusivist community, of what might be understood as the distinct participating in each other. Nonexclusive community is also staged in the depiction of the close friendship between Tissa and Saha, who take great pains to look out for each other. It is Tissa who arranged for Saha to lodge with the Wijepalas when he had nowhere to go. Saha, in return, was often an accomplice in Tissa's romantic escapades; his first thought, when he heard of Goonesinha's beating, was to go help his friend. In so doing, and this is the critical point to notice, the actants speak to each other, abide by each other, participate in each other, in the sense of these terms used in this study (and explained in the Introduction). Saha, after all, could have walked away from S.W., the old man, after Prema died, leaving him to fend for himself. He did not. The Sinhalese couple need not have (re)educated the Tamil lodger; they could have taken his rent and otherwise left him alone. They did not. What is the point being made here? It is that these narrative units could always be read as just elements in a story, but, to the reader convinced that literature could have a useful social function if read patiently, they signify something very different; they allow themselves to be read not just as abiding by Sri Lanka, which they do, but, more importantly, as so doing in the most useful of ways: as interrupting the Sri Lanka of nationalism and as imagining enabling community.

A commitment is also made by the two Sinhalese to the UpCountry Tamil (Ramasamy) and Muslim (Sultan) actants. They refuse to be exclusivist, to work only for other Sinhalese. That they fail in this endeavor is of lesser consequence, to my reading, than the fact that such commitment is narrativized, for it is by depicting such participation in each other that *When Memory Dies* allows the patient leftist reader to reconceptualize the question of peace in Sri Lanka. The nationalist understanding of peace has already been noticed (as inadequate): in both Wilson and de Silva, it accepts the domination of some groups by others. *When Memory Dies*, however, simply refuses to narrativize community on such a basis. Read literally, of course, it is an account of the failure of multiethnic community. And it has often been and sometimes still is fashionable to read literature "on its own terms," without reference to the other knowledges that inform, mark, or shape it. But, quite apart from the inadequacy of such a reading strategy in general, which would simply ignore the social function of literature, it must be insisted that, in this instance, the text itself, as was noted, guides its reader toward these other knowledges—especially history, both labor and nationalist. The text itself insists that it is not "mere" fiction but entangled with the social. And, when read against the nationalist histories, when read as an intervention into the Sri Lankan debate, rather than just a story that could simply be enjoyed and then placed back on the shelf, *When Memory Dies* appears in its political complexity. It allows the reader to learn from it, to put the novel to work, to make it the leftist's accomplice. Where history has failed, despite its promise, to provide the ground for peace, this text does not despair that, therefore, peace may be impossible. Rather, it accepts the failure, takes up the challenge, argues, in a properly postcolonial spirit, that history is impossible after colonialism—and turns to fiction to provide an alternative. This is both the novel's promise, its strength (from the perspective of this study), and its most limiting weakness. On the one hand, it is not empiricist; it refuses to make its case on the basis of the facts and will not cede that ground to history. Indeed, it will revise the record. This, of course, is an intellectually radical move the consequences of which, however, the text does not follow through with. For, on the other hand, *When Memory Dies* works within the logic of historicism, holds that the past will determine the present. Since the past of nationalism is politically unacceptable, and the past of a colony unrecoverable, anyway, fiction becomes the ground where a different and more enabling past might be imagined, which in turn might produce a different and more enabling present, except that, of course, with the present, the text's narrative moment—both Sri Lanka according to de Silva and Wilson and *When Memory Dies*'s book 3—leaves very little room for optimism and the novel's past, too, appears hopeless. There isn't multiethnic community in the present. Was it possible in the past? Could it be imagined? Not really.

When Memory Dies can be read, then, as the product of the failure of the imagination; which, in turn, can be accounted for as consistent with the novel's historicism: since the past produces the present and the present is hopeless, the past must have contributed to this and so must be hopeless, too. Thus book 1 must ultimately fail to produce effective, successful, stable, and lasting multiethnic Sri Lankan community, the distinct participating in each other, despite its attempt to imagine otherwise. Thus Goonesinha must, given the logic of the narrative, betray Ramasamy and—even when given a second chance, as it were—Sultan too. While I wouldn't disagree with such a reading, one learns very little from remaining there, from not situating the text within the larger Sri Lankan debate. Read after Wilson and de Silva, the novel should, from the perspective of this study, be understood not only as depicting a success or a failure but as useful—intellectually and politically—as being the leftist reader's accomplice, something she can work with, and therefore a "good" story. For one thing, it allows itself to be read as operating within the notion of peace held by this study, if not of leading this study to its understanding of peace. For another, it makes its claims through the singular and unverifiable. Quite apart from being unverifiable by definition, as it were, its response to history, the verifiable, has already been noted: although historicist in structure, it both draws attention to the record and takes liberties with it. Therein lies the significance, for instance, of its (revisionary) depiction of the actant Marshall; it allows *When Memory Dies* to produce itself, quite deliberately, as the work of imagination, the unverifiable—even while gesturing toward the record. Then, where de Silva would see the northeastern Tamils, Muslims, and not UpCountry Tamils but in his case Sinhalese Christians, as analogous minorities; where *Reaping the Whirlwind* clearly implies that in the fate of two hegemonized minorities, the Sinhalese Christians and Muslims, lies that of the third, the Tamils; *When Memory Dies* instead takes great care to respect their singularity. The stories of Saha, Ramasamy, and Sultan—all male, it must not be forgotten—are both similar and different; they rhyme. Ramasamy, at the end of his story, has no place to call home in Sri Lanka and is forced to leave the country. This is a possibility neither Sultan nor Saha ever have to face. Saha may be itinerant all over Sri Lanka, but he also has family back in the north, family that never lose their land. The northeastern Tamil, that is, is firmly rooted, almost literally, in the country (but it is necessary to notice here that, by leaving the northeast, Saha becomes what Wilson would call a "Colombo Tamil"). So is the Muslim, even if, in this instance, he is without property. However, if the northern

Tamil has many familial connections, which enable many opportunities, educational and otherwise, the Muslim has few, if any; Muslim prospects for social mobility are limited. The stories of the Tamil and the Muslim may be comparable on one register but not another. Their stories are not analogous; they just rhyme.

To appreciate the work of the singular, then, one must pay attention to the detail, for it is in the detail that the text's critique of history, its postcoloniality, its exemplary commitment to organized labor in an epistemological moment when postcoloniality often appears to have forgotten it, its signal contribution to reconceptualizing the question of peace in Sri Lanka, as well as its less enabling elements—its dogmatic Marxism, its historicism, its opposition to subalternity and feminism—are to be found. And detail, of course, is only visible to the patient reader, one who has acquainted herself with the Sri Lankan debate, who can read literature against social science. Thus, it is also by paying attention to the detail that one learns that this text insists, or could be read as insisting, that the Muslim and UpCountry Tamil be spoken to, participated with, and that peace in Sri Lanka would be impossible without these concerns being taken into account. This insistence, as said before, is this text's great strength to the leftist reader: it imagines multiethnic community outside the logic of dominance, refuses to place significance in number, produces an alternative to the exclusivism of de Silva and Wilson, and hints at what form a peaceful Sri Lanka might take. Its weakness, to the postempiricist, is its historicism: its inability to actually imagine peace as a stable or lasting possibility, because the past determines the present and neither provide much hope. For this reason *When Memory Dies* must be supplemented by other stories, in this case, by a reading of an antihistoricist text that also opposes the finding of significance in number: Ernest Macintyre's *Rasanayagam's Last Riot.*

Making History Irrelevant: Rasanayagam's Last Riot

If *When Memory Dies* does not—or perhaps cannot, given its allegiance to a certain type of Marxism—break with historicism, a moment in *Rasanayagam's Last Riot*, Macintyre's play set during the "riots" of July 1983, narrativizes, enables the imagination of, precisely such a possibility. More importantly, it also offers the postempiricist leftist reader an account of the necessity, in the Sri Lankan context, of such a break—a fictional one, of course, but one that rhymes nevertheless with the argument of David Scott discussed in chapter 3. To say this is not to contend that the play itself is antihistoricist

or opposed to history. Indeed, it relies very much on a particular interpretation of Sri Lankan history, emplotted iteratively, as the recurrence
of a particular event, the anti-Tamil riot. In so doing, perhaps inevitably,
it rhymes strongly with the narrative of Tamil separatism. But, at one pivotal moment, it opens itself to be read differently by—yes, I hope I am
predictable by now—someone prepared to pay attention to the detail,
who is familiar with the Sri Lankan debate, and who would know, upon
reading it, that the play is a complicated intervention into the argument
between Sinhalese and Tamil nationalisms that refuses to ally itself with
either position (even if it is more sympathetic, as is only to be expected,
to the Tamil narrative). It is an intervention that, in so doing, takes its
reader not into a situation of frustration and pessimism about peace, because it doesn't see that question as having only two possible answers,
both nationalist: Sinhalese nationalist hegemony or Tamil separatism.
Rather, it imagines—perhaps even insists upon—the possibility of alternative community in Sri Lanka, stages some of the conditions indispensable for such an eventuality, and even raises some important questions
about subject-positions the debate has ignored. If, like *When Memory Dies*,
it fails to imagine peace as a lasting possibility, in staging this failure it
provides the postempiricist leftist reader with some important ideas that
she can work with in the task of reconceptualizing peace in Sri Lanka.

Rasanayagam's Last Riot is emplotted fairly straightforwardly: during
the riots, Rasanayagam, described as "a middle-aged Tamil living and
working in Colombo," seeks refuge with Philip Fernando, "Rasanayagam's
university roommate in the mid-fifties and his good friend ever after," and
Sita Fernando, described with surprising brevity as "Philip's wife." (She
turns out, however, to be in many respects the most significant actant
in the play, which, actually, enables if not demands a feminist reading.)
This has become something like a perverse habit for Rasanayagam: he
has sought refuge with the Fernandos before, in " '56, '58, '61, '74, '77, '81."
Rasanayagam's Last Riot, then, is informed by the trope of violence. It sees,
or emplots, the Tamil predicament in Sri Lanka and postcolonial Tamil
history as punctuated if not defined by riot after riot directed against it.
Does this make the text anthropological in inspiration, the ally of Tambiah
and Daniel? Is it shaped by such a disciplinary level? To some extent, it
inevitably must be. How could it be seen then as abiding by Sri Lanka?
Is my reading of it somewhat forced, strong even? No, not really, because
it is better situated as resonating with a certain strand in Tamil nationalism that justifies separatism precisely on the grounds that the Tamils
are victims of attack after attack tantamount to genocide. However,

it is important to note that *Rasanayagam's Last Riot* is not a separatist text; it does not believe in an exclusivist notion of community; none of its actants promote one. Indeed, they all explicitly distance themselves from it. Like *When Memory Dies*, it advocates—not in a didactic sense but in the sense of a lesson to be learned by reading it from the perspective of this study—the distinct participating in each other. That, of course, is one critical reason *Rasanayagam's Last Riot* is a text good to work with and becomes my accomplice, my partner in crime. A second reason, as implied above, is its moment of antihistoricism, its critique of the work of history in the Sri Lankan debate, and its argument that the past should not determine the present. A third is its raising of a question that the debate over peace in Sri Lanka has yet to adequately recognize: its narrativization of the contradiction between gender and nationality and its insistence that the debate on peace *must* take women's concerns into account.[32] And a fourth—which, like the third, is another question, another subject-position the debate has ignored—is that of the southern Tamil. In raising this last question, *Rasanayagam's Last Riot*, unlike the debate over peace in Sri Lanka, turns out to be intervening from a position that questions the finding of significance in number.

As the play opens, at the beginning of the riots, the Fernandos, newly retired from their jobs, are preparing to emigrate to Australia. As always during such a riot, they await the arrival of Rasanayagam. To Philip, the friendship between the two old university mates "transcends" politics, which they never talk about. That is to say, the friendship is only possible by the repression of politics. This is not to imply that Philip is uninterested in politics. Philip "thrashes out" the "Tamil problem," as he puts it, with his Sinhalese friends, those who presumably have a position similar to his. With Rasanayagam, in contrast, he talks only about their old university days, assuming, again presumably, that Rasanayagam, being Tamil, would hold an opposing position. Sita has not complained about this before or even found it strange, but 1983 is different. The career of Sinhalese nationalism is beginning to disturb her now, although it hadn't before. Until recently, she tells her husband, she had behaved as a "nominal Tamil . . . like all my Colombo Tamil friends and relatives." She laughed and cried "only in English." Sita, in her self-conception, is a Tamil in name only, or even something less than that, since she actually changed her surname upon marriage. She says, "I have never taken an interest in the language policy, the colonization schemes, the university admissions system, the employment ratios in the public service, Tamil kingdoms of the past, and the so-called traditional homelands and all that kind of thing. I have no feel for these things" (9). She didn't, in short, identify with the Tamil narrative of discrimination. It didn't affect her. But then came the burning of the Jaffna public library in 1981—an event, by the way, to be found in the record.[33] After that, things changed. She realized that to be a "real" Tamil, as opposed to just a nominal one, was to identify with that narrative of discrimination, which resonates with Wilson and even more with Ponnambalam, to "feel" for it, perhaps abide by it, and to share this feeling with other Tamils. Identity, here, is about active socio-political identification, almost self-conscious acknowledgment of interpellation, and is not simply an inherited state; it is understood—or staged—as performative. But this identity has been denied Sita since marriage—mostly on account, she feels, of her own doing, which has also reinforced other Tamils' perceptions of her:

> There was a meeting of the committee of the OGA on the day the news of the burning of the Jaffna Library reached Colombo . . . The Tamils in the committee had arrived first . . . I could hear them talking passionately about the burning . . . and there were some powerful Tamil sentiments bursting out from those unlikely, deracinated women, like me . . .

> I could feel myself rushing forward to join them, to satisfy my own urge to express communally, which I never knew existed. I ran and went stumbling forward toward them . . . and then . . . when they saw me . . . they stopped . . . (8)

Sita has her own understanding of why this happened: "I'm sure they felt no malice towards me . . . They are too deracinated for that. It was some sort of misplaced deference for my marriage. I suppose they take it that when a female marries into the other nationality, she opts out of everything else into a special category called 'Domestic Bliss Only'!" (8).

This ironic statement gets to the very heart of one of the contradictions between gender and nationality. Sita may not have identified herself as Tamil before, but then, apparently, neither have her other female "Colombo Tamil" friends, whom she considers deracinated like herself. Nevertheless, at this critical moment, when one of the great symbols of Tamil learning has been destroyed—and one might remember here that it was the search for learning, education, that took Saha out of Jaffna in *When Memory Dies*—they rediscover, as it were, their ethnicity and perform or produce again their Tamilness. Sita wants to do so, too; she wants to be interpellated as Tamil—and to acknowledge such interpellation (even if she understood so doing, then, as being "communal"). She rushed forward, but stumblingly—something to be understood here as signifying not hesitation so much as, perhaps, almost a collapse under the burden of repression—to echo the sentiments of the group, needing their recognition, for identity is always a social as much as it is an individual affair. Sita cannot be a Tamil if she is not acknowledged as such by other Tamils (or the census, or some interpellating agency). But they refuse to see her as Tamil, refuse to let her produce such an identity that, within this heteronormative and patriarchal logic, has been lost due to her marriage to a non-Tamil. This is a burden that falls unequally upon the woman; a man in a "multiethnic" marriage is not deemed by such logic to lose his identity, much less expected to change his name. Reflecting upon this experience, Sita tells her husband, while the two of them wait for Rasanayagam's arrival, that he had "always had two sides to your life, yourself as a person with an identity as father, husband, friend, within our family and also as a person with an identity as a Sinhalese in the wider circle of Sinhalese people, which is the normal condition of most mankind" (10). She, in contrast, did not. Her life, it is implied in a most powerful formulation, is not "normal"—and has not been throughout her marriage, when she did not have an ethnic identity, when it happened to get repressed. Is there something to be learned from this story—this singular and unverifiable story, one might add—by the leftist reader trying to reconceptualize peace? Is Macintyre trying to tell her something? Is this just a moment in a story, or does it intervene in the Sri Lankan conversation on peace?

In the debate over constitutional reform in Sri Lanka, the conflict is understood as one between the Sinhalese and the Tamils (and, in some accounts, the Muslims), so it follows that it should be settled by the Sinhalese and the Tamils (and, in some accounts, the Muslims). To conflict management, and the disciplines that authorize it—political science, constitutional law—the women in these groups do not have, could not have, substantial interests that differ from, let alone contradict, that of the men. Such a perspective, of course, has had a long career outside conflict management, one complicit—to cut a long story short—with nationalism, and it is not surprising to find it echoed in Wilson and de Silva (although one expected more from Sivanandan). In their understanding, ethnicity, as a category, is unmarked by gender—or class. If *When Memory Dies* interrupts nationalism by both exposing its exclusivism and foregrounding the issue of class, *Rasanayagam's Last Riot* reminds its reader that the gendered nature of identity must be taken into account by any leftist seeking to reconceptualize peace. Sita wants to be able to assert and affirm her identity without her marriage—or, to be precise, a patriarchal coding of it—being a hindrance. This assertion is not, it is important to note, a simple matter of demanding equal rights for women. Sita insists, much more significantly, that the distinct participate in each other, address the question of difference, that the man *speak to* the woman and the Sinhalese speak to the Tamil, that Philip stop "thrashing out" the ethnic problem with his Sinhalese friends and instead talk to, listen to, and take into account the arguments of Sita and Rasa: "what is there to trash out the Tamil problem with the Sinhalese; you've got to thrash it out with the Tamils" (6). The woman, in other words, takes the initiative to begin a dialogue, begin speaking to, without which peace would be impossible. (And, in so doing, she reminds the reader of the courageous work of the organization Women for Peace, among others.) Whereas the man is secure in his identity, the woman is not and cannot be; whereas the structures that undergird the performance or production of identity allow the man to be so secure, they do not offer the same to the woman: this lack of security makes the woman, in this instance, question exclusivist identity and its consequences.

So, at Sita's insistence, Philip agrees to have a conversation with Rasa, though only if she instigates it. It's better, he feels, if a Tamil begins the political conversation with another Tamil. Sita does so, somewhat reluctantly; after all, Philip is the friend. However, Rasanayagam is reluctant to speak when questioned. Indeed, in what one is meant to understand as typical patriarchal fashion, he asks Sita to retire as she has done in past riots, leave the men to their reminiscences. The woman, however, is not to be denied; if reluctant initially, she is determined now to seize her opportunity. She will not "know her place." Or, if you like, the play stages her subjectivity as (proto)feminist. So, Sita asks Rasa, straightforwardly, when Philip is out of the room, "what are your feelings on the racial question?" He replies, equally straightforwardly, "every grievance and discrimination that the Tamils are claiming, I subscribe to, but that does not mean I'm not a Sri Lankan . . . I'm a Sri Lankan Tamil" (34). Rasanayagam, the reader has been told, "was not really an anglicized Colombo man. True, his education at Peradeniya was 'Western' . . . But it was his growth at Jaffna Hindu College . . . that became the important part of his being . . . The core of Rasanayagam remained Jaffna peninsular" (19). Rasanayagam, then, is more than a "nominal" Tamil. He may have lived most of his adult life in the south of Sri Lanka, but this has not "deracinated" him. He identifies with the Tamil narrative of discrimination completely, but that doesn't make him renounce a claim upon Sri Lanka or make him separatist. Or, to put this differently, through the figure of Rasanayagam, the text stages an encounter between Tamil nationalism of a nonseparatist variety and hegemonic Sinhalese nationalism (in the figure of Philip Fernando). It tries, one might say, to make these two positions speak to each other and imagines such a possibility. It stages, without sentimentalizing the issue or depicting any easy resolution of the conflict, the difficulties involved, somewhat like the confrontation staged in this study between Sinhalese and Tamil nationalisms.

As the conversation progresses, Rasanayagam makes his critique of what must be understood as the limitations of historicism. He has, at this moment in the play, distanced himself from separatism: "I'm not for encouraging the break-up of the island, in fact that is impossible, we live in the same island" (37). Philip, predictably enough, greets this announcement with encouragement. This is precisely what Sinhalese nationalism desires. But Rasa is not done yet: "at the same time it is obvious that we can't go back to the past, too much has happened . . . and it's a fact that the Tamil-speaking people actually live in a separate part of the country, so that amount of separation has always existed" (37). The leftist reader, of course, will pause at the text's deployment of the term "the Tamil-speaking people." Since it is uttered by the text's ethical center and not rebutted by another actant, this amounts to an endorsement of the term, a denial of Muslim difference. Unlike Sivanandan, clearly, and like de Silva and Wilson, Macintyre cannot narrate the specificity of Muslim difference; not only does *Rasanayagam's Last Riot* not have Muslim (or UpCountry Tamil) actants, it doesn't see the conflict as involving these groups at all. It is happening between just two principals. The leftist reader must notice and object to this, even while she insists that no text could be perfect. To return, then, to the narrative: Philip rejects Rasanayagam's statement on historical grounds: "archaeological evidence shows the ruins of Buddhist temples strewn all over the north and east." Where Philip would look back, his position rhyming with de Silva's, Rasanayagam would not; where Philip's claims upon the present (politics) are based upon the past (history), Rasanayagam's are not, and with good reason. Indeed, I find this the moment in the text of immense significance, for the Tamil responds to his friend: "they are ruins, Philip, we have to deal with the situation that exists now" (37). Like Wilson against de Silva, or Dharmadasa against Gunawardana for that matter, Rasa could have met archaeology with archaeology; he could have maintained—as some scholars do—that Tamil ruins in the north and east of the country predate the Sinhalese ones. Significantly enough, though, he does not. It is the present, "the situation that exists now," that he insists demands attention. One could, he implies, keep talking endlessly about what really happened in the past—endlessly and, as Scott might interject, inconclusively—or one could deal with the present, the fact that Tamils are being killed by Sinhalese nationalist mobs. The past is irrelevant in that context; regardless of whether those Buddhist temples actually predate the Tamil presence in Sri Lanka or even whether, as many Sinhalese nationalists apparently believe, Buddha actually visited Sri Lanka three times in previous incarnations, flying—or whatever—across the water, and blessed the island as the one in which his religion would flourish, the past does not justify Sinhalese nationalist mobs attacking Tamil civilians. The present has to be responded to on ethical and political grounds, not on historical grounds. That is one of the (antihistoricist) lessons the leftist postempiricist reader might—perhaps even must—learn from Rasanayagam and take from this play.

Philip, however, is unmoved by Rasa's arguments. But their disagreement is interrupted by the news of a massacre at the main Colombo jail of some Tamil prisoners. Among those killed is a friend of Rasanayagam, a community activist from the north. The news of the murder shatters the Tamil and he decides, not long after, to leave the Fernandos' house for a nearby refugee camp. The Sinhalese cannot protect the Tamils any more; if they cannot safeguard prisoners, of all people, they clearly can no longer be trusted. Rasanayagam wants, instead, to be with his "own." That appears to be the only option remaining for the Tamils. This can be read, of course, as a separatist or at the very least an exclusivist gesture, a repudiation of his earlier commitment to Sri Lanka, but, as will be seen, eventually it doesn't add up to one. For his part, Philip protests the decision adamantly: "I know I can protect Rasa better here" (40). He is overruled by the two Tamils; Sita, too, is convinced that Rasanayagam should leave. The Tamils conclude that the Sinhalese can no longer protect them. A police escort is arranged to make sure he gets to the camp safely, a luxury made available to him due to the intervention of another old university friend, a senior police officer. Along the way, they are met by a Sinhalese nationalist mob who want to determine, to test, his identity, as they had been doing with hundreds of Tamils all that day. The text makes it clear that Rasanayagam could have easily escaped the mob; all he had to do, as Jeganathan understands it, was "perform his Tamilness as Sinhalaness."[34] He had already done so, without pause, earlier in the day; he recounted so doing, once he got to the Fernandos, with enthusiasm. This time, however, Rasanayagam refuses—and is killed, burned to death by the mob. The text does not explicitly suggest why this happened, whether, for instance, the narrative event is to be read as a suicide. (Rasanayagam, after all, was single, without family and retired.) The responsible reader, however, cannot avoid the question. She must ask not so much why did he let himself be killed—a question without an answer, since the Tamil is an actant in a play, a fictional product whose head cannot be gotten into because it never existed—but what does Rasanayagam want? What does his death signify? Why does the text stage his death, and under such circumstances? Does it constitute some kind of statement on the Sri Lankan debate, draw attention to something missing in the way it has been polarized between Sinhalese and Tamil nationalisms? Can the leftist reader learn anything from it?

To answer these questions one must get back to the rest of the conversation between Rasa and Philip, during which the Tamil offers the Sinhalese what sounds like a deal, a compromise, or a bargain, something political science might consider a new social contract:

> the traditional homelands of the Sri Lankan Tamils can become an ideal *buffer* between the fifty million Tamils of Tamil Nadu and the thirteen or so million Sinhalese of Sri Lanka, because the Sri Lankan Tamil culture belongs in Sri Lanka. But if pressure is applied to that culture by the Sinhalese it will move closer to Tamil Nadu for protection and *lose its distinctiveness.* And the Sinhalese will be deprived of their buffer of protection. (37; emphasis added)

Philip Fernando retorts that he does not understand his friend; the latter restates his case: "if the Sinhalese help to foster the distinctive culture of the Sri Lankan Tamils by guaranteeing it in the areas where they live, one day the Sinhalese may even depend on the Tamils of the north to be its front line of defence in the preservation of its own civilization" (37). In these two formulations, Rasanayagam brilliantly reverses the positions of the Sinhalese and the Tamil: *he minoritizes the Sinhalese!* And then the Tamil proceeds to offer the Sinhalese, in a delicious irony, protection even while being protected by him! In so doing, the Tamil is playing upon the Sinhalese nationalist fear (articulated by de Silva, among others) of being a minority in a larger southern Asian context. The occurrence of number in that unit is not coincidental. But Rasanayagam is not, it is important to notice, threatening to inflict those Tamil hordes, lying just a shallow and narrow sea away, as de Silva pointed out, upon the Sinhalese. Rather, he is making a radical plea that the leftist reader must learn from: he asks the Sinhalese to respect and foster Tamil distinctiveness. He wants the distinct to participate in each other. He is clear about one thing: Tamil culture is Sri Lankan and "belongs" in the country, but its remaining in the country, as it were, should not be taken for granted. He wants the Sinhalese to think of the Tamils as a buffer, a barrier, or a shield, as an ally and a friend against India. In short, he wants the Sinhalese to reconceptualize the way they have defined their relationship with the Tamils. They can treat the Tamils as minor in every sense: as a minority lesser in number and therefore significance and so not entitled to the rights guaranteed to the majority, and as a minor, as in not "of age" and therefore in need of protection. Or they can treat the Tamil as equal. They can, that is, continue with business as usual—in which case the Tamil will have no option but to resist and retaliate—or the Sinhalese can change.

What the Tamil wants to know, quite simply, is whether the Sinhalese will continue to apprehend the Tamils as quantity, within the terms of arithmetic, or whether they are prepared to relate to the Tamils within the terms of (e)quality, of geometry. Rasanayagam's position is quite clear: to him—like Ramanathan and Ponnambalam before—the minority perspective is one that rejects the placing of significance in number, and rejects the notion—one shared both by Philip Fernando and the United Nations—that the minority, as such, must be protected.[35] To him, rather, the Tamils must not be conceived as minor but be allowed to determine their own fate, fortune, and future. One option along these lines, of course, is separatism, the production of Tamil subjectivity in national terms. But Rasanayagam not only refuses, as he puts it, to be "pushed back" to Jaffna (33), he also refuses the security of the exclusively Tamil refugee camp (whose denizens, it is important not to forget, were supposed to be shipped to Tamil-dominated Jaffna the next day). He wants, one might say, to be able to produce his Tamilness as Tamilness, under any circumstances and without fear, not just in the northeast but everywhere in Sri Lanka (as does, not coincidentally, Sita Fernando). Rasanayagam will not compromise on this. Compromise is an option the play argues is unavailable to him (to them), to those Wilson calls Colombo Tamils, not only because Sinhalese nationalism now refuses to "protect" them but also because, as seen in the last chapter, they were "written off" by Tamil nationalism too. This option has, incredibly enough, not even been raised in the Sri Lankan debate, which has pivoted only around the question of regional autonomy but has not addressed the question of the rights, the future, or the fears of southern Tamils, who would remain outside the northeast even after regional autonomy. In thus staging Rasanayagam's death, then, the play, like *When Memory Dies*, tells its reader that its narrative moment is pessimistic; it does not see much hope for peace in Sri Lanka. But, in so doing, it also draws the leftist reader's attention to those things necessary for peace: to the dangerousness of historicism as a response to the question of peace in Sri Lanka; it insists that women's concerns—as *women's* concerns—must be addressed by the debate as central, not incidental, to any discussion of peace; it insists that the distinct must participate in each other, speak to each other, and abide by each other for peace to happen; it also suggests—through this singular and unverifiable moment—that peace is impossible as long as community is defined through and significance is found in number; it insists that the Colombo Tamil, even if lesser in number than those domiciled in the northeast, cannot and should not be ignored and that, to phrase this differently, the methods, protocols, and categories of social science, which quite literally cannot see this Tamil because she does not count, could be argued to stand in the way of peace. The postempiricist postcolonial reader ignores these lessons at her peril.

Conclusion

To the quandary that bedeviled me as a child and bemuses me still—the chicken or egg question—I really have no answer. Did my understanding of the question of peace in Sri Lanka and of the shape peace should take, the one that informs this study, come before or after reading Adorno? Did Adorno articulate something I understood intuitively? Did reading Sivanandan help me better understand Adorno, or did it work the other way around? Surely, before reading Sivanandan or Adorno, I must have known the limitations—ethical and political—of de Silva and Wilson, of Sinhalese and Tamil nationalisms? The Sri Lankan leftist critique of nationalism—the work of Gunasinghe, Gunawardana, Jayawardena—must have shaped my thinking here. Then, surely, Macintyre could not have been necessary to appreciate the inadequacies of historicism? After all, the French critique of history, not to mention Scott's intervention into the Sri Lankan debate, has been cited. Surely I knew, again before encountering Macintyre, that a feminist argument about peace might raise specific issues no other position would or could? The work of Jayawardena, if not that of many other feminists, has also been cited. Which is another way of getting at this question: does literature—understood as a verb—really make a difference? Does it enable something social science does not and, more importantly, cannot? Are literary critics, readers, especially privileged subjects—with postempiricists being even more privileged than others? Could some of these conclusions have been reached without reading fiction? Is this study making too grand a claim for literature, for reading?

The only proper answer to those questions is "yes and no." For, what is defended here, or advocated for perhaps, is not literature as a material object, and certainly not the discipline, but reading as a method, reading postempirically and postcolonially, reading fiction against social science. What matters to that project is the refusal to be limited by empiricism and historicism, by the apparent fixity of the present, or by the failure of the imagination. That is where both Macintyre and Sivanandan make their crucial contributions to the question of reconceptualizing peace and offer the leftist an alternative, something new to think about; it is where Wilson and de Silva, even Jayawardena and Gunawardena, do not. For, no one will ever really know whether the historical Marshall Wickremasinghe was a communalist. In conceiving the fictional actant Marshal Appu otherwise, in making his story rhyme with that of S.W. and making S.W.'s story rhyme in turn with Tissa's, in also staging the travails of Ramasamy and the death of Sultan, *When Memory Dies* asks its patient reader, who is prepared to read that text against the Sri Lankan debate, whether the kind of nonexclusivist community it tries to imagine—which it must *imagine* because the record does not allow such an argument—is not more enabling to the leftist than that of Wilson and de Silva. *Rasanayagam's Last Riot*, for its part, in staging the conversation between Philip Fernando and Rasanayagam, calls into question the limits of historicism—whether in de Silva, Wilson, or Sivanandan—as a response to the present. It suggests, in a Nietzschean spirit, that we may need to forget the past, always contestable anyway, in order to live in the present. Through the figure of Sita Fernando, it calls into question the inadequacy of any understanding of ethnic identity that doesn't take gender into account; peace, it suggests, is always gendered. And, in staging the death of Rasanayagam and his refusal to compromise on his desire to perform or produce his Tamilness as Tamilness anywhere in Sri Lanka, it calls into account not only Sinhalese nationalism's brutalities but Tamil nationalism's refusal to protect its own nationals—its passing a poison off as a medicine.

Or, to be precise, these two texts enable themselves to be read as such, since they don't actually make these arguments in any explicit or analytic form. Literature, then, enables the putting to work of the imagination; and reading, optimism. Yes, the texts themselves may have produced their narrative moments pessimistically, but they need not be read that way. Or, for that matter, optimism need not be understood thus. To the leftist who begins from the position that peace cannot be proclaimed to have burst out merely because there is no war but, rather, that it requires an end to domination and mutual participation, these texts enable the theoretical argument that such proclamations must be examined through the perspectives of ethnicity, gender, and class before they become persuasive; that, after all, is the work of theory. The role of literature is to both enable and complicate it. When conflict management says, "yes, we know the problem in Sri Lanka and what to do about it," literature responds, "oh, really? Have you considered the consequences of this, that, and the other?" To conflict management, as will be seen in the concluding chapter, conceptualizing peace in Sri Lanka is very easy: all it requires, and there is consensus on this, is making the two parties, the Sri Lankan state (Sinhalese nationalism) and the LTTE (Tamil nationalism), compromise. This might pose several practical problems, and indeed it will; but what peace would ultimately look like is not in doubt: some form of regional autonomy for the Tamils, for the northeast. (In most versions of this thesis, there is a footnote to the effect that Muslim interests must also be taken into account.) This consensus has been interrupted from sections of the left—the empirical, social scientific left. How reading enables one to reconceptualize peace will be discussed in the final chapter.

Conclusion

Does Democracy Inhibit Peace?

Who says a chicken feather can't rise to heaven?

—Mao Tse-tung

This study has approached the question of peace in Sri Lanka, perhaps somewhat insistently, not just from a postempiricist and postcolonial but also from a leftist perspective. The script the study is produced by—its inheritances, convictions, and commitments, whether theoretical, ethical, or political—has enabled no alternative, no other "choice." Upon reading the texts, the histories, of Tamil and Sinhalese nationalisms from these perspectives and positions, many conclusions have been reached, some more important than others. Obviously, the first of these is that there are texts that abide by Sri Lanka and texts that don't. The latter texts are Western/Eurocentric/anthropological or, more accurately, address the—largely culturalist—concerns of the West, which sees Sri Lanka as a (violent) place of difference. In the former group are those texts that address and intervene within the political debate of a place called Sri Lanka, and effectively understand the country as a place of singularity (repetition with a difference). Texts in the former group (those that do abide by Sri Lanka) would include, ironically and unfortunately enough, writers whose work could be considered leftist, and the latter—as has been seen with Wilson and de Silva—right-wing writers. Thus, while the anti-Eurocentrist reader would acknowledge, even appreciate, the difference between the interventions of de Silva and Wilson and that of the likes of

Daniel, the leftist reader would be opposed to the former. Still, the concern remains: to what end? The questions were asked in chapter 2: is it in the interest of the leftist to accept, to advocate even, a continuing role in a *peaceful* Sri Lanka for Sinhalese nationalism—a project that, as I hope my reading has demonstrated, is hegemonic at best, genocidal at worst, and which therefore could be characterized as embodying the *différance* of peace? Is Sinhalese nationalism at all compatible with peace (as understood by this study, after the Adornean formulation)? In chapter 3, Tamil nationalism was also found to be incompatible with peace since it, too, did not foresee or promise an end to domination and was not interested in mutual participation either. Indeed, it was argued that Tamil nationalism is best understood as *pharmakonic*, as a medicine that is also a poison and thus at best an inadequate response to the criminal career of Sinhalese nationalism. If successful, it would "liberate" some Tamils in the northeast of Sri Lanka, leave the Tamils in the rest of the country to an uncertain fate, and minoritize the northeastern Muslims. Consequently, other questions arose. Does the leftist seek to eliminate these nationalisms, to marginalize them, or to consign them to some position in between? Would it be naively and irresponsibly utopian to prefer the first alternative, to wish the nationalisms away? Or, would it be extreme, mirroring one's opposition, to desire such a consummation devoutly? The aporia, in other words, is this: is it ethical to seek compromise with a genocidal nationalism (two in this case, given not just Sinhalese nationalism's response to the Tamils but also Tamil nationalism's response to the Muslims)? On the other hand, is it ethical to seek to eliminate it? These are not easy questions, and, quite frankly, I have been grappling with them, without finding satisfactory answers, for years. I do not know, to phrase the matter as concisely as possible, whether one's ethics should overdetermine one's politics or vice versa, or whether they should exist in a productive tension. Nevertheless, I will address these questions in this chapter, by way of a reading of an effectively ethical position on the contemporary Sri Lankan moment, of the University Teachers for Human Rights (Jaffna) and two explicitly political or pragmatic positions—those of Jayadeva Uyangoda and David Scott. Before that, some other conclusions of this study must be noted.

I have also argued in this study that history, inasmuch as the discipline produces itself as an unbiased recitation of the facts, cannot produce peace in Sri Lanka, as the nationalisms insist. The two different (symptomatic) histories—Sinhalese and Tamil nationalist—read closely here turn out not to be the product of the disciplinary level exclusively, as they claim, but are overdetermined by the narratological and, even more crucially, the abiding/political levels. They claim to deal with the facts alone but rely on literary devices to tell their story. They emplot and narrativize the "same" events very differently. They produce identity where another reader could quite easily notice difference. The hero in one account is the villain of the other. If history were as objective as they claim, a mere mirroring of the event, this should be impossible, which leads to another conclusion: either the histories read here are bad, unprofessional, and unworthy of the disciplinary label or there is a problem, as the French critique demonstrates, with the discipline itself. Since the postempiricist position is against the notions of good, bad, better, and so on—which all derive sustenance from the notion of the canon—and since the French critique has been persuasive to this study, the latter alternative has to be the case. (By the way, it is when faced with a question such as this that the orthodox leftist would get caught in an unresolvable contradiction: being an empiricist, she would believe in the possibility of a good or better history but, being a leftist, would be opposed to the canon!) This led to the conclusion that not just nationalist history but the very discipline itself must be deauthorized. Yes, we live, as Foucault argues, in the age of history, but that age, or disciplinary moment, of the sovereign subject has been brought to crisis by what I have been calling postempiricism. To seek to deauthorize history is to seek to intensify that crisis, consolidate its epistemological gains, and, in so doing, finish the critique of Eurocentrism.

Another crucial position arrived at in this study is rethinking the notion of the minority position. It is best understood, as argued in chapter 3, not as the perspective of the position lesser in number but as the one opposed to finding significance in number. Such a perspective would be opposed, therefore, to social science, which can only find significance in grouping things together, producing identity out of difference, working with arithmetic, and understanding analogy as self-evident, as opposed to a literary trope. All of this led, of course, to questioning democracy, specifically representative democracy, which works upon the majoritarian principle. If, as has been argued here, democracy is structurally repressive of the minority, how does the leftist respond to such a conclusion? Does she seek to refashion democracy, as a Lani Guinier might desire, or move beyond it? Does she accept that, despite its flaws, democracy is the best political structure we can conceive, as democracy's advocates (like Robert Dahl) insist, or does she think it possible to imagine otherwise? If the conclusions of this study are persuasive, does the leftist have any choice but to imagine otherwise?

Political theory, of course, has conceived alternatives to majoritarian democracy. Consociationalism is one such. While Wilson conceived of it narrowly as cooperation between elites, one of its best-known advocates, Arend Lijphart, understands it in somewhat greater depth. To him, consociationalism is predicated upon the belief that, to function effectively and frictionlessly, a plural or heterogeneous society needs political institutions and arrangements different from a homogenous one. These institutions and arrangements would also be democratic but not necessarily take the form familiar to the Anglo-American world. Such a claim, obviously, is impossible without the prior proposition, or belief, that some societies are homogenous and others are not. But this, of course, is not self-evident, at least not to the postempiricist reader. In working from and with such a distinction, Lijphart draws upon the writings of the influential U.S. political scientist, Gabriel Almond, who made his claim on an apparently geographic basis: to him, Anglo-American culture was homogenous, whereas continental European culture was not. Lijphart concurs with both the empirical claim and its ground because he finds Almond's a "theoretically rich, well-integrated, and economically formulated typology."[1] Once again, one should pause here and note the categories through which social science produces knowledge. Types—should one call them stereotypes?—are what is sought to be created, and the more economical the scheme, i.e. the fewer the types, the better. That is to say, to repeat a point made earlier, social science is allergic to the singular; it must repress difference. Where it cannot analogize, it will not find significance. It must produce identity out of difference, count, and cluster objects together to make sense. This was seen in de Silva and Wilson, Horowitz and the economics textbook (Mansfield and Yohe), and now in Almond and Lijphart. And yet social science is betrayed by its own rhetoric. For Lijphart adds that, despite its theoretical magnificence, Almond's scheme has one "major weakness": it "does not deal satisfactorily with the smaller European democracies," four in number, which don't fit into either type, not being quite Anglo-American or continental. These four Almond dismisses from consideration. This might suggest that political science finds significance only in magnitude, forgets the small, and is opposed to the minority perspective, but Lipjhart doesn't make such a critique. He desires inclusion. The logic at work here is quite simple: your typology is okay, even if incomplete, as long as it could include, make room for, or be stretched in order to make room for my types; exceptions do not break, or even require an alteration of, the rules. Of course, the notion that exceptions might actually lead to typology itself being called into question is not something that could be entertained. If it were, social science would make itself impossible.

But, still, and remarkably enough, it cannot repress the singular, not entirely. For Lijphart, after looking at the countries of Western Europe on an almost case-by-case basis, is ultimately forced to concede that the "fundamental error committed by much of the theoretical literature on political development is to exaggerate the degree of homogeneity of the Western democratic states."[2] This is a statement that must be paused at, for it constitutes a quite stunning critique, ultimately, of the method of his own discipline—producing homogeneity out of heterogeneity, identity out of difference—which Lijphart finds to be based on a fundamental mistake: not so much a falsehood but, near enough, an exaggeration. Indeed, upon consideration, Lijphart admits that even "Almond's Anglo-American type" doesn't describe a truly homogenous society and, going one step further, that the only homogenous society that could be considered to exist is not a society that actually exists but, perversely enough, "an idealized [exaggerated?] version of British society." No society, then, could be considered homogenous, not in the strict sense. Lijphart is prepared to concede this. He is a good empiricist and must respect the evidence. But then, after doing so, he proceeds, stunningly enough, as if the distinction is tenable—despite calling it a fundamental error, the most basic of mistakes, the most elementary of inaccuracies. Shame, I ask again, but this time with my tongue in my cheek, where is thy blush? Can one take social science seriously after claims like this? Of course, political science must maintain the distinction, insist upon the existence of homogenous societies—but for ideological, perhaps even racist, reasons, not for intellectual ones. Consociationalism, in this argument, is only necessary for heterogeneous or segmented societies. If all societies are actually heterogeneous, as the evidence seems to suggest to Lijphart, they might all need to consider consociationalism as an option. *All* of them, including Britain and the United States (which would require the white majority to contemplate sharing power—what a thought!). Such a move would be extremely radical but is one that Lijphart cannot make. He can't place democracy itself on the table, even if his own argument leads in that direction.

The question of democracy is not the only moment in the text where the singular emerges, deconstituting Lijphart's claims. It does so in many other places. Consistent with the arithmetical drift in political science, Lijphart develops an "index of fragmentation" by breaking down his societies into their various segments, on the basis of the size, number, and so on of their ethnic groups and then formulating a mathematical index. This is intended to measure "the probability that a randomly selected pair of individuals in society will belong to different groups."[3] His next step is to fit the four "smaller" countries of Europe into this scheme. Austria and the Netherlands "fit . . . quite neatly." Switzerland, however, "cannot be assigned without difficulty." This might suggest, as with all typologies, that it is the method underlying such indexes that needs to be interrogated, not that there is a problem with unwieldy Switzerland. But Lijphart cannot explore such a possibility, despite the fact that even Belgium, his fourth example, also doesn't quite fit the scheme: "Belgium fits combination 5. But . . . it is probably best to consider Belgium an instance of combination 4"—ahem, with some exceptions.[4] Exceptions, again. Why don't these exceptions suggest that the rules themselves may need alteration? Of the four smaller European countries Lijphart tries to tabulate, only two, by his own admission, appear to be tabulatable. Just half. This should indicate, to a mathematically oriented method, that the method itself isn't working. But for some reason—disciplinary, not intellectual—it does not. It cannot.

If its flaws are typical of social science, consociationalism is also a challenge to political science, or at least to its Anglo-American incarnation, for it presents an alternative to the Anglo-American conception of (representative) democracy. In segmented countries, consociationalism requires the following: "a grand coalition of the political leaders of all significant segments of the plural society"; "mutual veto or 'concurrent majority' rule"; "proportionality as the principle standard of political representation, civil service appointments and allocation of public funds"; and "a high degree of autonomy for each segment to run its own affairs."[5] The first feature is the most crucial—and the most elitist. The political leaders, not their supporters, are envisaged as coming together, forming a coalition, indulging, if you like, in an exclusive and elitist kind of mutual participation. But, Lijphart is quick to point out, this doesn't make consociationalism something unusual. Representative democracy is elitist, too, even if it doesn't admit it: "the elitism of consociational democracy should not be compared with a theoretical—and naive—ideal of equal power and participation by all citizens but with the degree of elite predominance that is the norm in democratic regimes of all kinds."[6] Even liberal democracy, that is, cannot be considered egalitarian. In making that statement, once again, Lijphart comes close to a fundamental critique of democracy itself, as a system that is structurally elitist, but pulls back from actually doing so. He verges upon the insight that parliamentary representation, based as it is upon a distinction and distance between representer and represented, a substitution by the former of the latter, a deferral by the latter to the former, should therefore be considered elitist. The consequences of following that lead, however, he cannot tolerate; they are ideologically unacceptable, too dangerous, and might lead to a critique of democracy itself. So, tamely, he detours.

Or, rather, he proceeds with the argument that, for plural or segmented societies, at any rate, elitism is a good and necessary thing. Lijphart understands segmentation, following J. S. Furnivall, as "in the strictest sense a medley [of peoples], for they mix but do not combine." In such segmented and conflicted societies, it is too much to expect the people to come together—thus the pragmatism and elitism of consociationalism; but, unlike the people, the elites might be expected to combine for the sake of peace. If they work together on the basis of "mutual veto," the second most significant feature of consociationalism, they'll manage conflict "by co-operation and agreement among the different elites, rather than by competition and majority decision."[7] Mutual veto, or concurrent majority rule, is a system in which a majority of the representatives of all the segments of a society have to approve legislation before it is passed. To that extent, it doesn't escape the logic of majoritarianism, but, it is important to notice, it is instituted to prevent just one majority, understood as *the* majority produced by the abstraction of number, dominating a legislature. To that extent, it is premised and predicated against majoritarianism. It is thus possible, I think, to read mutual veto, in Adornean terms, as an instance of the maintenance of distinction with mutual participation (if not a completely satisfactory participation). Lijphart, however, calls it an instance of "negative minority rule," which sounds like, to fall back on a term from advertising, really bad packaging. For Lijphart isn't just a describer of consociationalism, he's also an advocate. And suggesting a form of minority rule as an alternative to majoritarianism is unlikely to appeal to the advocates of the latter, those whom one is trying to convince to compromise. But consociationalism's unfamiliarity, within political science or outside, is not really from its inability to make itself attractive. Lijphart himself complains that "the entire body of political development theories . . . [is] uniformly indifferent or hostile to the possibilities of consociational democracy."[8] It is not difficult to figure out why. To Lijphart, "consociational democracy is more concerned with the equal or proportionate treatment of groups than with individual equality."[9] That may be; but what it suggests, even if it refuses to foreground it as its theoretical base, is that all societies are heterogeneous and that all societies consist of groups, not individuals. Consociationalism may be too timid, for good ideological reasons, to take on the bases of liberalism and liberal democracy, but its own arguments lead in that direction. Because of this, and because it derives its examples from "small" and Third World countries, the discipline, predicated as it is upon the sovereign subject, or free individual, and the significance of number, must and will marginalize, repress, and minoritize it.

In the Sri Lankan instance, consociationalism was first introduced into the debate on peace by Jayadeva Uyangoda. Surveying the debate in 1993—a decade after Gunasinghe—he implied that Sri Lanka, correctly in my view, badly needed new ideas about peace and constitutional reform—and he had one: consociationalism. Enterprisingly enough, he located this idea not just in recent political science, or G. G. Ponnambalam's "fifty-fifty," but in the thought of the young S. W. R. D. Bandaranaike, whom he called a "proto-consociationalist." Bandaranaike had argued in a 1926 speech that the ethnic divisions of Sri Lanka demanded a federalist form of government. Uyangoda interpreted this, creatively—if not paradoxically, as Scott sees it—as a nascent form of consociationalism (paradoxically because, even though Scott doesn't make this point, consociationalism emphasizes mutual participation—as opposed to federalism, which effectively emphasizes separation). It is, though, not of particular concern here whether Bandaranaike was indeed a consociationalist or could be interpreted as such. The point is that Uyangoda found consociationalism "appropriate for societies [like Sri Lanka] which were ethnically divided and faced problems concerning democracy." The greatest culprit was what he called "ethnic majoritarian democracy . . . [which] tended to exclude ethnic minorities from the political process."[10] Identifying Sri Lanka as an instance of such democracy, Uyangoda argued that the work of Lijphart provided a way of imagining the beginnings of a solution to the country's problems, of a way to include the minorities in the political process. Until this point, the Sri Lankan debate on peace pivoted, almost exclusively, around the question of regional autonomy/federalism/separatism; around, that is, the quantum or form of autonomy or sovereignty the Tamils were entitled to. With Uyangoda's intervention, other issues were placed, as they say, on the table. Autonomy alone, he implied, wouldn't solve the minority problem; indeed, consociationalism meant an opposition to the philosophical basis of autonomy—separatism, majoritarianism, or exclusivism. Uyangoda's argument raised the prospect of radically reimagining the country through the notion of power sharing or, if you like, of mutual participation.

It is nevertheless important to notice that Uyangoda, despite finding inspiration from it, wasn't an uncritical admirer of consociationalism:

> Consociationalism is essentially a utilitarian enterprise; it premises [sic] that the political institutions can and should be manipulated for the maximum benefit of the largest possible number. This is a dangerous premise, both politically and philosophically. The consociational alliance and the sharing of power among leaders of ethnic communities are pragmatic enterprises, which may often lack lasting moral bases required for and by the polity.[11]

This understanding of consociationalism as majoritarian and utilitarian, while not entirely incorrect, can be recast. But the significant point here is that Uyangoda's objection to consociationalism is ethical (he calls it moral). He finds it elitist and pragmatic in its basic approach, seeking to manage conflict, not to solve it. He cannot endorse it for these reasons, since it wouldn't address the underlying reasons for the conflict and also because it lacks a "lasting moral basis." Such a basis, he contends, must be found, and he proceeds to do so in the notions of "ethnic fairness and justice." Again, one might contend that consociationalism was conceived precisely in order to achieve those notions, but Uyangoda ignores the possibility. And then, again paradoxically enough, he argues that what he sees as the utilitarianness of consociationalism be blended with the very liberal notion of the social contract so as to give it a firmer (legal-constitutional) basis than the merely pragmatic or political. Consociationalism, actually, emerged to address the failure of liberalism, grounded as it is upon the category of the unmarked individual, to adequately respond to the problems facing heterogeneous societies, which are grounded, at least according to those who understand society thus, upon not individuals but groups or collectivities. In other words, it constitutes a critique, theoretical and political, of the assumptions of liberalism. To Uyangoda, however, liberalism could actually save it! This is his summary of the ideal consociational contract for Sri Lanka:

> It means that all ethnic groups in the polity are moral equals and equally valued. When the ethnic groups join the association of the state through this contract, they do not consider their ethnic identity; to be equal and equally valued they disregard whether they are Sinhalese, Tamils or Muslims. The communities enter the contract with the privilege of ignorance of their ethnic identity . . . [This] enables them to choose the principles of ethnic justice/injustice while being in a position to define "fairness" untainted by ethnic interests and prejudices.[12]

By refusing to find significance in number, by considering all ethnic groups equal—as opposed to a majority and minorities—and by advocating mutual participation, Uyangoda's understanding of peace seems to coincide with mine, and to a significant degree, it does. But Uyangoda is quite unable to decide whether it is ethnic groups or unmarked individuals who are the constitutive elements, or agents, of his proposed contract. The passage begins by stating that it should be ethnic groups and ends by desiring the unmarked individual. The shift is unexplained, and many questions are begged in the process: if the Sri Lankan conflict, as understood by Uyangoda, is ethnic in nature, how could a denial of ethnicity resolve it? Indeed, how on earth could a sudden denial of their ethnicity by the parties to the conflict be expected at all? Then, if his agents are to disregard or deny their own ethnicity, how could they be expected to see it in others? If his agents see themselves as unmarked, wouldn't they see others as unmarked, too—especially if they, too, enter the contract after shedding their ethnicity? But other, prior questions, also arise: in the first place, can ethnicity be shed so easily? Can we, as Spivak asks somewhere, just walk out of the scripts that produced us? Even if possible, is it ethical to make this demand, to argue for the eradication of difference? Surely the question of ethnicity must be confronted, not evaded or erased, by the Sri Lankan desiring peace?

Scott, one of the few to actually engage with Uyangoda, argues somewhat along these lines in his important response to this position. For a start, he points out that the denial of ethnicity, the production of unmarked Sri Lankan citizens voting, like all modern civilized subjects, on the basis of their economic interest alone, was what the Donoughmore Commission, what he calls "an experiment in colonial governmentality," sought to achieve in the 1930s. The experiment palpably failed (if it had succeeded, there wouldn't have been an "ethnic conflict" in the first place). Scott situates this failure not in the particular, not in the hegemonic project of Sinhalese nationalism, but more generally—and correctly, in my view—within the larger project of the Enlightenment, thus making his argument postcolonial. To him, the Enlightenment is unable to think its way out of the historical impasse we inhabit. This impasse . . . presents itself in the demand on the part of minorities that the liberal-democratic desire for an abstract principle—the principle of number—as the adjudicating principle of political community be recognized as at best incoherent because it denies their difference."[13] Number, or more correctly counting and arithmetic, works against difference. It produces the majority and minority as self-evident facts when they are constructs of the logic of democracy, constructs that, moreover, place value upon the greater number, conflate quantity with quality, and effectively leave the minority of no count. Why is this logic incoherent? Because, to the majoritarian perspective, all numbers are the same: the Sinhalese and Tamils are comparable because what matters about them, as voters in a democracy, is not their ethnicity but the fact that they are unmarked subjects. After all, at an election, all voters, regardless of ethnicity, get just one vote, making every vote equal to every other. So, in the Sri Lankan instance, that the majority of representatives elected is consistently Sinhalese and the minority always Tamil becomes irrelevant, a matter of mere detail. To the minority perspective, however, all numbers are not the same. Tamils are not comparable to the Sinhalese because they are not unmarked subjects. It is a matter here not of arithmetic but of geometry. Ethnicity matters because the Tamils are an oppressed group and the Sinhalese, the oppressor. Scott, like Uyangoda, agrees with this, disagrees with the logic of majoritarianism; but he goes on to argue, instead, that difference should be "embraced," not disavowed, for there to be peace in Sri Lanka. His innovative, if ultimately unpersuasive, suggestions lead one to conclude that what really characterizes Uyangoda's intervention is a failure of the imagination. The argument begins quite daringly with a new and radical idea but cannot follow through on the consequences of that idea, cannot be truly creative or committed to a reconceptualization of the Sri Lankan social, cannot fully explore the implications of consociationalism, recasting it if necessary. Instead, it falls back on an old and thoroughly critiqued theoretical basis: liberalism. Consociationalism is a critique of liberalism; the latter cannot therefore be deployed to shore up perceived inadequacies in the former. Indeed, by arguing that the agents of his contract think of their subjectivity not in ethnic but in unmarked terms, Uyangoda, though he doesn't seem to realize it, is no longer advocating consociationalism in any form but straightforward, unalloyed liberalism.

In contrast, Scott calls for something that could be read as mutual participation. He situates his argument as coming out of a consideration of Sri Lanka but as not pertaining exclusively to it:

> In the late modern political world we inhabit it appears self-evident to us that rule ought to be in the hands of the largest number . . . the majority. There is a relationship between abstract number and political representation that we take for granted as defining the field of possible argument about justice . . . Moreover we instinctively recoil from those who appear to resist this transparent principle of political arithmetic inasmuch as what seems necessarily to be implied by such resistance is that rule ought then to be in the hands of the lesser number, the minority.[14]

To Scott, minority rule is not the only alternative to majority rule. More importantly in the context of the Sri Lankan debate, he interrogates the production of the terms "majority" and "minority," through a reading of de Silva and the logic of what he calls "political arithmetic" (thus conceding that it is not the abstraction of number but the politics of counting, arithmetic, a discipline or method, that is at stake here). To de Silva, the notion of a democratic majority is unmarked. That, in the Sri Lankan context, democratic elections, working through the abstract and disinterested principle of number, produce a Sinhalese parliamentary majority every time is a sheer and unremarkable accident that the Tamils have to live with—even if it makes them of no count; de Silva, as a Sinhalese himself, has no stake in it, since he writes not as a Sinhalese but as a historian. Understanding de Silva, somewhat generously, though not necessarily inaccurately, as a liberal democrat and not as a Sinhalese nationalist, Scott goes on to ask whether liberal theory, which grounds de Silva's claims, even in its new and improved incarnation à la John Rawls, can accommodate difference and concludes, after examining Rawls, his supporters, and his critics, that it cannot. Scott further concludes that, coming back to the Sri Lankan instance, the "seeming democratic priority of abstract number masks the operations of an ethnic dominance."[15] In other words, abiding by Sri Lanka doesn't make Scott, an anthropologist by training, unlike Daniel and his ilk, lapse into a culturalist explanation of Sinhalese nationalism (or, indeed, any explanation or interpretation of it, at all). Rather, it takes him to a questioning of the Enlightenment itself and its epistemological and political legacy—as such, and in the (post)colony. He finds part of that legacy, modern liberal democracy, to be inseparable from the majoritarian principle and argues that it cannot be the horizon of a reimagining of Sri Lanka, cannot be the answer to the question of peace, since majoritarianism, democracy, is what produced the problem in the first place. The significance of this contention cannot be stressed too much: *to Scott, the problem facing Sri Lanka*, the cause if you will of the lack of peace, is not hegemonic Sinhalese nationalism or Tamil terrorism but *democracy itself.*

This is a very radical idea (although, unfortunately, Scott doesn't move from here to an interrogation of democracy as such), and it clearly has profoundly inspired, if not enabled, my own study, which would be quite impossible without it (though Scott's argument would be more persuasive if accompanied by a critique, or even an examination, of the career of Sinhalese nationalism and how it worked as the accomplice of democracy). Scott's suggestion is that, for peace in Sri Lanka, liberal democracy and all its assumptions be given up and, instead, a situation created where "Tamils, Sinhalas and Muslims . . . [are] able to argue within their own discursive traditions about who they are respectively and what they want," and to continue this argument in nonstate "public spaces in which these traditions [could] meet, in which disagreement and discord can be voiced, claims and counterclaims negotiated, and accommodations, compromises—i.e., settlements (albeit temporary ones) arrived at."[16] This sounds remarkably like mutual participation. However, it ignores history or, in my terms, is possible only by a deliberate repression of the autobiography and career of Sinhalese (and Tamil) nationalism. No, I am not suddenly reversing direction here and falling back on history to make my case. Rather, it should be pointed out that Scott understands identity and community historically. A discursive tradition, to him, is an "ongoing embodied argument . . . in which the historical forms of a common life carry on a normative moral debate about who they are, why they are who they are, and what will enable them to remain who they are."[17] Take these three last concerns to a reading of *any* text of Sinhalese nationalism, and one will discover, as was argued in chapter 2, that it will state, explicitly or otherwise, in some form or another, that the Sinhalese are who they are because of history, having been wounded by colonial and precolonial oppression, and can only remain who they are, victims working through those wounds, as a consequence of that history, through (majoritarian) democracy in Sri Lanka. If they compromise upon this, come to some accommodation with Muslims and Tamils, as Scott correctly says they should, the Sinhalese—as Scott, amazingly enough, does not seem to realize—could no longer remain who/what they now are and will, indeed, also have to renarrativize their story, change their minds about why they are who/what they are and want.

My point, it is important to stress, is not that Sinhalese nationalism will be around forever and will always want to dominate Sri Lanka. Rather, I wish to point out that Scott's position is only possible by deliberately repressing the career of Sinhalese nationalism—which he does despite holding that particular or discrete histories must be engaged with. He must do so in order to make his more general call for an "argument" between the Muslims, Tamils, and Sinhalese seem plausible and possible. But, once the particular or specific is attended to, one sees that the general call cannot hold, at least not as Scott articulates it. It is, quite simply, impossible to ask a Tamil opposed to Sinhalese hegemony, or to being minoritized, to let the Sinhalese hegemonist remain who she is. If she did so, the Tamil antihegemonist couldn't remain who she is. The two positions plainly contradict each other. That is to say, if peace requires a certain conversation or argument and accommodation, as Scott contends it does, then such conversation must be predicated upon the possibility that some or even all parties to the conflict might not remain who they are at its end. I am with Scott's call for such an argument, completely and enthusiastically, but insist that it must be conceived as an open-ended one. For it to work, as opposed to being a shouting match where contending positions are merely asserted and where nothing changes as a consequence of the shouting, the parties must be prepared to truly speak to the other, which means being open to the possibility that one might end up renouncing some or all of one's convictions and not remain who/what one is/was when it is over. This is not a liberal argument against difference, it does not mean that such a renunciation must or will or should take place, inevitably, as a consequence of such an argument. I am extremely doubtful that I could be persuaded that any of the positions I hold in this book— whether on postempiricism, postcoloniality, democracy, or the left—are those that I should or would change. I am, though, always prepared to listen to an argument that seeks to persuade me otherwise—with, of course, the exception of anthropology!—provided my interlocutor is similarly open. This, I think, is what Emmanuel Levinas means when he asks us to understand peace not as "the absorption or disappearance of alterity," as in the Uyangoda position where difference must disappear to make possible a peaceful Sri Lanka, but as "the fraternal way of a proximity to the other," with the other being understood as a "neighbor": literally, someone who is not distant or radically different but who is proximate or close by, who lives next door.[18] In such a conception of peace, which is not inconsistent with the Adornean formulation this study has worked with, one would not confirm "oneself in one's own identity," or be exclusivist, but be prepared to put "that identity itself in question."[19] That is to say, it is ultimately committed neither to identity (Uyangoda) or to difference (Scott). (And so eventually departs from Adorno, in whose formulation one cannot think beyond identity.)

Scott cannot hold this position because he is ultimately and profoundly conservative (as opposed to a leftist; and it is not, I think, coincidental that he holds that the distinction between left and right is no longer tenable in the post-Soviet conjuncture. I cannot imagine any leftist arguing thus—there is just too much at stake to the leftist in insisting upon the distinction). Communal identity—what he calls a historically embodied tradition—is an object he understands quite rigidly as an uncontaminated and uncontaminatable whole, something he cannot not cathect. Thus his paradoxical position that the Sinhalese, for instance, seek both to compromise with their neighbors and somehow remain who they are. My own problem with such a conception of identity, for a start, is that it is always exclusivist. And a leftist cannot endorse exclusivism. Second, of course, in Scott's conception it is historical, the product of an argument over time—and no doubt one that could be verified. Quite apart from the fact that this study holds history to be only a story (albeit an authoritative one), one of Scott's own most powerfully articulated conclusions in his book, one that my study is obviously sympathetic to, is that we must give up "the Enlightenment project as such."[20] It is consequent to this political and epistemological critique of the Enlightenment that he comes to his conclusions about democracy. But he simply fails to notice, or perhaps must repress, that disciplinary history, too, is a product of the Enlightenment, dating from no earlier than the nineteenth century. If it is Scott's position that we must, for good epistemological reasons, give up the Enlightenment project *as such*, then it is simply inconsistent to somehow seek to recover one object, history, from it. To be consistent with his own position, Scott should have conceived identity in terms other than as a historically embodied argument. Indeed, he also holds that these identities, at least in the Sri Lankan instance, are the products of a peculiarly colonial modernity. That is to say, if they are historical, their history is quite recent—and, once again, inextricable from the Enlightenment (the larger moment of colonialism). What, then, are they doing in the post-Enlightenment project he calls for? Like Uyangoda, Scott ultimately ends up being less than daring. He cannot follow through on the conclusions of his own position, his own insight. Or, one might say, his position is undertheorized. His theoretical convictions should lead him to disavow identities that his political (affective and ethical) commitments affirm, but they don't. Ultimately, his politics triumphs over his theory. Uyangoda's theory, in contrast, overdetermines his politics, undermines his commitment to difference.

By 2003, Uyangoda had transformed himself into a hardheaded pragmatist. His writings by then don't mention consociationalism, or anything radical or new, or have an ethical level, but speak of peace in realist, what Scott would term Hobbesian, terms. There is a tiredness in Uyangoda's prose; it reads almost as if he, like many others after a decade of consistent and courageous intervention into the debate, had run out not just of new ideas but of patience and so just wanted peace, understood as the absence of war, at almost any cost. Here is a symptomatic instance from a text in which he responds to a leftist/human-rights critique of those who, like him, advocate compromise with the LTTE:

The greater opposition to the ceasefire agreement emerged from some human rights groups in Colombo, on the assumption that it legitimized the LTTE's "totalitarian rule" in the Northern and Eastern provinces . . . Many human rights groups in Colombo expressed serious doubts about the wisdom of the very idea of an interim administration under LTTE hegemony because of its likely disastrous consequences for human rights, democracy, pluralism, accountability and the rights of the regional minorities. The University Teachers for Human Rights (UTHR-Jaffna) in a recent report have dramatically highlighted these concerns by branding this negative trajectory as "totalitarian peace." At the heart of this debate is a profoundly complex issue: how should the Sri Lankan state in search of peace handle the militaristic LTTE, which has also joined the peace process on its own terms?[21]

Very subtly but deliberately, perhaps even cunningly, Uyangoda delegitimizes the UTHR(J) in that passage. Its name may imply that it is based in Jaffna, but, by stating that the opposition to the ceasefire came from "human rights groups in Colombo," not Jaffna, the organization's authenticity is questioned. It is, one might notice, the only group specified in the passage. The implication, clearly, is that the group pretends to be based in Jaffna, by naming itself thus, but that it actually operates from Colombo. A more substantial, persuasive, forceful critique would have taken on the group's positions themselves, not its name or authenticity. Nevertheless, it would appear that Uyangoda, despite himself, is actually quite sympathetic to the UTHR(J)'s arguments, though not to the conclusions they arrive at.

For instance, in the passage quoted above, Uyangoda finds it "likely" that "an interim administration under LTTE hegemony" would have nothing short of "*disastrous consequences* for human rights, democracy, pluralism, accountability and the rights of the regional minorities." The LTTE, then, would not be unfortunate or inopportune but a catastrophe for the northeast. Furthermore—if, that is, there could be anything worse than a catastrophe—he is prepared to concede that:

The enduring commitment to the goal of a separate state, the unwavering belief in the efficacy of the military path to achieving that goal, subjugation of political options to military objectives, ruthlessness in the deployment of violence, terror and deception as means to power, and the calculated disregard for even elementary norms of democracy, human rights and pluralism are often posited to be some key characteristics of this unique movement called the LTTE. These certainly are also some of the key features that have distinguished the LTTE from all other militant Tamil groups.[22]

Nevertheless, he will not concur with the UTHR(J)'s judgment—and that, by the way, of much of the Sri Lankan left—that this would make the LTTE fascist or totalitarian. He merely finds the group, amazingly enough, "illiberal." It is "certainly" violent, terroristic, untrustworthy, and has a "calculated disregard for even elementary norms of democracy, human rights and pluralism." This makes the LTTE sound not much better than a bunch of thugs. Despite this, Uyangoda can only characterize the organization as "illiberal." This move, if dubious to the leftist, is by its own logic brilliant, for Uyangoda in the article also characterizes the Sri Lankan state as illiberal.[23] By so doing, he can, in all good conscience, proceed to advocate compromise between the two (similar) objects. If he accepted the UTHR(J)'s characterization of the LTTE as totalitarian, of course, he couldn't take such a position. No ethical subject could advocate compromise with totalitarianism.

Uyangoda's, then, is one response to the question: could the leftist advocate compromise with (in this case Tamil) nationalism? Seeing Sinhalese nationalism as a spent force, he contends that some political agreement between the state and the LTTE, despite the latter's career, is not just necessary and pragmatic but good and ethical because it could eventually turn what he calls a "transitional" peace into a "transformative" one. Significantly enough, he neglects to say how the LTTE, which would control a transitional peace, could be made to lose control (without, that is, a new war) or what a transformative peace might or should look like: would it take the form of federalism, or consociationalism, for instance? But my quarrel with Uyangoda's position, ultimately, is an ethical one. Even though he isn't entirely satisfied with his own position—thus his desiring a transformative peace—he approaches peace from an elitist perspective. He finds at "the heart of th[e] . . . debate," to repeat that sentence, "a profoundly complex issue: how should the Sri Lankan state in search of peace handle the militaristic LTTE, which has also joined the peace process on its own terms?" This is not the pivotal question—at least, not to the leftist. Again deploying an excellent narrative strategy, Uyangoda has shifted focus. A passage that begins by addressing the Sri Lankan human-rights critique of the LTTE suddenly and without warning perceives the LTTE not from that critique but from the perspective of the Sri Lankan state. By so doing, one can easily advocate pragmatism. After all, what else could the ethical subject ask of the Sri Lankan state, given its career vis-à-vis the

Tamil, but that it pursue peace? How comfortable, though, can the leftist be with this? Is she supposed to read the world from the perspective of an elitist state? Does she have no alternative, as Uyangoda implies, but to support the peace process as defined by the state and the LTTE? On the other hand, would not so doing, for whatever reason, make her complicit with extremist Sinhalese nationalism, which is also opposed to the peace process? Is support or opposition (of the state and/or LTTE) the only two options facing the leftist or anybody else seeking to abide by Sri Lanka?

The UTHR(J) would say no. A detailed reading of its many interventions over the years is not necessary here (I do invite the reader, once again, to at least visit its Web site) since the burden of this chapter is to develop a minority/leftist perspective on the question of peace and democracy, so a look at one of its more recent reports, on the human rights situation in the northeast during the ceasefire, will be adequate, both to capture its response to the Uyangoda position and to further develop the minority perspective. The report carries this story:

> Mr Puvaneswaran from Kokkadichcholai cultivated lands and owned a textile shop. The LTTE demanded a child from him after it started forced conscription last August. The man who had dealings with the LTTE refused and pointed out that the organization owed him Rs 4 lakhs for textiles he has supplied to them. In reply the LTTE removed his tractor and took over his paddy fields.
>
> Later, Thurai, the local LTTE man in charge of conscription, came to Puvaneswaran with some young underlings. Thurai watched as the underlings assaulted Puvaneswaran on his orders. Hearing about her father's plight, Puvaneswaran's daughter, who was schooling in Batticaloa, came home and gave herself to the LTTE. Then Puvaneswaran's goods and the Rs 4 lakhs owed to him were returned.[24]

Much of the left outside Sri Lanka still understands the LTTE as, at least, a fellow traveler because it is a liberation organization resisting national oppression. Its "calculated disregard for even elementary norms of democracy, human rights and pluralism" is increasingly documented, even by international human rights groups. But this left dismisses those reports, even as it represses the ugly detail that the LTTE actually physically exterminated—murdered wouldn't be too strong a word—much of the Tamil left, and indeed much of the liberal Tamil opposition it couldn't coopt or coerce into a coalition. The leftist who would abide by Sri Lanka, however, cannot take this position or make this choice. To do so would be to sacrifice ethics to the most uninformed if not the most opportunistic politics, an elitist politics that would take the perspective of the state and LTTE and ignore the story of Puvaneswaran and his unnamed daughter because they are insignificant and do not matter in the context of the greater good.

Clearly a fairly rich farmer and businessman, one would not call Puvaneswaran subaltern. But his story and that of his daughter are certainly minoritized in the Sri Lankan debate on peace (if not quite subalternized). As long as one understands that debate as essentially between the Sri Lankan state and the LTTE, their stories can only be consigned to insignificance. In the context of the "larger picture," the beating of one Tamil man, the forced recruitment of one Tamil girl into the LTTE, simply do not matter, do not count. And the courageous work of the UTHR(J) can be dismissed as, at best, an irritation, as Uyangoda effectively does. But, as should be clear by now, the leftist who does not find significance in number, cannot dismiss that story. Or this one:

> Kanthasamy was a farmer living in Unichchai in the interior of Batticaloa. During 1990, just after the Indian Army pulled out, his eldest son was meddling with a shell stuck at the edge of the tank. The shell exploded killing the boy and wounding his sister. The LTTE went to Kanthasamy's house on 23rd March 2002 and demanded a surviving son. Upon Kanthasamy's firm refusal, he was taken to the punishment farm in Tharavai. The LTTE released him on 30th March with orders to bring his son or face severe punishment. Kanthasamy committed suicide by taking poison near 8th Mile Post on the Badulla Road, where the road crosses a stream. His body was cremated by relatives who found it at 8 o'clock the morning after.[25]

At first glance, this is classic empiricist prose of the kind this study has critiqued in de Silva and Wilson, saturated by detail—Barthes's narrative luxury—unnecessary to the plot. After all, does it really matter to the reader exactly where Kanthasamy committed suicide, or that, on its eighth milepost, the Badulla Road crosses a stream? Again, those familiar with the prose of metropolitan human-rights groups will see in this an attempt at imitation. And, without a doubt, this report is complicitous with that discourse. But it cannot, I suggest, be read as simply derivative or mimetic. For a start, there is something moving in this story that one never finds in the professionalized prose of human-rights discourse. The careful reader would have noticed that the last sentence states that the body of Kanthasamy was discovered after it was cremated. Such semantic impossibilities would be fact-checked out of a final report from the metropolis. More importantly, though, unlike metropolitan human-rights discourse,

the UTHR(J) does not present its work as objective reportage. It foregrounds its politics and will abide by the place it writes about. It will call
for change. It will take on the LTTE—and anybody else, if necessary—
however dangerous the enterprise.

To the UTHR(J), "What LTTE politics has brought to the Tamil
people is the destruction of everything good in society."[26] This is a most
unnuanced, if not an absurdly hyperbolic statement, the kind one is
tempted to peremptorily dismiss. It should not, however, be dismissed—
on those or other grounds. Rather, it must be read patiently, not just in the
polemical but also in the ethical and political spirit that animates much of
the work of the UTHR(J), for its opposition to the LTTE is not oppor-
tunist but (mostly) based upon the belief that, inasmuch as the LTTE has
since the mid-1980s sought to silence all dissent and opposition by physically exterminating it, the peace it seeks is a "totalitarian" one: the complete domination, through terror, of all aspects of life of the Tamil (and
Muslim) population of the northeast. It fails to find anything redeeming
in the actions and statements of the LTTE: the continuing recruitment of
children as soldiers, despite protests from their parents (and others), the
continuing harassment of Muslim civilians, despite protests from Muslims
(and others), and the harassment, intimidation, and murder of Tamil civilians and political opponents only makes its revulsion of the group greater.
Admitting to all this, Uyangoda might nevertheless ask (with Scott presumably agreeing, given his pragmatism): but what choice do we have
except to make peace with the LTTE? He might even cite that well-worn
cliché of political science and insist that one makes peace with one's ene-
mies, not one's friends. To which the UTHR(J) would reply: is the peace
you desire a totalitarian one? Could you consider that a peace at all? In so
asking the irritating and troubling questions, in refusing to be silenced, in
consistently resisting the seductions of pragmatism, the UTHR(J) provides a superb example to the leftist seeking to abide by Sri Lanka, for the
UTHR(J), too, in a certain sense, is irrelevant. And that is why it is both
supremely necessary and utterly relevant—to this study, to those who
seek to abide by Sri Lanka from the left. Peace, to this study, has never
meant the absence of war, a ceasefire between the state and its chief military rival, the LTTE, producing the continuing legitimated domination
of the Sri Lankan population by two governmental entities (for a change)
instead of one. Thus, while I am not opposed to ceasefires, I do not feel
obliged or compelled to support them, either. I hold that the leftist who
would abide by Sri Lanka need not take one or the other position, need
not subscribe to a for or against, an either/or politics. Indeed, anybody

whose politics is governed—or at the very least underlined—explicitly by an ethics should not, perhaps even cannot, do so. The task, instead, lies elsewhere.

We are still left, then, with the questions we began with: can one make peace with the LTTE? Could there be peace without it? If one understands peace as this study has done, the answer is quite clear. But, then, it could also be asked: is the Adornean formulation particularly helpful? Is its deployment here designed to exclude the LTTE—and Sinhalese nationalism? Was it imposed upon this study from outside, or did it emerge as a consequence of its readings? The answer, of course, is both. Upon reading these histories—these essentialist, exclusivist, hegemonic narratives—I find their understandings of peace unacceptable. However, I did not, it is perhaps important to insist, receive my understanding of terms like "essentialism" and" hegemony" from these texts but from what, for want of a better word, goes by the name "theory." My critique of nationalism is, if you like, based on a combination of the inductive and deductive. So, nothing that has been said here so far should lead the reader to expect compromise with Tamil and Sinhalese nationalisms to be advocated. Nevertheless, although I do not support the pragmatic (Uyangoda/Scott) position, it must be stressed that I am not entirely opposed to it, either (for these are, needless to add, not the only choices). And it is equally necessary to point out that, while being much more sympathetic to the UTHR(J) position, I am not entirely with it, either. Sometimes, the necessary has to give way to the possible. But, only sometimes. Thus my greater sympathy for the UTHR(J) position as opposed to the Scott/ Uyangoda position; or, put differently, this is why Adorno has to be supplemented with Levinas. The Adornean formulation doesn't enable even the possibility of getting beyond identity (where Scott rests); the Levinasian insists we must. Sinhalese and Tamil nationalism, of course, do not come anywhere near even the former, the "state of distinctness without domination with the distinct participating in each other." Not only do the nationalisms not advocate mutual participation, they do not even desire the first step toward it, speaking to each other. They are not prepared to listen to each others' stories or to any story but their own. So, while I don't wish nationalisms away, I do want them to change. At the very least, I would like them into enter into a conversation predicated on the possibility that they may get out of it having changed.

It is hoped such a conversation would also enable a more daunting project: retheorizing democracy. Ultimately, representative democracy must be questioned not just because it is majoritarian but also because it works by passing a metaphor (or a relation of substitution) for a metonym (a relation of continuity). The representative ("of the people") is produced by democracy as being in a relation of seamless continuity with the people; but, in my reading, this relationship is better understood as one of substitution. The representative takes the place of the people, displaces them, is their *différance*. She is not only different from them but makes them defer; the people must both submit to her authority and put aside the possibility of taking her place. That there is a structural similarity between democracy and anthropology—the anthropologist produces herself as in seamless continuity with her object of study but is better read as taking its place—only buttresses my conclusion that postcoloniality, or finishing the critique of Eurocentrism, is the accomplice of postempiricism, which requires, among other things, asking the question of democracy. Or, at least, that is the conclusion this study has reached while seeking to abide by Sri Lanka.

Notes

INTRODUCTION

1 Gunasinghe 1996, 204; emphasis added.
2 Ibid., 205.
3 Readers familiar with Derrida would know that, in "Signature, Event, Context," he sees his project, as it were, as interventionist.
4 To mention only Sri Lankanists I have had a drink with here, the others would include Ananda Abeysekera, Mala de Alwis, R. A. L. H. Gunawardana, Rajan Hoole, Pradeep Jeganathan, Ram Manikkalingam, Vasuki Nesiah, Gananath Obeysekere, David Scott, Serena Tennekoon, Rajani Thiranagama, and, most of all, Kumari Jayawardena.
5 It is perhaps necessary to add here that conversations along these lines were taking place at the Social Scientists' Association for a while. See, for instance, the Introduction to *Ethnicity and Social Change* (Social Scientists' Association 1984).
6 Mowitt 1992, 3.
7 For a similar, and quite brilliant, argument, also from the left but at a very different conjuncture, see Abhayavardhana 1962. It is perhaps unnecessary to remind readers of this book that the Sri Lankan left has had a long and remarkable career, intellectually and politically.
8 The "advances" that have most shaped this study are, for the critique of empiricism, Althusser 1997, Barthes 1986, de Certeau 1988, Derrida 1978, and Mowitt 1992; for postcoloniality, after Fanon 1963 and Said 1979 opened the door, Spivak 1988 and 1999 and Chatterjee 1993 most particularly, and the volumes of *Subaltern Studies* more generally.
9 Derrida 1978, 281.
10 Ibid., 288.

11 This term is taken from Rancière 1999, though its deployment here differs from his. It allows one to conceive of a relation of sameness and difference simultaneously.

12 See Mowitt 1992.

13 See Jeganathan 1998a.

14 Foucault 1984, 382.

15 When coded differently it is not the same object that will be perceived. Those who understand the problem as about terrorism, and those who understand it as national oppression or genocide, do not really see the same thing. That, from a postempiricist perspective, is why a problem exists in the first place.

16 It is perhaps necessary to point out here that I hold, with Barthes (1977), that the task of the postempiricist is to diminish the distance between reading and writing.

17 That is to say, I didn't really select it.

18 Watson 1997, 1.

19 The problem with "experience" as an authorizer of knowledge is not just that it is a foundational category, as Joan Scott (1992) has argued, but that it sees such knowledge as outside language and signification.

20 This is probably the best place to stress that I do not see academic knowledge production on Sri Lanka in binary terms, as divisible into two kinds, Western and Sri Lankan, based upon their relation to the object of study. I could identify at least one other mode, as it were, of academic production: "Indian" texts on Sri Lanka, which would fall into neither category. Exploring the content and work of that category would necessitate situating "India" and "Sri Lanka," as epistemological spaces, not only in relation to each other, and the West, but also to another, "South Asia," all understood in nongeographic terms, of course. (And it is no doubt unnecessary to add here that it is not just places called "India" and "Sri Lanka" who have a stake in the term "South Asia.") Such work, while imperative, is beyond the scope of this study. Two broad "Indian" approaches to Sri Lanka, however, might be somewhat schematically identified here: one situates Sri Lanka within a South Asian frame and opens itself up to an exchange (see Krishna 1999); the other situates Sri Lanka within a hegemonic Indian frame (see Muni 1993).

21 See Foucault 1973.

22 See Spivak 1988.

23 That is to say, this text thrust itself upon me.

24 Spencer 1990, 4. These are the people, the unit continues, "who will decide the fate of *all* attempts to find a peaceful settlement" to the conflict (emphasis added). This populist, romantic and antisubalternist representation of subalternity betrays, of course, a most naive understanding of power.

25 Watson 1997, 1.

26 Spencer 1990, 3.

27 It has long been a fantasy of mine to write to some anthropology departments in the United States and ask their chiefs whether they would let me study their rituals. I don't, of course, expect to get permission. What I wonder is whether any of the letters would be replied to at all.

28 Daniel 1996, 9.

29 See Barthes 1977.

30 This is the place to mention that my understanding of place has been powerfully

shaped by de Certeau (1988), who does not understand the concept geographically but institutionally.

31 Spencer 1990, 4.

32 Daniel 1996, 10. I prefer, by the way, to call this group "UpCountry Tamils." Daniel has a very interesting discussion of their naming, in his chapter 1. In the rest of my study, when the term "Tamil" appears unmarked, it can be assumed that I refer to the northeastern Tamils.

33 Indeed, Daniel's text is at its most moving and intellectually rich when it works within this "bias" for a subaltern group. Unfortunately, though, this is not consistently done and, in any case, signifies a commitment to a subjectivity and identity rather than a politics. This is not to imply that the one is not implicated in the other, but it does further indicate why my sympathy for Daniel's efforts is very limited.

34 Daniel 1996, 10.

35 Ibid., 5.

36 Appadurai 1989, 37.

37 Those familiar with Spivak's work will realize how much the concept of abiding owes to it.

38 Spencer 1990, 4. This, by the way, is a serious misrepresentation of the work of two of his contributors, R. A. L. H. Gunawardana and Serena Tennekoon, who make powerful critiques of Sinhalese nationalism, critiques originally published in Sri Lanka that have made lasting impressions on the debate.

39 Some key texts here are Obeyesekere 1970, 1979, 1981, 1984, and 1990; and Obeyesekere and Gombrich 1988.

40 I want to stress here that the importance of David's work and example to this study, especially his thinking on the questions of number and democracy, cannot be overstated. My work would, quite simply, be impossible without his— something that will become clear only in the Conclusion of this book.

41 It should be stressed here that abiding by Sri Lanka doesn't necessarily happen only within a strictly "national" frame of reference. Those Asian activists, for instance, working to establish the rights of migrant workers, in the Middle East and elsewhere, also abide by Sri Lanka.

42 According to his publisher, de Silva "held the chair of Sri Lanka History at the University of Ceylon, later the University of Peradeniya, from 1969 to 1995."

43 According to one of his publishers, Wilson "held the founding Chair of Political Science at the University of Ceylon (now Peradeniya) before being appointed Professor of Political Science at the University of New Brunswick."

44 See Althusser 1997.

45 See Mowitt 2002.

46 The most significant texts are Althusser 1997, Barthes 1986, de Certeau 1988, Foucault 1973, Rancière 1994, and Rancière 1999. I cannot, obviously, rehearse their arguments here, but they are somewhat brutally summarized at the beginning of chapter 3.

47 See Foucault 1973.

48 My thinking on this question has been deeply shaped, as discussed in chapter 2, by Scott 1995.

49 This formulation may sound like a concession to literature, since the text emerged precisely in order to challenge, to displace the notion. I would rather it be read, though, as an attempt to reclaim the term for textuality.

50 Spivak 2005.

51 Aristotle 1998. For a brilliant reading of this text, see Rancière 1999. Geometry brings together the incommensurable: a circle and a straight line, say, things inaccessible to arithmetic, which cannot compare them. Or, in the Sri Lankan instance, such thinking, outside the logic of number, would seek, for a start, to speak of all four ethnic groups together, without calling one (or two) major and the others minor.

52 Arato and Gebhardt 1993, 500. The title of the Adorno essay is "Subject and Object." It asserts the primacy of the object/ive and thus may seem an unlikely text for an avowed postempiricist reader to find inspiration in. But it is also a brilliant recasting of the dialectic that seeks, without being unfaithful to Marxism, to reconceptualize "reconciliation," enabling therefore a catachrestic reading as being concerned with conceptualizing peace more generally. It is, of course, such creativity that makes Adorno a more enabling thinker than, say, a Lukács.

53 See Guha 1997.

54 The best example of Barthes's seminal arguments are to be found in some of the essays in *The Rustle of Language*. I presume they are too well known to be rehearsed here.

55 See Mowitt 1992.

56 Kadirgamar 2001, 266. He also reminds his readers that, while the conventional story locates the birth of the organized Sri Lankan left with the Lanka Sama Samaja Party in the 1930s, the anti-imperialist Jaffna Youth Congress, led by Handy Perinbanayagam, was active (mainly in the north) in the 1920s.

57 Marx 1994, 15.

58 The reference is to Lazarus 1999.

59 See especially Guha 1997.

1. BETTER THINGS TO DO

1 Daniel 1996, 3.

2 Ibid., 5.

3 Ibid., 4. By the way, this begs the question of pornography. It is not self-evident that pornography is a bad thing.

4 To be found in Geertz 1973.

5 Tylor 1958, 1. This book was first published in 1871.

6 Geertz 1973, 16; emphasis added.

7 Ibid., 9.

8 Ibid., 10; emphasis added.

9 This is made absolutely clear in Gadamer 1987.

10 Ibid., 18; emphasis added.

11 Ibid., 16.

12 Ibid., 14; emphasis added.

13 Ibid., 30.

14 Chatterjee 1993, 17.

15 Geertz 1973, 5; emphasis added.

16 The interpretive turn was responding most of all to *Orientalism* and Fabian's important *Time and the Other*. Said 1989 and Spivak 1988 must also be mentioned here.
This study sees itself as very much in the wake of Said 1989, in which he finds
the interpretive turn an attempt to "anesthetize" the critique of anthropology by
postcoloniality.

17 Clifford 1986, 2; emphasis added.

18 Ibid., 11.

19 Ibid., 19.

20 Thus, for instance, Clifford will state, "Literary processes—metaphor, figuration,
narrative—affect the way cultural phenomena are registered" (ibid., 4). Culture,
in this understanding, is not constituted by language but exists, empirically, outside it. Once again, this sounds like Geertz.

21 Lila Abu-Lughod makes a similar, important and powerful argument in "Writing
against Culture," that culture is not self-evident but "the essential tool for making
other" (1991, 143). Unfortunately, she negates the force of her own critique by
compromising with eurocentrism; by casting her lot, eventually, with what she
calls a "tactical humanism." This is a tactical resolution of a theoretical problem,
and so unpersuasive. For, after Bhabha's powerful argument (1994) that all humanism can offer the native is to be not white, not quite, it cannot be an option for
postcoloniality.

22 Clifford 1986, 1.

23 Spivak 1988, 308.

24 If not, it should be put there. And, after a while, cremated. There is no compelling
need for this particular object to be gazed at too long.

25 Derrida 1978, 282.

26 See Boas 1901 and 1911.

27 To say this, of course, is not to imply that there has been no critique of colonialism
from within anthropology; one thinks, here, of the work of Johannes Fabian, Lila
Abu-Lughod, and Nicholas Dirks.

28 Daniel 1996, 50.

29 Apart from Wilson, discussed at length in chapter 2, see also Balasingham 1983
and Ponnambalam 1983. A long bibliography of recent Tamil nationalist histories
could be provided here, but that, presumably, would be unnecessary.

30 Daniel 1996, 13.

31 Jeganathan 1998a, 11. Jeganathan records a long bibliography. By now, of course,
it must be even longer. One wonders how many trees might have been spared if
these scholars had acted responsibly.

32 Ibid., 28.

33 On emplotment, or the making of plot, see Ricoeur 1984 and White 1978. They
draw, of course, upon Aristotle, who in his *Poetics* first insisted that stories don't
narrate themselves but are made, or emplotted.

34 Jeganathan 1998a, 46.

35 See Lazarus 1993. However, the best theoretical response to Ahmad is Prasad 1997.

36 See, for instance, Young 2001.

37 Dirlik 1997, 501. For a critique of his position see, for instance, Young 2001.

38 While Chatterjee 1993 and Spivak 1988 remain my major sources of inspiration
here, I should also acknowledge other texts from the collective that have strongly

shaped my thinking on postcoloniality: Amin 1995; Guha 1981, 1997, and 2002; and Pandey 1990.

39 Spivak has described *Subaltern Studies* as an "instrument of study which participates in the nature of the object of study."

40 The reference is to Lazarus 1999, chapter 2.

41 Lazarus approves of, unsurprisingly enough, some of Guha's early work, in which he tries to speak for the subaltern.

42 Lazarus 1999, 89, 89, 93, 94.

43 Ibid., 120.

44 Ibid., 123.

45 Althusser 1997, 105.

46 Ibid., 59.

47 This question is addressed at length in Ismail 2000.

48 Guha 1994, 7; emphasis added.

49 The reference here is Guha 1997, especially the second chapter.

50 Lazarus 1999, 75.

51 This can be seen quite starkly when reading Lenin on anticolonial nationalism. He is absolutely clear that, theoretically, the Marxist must be opposed to nationalism because it is a bourgeois ideology and does the work of enabling capitalist revolution. However, when the bourgeois in question is anti-imperialist, such nationalism must be supported strategically. This implies a quite bizarre relation between theory and practice: that the one has no consistent relation to the other.

52 Indeed, we are told, without the slightest trace of irony, that this anthropologist, Peter Rigby, is a "consecrated cultural insider" (Lazarus 1999, 115) in relation to his tribe.

53 Ibid., 114.

54 Ibid., 143.

55 Derrida 1986, 10. The same point is also made, in passing, in "Différance."

56 Political theory has long been aware of this. See, for instance, Tussman 1960. Indeed, it could be argued that Hobbes takes the same position.

57 Spivak 1988, 295; emphasis added.

58 The most powerful response from queer theory to this argument is, of course, Butler 1997.

59 Chatterjee 1993, 38; emphasis added.

60 Young 2001, 10.

61 Sitze 2003.

62 Young 2001, 9.

63 Bhabha 1994.

64 Fanon 1963, 235.

65 Ibid., 311–15.

66 Likewise, for him, whiteness—expressed in that memorable formulation, "you are rich because you are white, you are white because you are rich" (Fanon 1963, 40)—has nothing very much to do with skin color. Whiteness, here, emerges as a discursive construct that richness—a synonym for power—enables.

67 Ibid., 316.

68 My argument here, of course, rhymes with that of Gyan Prakash (1997).

69 Chatterjee 1993, 38.

70 The reference here, of course, is to Chakrabarty 2000.

71 Ibid.,17.

72 Ibid., 35.

73 He explains his refusal to address the Muslim question as a consequence of his Hindu imagination. This hasn't, though, prevented him working with Marx and Heidegger. Of course, they might have been Hindus in a previous birth.

74 Prasad 1997, 143.

75 Spivak 1988, 295.

76 Lazarus 1999, 113.

77 Spivak 1988, 295.

78 This is only an apparent contradiction because, when invoking her positionality at the beginning of the essay, she states that, for politically interested reasons, she will refuse to push to the limit the consequences of her theoretical position. That is to say, her political commitments require information retrieval, even while her theoretical ones insist upon its dangerousness.

79 He does state, though, in his chapter on Gandhi, that Gandhi "did not even think within the thematic of nationalism" (1993, 93), which is also the thematic of Eurocentrism. Nevertheless, Lazarus somehow manages to assert that, to Chatterjee, the thematic of Eurocentrism is "untranscendable" (1999, 124). In the course of this rather sorry misreading he also, and quite disingenuously, calls Chatterjee Foucauldian, whereas the primary theoretical inspiration for *Nationalist Thought* is explicitly situated in Gramsci.

80 Needless to add, this position is a critique of Appiah 1997.

81 Lazarus 1999, 241.

82 Ricoeur 1988, 206.

2. MAJORITY RULES

1 I have in mind, most particularly, de Silva 1981, 1986, 1987, and 1993.

2 This is not to argue that we can do without generality. That would, among other things, make politics impossible. Rather, such a reading strategy seeks to draw attention to what is deferred, shunted aside, suppressed when easy, unself-conscious claims are made upon the general.

3 Mowitt 1992, 75.

4 See White 1981, 7. Another, and better, way of saying "one central subject plus identifiable narrative voice," as will be seen later, is through a formulation of A. J. Greimas, that a work of history cannot narrate what he terms "synchronic diversity."

5 Althusser 1997, 27.

6 Barthes 1986, 132.

7 Chakrabarty 2000, 13.

8 Chatterjee 1993, 42.

9 Asia Watch 1987, 18.

10 Carr 1961, 29.

11 To say this, of course, is not to imply that history has no politics; though it must affirm that it doesn't.

12 Althusser 1997, 34; emphasis added.

13 See Barthes 1981.

14 Althusser 1997, 100.

15 My debt to Nietzsche here, and throughout this study, should be obvious. "Monumental history deceives by means of analogies" (Nietzsche 1995, 100).

16 It is important to record here that, within the historicist problematic, this under-standing of Sinhalese identity has been contested, brilliantly and with great rigor, by R. A. L. H. Gunawardana (1984). His argument is discussed in the next chapter.

17 Nature itself is commandeered to assist here: the waters separating Tamilnadu and Sri Lanka are just a "shallow and narrow" sea to de Silva, further emphasizing the closeness between Jaffna and Tamilnadu. Those places may be cartographically distinct, parts of two different countries, but they are so close they could be con-sidered a single entity.

18 It is not incidental to notice that, to *Reaping the Whirlwind*, the duration of the Sinhalese presence in Sri Lanka is a matter of "belief" to historians, not one of record. There is, in other words, no disciplinary certainty about this.

19 I have argued that Muslim identity could be understood otherwise; see Ismail 1995.

20 De Silva's bibliography, though extensive, does not contain any reference to Sowell, and the Weiner citation doesn't discuss the Sri Lankan conflict. Horowitz does, and is examined later in this chapter.

21 It must be noted here that, to de Silva, the UpCountry Tamils are even more in-significant to the Sri Lankan story than the Muslims.

22 Greimas and Courtes 1982, 5.

23 Kemper 1991, 195.

24 This, by the way, is an instance of Scott's intellectuo-political courage. Courage, here, lies in the refusal to be anthropological, to inform the West of the non-West, to be fashionable and address only Western concerns; rather, he performs the dif-ficult work of abiding by Sri Lanka.

25 On emplotment, making "the intelligible spring from the accidental," as said in the previous chapter, see Ricoeur 1984, especially chapter two, and White 1978.

26 This account, significantly enough, strongly echoes the British colonial account of ancient Sri Lankan history, more usually found in popular Sinhalese nationalist history rather than the academic variety. The dominant colonial text is Tennent 1996, whose story, in turn, draws exceedingly, and uncritically, from Turnour's translation of the ancient chronicle, the *Mahawamsa*. My point is that the pres-ent authority of the *Mahawamsa*, a text largely unknown in the mid-nineteenth century, arises to a significant degree not from the text itself so much as from its stamp of approval by Tennent/colonialism as a work of "authentic" history (as op-posed to myth). Work on this question, the colonial construction of the Sinhalese past, and its subsequent appropriation by Sinhalese nationalism is sorely lacking, except for an important paper by Pradeep Jeganathan (1995). He points out that, in the colonial account, an old text that had to be produced within a different problematic becomes modern positivist history.

27 Greimas 1990, 19.

28 See Genette 1980, 106–9.

29 It is perhaps relevant to mention here that among the things listed in De Silva's CV would be writing the official biography of Jayewardene.

30 Leary 1984, 9.

31 The narrative, though, grants one sentence to a rebellion of "1797–98."

32 He does find, though, if only in a passing remark, that the Muslims were victims of the Portuguese.

33 Macherey 1978, 85–87.

34 White 1978, 84.

35 De Certeau 1988, 68.

36 "Sinhalese Only" is the term for the position that wanted English to be replaced by Sinhalese exclusively, as opposed to Sinhalese and Tamil, as the official language of the postcolonial Sri Lankan state.

37 See Guha 1997, 23. Gramsci, to Guha, presents "dominance" and "hegemony" as antinomies. The force of Guha's (re)formulation is his understanding hegemony as a relation of dominance.

38 Greimas and Courtes 1982, 371.

39 Greimas 1990, 77.

40 Tocqueville 1988, 247. The philosophical authority for this position might well be that conjuncture's most influential thinker, Hegel: "The particular is for the most part of too trifling value as compared with the general" (1956, 33). In that text, of course, Hegel justified the principle of majority rule.

41 Genette 1980, 116.

42 Frege 1980, 44.

43 Horowitz 2000, xv. "Ethnic conflict" emerges in this text as something that happens out there, in the Third World, Asia and Africa in particular. Horowitz finds it "inconvenient" and "difficult" to include the West in his study, despite admitting several Western instances of such conflict (which cannot surprise the reader informed of the career of this discipline). Reading Horowitz after Jeganathan's discussion of violence and Gyan Pandey's superb mapping (1990) of British colonialism's deployment of "communalism" as an explanatory category, which actually orientalizes India, one begins to feel that "ethnic conflict," too, is an indice: not an accurate description of some existing Third World reality but a Eurocentric term that works, as an ally of anthropology, to other the Third World, to produce it as the (continuing) site of cultural/civilizational chaos, the nonmodern, as something noncoeval with the West. Exploring that possibility, a fuller reading of Horowitz, though no doubt important, is beyond the scope of the present study. However, I have to, even though weary of the term, call his text racist.

44 Frege's citation of W. S. Jevons might be usefully repeated here: "Number is but another name for *diversity*. Exact identity is unity, and with difference arises plurality . . . It has often been said that units are units in respect of being perfectly similar to each other; but though they may be [so] . . . they must be different in at least one point, otherwise they would be incapable of plurality. If three coins were so similar that they occupied the same place at the same time, they would not be three coins but one" (Frege 1980, 46). Thus Frege's insistence, throughout his text, that the distinction between a concept and an object must not be forgotten.

45 De Man 1979, 154. This, of course, resonates with Jevons, cited above.

46 Modern social science, it is worth noting here, emerged with nationalism.

47 Nancy argues, "What I have in common with another Frenchman is that I am *not* the same Frenchman as him" (Nancy 2000, 155). Frenchness, and the same would hold for any other identity—national, ethnic, sexual, political—is to be understood

as simultaneously singular and plural. This, of course, follows from the critique of essentialism.

48 Nietzsche 1994, 34.

49 Horowitz 2000, 17.

50 Within disciplinary Sri Lankan history, the critique of the *Mahawamsa*, and therefore the colonial deployment of it, as unreliable, is quite old. See, for instance, Mendis (n.d.).

51 Scott 1999, 174.

52 See, for instance, Ginzburg 1994 and LeGoff 1992. This question is discussed at some length in the next chapter, through the work of Appleby et al. (1995).

53 White 1984, 85.

3. MINORITY MATTERS

1 See, especially, Wilson 1974 and Wilson 1980.

2 Apart from *The Break-Up of Sri Lanka*, I have in mind, most particularly, Wilson 1994a, Wilson 1994b, and Wilson 2000.

3 The work I would recommend to the leftist seeking an alternative account of the Tamil story is Hoole et al.'s *Broken Palmyrah*. I cannot think of a finer instance of committed scholarship. Its emphasis, however, is on events in the 1980s. On the earlier part of the twentieth century, see Ponnambalam 1983.

4 I argue, in Ismail 2000, that a subject interpellated by nationalism is best termed a "national."

5 Chatterjee 1993, 42.

6 Althusser 1997, 28.

7 Wilson uses the term "elite" consistently in *The Break-Up of Sri Lanka*, so I follow his usage; my sense of the term, though, derives from Guha (1994) and is not therefore to be understood as merely descriptive.

8 Identifying agency in these terms, within the logic of liberal individualism, constitutes one element of this text's right-wing allegiance.

9 Here is the whole quotation: "I went out of my way to join the Congress at a time when the whole Muslim community was against the Congress. . . . I can tell my honorable friends that during the elections it was put to me that I could have the support of my community if I gave up the Congress. If I was actuated by selfish motives, I would have given up the Congress" (12).

10 Sivathamby 1987; on this question, see also Ismail 1995.

11 I am constrained to point out here that Wilson's "conscience" is a most partial one: nowhere does this text discuss the LTTE's treatment of the Muslims (on which the reports of the UTHR are especially detailed); de Silva, the reader might remember, termed it "ethnic cleansing."

12 Unfortunately, "fifty-fifty," a truly original idea, has been ignored by the Sri Lankanist literature, except for a chapter in Jane Russell (1982). De Silva's student, she blithely dismisses Ponnambalam as "communalist."

13 For a classic instance of such an understanding, see the United Nations "Declaration on the Rights of Persons Belonging to National or Ethnic, Religious or Linguistic Minorities." It proceeds on the assumption that what constitutes a minority need not be stated, presumably because it is so well known.

14 For more on the contradictions of Tamil nationalism, see Ismail 2000.

15 The reader is even told that Ponnambalam "was not from a reputable family . . . nor did he have wealth in his own right at the time of his political debut, although he acquired considerable wealth by marriage" (61). The relevance of such detail, to an account of the break-up of Sri Lanka as opposed to say a biography of Ponnambalam, is difficult to fathom.

16 I am not particularly sympathetic to the idea that biographical information is a useful aid to reading. In this instance, however, given Wilson's refusal to be in any way critical of Chelvanayakam, the reader may find it interesting to know that Wilson was married to the Federal Party leader's daughter.

17 The term "traitor" is not used, directly or indirectly, to describe Ponnambalam; but, after Mahadeva, the implication that the TC leader's actions were treacherous is hard to miss.

18 Cited here are de Silva, Jane Russell, and Howard Wriggins.

19 It is symptomatic of Wilson's privileging the "Ceylon Tamil" perspective that the consequences of the actions of the state against the UpCountry Tamils are seen from the former perspective, that of the "principal minority"; BSL does not address the impact this had on the UpCountry Tamils themselves. On this important question, see Nadesan (1993).

20 See Jalal 1985.

21 Compare Wilson's with Ponnambalam's quite emotive rhetoric and detailed narration: "Sinhalese mobs went on the rampage, stopping trains and buses, dragging out Tamil passengers and butchering them. Houses were burnt with people inside, and there occurred widespread looting in all areas where Sinhalese and Tamils lived together. A Hindu priest performing pooja ceremonies . . . was . . . burnt alive" (Ponnambalam 1983, 113). My point, of course, is that the "same" events can be emplotted quite differently by different narratives. When this happens, they cannot really be deemed to be the same events, or objects—not by the postempiricist reader.

22 Balasingham 1983, 17; emphasis added.

23 For a fuller reading of this text and other cardinal texts of organized Tamil separatism, including what Wilson calls the "Pannakam Resolution," see Ismail 2000.

24 This, of course, suggests that, at least between 1958 and 1965, Tamil demands did not escalate but were reduced; nevertheless, Wilson proceeds with his plot without so much as a hiccup.

25 Wilson cites an article by Kingsley de Silva to the effect that, as a consequence of standardization, Tamil students had to get higher marks to enter the university than did Sinhalese students.

26 Senanayake, here, could not agree to implement the B-C Pact in 1960 because he had promised the Sinhalese voter that he was against it. In 1965, he promised Chelvanayakam, as a politician who never broke his word, to implement something like it. This should have prompted Wilson to ask Chelvanayakam how he could have trusted Senanayake, but, apparently, it did not.

27 Barthes 1986, 141.

28 See Genette 1980, chapter 2.

29 Appleby, Hunt, and Jacob 1995, 4.

30 Ibid., 229.

31 Trouillot 1995, 22.

32 Ibid., 11.
33 Scott 1995, 11.
34 Ibid., 14.
35 Gunawardana 1984, 87.
36 Scott 1995, 20.
37 Scott's argument, it is important to note, has begun to resonate with that of other scholars. Sumanasiri Liyanage (1996), while not citing Scott, has contended that in order to reach a consensus solution to the national question we must "forget our own interpretations of history"; this is another way of saying that the past must be disconnected from the present. Liyanage's work, as even a superficial acquaintance with it would reveal, is by no means postempiricist. Neither is that of Michael Roberts. In his inimitable style, Roberts too—again, not citing Scott— has recently argued (2000) that history in Sri Lanka has proved itself to be "dynamite," that the project of "multi-cultural tolerance" requires that we "fence-off and restrain" history before it blows us all up. Perhaps Roberts does not cite Scott because the former has argued, elsewhere, that history cannot be dehistoricized.
38 This may help explain why, when the essay gets reproduced in his book (1999), it sits, paradoxically and remarkably enough, with a series of profoundly historicist essays.
39 Scott 1995, 20.
40 Wilson 1994, 140; emphasis added.
41 I address this question at some length, especially in relation to the LTTE, in Ismail 2000).
42 Fanon 1963, 46.

4. WHAT, TO THE LEFTIST, IS A GOOD NOVEL?

1 For a superb account of "interference," see the Introduction to Casarino 2002.
2 I was introduced to this phrase of Blake's during a talk given at the University of Minnesota by Sari Makdisi.
3 For a recent argument about understanding Sri Lankan identity as hybrid, see the collection edited by Silva (2002).
4 Mansfield and Yohe 2000, 15; emphasis added.
5 A classic instance of this in the Sri Lankan debate is, alas, Manikkalingam 2003b. While conceding the existence of "Muslims and Hill-country Tamils" as "prominent ethnic communities," he proceeds to narrativize the conflict, for the sake of "brevity," as between a variety of exclusively Sinhalese and Tamil positions. This statement is included here only because one is especially saddened when one gets minoritized by one's friends.
6 This might, of course, explain why economics gets it "wrong" so often.
7 There is, of course, a minoritized argument within social science that takes language seriously; see, for instance, McCloskey 1994. Thanks to Jay Coggins for bringing this text to my attention.
8 A genealogy of this way of understanding literature would have to include Shelley's "A Defence of Poetry." But, where he understands the work of imagination as enabling a "man . . . to put himself in the place of another," a move that resonates with representation as speaking for, the work of imagination, to this study, is to enable speaking to.

9 Sidhwa 1991, 94.

10 This, no doubt, is the moment in this study where I must state that I look forward to Ajay Skaria's (re)reading of Gandhi.

11 For feminist readings of Gandhi see, for instance, Katrak 1992 and Kishwar 1985.

12 See Eagleton 1983.

13 See Viswanathan 1989.

14 Macaulay 1971, 190.

15 Perera 1997, 14.

16 One thinks, for instance, of the output of James Goonewardena.

17 Romesh Gunasekera's fiction would fall into this category.

18 Though not using my terms, Suvendrini Perera (1999) makes a similar argument: the novel must be read in the context of other anticommunalist writings on Sri Lanka.

19 The reference, of course, is to Jayawardena 1972.

20 I have discussed the relation between nationalism and nostalgia at some length in Ismail 2000.

21 Ponnambalam 1983, 75.

22 Nadesan (1993) might remind the reader here that UpCountry Tamils were eventually granted citizenship in the late 1980s.

23 Fanon 1963, 210. Within postcoloniality, this line of thought has been developed by Chakrabarty (2000). However, he also holds, in an anthropological spirit, that some sort of authentic native cultural space untouched by colonialism can be recovered, a position Fanon was very critical of. Funnily enough, this position is also held by Lazarus (1999), an otherwise severe critic of Chakrabarty.

24 For the purposes of this section, by "record" I mean Jayawardena's meticulously researched *The Rise of the Labor Movement in Ceylon.*

25 Indeed, by the standards of elitist or Leavisite criticism, this novel is "flawed." Regi Siriwardena has argued along these lines: "A kind of prologue in the first person, then third person, first person, third person—that's the structure of the novel. I can see no explanation for it" (Siriwardena 1997, 75). A good reader can, of course, find explanations.

26 Barthes 1986, 131.

27 See, for instance, Ali 1981.

28 Sivanandan 1984, 1.

29 Genette 1980, 110.

30 See Guha 1994.

31 In this connection, one is constrained to remark on the narrative's use of the term "low caste," as if some groups of people were indeed, self-evidently "low." Other, more politically sensitive terms, like "depressed" and "oppressed," are, of course, available.

32 Women's groups, of course, have been raising these questions for years and the literature on it is extensive.

33 See Ponnambalam 1983.

34 Jeganathan 1998b, 99.

35 See, for instance, "Declaration on the Rights of Persons Belonging to National or Ethnic, Religious, or Linguistic Minorities," http://www.unhcr.ch/html/menu3/b/d_minori.htm.

CONCLUSION

1 Lijphart 1977, 14. He concedes that Canada, a part of the "Anglo-American" world, is not homogenous.
2 Ibid., 21.
3 Ibid., 59.
4 Ibid., 61.
5 Ibid., 25.
6 Ibid., 50. All the dominant theorists of representative democracy—Madison, Mill, and so on—concede that it is elitist.
7 Ibid., 5.
8 Ibid., 142.
9 Ibid., 49.
10 Uyangoda 1993, 6.
11 Ibid., 9.
12 Ibid., 10.
13 Scott 1999, 182.
14 Ibid., 162.
15 Ibid., 176.
16 Ibid., 186.
17 Ibid., 185.
18 Levinas 1999, 137.
19 Ibid., 141.
20 Scott 1999, 155.
21 Uyangoda 2003, 64.
22 Ibid., 65.
23 He does, though, qualify this statement by calling the LTTE "essentially" illiberal and the Sri Lankan state only "relatively" so.
24 UTHR(J) 2002a, 31.
25 Ibid., 24.
26 Ibid., 45.

Bibliography

Abeysekera, Charles, and Newton Gunasinghe, eds. 1987. *Facets of Ethnicity in Sri Lanka.* Colombo, Sri Lanka: Social Scientists' Association.

Abhayavardhana, Hector. 1962. "Categories of Left Thinking in Ceylon." Paper presented at the annual sessions of the Ceylon Association for the Advancement of Science, Colombo, Sri Lanka.

Abu-Lughod, Lila. 1991. "Writing against Culture." In *Recapturing Anthropology: Working in the Present*, ed. Richard G. Fox, 137–62. Santa Fe, NM: School of American Research Press.

Ali, Ameer. 1981. "The 1915 Racial Riots in Ceylon (Sri Lanka): A Reappraisal of Its Causes." *South Asia* 4, no. 1: 1–20.

Althusser, Louis. 1997. *Reading Capital.* Trans. Ben Brewster. New York: Verso.

Amin, Shahid. 1995. *Event, Metaphor, Memory: Chauri-Chaura, 1922–1992.* New Delhi: Oxford University Press.

Appadurai, Arjun. 1989. "Putting Hierarchy in Its Place." *Cultural Anthropology* 3, no. 1: 36–49.

Appiah, K. Anthony. 1997. "Is the 'Post-' in 'Postcolonial' the 'Post-' in 'Postmodern'?" In *Dangerous Liaisons: Gender, Nation, and Postcolonial Perspectives*, ed. Anne McClintock, Aamir Mufti, and Ella Shohat, 420–44. Minneapolis: University of Minnesota Press.

Appleby, Joyce, Lynn Hunt, and Margaret Jacob. 1995. *Telling the Truth about History.* New York: Norton.

Arato, Andrew, and Eike Gebhardt, eds. 1993. *The Essential Frankfurt School Reader.* New York: Continuum.

Arendt, Hannah. 1973. *The Origins of Totalitarianism.* New York: Harvest.

Aristotle. 1998. *The Nichomachean Ethics.* Trans. David Ross. New York: Oxford University Press.

Asia Watch. 1987. *Cycles of Violence: Human Rights in Sri Lanka since the Indo–Sri Lanka Agreement.* New York: Asia Watch.

Balasingham, A. S. 1983. *Liberation Tigers and Tamil Eelam Freedom Struggle*. LTTE Publications.

Balasingham, Adele. 2001. *The Will to Freedom*. Mitchum, UK: Fairmax Publications.

Barthes, Roland. 1986. *The Rustle of Language*. Trans. Richard Howard. Berkeley and Los Angeles: University of California Press.

———. 1985. *The Responsibility of Forms*. Trans. Richard Howard. Berkeley and Los Angeles: University of California Press.

———. 1981. "Theory of the Text." In *Untying the Text: A Post-Structuralist Reader*, ed. Robert Young, 31–47. Boston, MA: Routledge.

———. 1977. *Image-Music-Text*. Trans. Stephen Heath. New York: Hill and Wang.

———. 1971. *Problems in General Linguistics*. Trans. Mary Elizabeth Meek. Coral Gables, FL: University of Miami Press.

Bhabha, Homi. 1994. *The Location of Culture*. Routledge: New York.

Boas, Franz. 1911. *The Mind of Primitive Man*. New York: Macmillan.

———. 1901. "The Mind of Primitive Man." In *Annual Report of the Smithsonian Institute*, 451–60. Washington, DC: Smithsonian Institute.

Butler, Judith. 1997. "Merely Cultural." *Social Text* 52/53: 265–77.

Carr, Edward Hallett. 1961. *What Is History?* New York: Vintage.

Casarino, Cesare. 2002. *Modernity at Sea: Marx, Melville, Conrad in Crisis*. Minneapolis: University of Minnesota Press.

Chakrabarty, Dipesh. 2000. *Provincializing Europe: Postcolonial Thought and Historical Difference*. Princeton, NJ: Princeton University Press.

Chatterjee, Partha. 1993. *Nationalist Thought and the Colonial World: A Derivative Discourse?* Minneapolis: University of Minnesota Press.

Clifford, James. 1986. Introduction to *Writing Culture: The Poetics and Politics of Ethnography*, ed. James Clifford and George E. Marcus. Berkeley and Los Angeles: University of California Press.

Dahl, Robert A. 1998. *On Democracy*. New Haven, CT: Yale University Press.

Daniel, E. Valentine. 1996. *Charred Lullabies: Chapters in an Anthropography of Violence*. Princeton, NJ: Princeton University Press.

De Certeau, Michel. 1988. *The Writing of History*. Trans. Tom Conley. New York: Columbia University Press.

De Man, Paul. 1979. *Allegories of Reading: Figural Language in Rousseau, Nietzsche, Rilke, and Proust*. New Haven, CT: Yale University Press.

Derrida, Jacques. 1986. "Declarations of Independence." *New Political Science* 15: 7–15.

———1982. "Différence." In *Margins of Philosophy*. Trans. Alan Bass. Chicago: University of Chicago Press.

———. 1978. "Structure, Sign, and Play in the Discourse of the Human Sciences." In *Writing and Difference*, 278–94. Trans. Alan Bass. Chicago: University of Chicago Press.

De Silva, Kingsley Muthumani. 1998. *Reaping the Whirlwind: Ethnic Conflict, Ethnic Politics in Sri Lanka*. New Delhi, India: Penguin.

———. 1987. *Separatist Ideology in Sri Lanka: A Historical Appraisal of the Claim for the "Traditional Homelands" of the Tamils of Sri Lanka*. Kandy, Sri Lanka: International Center for Ethnic Studies.

———. 1986. *Managing Ethnic Tensions in Multi-Ethnic Societies: Sri Lanka 1880–1985*. Lanham, MD: University Press of America.

————. 1981. *A History of Sri Lanka.* New Delhi, India: Oxford University Press.

De Tocqueville, Alexis. 1988. *Democracy in America.* Trans. George Lawrence. New York: Harper-Collins.

Dirks, Nicholas. 1992. "Castes of Mind." *Representations* 37: 56–78.

Dirlik, Arif. 1997. "The Postcolonial Aura: Third World Criticism in the Age of Global Capitalism." In *Dangerous Liaisons: Gender, Nation, and Postcolonial Perspectives,* ed. Anne McClintock, Aamir Mufti, and Ella Shohat, 501–28. Minneapolis: University of Minnesota Press.

Eagleton, Terry. 1983. *Literary Theory: An Introduction.* Minneapolis: University of Minnesota Press.

Edrisinha, Rohan. 1998. "A Critical Overview: Constitutionalism, Conflict Resolution, and the Limits of the Draft Constitution." In *The Draft Constitution of Sri Lanka: Critical Aspects,* ed. Dinusha Panditaratne and Pradeep Ratnam, 13–37. Colombo, Sri Lanka: Law and Society Trust.

Fabian, Johannes. 1983. *Time and the Other: How Anthropology Makes Its Object.* New York: Columbia University Press.

Fanon, Frantz. 1963. *The Wretched of the Earth.* Trans. Constance Farrington. New York: Grove Weidenfield.

Foucault, Michel. 1984. "Polemics, Politics, and Problemizations." In *The Foucault Reader,* ed. Paul Rabinow, 381–90. New York: Pantheon.

————. 1973. *The Order of Things: An Archaeology of the Human Sciences.* New York: Vintage.

Frege, Gottlob. 1980. *The Foundations of Arithmetic.* Trans. J. L. Austin. Evanston, IL: Northwestern University Press.

Gadamer, Hans-Georg. 1987. "The Problem of Historical Consciousness." In *Interpretive Social Science: A Second Look,* ed. Paul Rabinow and William M. Sulliwan, 82–140. Berkeley and Los Angeles: University of California Press.

Geertz, Clifford. 1973. *The Interpretation of Cultures.* New York: Basic Books.

Genette, Gerard. 1980. *Narrative Discourse: An Essay in Method.* Trans. Jane E. Lewin. Ithaca, NY: Cornell University Press.

Ginzburg, Carlo. 1994. "Checking the Evidence: The Judge and the Historian." In *Questions of Evidence: Proof, Practice, and Persuasion across the Disciplines,* ed. James Chandler et al., 290–303. Chicago: University of Chicago Press.

Greimas, A. J. 1990. *The Social Sciences: A Semiotic View.* Trans. Paul Perron and Frank H. Collins. Minneapolis: University of Minnesota Press.

Greimas, A. J., and J. Courtes. 1982. *Semiotics and Language: An Analytical Dictionary.* Bloomington: Indiana University Press.

Guha, Ranajit. 2002. *History at the Limit of World History.* New York: Columbia University Press.

————. 1997. *Dominance without Hegemony: History and Power in Colonial India.* Cambridge, MA: Harvard University Press.

————. 1994. "On Some Aspects of the Historiography of Colonial India." In *Subaltern Studies I,* ed. Ranajit Guha, 1–8. New Delhi, India: Oxford University Press.

————. 1981. *A Rule of Property for Bengal: An Essay on the Idea of Permanent Settlement.* New Delhi, India: Orient Longman.

Guinier, Lani. 1994. *The Tyranny of the Majority: Fundamental Fairness in Representative Democracy.* New York: Free Press.

Gunasinghe, Newton. 1996. *Selected Essays*. Colombo, Sri Lanka: Social Scientists' Association.

Gunawardana, R. A. L. H. 1995. *Historiography in a Time of Ethnic Conflict: Constructions of the Past in Contemporary Sri Lanka*. Colombo, India: Social Scientists' Association.

———. 1984. "The People of the Lion: Sinhala Consciousness in History and Historiography." In *Ethnicity and Social Change*, 55–107. Colombo, Sri Lanka: Social Scientists' Association.

Gupta, Akhil, and James Ferguson. 1997. *Culture, Power, Place: Explorations in Critical Anthropology*. Durham, NC: Duke University Press.

Hegel, G. W. F. 1956. *The Philosophy of History*. Trans. J. Sibree. New York: Dover Books.

Hoole, Rajan. 2001. *Sri Lanka: The Arrogance of Power*. Colombo, Sri Lanka: University Teachers for Human Rights.

Hoole, Rajan, et al. 1990. *The Broken Palmyrah: The Tamil Crisis in Sri Lanka—An Inside Account*. Claremont, Sri Lanka: Sri Lanka Studies Institute.

Horowitz, Daniel L. 2000. *Ethnic Groups in Conflict*. Berkeley and Los Angeles: University of California Press.

Ismail, Qadri. 2000. "Constituting Nation, Contesting Nationalism: The Southern Tamil (Woman) and Separatist Tamil Nationalism." In *Subaltern Studies XI*, ed. Partha Chatterjee and Pradeep Jeganathan, 212–72. New Delhi, India: Permanent Black.

———. 1999. "Discipline and Colony: *The English Patient* and the Crow's Nest of Post-Coloniality." *PostColonial Studies* 2, no. 3: 403–36.

———. 1995. "UnMooring Identity: The Antinomies of Elite Muslim Self-Representation in Modern Sri Lanka." In *UnMaking the Nation: The Politics of Identity and History in Modern Sri Lanka*, ed. Pradeep Jeganathan and Qadri Ismail, 55–105. Colombo, Sri Lanka: Social Scientists' Association.

Jalal, Ayesha. 1985. *The Sole Spokesman: Jinnah, the Muslim League, and the Demand for Pakistan*. Cambridge: Cambridge University Press.

Jayawardena, Kumari. 2000. *Nobodies to Somebodies: The Rise of the Colonial Bourgeoisie in Sri Lanka*. Colombo, Sri Lanka: Sanjiva Books.

———. 1985. *Ethnic and Class Conflicts in Sri Lanka: Some Aspects of Sinhala Buddhist Consciousness over the Past One Hundred Years*. Colombo, Sri Lanka: Center for Social Analysis.

———. 1972. *The Rise of the Labor Movement in Ceylon*. Colombo, Sri Lanka: Sanjiva Prakashana.

Jeganathan, Pradeep. 1998a. "'Violence' as an Analytical Problem: Sri Lankanist Anthropology after July 1983." *Nethra* 2, no. 4: 7–47.

———. 1998b. "In the Shadow of Violence: 'Tamilness' and the Anthropology of Identity in Southern Sri Lanka." In *Buddhist Fundamentalism and Minority Identities in Sri Lanka*, ed. Tessa Bartholomeusz and Chandra de Silva, 89–109. Albany: State University of New York Press.

———. 1995. "Authorizing History, Ordering Land: The Conquest of Anuradhapura." In *UnMaking the Nation: The Politics of Identity and History in Modern Sri Lanka*, ed. Pradeep Jeganathan and Qadri Ismail, 106–36. Colombo, Sri Lanka: Social Scientists' Association.

Jeganathan, Pradeep, and Qadri Ismail, eds. 1995. *UnMaking the Nation: The Politics of Identity and History in Modern Sri Lanka*. Colombo, Sri Lanka: Social Scientists' Association.

Kadirgamar, Santasilan. 2001. "The Left Tradition in Lankan Tamil Politics." In *Sri Lanka: Global Challenges and National Crises*, ed. Rajan Philips, 265–94. Colombo, Sri Lanka: Social Scientists' Association.

Kandiah, Thiru. 1984. "'Kaduwa': Power and the English Language Weapon in Sri Lanka." In *Honoring E. F. C. Ludowyk: Felicitation Essays*, ed. Percy Colin-Thome and Ashley Halpe, 117–54. Dehiwela, Sri Lanka: Tisara Prakasakayo.

Katrak, Ketu. 1992. "Indian Nationalism, Gandhian 'Satyagraha,' and Representations of Female Sexuality." In *Nationalisms and Sexualities*, ed. Andrew Parker et al., 395–406. New York: Routledge.

Kemper, Steven. 1991. *The Presence of the Past: Chronicles, Politics, and Culture in Sinhala Life.* Ithaca, NY: Cornell University Press.

Kishwar, Madhu. 1985. "Gandhi on Women." *Economic and Political Weekly* 20, no. 40: 1691–1702.

Krishna, Sankaran. 1999. *Postcolonial Insecurities: India, Sri Lanka, and the Question of Nationhood.* Minneapolis: University of Minnesota Press.

Lazarus, Neil. 1999. *Nationalism and Cultural Practice in the Postcolonial World.* Cambridge: Cambridge University Press.

———. 1993. "Postcolonialism and the Dilemma of Nationalism: Aijaz Ahmad's Critique of Third Worldism." *Diaspora* 2, no. 3: 373–400.

Leary, Virginia. 1984. *Ethnic Conflict and Violence in Sri Lanka.* Geneva, Switzerland: International Commission of Jurists.

LeGoff, Jacques. 1992. *History and Memory.* Trans. Steven Rendall and Elizabeth Claman. New York: Columbia University Press.

Lenin, V. I. 1994. *State and Revolution.* Originally published in 1918. New York: International Publishers.

Lenin, V. I., and J. V. Stalin. 1970. *Selections from Lenin and Stalin on National Colonial Question.* Calcutta, India: Calcutta Book House.

Levinas, Emmanuel. 1999. *Alterity and Transcendence.* Trans. Michael B. Smith. New York: Columbia University Press.

Lijphart, Arend. 1977. *Democracy in Plural Societies: A Comparative Exploration.* New Haven, CT: Yale University Press.

Liyanage, Sumanasiri. 1996. "Towards a Compromise Solution." In *Sri Lanka: The Devolution Debate*, 45–54. Colombo, Sri Lanka: ICES.

Macaulay, Thomas Babington. 1971. "Minute on Indian Education." In *Imperialism*, ed. Philip D. Curtin, 178–91. New York: Harper and Row.

Macherey, Pierre. 1978. *A Theory of Literary Production.* Trans. Geoffrey Wall. New York: Routledge.

Macintyre, Ernest. 1993. *Rasanayagam's Last Riot.* Sydney, Australia: Worldlink.

Madison, James, Alexander Hamilton, and John Jay. 1987. *The Federalist Papers.* New York: Penguin.

Manikkalingam, Ram. 1995. *Tigerism and Other Essays.* Colombo, Sri Lanka: Ethnic Studies Group.

Mansfield, Edward, and Gary Yohe. 2000. *Microeconomics.* New York: Norton.

Marx, Karl. 1994. *The Eighteenth Brumaire of Louis Bonaparte.* New York: International Publishers.

McCloskey, Donald. 1994. *Knowledge and Persuasion in Economics.* Cambridge: Cambridge University Press.

Mendis, G. C., n.d. *Problems of Ceylon History*. Colombo, Sri Lanka: The Apothecaries'.
———. 2000. "Trauma Envy." *Cultural Critique* 46:272–97.
———. 1992. *Text: The Genealogy of an Antidisciplinary Object*. Durham, NC: Duke University Press.
Muni, S. D. 1993. *Pangs of Proximity: India and Sri Lanka's Ethnic Crisis*. New Delhi, India: Sage.
Nadesan, S. 1993. *A History of the Upcountry Tamil People*. Colombo, Sri Lanka: Nandalala Publishers.
Nancy, Jean-Luc. 2000. *Being Singular Plural*. Trans. Robert D. Richardson and Anne E. O'Byrne. Stanford, CA: Stanford University Press.
National Joint Committee. 1998. *Report of The Sinhala Commission*. Colombo, Sri Lanka: National Joint Committee.
Nietzsche, Friedrich. 1995. "On the Utility and Liability of History for Life." In *Unfashionable Observations*, trans. Richard T. Gray, 83–168. Stanford, CA: Stanford University Press.
———. 1994. *On the Genealogy of Morality*. Trans. Carol Diethe. Cambridge: Cambridge University Press.
Obeyesekere, Gananath. 1990. *The Work of Culture: Symbolic Transformation in Psychoanalysis and Anthropology*. Chicago: University of Chicago Press.
———. 1984. "The Origins and Institutionalization of Political Violence." In *Sri Lanka in Change and Crisis*, ed. James Manor, 153–74. London: Croom Helm.
———. 1981. *Medusa's Hair: An Essay on Personal Symbols and Religious Experience*. Chicago: University of Chicago Press.
———. 1979. "The Vicissitudes of the Sinhala Buddhist Identity through Time and Change." In *Collective Identities, Nationalisms, and Protest in Modern Sri Lanka*, ed. Michael Roberts, 279–313. Colombo, Sri Lanka: Marga.
———. 1970. "Gajabahu and the Gajabahu Synchronism: An Inquiry into the Relationship between Myth and History." *Ceylon Journal of the Humanities* 1, no. 1: 25–56.
Obeyesekere, Gananath, and Richard Gombrich. 1988. *Buddhism Transformed: Religious Change in Sri Lanka*. Princeton, NJ: Princeton University Press.
Pandey, Gyanendra. 1990. *The Construction of Communalism in Colonial North India*. New Delhi, India: Oxford University Press.
Pateman, Carole. 1988. *The Sexual Contract*. Stanford, CA: Stanford University Press.
Perera, Suvendrini. 1999. "Unmaking the Present, Remaking Memory: Sri Lankan Stories and a Politics of Coexistence." *Race and Class* 41, no. 1/2: 189–96.
Perera, Walter. 1997. "Attempting the Sri Lankan Novel of Resistance and Reconciliation: A. Sivanandan's *When Memory Dies*." *The Sri Lanka Journal of the Humanities* 23, no. 1/2: 13–27.
Philips, Rajan, ed. 2001. *Sri Lanka: Global Challenges and National Crises*. Colombo, Sri Lanka: Social Scientists' Association.
Pitkin, Hanna Fenichel. 1967. *The Concept of Representation*. Berkeley and Los Angeles: University of California Press.
Ponnambalam, Satchi. 1983. *Sri Lanka: The National Question and the Tamil Liberation Struggle*. London: Zed.
Prakash, Gyan. 1997. "Postcolonial Criticism and Indian Historiography." In *Dangerous Liaisons: Gender, Nation, and Postcolonial Perspectives*, ed. Anne McClintock, Aamir Mufti, and Ella Shohat, 491–500. Minneapolis: University of Minnesota Press.

Prasad, Madhava. 1997. "On the Question of a Theory of (Third) World Literature." In *Dangerous Liaisons: Gender, Nation, and Postcolonial Perspectives*, ed. Anne McClintock, Aamir Mufti, and Ella Shohat, 141–62. Minneapolis: University of Minnesota Press.

Rancière, Jacques. 1999. *Disagreement: Politics and Philosophy*. Trans. Julie Rose. Minneapolis: University of Minnesota Press.

———. 1994. *The Names of History: On the Poetics of Knowledge*. Trans. Hassan Melehey. Minneapolis: University of Minnesota Press.

Ricoeur, Paul. 1988. *Time and Narrative*. Vol. 3. Trans. Kathleen Blamey and David Pellauer. Chicago: University of Chicago Press.

———. 1984. *Time and Narrative*. Vol. 1. Trans. Kathleen McLaughlin and David Pellauer. Chicago: University of Chicago Press.

Roberts, Michael. 2000. "History as Dynamite." *Pravada* 6, no. 6: 11–13.

Russell, Jane. 1982. *Communal Politics under the Donoughmore Constitution*. Dehiwela, Sri Lanka: Tisara Prakasakayo.

Said, Edward W. 1989. "Representing the Colonized: Anthropology's Interlocutors." *Critical Inquiry* 15: 205–25.

———. 1979. *Orientalism*. New York: Vintage.

Schmitt, Carl. 2000. *The Crisis of Parliamentary Democracy*. Trans. Ellen Kennedy. Cambridge, MA: MIT Press.

Scott, David. 2000. "Toleration and Historical Traditions of Difference." In *Community, Gender, and Violence: Subaltern Studies XI*, ed. Partha Chatterjee and Pradeep Jeganathan, 283–304. New Delhi, India: Permanent Black.

———. 1999. *Refashioning Futures: Criticism after Postcoloniality*. Princeton, NJ: Princeton University Press.

———. 1995. "Dehistoricizing History." In *UnMaking the Nation: The Politics of Identity and History in Modern Sri Lanka*, ed. Pradeep Jeganathan and Qadri Ismail, 10–24. Colombo, Sri Lanka: Social Scientists' Association.

Scott, Joan. 1992. "Experience." In *Feminists Theorize the Political*, ed. Judith Butler and Joan Scott, 22–40. New York: Routledge.

Shanmugathasan, N. 1974. *A Marxist Looks at the History of Ceylon*. Colombo, Sri Lanka: privately published.

Sidhwa, Bapsi. 1991. *Cracking India*. Minneapolis, MN: Milkweed.

Silva, Neluka, ed. 2002. *The Hybrid Island: Culture Crossings and the Invention of Identity in Sri Lanka*. Colombo, Sri Lanka: Social Scientists' Association.

Siriwardena, Regi. 1997. "When Memory Dies." *Nethra* 1, no. 4: 74–81.

Sitze, Adam. 2003. *Articulating Truth and Reconciliation in South Africa: Sovereignty, Testimony, Protest Writing*. PhD diss., University of Minnesota.

Sivanandan, Ambalavaner. 1997. *When Memory Dies*. London: Arcadia.

———. 1984. "Sri Lanka: Racism and the Politics of Underdevelopment." *Race and Class* 26, no. 1: 1–38.

Sivathamby, Karthigesu. 1987. "The Sri Lankan Ethnic Crisis and Muslim-Tamil Relationships: A Socio-Political Review." In *Facets of Ethnicity in Sri Lanka*, ed. Charles Abeysekera and Newton Gunasinghe, 192–225. Colombo. Sri Lanka: Social Scientists' Association.

Social Scientists' Association. 1984. *Ethnicity and Social Change*. Colombo, Sri Lanka: Social Scientists' Association.

Spencer, Jonathan. 1990. *Sri Lanka: History and the Roots of Conflict*. London: Routledge.

Spivak, Gayatri Chakravorty. 2005. *Other Asias.* New York: Blackwell.

———. 1999. *A Critique of Postcolonial Reason: Toward a History of the Vanishing Present.* Cambridge, MA: Harvard University Press.

———. 1993. *Outside in the Teaching Machine.* New York: Routledge.

———. 1989. "The New Historicism: Political Commitment and the Postmodern Critic." In *The New Historicism,* ed. H. Aram Veeser, 277–92. New York: Routledge.

———. 1988. *In Other Worlds: Essays in Cultural Politics.* New York: Routledge.

———. 1988. "Can the Subaltern Speak?" In *Marxism and the Interpretation of Culture,* ed. Cary Nelson and Lawrence Grossberg, 271–316. Urbana: University of Illinois Press.

Tennekoon, Serena. 1987. "Symbolic Refractions of the Ethnic Crisis: The *Divaina* Debates on Sinhala Identity." In *Facets of Ethnicity in Sri Lanka,* ed. Charles Abeysekera and Newton Gunasinghe, 1–59. Colombo, Sri Lanka: Social Scientists' Association.

Tennent, James Emerson. 1996. *Ceylon: An Account of the Island Physical, Historical, and Topographical with Notices of Its Natural History, Antiquities, and Production.* New Delhi, India: Asian Educational Services.

Trouillot, Michel-Rolph. 1995. *Silencing the Past: Power and the Production of History.* Boston, MA: Beacon.

Tussman, Joseph. 1960. *Obligation and the Body Politic.* New York: Oxford University Press.

Tylor, E. B. 1958. *The Origins of Culture: Part I of "Primitive Culture."* New York: Harper.

University Teachers for Human Rights (Jaffna) [UTHR(J)]. 2002a. *Towards a Totalitarian Peace: The Human Rights Dilemma.* Kohuwala, Sri Lanka: Wasala Publications.

———. 2002b. *The Plight of Child Conscripts, Social Degradation, and Anti-Muslim Frenzy.* Kohuwala, Sri Lanka: Wasala Publications.

———. 1993a. *A Sovereign Will to Self-Destruct.* London: n.p.

———. 1993b. *Rays of Hope amidst Deepening Gloom.* London: n.p.

———. 1992. *The Trapped People among Peacemakers and War Mongers.* Jaffna, Sri Lanka: n.p.

———. 1990. *The War and Its Consequences in the Amparai District.* Jaffna, Sri Lanka: n.p.

Uyangoda, Jayadeva. 2001. *Questions of Sri Lanka's Minority Rights.* Colombo, Sri Lanka: International Centre for Ethnic Studies.

———. 1999. "Sri Lanka: The Question of Minority Rights." Paper presented at the International Centre for Ethnic Studies workshop on Minority Protection in Sri Lanka, August 14, 1999, Colombo, Sri Lanka.

———. 1993. "Sri Lanka's Crisis: Contractarian Alternatives." *Pravada* 2, no. 8: 6–11.

Viswanathan, Gauri. 1989. *Masks of Conquest: Literary Study and British Rule in India.* New York: Columbia University Press.

Watson, I. B. 1997. "Preface." *Conflict and Community in Contemporary Sri Lanka.* Special issue of *South Asia* 20: 1–2.

White, Hayden. 1984. *Tropics of Discourse: Essays in Cultural Criticism.* Baltimore: The Johns Hopkins University Press.

———. 1981. "The Value of Narrativity in the Representation of Reality." In *On Narrative,* ed. W. J. T. Mitchell. Chicago: University of Chicago Press.

———. 1978. *Tropics of Discourse: Essays in Cultural Criticism.* Baltimore, MD: The Johns Hopkins University Press.

Wilson, Alfred Jeyaratnam. 2000. *Sri Lankan Tamil Nationalism: Its Origins and Development in the Nineteenth and Twentieth Centuries.* Vancouver: University of British Columbia Press.

———. 1994a. *S. J. V. Chelvanayakam and the Crisis of Sri Lankan Tamil Nationalism, 1947–1977.* London: Christopher Hurst.

———. 1994b. "The Colombo Man, the Jaffna Man, and the Batticaloa Man." In *The Sri Lankan Tamils: Ethnicity and Identity,* ed. Chelvadurai Manogaran and Bryan Pfaffenberger, 126–42. Boulder, CO: Westview.

———. 1988. *The Break-Up of Sri Lanka: The Sinhalese-Tamil Conflict.* Honolulu: University of Hawaii Press.

———. 1980. *The Gaullist System in Asia: The Constitution of Sri Lanka, 1978.* London: Macmillan.

———. 1974. *Politics in Sri Lanka, 1947–1973.* London: Macmillan.

Wriggins, Howard. 1960. *Ceylon: The Dilemmas of a New Nation.* Princeton, NJ: Princeton University Press.

Young, Robert. 2001. *Postcolonialism: An Historical Inquiry.* Oxford: Blackwell.

Index

QADRI ISMAIL teaches postcolonial studies at the University of Minnesota.